ENVIRONMENTAL INTERIORSCAPES

ENVIRONMENTAL INTERIORSCAPES

A DESIGNER'S GUIDE TO INTERIOR PLANTSCAPING AND AUTOMATED IRRIGATION SYSTEMS

STUART D. SNYDER

Whitney Library of Design

An imprint of Watson-Guptill Publications

New York

Acknowledgments

This undertaking could not have been accomplished without the input and cooperation of quite a few people. All have my deepest gratitude. I would like to express my special thanks to Bob Johns, architect, interior designer, and inventor who reviewed this text with a critical and understanding eye; to Dr. Bill Wolverton of Wolverton Environmental Services, Space Technology Hall-of-Famer who introduced me to some of the latest findings in bio-environmental research; to Dr. Norman Salansky, professor of aerospace science at the University of Toronto who helped me understand the depth of Soviet research in life support and biospheric sciences; and to the staffs of Florida Atlantic University Library in Boca Raton, Boca Raton Public Library, Broward County Library in Fort Lauderdale, and Palm Beach County Library in West Palm Beach who were exceedingly helpful in rooting out masses of research material. Thanks also to Mrs. Jan Roy of the Plants for Clean Air Council for furnishing newly acquired research reports, and to Roberto de Alba of Whitney Library of Design for having confidence in this project and providing me the opportunity to speak to so many through this book. Another special acknowledgment is directed to Whitney editor Micaela Porta who skillfully helped me shape this document and was a true pleasure to work with.

My deepest feelings of appreciation are directed to Harriet Victoria Ayers, without whom this book could not have been written. Her help, understanding, consideration, love, and encouragement were profound.

Copyright © 1995 by Stuart D. Snyder

First published in the United States in 1995 by Whitney Library of Design, an imprint of Watson-Guptill Publications, a division of BPI Communications, Inc., 1515 Broadway, New York, NY 10036.

Library of Congress Cataloging-in-Publication Data

Snyder, Stuart D., 1932-
    Environmental Interiorscapes: a designer's guide to interior plantscaping and automated irrigation systems / Stuart D. Snyder.
        p.   cm.
    Includes bibliographical references and index.
    ISBN 0-8230-1604-8
    1. Interior landscaping. 2. Buildings—Irrigation—Automation. 3. House plants—Irrigation. 4. Indoor air pollution. 5. Plants as sanitary agents. I. Title.
    SB419.25.S686 1995   95-45556
    747'.98—dc20   CIP

Distributed in the United Kingdom by Phaidon Press, Ltd., 140 Kensington Church Street, London W8 48N, England.

Distributed in Europe (except the United Kingdom), South and Central America, the Caribbean, the Far East, the Southeast, and Central Asia) by Rotovision S.A., Route Suisse 9, CH-1295 Mies, Switzerland.

Manufactured in the United States
First printing, 1995

1 2 3 4 5 6 7 8 9 / 02 01 00 99 98 97 96 95

Senior Editor: Roberto de Alba
Associate Editor: Micaela Porta
Production Manager: Ellen Greene

Contents

Preface

The road we travel in this book has been shaped by time and the vagaries of evolution. Ours to explore after eons of change, use, abuse, revelation, indifference, and doubt, its foundation is the complex of living systems we call nature. Many believe its beginning was willed by a supreme being, others believe it resulted from the forces shaping our globe during its formative years, ultimately creating wonders beyond our imaginings. The destination of our world will be determined not only by those forces that brought it here, but also by those of us who populate it. That's a grave responsibility, but here we are, trying to grapple with what it all means. The important question before us is, How do we advance our lifestyle and commercial endeavors without destroying the exquisitely complex, natural system that sustains us? Clearly, we must show greater prudence and vision, for without it life on Earth will eventually cease.

For decades, my profession as engineer led me through the halls of megacorporations. The goal at the time was simply to work effectively and make a contribution to my employer and society in the form of new and useful products. Many of those years were spent in one of the largest bastions of the chemical industry. Now age, broader environmental science, and, I hope, wisdom, have taught me that many of the improvements in our standard of living have come at a serious price—namely, the degradation of our environment and public health.

Six years ago, while researching and writing another book, NASA opened my eyes to a new brand of environmental study that promises to have a positive impact on the critical issue of indoor air pollution. I was put in touch with their Environmental Research Laboratory in Mississippi, and

with Dr. Bill Wolverton, its director and a pioneer in the field of bio-technical space research. There, in the epicenter of high technology, was a lab working with plants, trying to harness their wonderful properties for long space missions. These plants were being studied not for food, or decor, or shade, or medicinal purposes, but for their functional attributes in cleaning the air in confined spaces. NASA had found from earlier science that plants could soak up sunlight and polluted air and perform their chemical magic to purify the atmosphere. They were conducting studies to determine the usefulness of bio-systems in their space projects. If their experiments continued to yield positive results, many life-support problems could be solved. They also recognized the potential for keeping civilian shelters free of airborne contamination, and focused much of their research in that direction.

As NASA worked busily on the study, the Soviets were at least fifteen years ahead in their contributions to space science. The Soviets confirmed that the technology of nature is often far superior to humankind's devices. Through Dr. Wolverton I gained access to pertinent reports, papers, experimental data, and clippings, and after much investigation, I too became a believer in the abilities and potential of the photosynthetic process. The weight of evidence was compelling, yet relatively few people in the U.S. took it seriously.

A couple of years ago I spoke with a well respected environmental air quality official from California. When I asked her position on the use of plants for indoor air pollution control, she told me how cool they were toward the idea—that the scientific evidence did not weigh in favor of it. She said they'd studied the research of Dr. Wolverton's group at NASA, and that it was not complete or compelling enough for them. When asked if they'd seen the depth of research NASA had generated to that point—about six or eight studies—she became annoyed and told me that of course they had. Further questioning revealed only one NASA report was in their possession, and an early one at that. Obviously, the California group's investigation into the issue had been haphazard. It was also obvious that they were echoing the EPA party line, which is strongly biased toward electromechanical solutions. When I raised the issue that Soviet space research had gone even farther in this field, and validated in many ways what NASA was finding, she defended her position by telling me how unreliable Russian research is. In fact, the Russian space program is quite advanced. They accomplished most of their feats long before NASA. *Popular Science* magazine recently lauded their effort and leadership in a feature article ("Beyond Mir: The Soviet Union is dead, but the world's most successful space program lives on," August 1994). Perhaps their greatest contribution to space science lies in their studies of human physiology and psychology in space, and in their creation of closed, self-regenerating life-support systems based on natural processes. Despite these truths, many refuse to learn from that which the Soviets have to offer.

My experience with the arrogant environmental official who denigrated foreign scientific and technological achievement, as well as natural functional processes, is difficult to accept. It reflects the problem forward thinkers have had throughout history. Unfortunately, from lack of awareness, misinformation, or bias, most people are still subject to narrow visions of life as it really exists. When the misinformed also become our leaders, the resulting mindset can be harmful, for progress is hampered in many critical areas deserving attention. So it was with Dr. Wolverton's work in demonstrating how plants can make our enclosed environments healthier. While it continues to receive international acclamation, criticism is still forthcoming from segments of scientific and political communities resistant to change, often guided by financial pressure. Thankfully, the concepts that Dr. Wolverton, the Soviet space scientists, and others explored are finally beginning to take root in environmentally conscious projects. We are learning to design our own controlled ecological life support systems for the shelters we inhabit—and that's what this book is all about.

So here we are, traveling on this road created by nature and explored by science, about to delve into the subject of environmental interiorscaping, a new field of knowledge and expertise that could both further our careers and benefit mankind. In this book is contained not only information on the use of biological systems for shelter enhancement, but also on the modern, "high-tech," automated techniques that make them work. These systems range from the simple to extremely complex. In that spectrum the reader will find an installation suitable for any given purpose—be it an upscale commercial job, or a more modest residential commission. My hope is that readers will use this information for the improvement of their clients' health and the quality of their living and working environments. Ultimately, your work could make the world a better place. I am confident this book will contribute to that progress.

Stuart D. Snyder
Delray Beach, Florida
September 1995

Introduction

Only recently have we begun to appreciate the delicate balances in our ecosystem. Science has shed light on the destruction we have caused, as well as on the tragic consequences that lie ahead if our course is not reversed. This new store of knowledge is driving the environmental movement in which "ozone layer," "Brazilian Rain Forest," "CFCs," and "global warming" have become buzzwords of the decade. Among the most heinous of our crimes against the environment is the continuous destruction of trees and other greenery. As I will discuss in detail in the first half of this book, green plants perform the many services necessary for our survival.

Horticultural environmental research in the 1970s and early 1980s dealt mostly with outdoor growth in the form of trees, shrubs, crops, and grasses. Some studies focused on natural greenery functioning as biological pollution abatement systems in the global ecology. Those studies targeted HF, SO_2, CO, CO_2, NO, NO_2, Cl_2, HCl, and PAN as pollutants of interest because the focus was then on agricultural and urban environments. They provided early evidence that the photosynthetic process was an important ally.[1] One project, for example, demonstrated that alfalfa fields could remove 1/4 ton of nitrogen dioxide or sulphur dioxide per square mile of air each day.

Additional research with live plants weighs heavily in favor of their use indoors. Industry shipments of tested varieties of foliage plants used in interior landscaping have risen sharply in the past twenty-five years, currently about 1600% over 1970 levels. The popularity of designing with plants will be augmented not only by NASA's revelations into their usefulness in the control of indoor air pollution, but by other important attributes as well.

One has to do with the fact that as valuable as computers and other high-tech work tools are to our economy, they have been found to cause certain problems about which industrial psychologists, medical doctors, business efficiency experts, and corporate managers are becoming worried. The human spirit is having trouble adapting to the invasion of high-tech electronics and computer-age procedures, and in various ways we want to fight back. One manifestation of this is evident in the back-to-nature movement of the 1960s and 1970s. In his best-selling book *Megatrends,* John Naisbitt proposed that we can "straighten our heads" by rehumanizing our personal worlds. He says that for every technical advance there should be an equal and opposite modifying influence that would tend to rehumanize the world of those affected by the technology, so as to overcome the debilitating effects. He calls these rehumanizing, balancing influences "high-touch."[2] Mr. Naisbitt puts it this way:

> We must learn to balance the material wonders of technology with the spiritual demands of our human nature. . . . The need for compensatory high-touch is everywhere. The more high-tech in our society, the more we will want to create high-touch environments with soft edges balancing the hard edges of technology.

In the Naisbitt concept, high-touch takes many forms—biking, hiking, handwriting notes, socializing, handcrafting, decorating, and gardening, among other activities. As one of the strongest influences available for developing more comfortable and natural environments, live tropical plants are the ultimate in high-touch.

NASA has done extensive research into the use of live plants in spacecraft and space stations to modify emotional stresses on astronauts. Recognizing the value of natural environments, some space scientists recommend inclusion of miniature, natural landscapes as microenvironments in cabins and work areas.[3] Another consultant to NASA states in his book:

> The green experience is pervasive. Nature matters to people. The examples are endless and involve innumerable nooks and crannies in people's lives. They also provide hints of countless small changes that can make the human condition just a little more satisfying.[4]

The Soviet space program also made extensive use of natural scenes and working gardens to maintain morale in the stressful environments of Salyut and Mir space stations. A few years ago a study was conducted by a research group looking for guidance in designing spacecraft interiors. They interviewed a culturally diverse group of U.S. and Soviet astronauts and cosmonauts, asking for suggestions on interior decor options they would prefer. The responses indicated a strong, almost unanimous preference for having more plants and other natural elements in their high-tech orbital habitats.[5]

In the past, the mainstream design professions ignored many basic human needs by overlooking the elements that make buildings comfortable and functional for us. Their concentration on design elements created for purely aesthetic purposes incited criticism from many of the people who actually had to live and work in their creations. Much of the debate stems from old arguments over form versus function. In *Towards a Humane Architecture,* Bruce Allsopp observes:

> People want architecture which is warm and comforting to the senses, architecture which is pleasant to live with, which caters to man as he is and not for man as an abstraction, architecture which is seen to be appropriate to its purpose, bearing in mind the habitual attitudes and responses of people who have been brought up in a living society, not processed in a laboratory. The supreme fallacy of modern architectural thought is that if the architect designs what he knows, by his own introverted standards of pure architecture, to be best, the public ought to grow to like it. Why the hell should they?[6]

While this is a rough criticism of design practice at the time, similar critiques can be found in the writings of Lang, Burnette, Moleski and Vachon,[7] Mikellides,[8] and Walter Kleeman,[9] who ensures that interior designers don't escape criticism. In *The Challenge of Interior Design,* Kleeman explains the importance of a humanistic design philosophy:

> The studies cited in this book tell us as designers that there are behavioral implications in every one of our designs. Interior design can produce environmental habitability, a very important goal in terms of human well-being. The condition of the ultimate environment, the interiors where we live, love, work and play, cannot help but be one of the most important factors in our survival as rational, functional human beings.

Some of the more enlightened practitioners in the design professions have heeded the criticisms and directives leveled at them, and are now humanizing their structures, both architecturally as well as through interior design elements. Use of live tropical plantings is one of the important ingredients being used to achieve more

Plants as an element of
building architecture.

comfortable and natural interiors. Following the lead of such innovators as architect John Portman, many design professionals are using greenery in abundance to enrich our lives.

Merchants have found strong commercial value in greening their establishments because the restful environment they create helps to attract customers. As others have noted, it helps to rest the soul. We create comfort and high-touch by bringing a bit of nature indoors, with wallcoverings of grasscloth, wood paneling, stone, and brick. We use pine and floral scents to tease the nostrils, the trickle of a mini-waterfall or fountain to tickle the ear and invade our senses with a hint of the outdoors. Above all else, we surround ourselves with live tropical plants to give us back the feeling of earth, of growing things that evoke the memories of our agrarian past, and as some psychologists think, perhaps visions of exotic places.

The green color of tropical foliage is another desirable attribute. Psychologists consider it a cool color that has a restful influence on people. In its *Habitability Data Handbook,* NASA reaches the following conclusion about cool colors: "Dimness, quietness, and sedation of the senses in general are associated with the most active effect of cool colors."[10]

It has been postulated for more than one hundred years that being around plants can improve our emotional and psychological health. Master landscape architect Frederick Law Olmsted used this argument to sell his plan for the creation of New York City's Central Park. He was a strong proponent of using vegetation and other forms of nature to create urban oases where city dwellers could come for a respite away from everyday pressures. As he put it, an environment containing vegetation or other forms of nature, ". . . employs the mind without fatigue and yet exercises it; tranquilizes it and yet enlivens it; and thus through the influence of mind over the body, gives the effect of refreshing rest and revigoration to the whole system" (1865).

Most scientists feel these phenomena are evolutionary and stem from our long developmental past. Recent research has proven theories such as Olmsted's to be accurate, and, in fact, more beneficial than originally imagined. Many studies have shown significant stress reduction when people are around plants. This involves not only a psychological response, but also a

The glade-like atmosphere of indoor gardens relaxes patrons.

physiological one, for changes in body function always accompany emotional stress. In laboratory research, visual exposure to settings with vegetation has produced significant recovery from stress within only about five minutes, as measured by changes in physiological response, such as blood pressure, muscular tension, and brain wave activity.[11]

Another positive factor in the "greening" of American building interiors is the decorative value plants possess. By complementing other elements of interior design, plants forge a symbiotic relationship with the design that helps tie the interior elements together. No longer are design elements limited to surface treatments, furnishings, and architectural casework. Interior designers and architects have found that plants serve to unify the design elements, add color, and create interest and softness where none existed. Some have this to say about using plants in interior spaces:

> Plants are wonderful accessories. They are the quickest injectors of liveliness and freshness to a room, can add height, variety, colour, and drama all at once and are generally worth every penny you pay for them. There is almost no gap in a room that a plant cannot fill and improve, no piece of furniture that cannot be balanced by a spread of foliage. I really would not feel happy in a plantless room.—Mary Gilliatt, Interior Designer[12]

> An interior without living greenery is rather like a meal without salt or spices . . . It may serve its basic purpose, but is dull and uninspiring. Plants bring vitality and visual excitement to a room. They serve as much more than ornaments, thanks to the added dimension brought by their living, growing, ever-changing character and their subtle variations in tone and texture.—Michael Wright, editor, *The Complete Indoor Gardener*[13]

> Plants are living sculptures. They bring color, texture, and a variety of forms into the office. They enliven interior spaces by softening the regular geometry of buildings and furniture. In addition to their visual charms, plants bring some of the intangible delights of the outdoors into the office. They foster interest and provide the satisfaction of nurturing something and watching it grow and flourish. They are a welcome natural element in an artificial environment.—Judy Graf Klein, author, *The Office Book*[14]

> Plants produce fabulous results for rooms decorated on tight budgets. Hang lush plants from the tops of windows and place tall ones in the corners of rooms. Use them to fill in holes near tables or next to lamps . . . . Never, never use plastic plants. If insufficient light is a major problem, use baskets of dried flowers, dried grasses, dried hydrangeas, dried tree branches . . . anything at all as long as it's natural and organic. Plastic flowers look unreal and are deadly in any decorative scheme.—Norma Skurka, author, *The New York Times Book of Interior Design and Decoration*[15]

Plants' live presence tends to overcome the stark, monolithic feeling that a concrete, steel, and glass structure can generate. The tie with nature is returned to these construction materials, giving them a sense of compatibility with their new surroundings, as they had before being extracted from the earth.

Because the inclusion of greenery in interiors has been proven to have such a positive effect on people, it's no surprise that plants have been brought into the

workplace. For corporate managers, the benefits plants offer employees were seen not only as a plus for their "bottom line," but also as a "perk" for the employees themselves who constitute by far a company's largest expenditure. Over the life of a building, construction, decorating, and operating expenses account for only about 8% of company expenses. The remaining 92% goes toward the salaries and benefits of employees working inside the structure. It makes sense, then, to try to improve employee productivity by making the working environment pleasant and effective. A study was conducted in 1982 by the Buffalo Organization for Technological and Social Innovation (BOSTI) to determine the importance of working environments on employee satisfaction and efficiency. It was found to be very important—more than management had realized.[16]

European executives have been more advanced in these matters than their counterparts in the United States, however,

Plants as an element of interior design.

Plants used in
workstations,
conference rooms,
and reception
areas of offices.

particularly in Germany, Sweden, and The Netherlands. These countries have traditionally shown more concern and reverence for the worker, refusing to institute some of the working conditions commonly imposed here. Some years ago, a German management consulting/design group called the Quickborner Team was commissioned to see how it could adapt open office plans to European standards. The result was what they called *Burolandschaft,* which means office landscaping, or, the extensive use of live plants to humanize a dehumanizing space. Greenery was densely installed to screen areas, to define circulation routes, and to separate work stations. The visual and audible improvements provided beauty and decorative value, introduced the salutary benefits of natural elements, gave more privacy to the worker, and the special placement of plants was used to identify status in executive areas. These are the benefits common to all offices, but plants are so important to the German concept that the generic term for their open plan office layouts actually became burolandschaft.[17] Office management research indicates that use of ornamental plants in the office can improve employee efficiency by 10% to 15% aside from providing greater job satisfaction.[18]

Plant use in residential structures works just as well as in commercial ones, providing a finished look to any type of interior design project. The homeowner learned about the many benefits of plants long ago, although he or she may not have thought about them very seriously. Homeowners have always known that houseplants "dress" a house or apartment by adding color, unifying interior design elements, filling bare spaces, and providing relatively inexpensive decorative value. For ages, homemakers not only decorated with plants, but developed a sense of responsibility in caring for them, too. The term "green pets" aptly describes the relationship that developed between some plant owners and their prized houseplants. As with animal pets, emotional attachments are made with the beauty as well as the vulnerability and dependency of living plants.

Other reasons for having plants indoors are said to stem from our primitive need to grow something. Prehistoric man had to grow food in order to survive, and psychologists believe we still have some of that motivation stirring within us. Lacking the room outdoors, or the time for full-fledged gardening, plants are brought indoors where we can satisfy some of these needs. This is particularly true with apartment dwellers.

The need to grow things purely for diversion is another factor that has attracted the attention of space researchers on both

sides of the Atlantic. An excerpt from a NASA report states:

> Since the earliest days at Antarctic research stations, there has been an abiding interest in growing plants. Ryumin (1980) also describes the pleasure that he derived from tending the experimental garden aboard the Soviet Salyut 6 space station. The activity apparently transcended the experimental requirements and the cosmonauts found themselves devoting much of their leisure time to gardening . . . [which is] an activity that provides substantial gratification to many people in both isolated and non-isolated environments . . . .[19]

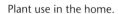

Plant use in the home.

The scientific work cited above is merely an extension of our everyday humanity—an attempt to make the space worker feel at home in the alien environment so far away.

In one form or another, gardening is a hobby shared by so many of us because of its salutary value. Its benefits are so well recognized that psychologists use plants as therapeutic tools to mollify various mental disorders. The Gallup Organization of Princeton, New Jersey, has been developing statistics for the U.S. Government and commercial interests. Their survey uncovered the fact that gardening is the number one leisure activity of American adults.[20] Indoor gardening accounts for a large part of that statistic. Other data they generated showed that 56% of the 83.3 million households in this country had 9 to 18 houseplants, with the average having 13. While these numbers seem a little on the high side, they nevertheless indicate the magnitude of involvement with live indoor plants in our homes.

Among the hurdles still preventing the widespread use of environmental interiorscapes is the fact that all too often planter design and supply contracts are given to landscape nurserymen and other professionals specializing in outdoor horticulture. While you will find that most of these growers and contractors are well intentioned, they simply do not have the expertise or "feel" to offer proper advice concerning interior projects. There is a great difference between these two branches of ornamental horticulture; conditions and problems are too diverse. Interiorscaping is a field unto itself, with its unique expertise, and must be recognized as such.

Another industry problem is that superior tropical plants have been developed by the specialty growers for interior applications, and advanced techniques for their care have been developed by interiorscape contractors and by industry. Few design professionals (outside of interior landscape specialists) are sophisticated in these matters, and so they tend to minimize their importance. The "team" or "collaborative" approach—namely, using specialists in these disciplines as part of the project task force—is not commonly used in most modern building projects. The outcome is that too many projects suffer aesthetically from the eventual degradation of plant materials, and financially from much greater plant maintenance costs spread over very long periods of time. If property and facility owners and managers were aware of the enduring costs being built into their real estate due to inexperience or lack of concern, more attention would be paid to these details.

In the preceding text we have summarized the many factors which promote the use of live plants indoors. From a humanistic standpoint, none are more important than their biological functional attributes, capable of improving our everyday physical environments in profound ways. In the next few chapters we will explore in detail environmental risk factors and the biological concepts coming out of space science which promise to help make our shelters healthier. We will also discuss why the designer is a critical player in this scenario.

As natural plants proliferate in our homes and businesses, so too does the need for more effective ways of caring for them. Advanced technologies have been developed for that purpose, and a large portion of this book will also deal with these new methods. They can significantly affect the practicality of architectural and interior design projects striving for environmental integrity.

ONE

Design in a Complex World

Modern technology brings with it countless advances and breakthroughs that improve the quality of our lives immeasurably. Those steps forward have come at a price, however, one that has been largely paid by our natural environment. There was a time when the design professional considered aesthetics and function as disparate as oil and water. Today, designers are forced to consider the functional—and ecological—implications of the projects they create in addition to the shapes those forms will take. What is the real value of a highly textured accent wall if it becomes a maintenance nightmare? How will planned wall partitions interfere with air flow? Should an automated lighting control system be used to maximize the dramatic effect of an object? Will the heat generated by a bank of drop lights cause discomfort or undue power expense? The answers to many of these questions should come from meetings with a design task force made up of professionals from various disciplines, including architecture, engineering, design, construction, and indoor horticulture.

The Designer's Changing Role

The role of today's design professional is infinitely more complex than in the past. Economic, social, and political forces have changed the way we live and work. Social research tells us we spend over 90% of our lives indoors. That makes the sheltered environment a supremely important factor in the quality of our lives, and one that is shaped in large measure by the design professional. Recent recessionary pressures, with resultant widespread layoffs, corporate downsizing, and trends toward greater utilization of temporary help, have kept more people at home. For many, the change appears to be permanent. Great numbers took early retirement, others started small businesses with offices at home, and some companies, in an effort to be in tune with the "green" spirit of environmental responsibility, have permitted many of their employees to work at home rather than expend energy commuting to the office. Businesses have slimmed and trimmed to more efficient proportions, and to fill the voids new technologies are replacing areas where human labor had prevailed. Robotics, computers, electronic mail, interactive appliances, electronic energy management and security systems are but a few of the advances of the past decades. With sophisticated automation entering the home as well, designers will play an even more significant role in our lives.

Concurrent to this technological advancement is the growing awareness that as we innovate, we also foul the natural world that created and sustains us. Most of the machines, methods, and materials we use have been developed with little regard for their impact on the environment—particularly the microenvironments we create indoors. Indoor air pollution has become one of the more serious consequences, and only now are we becoming aware of its environmental impact and predisposition to legal scrutiny. The design community is central to this dilemma, for with each project it shapes the conditions within which generations of people will live and work.

Green plants also have a role in this dilemma. NASA and the Soviet space program have shown that green plants are highly developed organisms which are capable of absorbing and eliminating from the local area many toxic gases, bacteria, and viruses. They can have an impact on a project's environmental integrity, helping to overcome the effects of some of the toxicity introduced by the design team and providing building owners with a number of advantages, not the least of which is a measure of liability protection. Designers seldom consider plants as functional entities. Few of us do. To most they are simply organisms that modify the decor, living sculptures that have a purely aesthetic value. Consider this, however: The image of green leaves is the most popular icon used to denote environmental concern. Using plants for functional purposes is a new concept which must be learned and explored.

Interior landscaping, or Interiorscaping, is a specialized field in which plants and state-of-the-art biotechnology are used to achieve healthy, beautiful, manageable interiors. Designers not possessing this expertise generally relegate horticultural details to specialists. Interiorscape irrigation is another specialty, and knowledgeable professionals in that field are also relied upon for active participation in interiorscape projects. The interior designer and architect generally specify size, shape, and location of planters as well as technical systems they consider important for long-term maintenance support. This can include lighting, shading, automated irrigation, and sometimes area ventilation. Specialists input the details of those systems, frequently under the project supervision of the designer, architect, builder, or engineer.

New awareness of our environmental problems tugs at the designer's conscience. How far should one go in using materials in building interiors that are known to be, or strongly suspected of being, toxic to human beings? With strong scientific evidence available to demonstrate that many of the products used in the construction and decoration of buildings are harmful, it puts the primary material specifiers—designers, architects, builders, building contractors, and engineers—at the vortex of the problem. With their responsibility to public health and the environment also comes a vulnerability none could have envisioned a few years ago. Litigation over environmental issues has swelled in the past five years. Indoor settings that are suspected health risks are under increasing legal scrutiny. Attorneys have targeted not only building owners and managers, but construction companies, contractors, designers, architects, real estate agents, product manufacturers, and engineers. Someday broad, protective regulation with tighter codes will inevitably ban many of the harmful materials and practices that are commonplace today. A start has been made, but the path will be long and bumpy.

The designers' hands are far from tied. Indeed, there are many things that can be done now to modify the harmful influences specified into interior microenvironments. One is to use the safer man-made materials—plastics, paints, and other products which are inherently safe or modified to lower toxicity—that are considered "environmentally friendly." Lots of guidance is available in this area. By using environmentally friendly materials, designers can influence manufacturers to market only the safest products.

Another important measure—and the subject of this book—is the greater use of natural, interior landscapes. There are many positive aesthetic, economic, environmental, social, and psychological reasons for doing so, from helping to maintain the life-giving biomass on the planet to soothing our nerves at the end of a workday. One of the most important reasons for practicing environmental interiorscaping is that live plants help maintain a healthier environment. Space scientists have discovered powerful air purification properties in many common tropical foliage plants of the types used indoors. Following the tenets of the new science of biospherics, these scientists urge the use of plants for healthier civilian environments and the creation of indoor ecological systems for more effective human life-support.[1] After all, our shelters are part of our self-crafted life-support system, and air conditioning (HVAC) does only part of the job while simultaneously creating another set of environmental problems. In rising to the challenge, the design professional must learn to use more innovative solutions for the creation of safe, functional, and beautiful interiors.

In the Beginning

Despite what we see around us, the Earth is not composed of Lexan, Dacron, Celotex, Scotchgard, Corian, and Formica. It was conceived as an amalgam of natural gases and mineral elements which eventually took form and gave life to organic species. We are one of the products of that metamorphosis. Between the primeval phases and man's entry on the scene a mere million or so years ago, plant life abounded. Over a period of hundreds of millions of years, through natural biological processes, green oceanic and terrestrial plants generated our oxygenated atmosphere. Through those same massive functional bio-systems, the greenery on earth now sustains the gaseous balance which sustains human life. Our careless tampering with that balance is threatening most forms of life on Earth. Science tells us the threat is extreme, and cautions that we had better preserve and augment these natural, biological systems that got us here, otherwise the globe will become uninhabitable for all aerobic (oxygen-breathing) organisms, including mankind.

The human body took tens of millions of years to evolve and contains hundreds of delicate, fine-tuned organic systems which developed very slowly through adaptation. The synthetic products and technological systems that surround us today came suddenly, only within the past century or so. Our minds and bodies, which necessarily act in harmony with the environment, haven't yet adapted to the serious physical and emotional stresses these alien influences place upon us every minute of our lives.

The indoor environment is one of the elements of life which we embraced in the latter stages of human development. In prehistoric times we were primarily hunters and agrarian beings spending our days in the open under the skies. With the coming of industrial and commercial revolutions, we gravitated to places where better livings were made—in factories, offices, shops, institutions, and laboratories. We became sheltered beings, relying on the design, construction, and function of buildings for our pleasure, efficiency, commerce, and comfort.

Until the early part of this century, materials used for construction and decor were naturally occurring products like wood, plaster, bricks, steel, stone, marble, and ceramics. Then, large chemical manufacturers developed and introduced the first plastics for furnishings, clothing, and construction.[2] No one could have foreseen the impact these synthetic products would have on our lives. Over decades the number of available synthetic chemicals grew to tens of thousands as the

marketplace embraced and absorbed them. More than seventy thousand are listed today. The number of different products made from them multiplied into the millions. Fabrics became tougher, colors more vivid, the shapes infinite, and structural elements stronger.

It is interesting to note, however, that early in the twentieth century public health began a gradual decline, and much of this is blamed on the toxic effects of synthetic products. One of the profound expressions of man's delicate relationship with the biosphere came from a great Native American almost a century and a half ago. Chief Seattle was a humanitarian, gifted philosopher, orator, and communicator of the Indian spirit and values. In 1854 he commented, "Man did not weave the web of life, he is merely a strand in it. Whatever he does to the web, he does to himself."[3] The post–World War II global community saw the introduction of an explosive array of consumer goods made in large part from synthetic materials. Not until recently did we learn that these plastics were capable of emitting gases from their constituent chemicals, many of which are harmful to human life. Since the 1950s, the medical community has had to cope with a growing variety and severity of illnesses. Incidence of allergies, cancer, birth defects, and other human diseases have all increased, despite billions of dollars spent on drugs, medical attention, and research. Meanwhile, other research has pointed to environmental factors as the cause, brought on in large part by the synthetic materials surrounding us. In the February 9, 1994, issue of the *Journal of the American Medical Association,* the medical establishment finally concurred, after many years of indecision and denial, that environmental factors related to jobs, food, water, and air are seen to be the probable cause of the growing incidence of non-smoking-related cancers over the past several decades.[4] Hundreds of prior studies had shown overwhelming evidence of environmental links to disease.

One of the many dangers is gaseous by-products of synthetic materials called VOCs (volatile organic compounds) which pollute the air we breath and are toxic to our systems. Our unconscious exposure to them in low concentrations consistently and over long periods of time causes toxins to accumulate in our bodies and interfere with immune functions and normal metabolism. The cases we hear about in the media are generally those involving acute exposure, like Sick Building Syndrome and Building Related Illness, where building occupants quickly become ill or irritated by high levels of VOCs, and are relieved when they escape to healthier air. These situations get most of the attention though they represent just part of the complex indoor air quality problem—probably the minor part, for long-term, chronic exposure is the most insidious and potentially damaging. We don't know it's there so we sit in it and absorb it, year after year. A broad range of illness from chronic headaches to cancer and other degenerative diseases, birth and genetic defects, and allergic and emotional disorders are the result of air pollution in its various forms.

A Glimpse into the Future

Because of the length of time we spend indoors, and the pervasiveness of toxic gases there, the Environmental Protection Agency (EPA) has called indoor air pollution one of the most serious health risks facing Americans.[5] Foreign environmental agencies have raised the same warning flags in their respective countries. A consortium of highly respected environmental and health researchers and educators is working diligently in the United States to increase awareness of the dangers.[6] It is a global problem that infects primarily the most developed nations which can afford to use modern, synthesized materials to build and decorate their shelters. The United Nations, NATO, and the World Health Organization are deeply involved in research and policy making.

Among other strategies to cope with the problem, the EPA calls for changing the materials we use in building interiors, as well as modifying ventilation practices. The sources of indoor toxins are not exotic or rare. They are, in fact, everyday materials like carpeting, cove molding, high pressure laminates (Formica-type products), paints, wallpaper, furniture finishes, fabric dyes, synthetic fibers in furnishings and clothing, adhesives, foam insulation, cleaning chemicals, furniture and cabinet cores, paneling, artificial plants, wiring, caulking compounds, copy machine solvents, pesticides, air fresheners, and electronic circuit boards in our TVs, stereos, and computers. That list only begins to touch the surface. Evidence of products gassing-off into the surrounding environment can sometimes be seen in carpet sections located in close proximity to Mica furniture for long periods. When the furniture is finally removed, a unique discoloration can be seen around the junction where furniture met carpet, different in color or shade from any fading the rest of the carpet might exhibit. Mica furniture is made of formaldehyde compounds (hence the name FORM-ica) which can cause dyestuff deterioration. If they can attack and destroy organic dyestuffs that effectively, we can be sure their toll on the human body is also significant. Highly toxic to humans, these compounds can cause nausea, respiratory problems, short-term memory loss, and cancer. A typical source of decoration, synthetic plants also contribute to the problem of indoor air pollution. Skeptics doubting the veracity of that statement should visit an artificial plant showroom, where the air is typically thick with fumes. Plastics, adhesives, fragrances, dyestuffs, and pigments used in their manufacture contain harmful constituents that gas-off into the atmosphere. In simple terms, artificial plants are harmful—live green plants are our friends.

While research is getting a better handle on it, we can only imagine the extent and effects of other synthetic products in our midst. The EPA estimates the American economy is drained of $60 billion a year by indoor air pollution.[7] This represents primarily the cost of lost work productivity, medical expenses for sickness, lost wages, death benefits, higher insurance costs, litigation expenses, and equipment and property damage.[8] Because of its seriousness, it is being studied in depth by researchers around the world. The most prominent project, called the TEAM (Total Exposure Assessment Methodology) Study, was carried out by the Environmental Protection Agency.[9] The EPA reported the dangers to Congress in 1989, after six years of in-depth research. They found literally hundreds of these pollutants in each of the hundreds of typical homes and commercial buildings tested around the United States *in much higher levels than one would find outdoors.*

Legislative reaction has been slow. An Indoor Air Quality Act has been drafted by both Houses, and the Senate version was passed in 1991 by an overwhelming vote of 88 to 4. However, the House version has been gridlocked for years, hampering progress.

As part of the movement to accommodate our human needs through more enlightened building design and engineering, more buildings will incorporate elements needed to counteract the harmful effects of high-technology while harnessing the beneficial ones. As articulated by John Naisbitt in *Megatrends,* we need counterbalancing influences in our daily lives to overcome the debilitating effects modernization has on our minds and bodies. "Softening" influences must be introduced into our work, home, and leisure environments. He calls these lifestyle and environmental modifiers "high-touch."[10] As key instrumentalists in providing us with high-touch, the architect, interior designer, building developer, real estate executive, and corporate office manager must rethink the importance of our surroundings. As part of this, we must be put into contact with elements that help to preserve our links with nature. The impersonal manifestations of our new technology are alien to us and must be tempered with the more familiar sights, sounds, and smells with which humans have become comfortable over the ages. This is part of the psychology behind the rapidly growing use of live, tropical plants in our interior surroundings. Science tells us it is restorative to be around plants, and the designer should have an appreciation of that aspect of shaping environments.

The designer's involvement with automated technologies for building "intelligence" is less well defined. There is a demand in the marketplace for buildings and facilities that are both beautiful and practical and that accommodate the needs of the occupants while easing labor and cost burdens associated with home and commercial building management. New electronic, "high-tech" helpers have been devised to meet these needs, but they are generally not part of the designer's area of expertise. In fact, the term "high-tech" may have a completely different connotation to a designer, frequently referring to a trendy, ultra-modern, decorative concept having little to do with function. In the practice of environmental interiorscaping, the high-tech we refer to always involves function. Common today in buildings are integral communication networks, automated lighting and air conditioning control, internal fiber-optic data networks, sophisticated elevator control, master energy management systems, interactive appliances, automated drapery and window controllers, computer-controlled fire safety and security systems, and the list goes on. The quest for useful, efficient, sophisticated, and aesthetically pleasing buildings stems in part from the need to accommodate the requirements of the computer and communication age we live in, as well as from the desire for freer and more productive lifestyles. The future will see more of these electronic marvels integrated into increasingly "intelligent" structures.[11]

In most cases architects and interior designers are not sufficiently trained to deal with the many technologies available, nor would they want to be. (Those professionals dealing with corporate office projects may be an exception.) The expertise of specialists is generally relied upon to accommodate project needs. There is an important competitive advantage, however, for the designer who has at least a nodding acquaintance with the various building control techniques at his or her disposal, for the knowledge provides a more rounded perspective of the requirements of a project and available input factors. Technologies could then be injected into projects as the informed designer perceives their merit. Some are capable of saving clients many times their cost over a period of years, and much more over the life of the building. Many systems turn mediocre shelters into highly marketable, advanced buildings. These should always be presented for clients' consideration. An informed design team is capable of doing so.

Now that we have briefly discussed the merits of environmental interiorscapes, the reader should note that as with all good things, there are counterbalancing influences. Broad use of tropical foliage tends to promote greater planter maintenance cost and expense. This, too, can be minimized through the use of advanced, automated systems devised for

interiorscape watering. It must be kept in mind that the largest cost of interiorscaping is not the purchase or leasing of plant stock, but the cost of maintaining the landscape over many years. The manual watering task is one of the most labor-intensive and expensive of those carried out by the interiorscape maintenance technician, and burdensome to the building or facility management.[12] Systems are currently available that have been developed to automate watering. Integrated into building structures, they make the extensive use of interior planters practical, and in doing so, support the concepts of indoor ecology for healthier environments. The designer should have an appreciation of how this can augment the practicality of a given project.

Automated interior plant care has many implications, having to do not only with horticultural issues, but also with building, interior, and irrigation design; building construction; real estate marketing and management; as well as corporate office management; hospitality industry management; and certain areas of office and marine product design. While the information presented in this book will be useful to architects, interior designers, landscape architects, engineers, interior landscape contractors, building owners and managers, corporate office managers, real estate agents and installers, do-it-yourselfers, or those who plan to become specialists in the technology of automated interior plant care, few designers will be inclined to study the subject in detail. Nevertheless, the intricacies are made available in later chapters to acquaint those technically inclined readers with the various possible interior applications, with plant-related factors, and with techniques available for achieving successful projects. The technical details can also be passed on to specialists being relied upon for design and installation.

TWO

The Indoor Air Quality Dilemma

In 1985, the *Louisville Courier-Journal* published a forty-five-page exposé resulting from eight years of investigative research into indoor pollution problems in Kentucky and Southern Indiana. The piece, called "The Menace Within: Indoor Pollution, A Crisis in the Making, Perils That Need Not Be,"[1] is a comprehensive and sweeping indictment of the health hazards in our homes and workplaces. The prophetic editor emphasized the general lack of support for improved interior environmental standards, saying, "environmentalists feared that emphasizing it [indoor pollution] might divert attention from urgent outdoor cleanups; and government officials weren't eager to uncover problems that would demand expensive anti-pollution campaigns."

Determining the Problem

Funding allocated to the study of indoor air pollution (IAP) has indeed been meager compared with the amount supporting outdoor air pollution projects. While the term "Sick Building Syndrome" has become commonplace, it alone does not encompass the enormity of the problem. Most unhealthy building incidents are actually disqualified from the "sick building" label, and those excluded represent the greatest potential danger to us, for they involve our typical homes and offices. More recent EPA studies have been clear and forceful in their conclusions. To quote from the EPA's 1987 TEAM Study: "The major finding of this study is the observation that personal and indoor exposures to these toxic and carcinogenic chemicals are nearly always greater . . . often much greater . . . than outdoor concentrations. We are led to the conclusion that indoor air in the home and at work far outweighs outdoor air as a route of exposure to these chemicals." We will explore this report in more detail, but suffice it to say that it came as the result of six years of detailed, scientific studies monitoring air in human habitats and its effects on occupants. Parallel research from around the world reaches similar conclusions.

How should we react to all of this? It has long been known that the interiors we frequent contain air that is less than wholesome. Anyone riding an elevator with a smoker, inhaling the aromas of a new house, or entering a room recently sprayed with pesticides knows it. When wood- and coal-burning stoves were common, evidence of soot on the walls indicated that the occupants were breathing in those substances as well. But it wasn't until miners and chemical industry workers came down with disabling diseases in increasing numbers that doctors and scientists began to see important correlations between work and home environments and health. Early signs of illness were also related to lead, asbestos, tobacco smoke, and radon. Despite the evidence, indoor air didn't become an issue on the national agenda until the mid-1970s.

Reacting to the severe fuel crisis of the time, with upwardly spiraling energy costs and the specter of depleted global reserves, standards were then set to seal our buildings from outdoor temperature extremes, producing tight, energy-efficient structures. An unwelcome by-product of this movement, however, was that unhealthy air became sealed within buildings to be continuously recirculated and contaminated with other pollutants. The effects on human inhabitants became increasingly noticeable as office employees complained of headaches, dizziness, respiratory problems, drowsiness, and worse. Correlations between building materials, indoor decorative materials, furnishings, air handling systems, and occupant activities were drawn against some of these illnesses. The issue was brought into sharper focus in 1976 by the tragedy in a Philadelphia hotel where 34 legionnaires attending a convention died from a bacteria nurtured in the building's air conditioning ducts, hence the name "Legionnaire's Disease."

At the same time laboratory research was proving the hazards of tobacco smoke. The seriousness and immensity of the problem was then more clearly defined and indoor air quality (IAQ) research was stepped up. In the late 1970s, research from Denmark further confirmed the extent and seriousness of indoor air pollution.[2] From that point the scientific community initiated a wide variety of studies aimed toward a better understanding of the problem in order to find ways of solving it. Projects were instituted by the National Institute for Occupational Safety and Health (NIOSH), the

American Lung Association (ALA), American Cancer Society (ACS), EPA, American Society of Heating, Refrigeration and Air Conditioning Engineers (ASHRAE), National Research Council (NRC), Swedish Council for Building Research, Danish Building Research Institute, German Institute for Water, Soil and Air Hygiene, World Health Organization, NATO, and a host of other organizations and agencies around the world.

NASA had also become involved in the early 1970s when it found severe atmospheric pollution inside the Skylab III spacecraft. Highly sensitive instruments for monitoring air quality within astronaut cabins and work spaces were used during Skylab space missions. The detection/analysis technique involved the use of a gas chromatograph coupled with a mass spectrometer to monitor air samples. These sophisticated instruments are capable of detecting extremely small quantities of gases in the atmosphere and quantifying the degree of their presence. Results from studies during the Skylab III mission demonstrated the presence of over 300 volatile organic compounds (VOCs) in the spaces occupied by the crew. Of these, 107 were identified and caused much concern because many were known to pose serious risks to human health. The gases came from common construction materials in the craft, as well as from electronic instrumentation, wiring, fabrics used for comfort or function, surface coatings, and a broad range of other materials. Others were bio-effluents resulting from human metabolism. Detected were acetone, toluene, xylene, ethyl acetate, benzene, benzaldehyde, freon, dichlorobenzene, and a host of other unwanted chemical fumes.[3] The revelations from Skylab III helped focus attention on our indoor environments here on Earth as well, for many of the same materials are used in constructing our homes and offices. From that time forward, NASA redirected some of its effort toward solving the similar problem of civilian pollution by using what it learned in those studies.

Still, today many refer to the problem of indoor air pollution as the "forgotten environment." Earth Day 1990 marked the 20th anniversary of the first international focus on environmental problems, and media coverage of indoor air quality issues during that period remained scant. By now, designing for environmental integrity should be a national commitment.

Figure 2.1: Skylab III. Source: McDonnell Douglas.

Federal Involvement in Indoor Air Pollution

The Clean Air Act was passed by Congress in 1970 to address the problems of urban environments, mostly in response to irresponsible industrial development and increased use of automobiles, both of which generated much of our outdoor air, soil, and water pollution. At that time the Act was interpreted as covering only outdoor air pollution, but during the early and mid-1970s several factors began to influence current thinking about the problem indoors.[4] Formaldehyde was said to cause acute irritant reactions and possibly cancer in occupants of homes insulated with urea-formaldehyde foam and/or large quantities of plywood and particleboard. Particularly vulnerable to the hazards were mobile homes. Asbestos was also raised as a hazardous material, and several federal programs were subsequently started to cope with the large number of contaminated buildings. Of particular concern were buildings where people spend large amounts of time, like residences, nursing homes, offices, and hospitals.

As urgency built, Congress appropriated small sums each year for EPA research into causes and remedies in the field of indoor air pollution. While grossly inadequate, it represented the first coordinated effort from the federal sector. By 1986, Congress was concerned enough about human risks from exposure to indoor air pollutants that it enacted Title IV of the Superfund Amendments and Reauthorization Act (SARA). SARA empowered the EPA to establish a serious research effort to determine the extent of IAP and its causes, and to develop strategies and methods for their elimination.[5] While Title IV was called the "Radon Gas and Indoor Air Quality Research Act," its scope was broad and

attempted to stimulate public eduction into indoor health hazards.

One of the first things done was to establish an Indoor Air Division within the EPA's Office of Air and Radiation which provides guidance, research coordination, and information dissemination functions. Among other things, it interfaces with other federal agencies working in the field, such as NIOSH, TVA, DOE, NASA, and with private sector research efforts (ASHRAE, National Research Council). By the end of 1987, the House of Representatives drafted a bill entitled the "Indoor Air Quality Act of 1987." Sponsored by Congressman Joseph Kennedy, it was an attempt to establish a properly funded federal effort to assess and solve indoor air quality problems. That bill languished in subcommittee, and has been reintroduced in each succeeding congressional session. It was finally passed in October 1994 with modifications which must be reconciled with the Senate. Fewer problems were encountered on the Senate side of Capitol Hill. Their Indoor Air Quality Act was sponsored by Senator George Mitchell, and in October 1991, was overwhelmingly passed (88 to 4 vote), and then passed again in October 1993. The preamble to both the House and Senate bills describes the serious issues involved, and concedes that: ". . . indoor air contaminants pose serious threats to public health (including cancer, respiratory illness, multiple chemical sensitivities, skin and eye irritation, and related effects)."[6] Despite Congressional awareness and general support, federal commitment to protecting the public from these pervasive health risks has diminished.

The EPA is by far the agency with the deepest research experience in the field of indoor air pollution. While many environmentalists contend it is not doing enough, its accomplishments in the face of very tight budgets and political difficulties have been impressive. EPA projects number in the hundreds, and all take many months, if not years, to complete. Lack of adequate funding and manpower as well as political tampering have slowed the development of projects considerably.

Other federal agencies are involved with IAP as well. The Department of Energy conducts research into the effects of radon contamination on humans. The U.S. Department of Health and Human Services (NIOSH, etc.) has broad studies in progress involving human exposure to cigarette smoke, mold, bacteria, dust mites, and other allergens, as well as radon studies. Its studies are conducted by monitoring commercial buildings suspected of being hazardous. The General Services Administration is studying indoor air quality policies for federal buildings, as well as radon- and asbestos-control techniques. Continuing its commitment to the study of IAP, NASA looked into bio-tech solutions using common decorative plants to remove formaldehyde, carbon monoxide, benzene, and other air pollutants from confined spaces, like building interiors. This was the prelude to their CELSS Project, under which self-regenerating life-support systems for long-voyage missions are being developed. The Tennessee Valley Authority has ongoing research in the detection and abatement of radon, VOCs, and nitrogen dioxide in residences and public buildings, while the Commerce Department (National Institute of Standards and Technology) is developing standards for VOCs in buildings, test methods for measuring air movement in and around large commercial buildings, and evaluating HVAC filtration devices. The Defense Department is assessing the magnitude of indoor air quality problems in Air Force facilities, including radon studies. The Department of Housing and Urban Development is studying radon as well, and in addition is assessing methods of identifying lead-based paints in buildings and moisture control in manufactured

housing. Geological studies are being used by the Department of the Interior to learn more about the characteristics of radon sources. The Department of Labor (OSHA) is at once studying ways of regulating levels of air pollutants in the workplace and investigating worker complaints. The Departments of State and Transportation also have minor studies in the works. This summary represents only a partial list of federal activity in IAQ issues.

One of the more important IAP studies to come out of federal research efforts was implemented by Walter Reed Army Institute of Research. A four-year study of acute respiratory diseases among army recruits concluded in 1988 that modern, energy-efficient living and work environments pose approximately a 50% greater health risk than older buildings with lesser structural integrity that use windows for main ventilation.[7] The results supported earlier studies and hypotheses that tight buildings with closed ventilation systems significantly increase risks of respiratory transmitted infections among congregated occupants. The study was notable because of its large population size (2.6 million trainee-weeks). Subjects came from highly controlled groups and were drawn randomly from around the country. They all received identical immunizations during processing, and were kept isolated from soldiers of other barracks.

Notwithstanding its efforts, the federal government has been widely criticized in the fight against cancer because of its concentration on diagnosis and treatment rather than on prevention.[8] A coalition of more than sixty authorities in the fields of preventive medicine, environmental medicine, public health, and cancer research claim the incidence of cancer has increased by 44% since 1950 (higher than reported by the government) because the most important causative factors—human exposure to industrial chemicals in air, water, food, and the workplace—have been

largely minimized and ignored by cancer research programs. They called for a reorganization of cancer-related priorities to put prevention on an equal footing with diagnosis and treatment. The cost of cancer care in the United States is more than $110 billion annually—nearly 2% of GDP. At a time when health care reform is high on the national agenda, disease prevention strategies should command more serious consideration. Control of indoor air pollution is an important element in disease prevention strategies.

Meanwhile, state and local governments have shown a growing awareness and interest in IAP, probably in response to federal leadership and litigious pressure. Among other catalysts are active unions which have forced higher indoor environmental standards in government offices.

Private Industry Involvement in Indoor Air Pollution

Corporate America's motivation in reacting to the IAQ issue is mainly economic. It has been estimated that the economic drain from IAP in the United States can be as high as $60 billion annually from the expense of sickness, lost wages, lost work productivity, death benefits, higher insurance costs, litigation expense, and equipment/property damage. The EPA related in its *Report to Congress on Indoor Air Quality:* "expenditures for improved indoor air quality could generate exceedingly high returns to the business community, where labor is an important cost category . . . ." In NATO's 1989 Pilot Study on Indoor Air Quality Report, other economic suggestions were forwarded: "It is clear, therefore, that from a profit and loss standpoint, (employee) productivity, not energy consumption, is the dominant consideration for office environments." The economics of clean indoor air are becoming clearer to the corporate executive, and will foster more activity in the private sector.

Indoor Air Quality Litigation and the Design Community

As more information about indoor air pollution is made available to the public, legal suits over building conditions and occupant illness will be brought to court. The real estate and construction industries are struggling with the problem, as many lawsuits have already been leveled against hotel chains, office building owners, schools, and nursing homes. Sickness and death have resulted from poor architectural planning, engineering deficiencies, and insensitive management. While millions of dollars in relief are being awarded to victims, insurance companies show increasing interest in IAP. With liability litigation over unhealthy building environments increasing in frequency and severity, plans are under consideration within that industry to offer incentives for achieving superior air quality. This will impact the design community in profound ways.

Because of the technical complexities in IAQ suits actual fault is sometimes difficult to determine, thus multi-defendant lawsuits are typically filed. The first of these cases was Buckley v. Kruger-Benson-Ziemer in 1987. The plaintiff sued approximately two hundred named and unnamed defendants for his personal injuries, allegedly sustained after he was exposed to pollutants in his confined workspace. The case was settled for $622,500.[9] Since 1987, architects, interior designers, engineers, property owners, major employers, and product manufacturers have all been the target of IAQ lawsuits by office workers. Such suits have alleged that these parties knew or should have known about the dangerous chemicals and toxins in office buildings, furnishings, and equipment. Recent awards have ranged from $660,000 to $3.5 million.[10] By 1987, the ASHRAE ventilation standard of 5 cubic feet of air exchange per minute (CFM) per person was proving itself to be unrealistic and hazardous. As the result of mounting research and litigation, in 1989 ASHRAE reestablished the original standard of 20 CFM. That same year also saw the publication of the EPA's *Report to Congress on Indoor Air Quality,* which greatly raised awareness of the issue of indoor air pollution and its health effects. Since then lawsuits have escalated. Lawyers found it was difficult for workers to sue their employers because worker's compensation contracts restrict suits of that type. However, the law in such cases is moving away from the concept that a building is the cause of IAQ problems and toward the notion that a building or a house is a product with a known liability, and responsibility is to be shared by architects, interior designers, engineers, construction companies, sub-contractors, real estate agents, product manufacturers and suppliers, maintenance companies, owners, and managers.

Litigation is not as pronounced in the residential markets because the average homeowner has little understanding of IAQ issues. Seldom are everyday health problems related to the buildings in which we live. The death of a family member is usually not related to acute or long-term chronic exposure to chemicals from a faulty HVAC installation, or from decorative paneling, the wrong type of insulation, or even furnishings. Science is showing, however, that these are frequently the realities. Because of their subtlety, the conditions are overlooked.

An exception is in the mobile home/formaldehyde controversy. More than two thousand formaldehyde-related lawsuits have been filed in the United States and many more in Canada, most against an array of multiple defendants. Some have led to jury verdicts exceeding one half million dollars. Many out-of-court settlements have also involved six-figure sums. Because of the multitude of products containing formaldehyde, many expect an eventual explosion in related litigation.

Chlordane and other pesticides have also undergone litigious pressure. One example is the 1988 case, U.S. v. Orkin Exterminating Co. They were charged with five criminal counts of violating federal pesticide laws and with involuntary manslaughter. Two homeowners died in the incident. Asbestos-containing products have been under heavy pressure for many years, as have other manufactured items containing lead and volatile organic compounds. Research is constantly turning up new offenders, which will lead to the discovery of further injury and new grounds for litigation.

Potential defendants are becoming sensitive to their vulnerability and quickly take steps to correct problems. Failure to do so can be interpreted as an act of negligence. Investigation and corrective action can be expensive, however, and frequent, frivolous claims can seriously affect profits. On the other hand, successful legal action against a company can be devastating. In the case of architects, engineers, and interior design firms, environmental awareness must become an important part of their training and experience as the moral, ethical, and legal issues that complicate their professions become more profound.

THREE

Indoor Air Pollution and Human Health Risk

Reactions to short-term exposure to environmental pollutants may be as innocuous as mild allergic symptoms, such as a runny nose or itching eyes. On the more serious side, pollution-caused cancers result in the deaths of hundreds of thousands of people around the world each year. Building interiors are now recognized as the most important source of human exposure to carcinogenic chemicals and other airborne contaminants; ironically it is indoors that our environmental health risk is the highest.[1]

Pollutants, Sources, and Health Effects

Lifestyles are such today that employed persons spend roughly 60% of their day at home, 30% at work, and 5% in transit. Work has largely shifted from a manufacturing environment to offices. Full-time homemakers spend up to 95% of their day indoors, with an average of 20.5 hours in their residence plus other locations. Children, the infirm, elderly, and business people working at home also spend approximately 95% of their time in the same shelter microenvironments.[2] It is estimated that 41 million American citizens currently work out of their own homes full- or part-time as entrepreneurial business people or employees of progressive corporations. The average time we spend indoors is most commonly quoted as 90% of our lives. Our indoor environments must therefore be relatively free of pollutants in order to minimize health risks. Otherwise, long-term exposures to these toxins will eventually take their toll.

As a practical matter, it is not possible to eliminate all contaminants from work and living spaces. In its studies of typical enclosed environments, the EPA showed that our inner surroundings are largely hazardous. Air quality samples from schools, homes, offices, rest homes, and hospitals showed significant evidence of benzene (a known human carcinogen), chloroform, trichloroethylene, tetrachloroethylene, carbon tetrachloride, formaldehyde, and p-dichlorobenzene—all known animal carcinogens and suspected human carcinogens as well. In fact, hundreds of toxic chemicals were found in each sample. Most of the pollutants promote mild reactions, such as runny noses, eye irritation, itching skin, headaches, irritability, depression, lethargy, dizziness, forgetfulness, loss of concentration, asthma, bronchitis, and other respiratory infections. While not usually life-threatening, these symptoms cause a great deal of human misery, high and frequent medical expenses, and often lead to more serious consequences, such as lung impairment, cancer, acute asthmatic conditions, emphysema, memory loss, heart disease, impairment of kidney function, liver function, and of the central nervous system, and depressed immune systems. Some pollutants are carcinogenic (causing cancer), some are known to be mutagenic (causing distortions or mutations in body cells), embryotoxic (toxic to developing fetuses), neurotoxic (toxic to the central nervous system), or allergenic (causing allergic reactions).

The quality of air indoors depends on a number of factors, each of which can be partially controlled:

- Sources of pollutants contained in the microenvironment

- Ventilation strength, direction, and interchange rates

- Concentration levels of pollutants

- Inherent moisture and temperature levels

- Locally absorbent materials

- Nature of foot traffic

Health risk assessment is a nebulous, imprecise science at best, for the early state of research in this field leaves many questions unanswered. Most health risk assessments have concentrated on cancer effects because of the greater media attention they garner. Lesser health risks are also important in many ways. Medical studies show progressive erosion of our immune system when subjected to toxic environments (even at low levels), making us vulnerable to all types of disease. Pollutant by-products invade and damage body cells and become involved in metabolic processes. Disease, loss of energy, premature aging, and memory impairment are but part of the legacy. The greatest unknown involves increased toxicity when certain combinations of pollutants are present. Researchers have seen frightening evidence of harmful synergistic combinations. The overall picture is one we can no longer ignore.

The list of individual indoor air pollutants and health repercussions is voluminous, covering literally hundreds of individual sources.[3] While it is beyond the purpose of this book to detail the subject, the following summary may broaden the reader's perspective.

Radon

Radon is a colorless, odorless gas that occurs naturally and is found everywhere, mostly at very low levels. When radon becomes trapped in buildings, it concentrates to harmful levels and is a major health concern. Its most common source is uranium in the soil or rock upon which houses or commercial buildings are built. As uranium breaks down it releases radon gas, which further degrades into radioactive decay products. Radon gas enters homes through foundation cracks, well water, and frequently through building materials containing radioactive elements. EPA studies indicate that as many as 10% of homes in the United States have levels of radon exceeding safe limits.

There are no immediate symptoms of radon exposure, yet lung cancer is the usual consequence of elevated radon concentrations in homes. Dust and other particulates are inhaled after becoming carriers for radon emissions, settling in the lungs and starting cell deterioration, which increases as the dosage accumulates. It is estimated that between 5,000 and 20,000 lung cancer deaths occur in the United States annually as a result of radon exposure.

Environmental Tobacco Smoke (ETS)

This comes from lit cigarettes, cigars, and pipes, and from smoke that is exhaled by a smoker. Environmental tobacco smoke is a complex mixture of 4,700 compounds and includes both gas and particles (including formaldehyde, nitrogen dioxide, and carbon monoxide), some of which are known or suspected human carcinogens. By measuring certain chemicals in a subject's breath, the EPA TEAM study demonstrated that smoking was responsible for greatly elevated breath concentrations of benzene and styrene, and significantly elevated breath concentrations of ethylbenzene, xylene, and octane. Having a smoker in the house was found to be a major contributor to heavier concentrations of these and other air pollutants. Studies by the National Academy of Sciences and others indict environmental tobacco smoke as a major cause of lung cancer, heart disease, and other serious health risks. It not only affects smokers, but is also harmful to non-smokers through passive smoking from polluted environments. ETS is the most highly concentrated pollutant in many home and commercial interiors. Some of its more immediate effects are eye, nose, and throat irritation, headaches, asthma, bronchitis and pneumonia in adults, and increased risk of respiratory and ear infections in children. Non-smokers who breath others' smoke show changes in heart rate, systolic blood pressure, carboxyhemoglobins, psychomotor function, and small airway dysfunction.

Biological Contaminants

There are many sources of biological contaminants, including bacteria; mold; viruses; animal dander, feces, and saliva; mites; and pollen. Carbon dioxide and other products of human metabolism are biological contaminants as well. We discharge more than one pound of body waste products through our skin daily. It is estimated that one third of all body impurities are excreted this way.[4] Additional air contaminants are expelled by normal respiration. Most pollens found indoors originate from flowering plants and are tracked into buildings from outdoors or enter with indoor/outdoor air exchange. Viruses are transmitted by people and animals, while bacteria are carried by people, animals, pests, soil, and plant debris. Household pets are the main sources of dander and saliva, and rodent urine is another source of airborne allergens. Mold, mildew, bacteria, and other microorganic contaminants can breed in central air handling ductwork, humidifiers, and air coolers, which eventually distribute them throughout a building. Standing water in toilet tanks, ice makers, and wet carpeting are often breeding grounds for molds, mildew, bacteria, and insects. House dust mites are in virtually all homes, particularly in carpeting and upholstery, and frequently trigger allergic reactions. Ventilation systems in schools, hospitals, homes, and office buildings can circulate viruses and other microorganisms, spreading respiratory diseases.

These pollutants are ubiquitous. Humans are an important source, harboring bacteria, fungus, and other microorganisms on the skin, in hair, nose, mouth, and every other orifice and transmitting them to the air around us. While seldom lethal, biological contaminants can have other very serious implications. Allergic reactions are the most prevalent health effects. These include allergic rhinitis, some types of asthma, and hypersensitivity pneumonitis. Infectious diseases, such as influenza, measles, and chicken pox, can be transmitted by these microorganisms. Symptoms include watering eyes, sneezing, coughing, shortness of breath, dizziness, lethargy, fever, and digestive problems. Legionnaire's Disease is lethal and is an extreme example of what can happen from microorganic air pollution.

A buildup of carbon dioxide and other gases given off by the human body can affect the health and performance of office workers as well, and must especially be monitored in crowded spaces. A product of human metabolism, CO_2 can become concentrated to levels greater than 1200 ppm (parts per million) in crowded buildings with poor circulation and/or ventilation. This situation causes sleepiness, headaches, and ultimately leads to inefficiency. Other by-products of human metabolism which invade indoor air are acetaldehyde, acetone, ammonia, butyric acid, ethyl acetate, hydrogen sulfide, methane, methyl alcohol, phenol, and toluene.

Several years ago there was concern that foliage plants might be a source of airborne, biological contamination. Hospitals refused gift plants for patients at the time to avoid complications. In 1983, however, a research study by the University of Michigan dispelled these concerns. Foliage plants (non-flowering) were found to cause little or no contamination. There was concern, however, that chronically overwet planter soil could contaminate the air by harboring microorganisms. Under the right conditions they can migrate into surrounding air, but this has more to do with plant-care practices than with the general use of plants.[5] Common decorative plants were finally deemed benign by these researchers and are no longer medically restricted, except in highly sensitive situations where extreme caution prevails. Other reports support this position.[6]

Lead
Once a serious problem in the home, lead had been recognized early as a pollutant and human health hazard. The means of exposure are many—through drinking water, air, food, contaminated soil, or dust. Airborne lead enters the body when particles are breathed or swallowed as lead

dust. Automobile exhaust was a major contributor to this type of pollutant. Lead-based paint was discovered to be a significant source of lead poisoning among children who ate paint chips and contract workers who breathed in lead-based paint dust while sanding surfaces. Proper removal techniques minimize risk.

Lead-based paints have been removed from the market, but some exposure persists from outdoor lead dust being tracked into buildings from soldering processes (plumbing and electronics), lead-containing glass bottles, and from the continuous heating of soldered components in active computers, TVs, and other electronics.

Lead is toxic to many organs of the human body even at low concentrations. It can cause serious damage to the liver, brain, kidneys, peripheral nervous system, and red blood cells. Elevated high blood pressure can also result, even from low doses. Children, infants, and fetuses are particularly vulnerable because lead is more easily absorbed by growing bodies. Lead exposure by expectant mothers can delay fetal development, both physically and mentally. Children damaged by lead exhibit lower IQ levels, have shortened attention spans, and are more likely to exhibit behavior problems. Also, organ disorders would be expected throughout their lives.

Combustion By-Products

Burning fuel in homes and businesses can produce carbon dioxide, carbon monoxide, sulphur dioxide, formaldehyde, hydrocarbons, nitrogen oxides, particulates, and polyaromatic hydrocarbons—and this is only a partial list. We will discuss the most potentially damaging.

Carbon monoxide is a colorless, odorless gas that interferes with the delivery of oxygen to the body. It is a combustion product most commonly escaping from inadequately vented or maintained wood stoves, leaking chimneys, fireplaces, water heaters or boilers, kerosene or gas space heaters, gas ranges and clothes dryers, and automobile exhaust. Some are the result of flame in confined chambers (such as boilers) lacking sufficient oxygen for complete combustion. It can seep into the home, hotel, or office suites from attached garages or building mechanical rooms. Several recent lawsuits by injured hotel guests and office workers have won multi-million-dollar jury awards, pointing to the prevalence of the hazard and vulnerability of those of us who take our surroundings for granted. Environmental tobacco smoke is also a major source of carbon monoxide.

At low concentrations, carbon monoxide can impede coordination and cause fatigue and some chest pain in people with chronic heart disease. At higher concentrations, carbon monoxide can cause dizziness, headaches, weakness, nausea, confusion, and disorientation. Even greater concentrations can lead to unconsciousness and death.

Nitrogen dioxide is another by-product of combustion, from generally the same sources as carbon monoxide, and so the two are frequently found together in the interior environment. Millions of homes are equipped with gas stoves. Studies show that NO^2 levels in a kitchen while cooking with gas routinely exceed 1 mg/m^3 (0.53 ppm). At those levels pulmonary function has been shown to be depressed, particularly in children. Immune system response and lung function are also impaired. Its health effects are eye, nose, and throat irritation through an irritation of the mucous membranes, impaired breathing, and increased respiratory infections, particularly in children. Studies indicate it may also lead to serious lung diseases, such as emphysema.

Asbestos

These solid pollutants are microscopic mineral fibers which are flexible, durable, and will not burn. The fibers are light and are therefore easily airborne. Because of their excellent insulating properties, asbestos fibers are used in many appliances and building products. Around the house they used to be common in roofing, flooring, wall and pipe insulation, cement, spackling compound, heating equipment, hair dryers, and acoustic tiles. Upon aging or product damage, the fibers tend to flake off and become airborne, at which point they become health hazards. Automobile and truck brake linings were commonly made from asbestos. Decades of vehicular traffic has deposited asbestos along streets, parking lots, and roadways to be eventually tracked into buildings by pedestrian traffic.

These tiny fibers are inhaled and become trapped in the lungs where they cause permanent damage. "Asbestosis" is a scarring of the lung tissue, which impairs its function. Lung cancer and other carcinomas are also common, serious diseases brought on by exposure to asbestos.

Particulates

Fine particles of incompletely burned materials also permeate the air we breath. Its sources are generally the same as carbon monoxide and nitrogen dioxide, including environmental tobacco smoke. Other sources are dust and dirt. Pollen and animal dander are examples of biological particulates.

Particulates cause eye, nose, and throat irritation, respiratory infections, and bronchitis. Lung cancer is another serious illness caused by particulates, particularly when other pollutants (such as radon and benzo-(a)pyrene, both carcinogens) become attached to them and are inhaled deep into the lungs.

Formaldehyde

This is a chemical used to manufacture a wide variety of building materials and decorative products, and is thus found in abundance indoors. It is also a by-product

of combustion and certain natural processes. Although formaldehyde is an organic compound like other VOCs, its importance accords it separate discussion status. It is present in relatively heavy concentrations both indoors and outdoors. It is a colorless, pungent gas emitted from solid products made of formaldehyde compounds. Sources of this pollutant in the home and office include smoking (a by-product of cigarette combustion) and poorly vented fuel burning fireplaces and appliances, such as gas stoves, dryers, and kerosene space heaters. Major sources of formaldehyde are pressed wood and paper products (wallboard, wallpaper, high-pressure laminates, etc.).

Urea-formaldehyde is a resin widely used to hold wood and paper products together as a binder or adhesive. It is used in many types of structural materials in furniture (chipboard, flakeboard, fiberboard, hardboard), subflooring, shelving, cabinetry, and plywood paneling, and is also found in books, office paper, paper towels, wallpaper, wallboard, and a host of other common products. Phenol-formaldehyde finds similar uses in decorative laminates, such as Formica. Other decorative materials in the home and office also contain formaldehydes. Urea-formaldehydes and melamine-formaldehydes are widely used in clothing and decorative fabrics to impart wrinkle resistance, and also in carpet backing. In the 1970s urea-formaldehyde foam had also been used as a building insulation. High gaseous emissions soon forced discontinuation of its use. Elevated interior temperatures and humidity cause an increase in the release of the gas, augmenting the health risks.

The health consequences resulting from formaldehyde exposure are varied. At elevated concentrations (above 0.1 ppm), it can cause nausea, watery and burning sensations in the eyes, nose, and throat, as well as difficulty breathing. Asthma attacks are a common response in people who are susceptible. Studies suggest that humans can develop chemical sensitivity after prolonged exposure to formaldehyde. Other studies confirm its carcinogenic effects on laboratory animals, and it is strongly suspected of causing cancer in humans as well. High incidence of cancer among mobile home owners prompted the implementation of federal standards regulating usage. Some work suggests that 1 ppm of formaldehyde in environmental air can affect the central nervous system, leading to short-term memory loss, anxiety, and decreased sensitivity to light. At that level the substance can be smelled. Other neurophysiological effects also start at that level. Upper airway irritation starts at 0.1 to 25 ppm. Lower airway and pulmonary effects start at 5 to 30 ppm. Pulmonary edema, inflammation, and pneumonia start at 50 to 100 ppm, and death can occur at 100 ppm or above.[7] Three commercial buildings tested in 1988 by a Georgia Institute of Technology research group typically showed formaldehyde concentrations over 25 ppm (25, 30, and 39 ppm).[8] Testing in homes typically showed average formaldehyde levels at about 0.05 to 0.08 ppm. Long-term exposure to these low levels can produce similar effects.

The reason these and other carcinogenic chemicals cannot gain confirmation as cancer-causing agents in humans is that highly controlled, scientifically valid laboratory and clinical experiments cannot be performed directly on humans for safety reasons.

Pesticides

The EPA conducted a survey several years ago to find out how many households use pesticides. The results show that pesticides are used in 9 out of 10 homes. Another of their studies suggests that up to 90% of human exposure to airborne pesticides occurs indoors at home and in the office. Yet another study monitored measurable levels of up to one dozen different pesticides in private homes.

Pesticides are residual products. They are made to be long-lasting, and can emit their gases for many years. Other local products, such as wood furniture, wallboard, carpeting, upholstery, and draperies absorb these gases and, in turn, emit them over time. Pest control companies use large quantities of these chemicals in regular applications. Even outdoor applications find their way into the structures through air exchange, as well as through being tracked in by pedestrian traffic. Applications in partitions easily gas off into adjoining rooms. Pesticides are sold as aerosol sprays, liquids for spraying, sticks, powders, crystals, balls, and foggers (or "bombs") to control insects (insecticides), termites (termiticides), rodents (rodenticides), and fungi (fungicides).

As a class, pesticides are dangerous chemicals. The "-cide" in pesticide means *to kill*. Some pesticides were found to be so dangerous that they were banned from the market. Chlordane, heptachlor, aldrin, and dieldrin were found to remain active for very long periods of time and are therefore hazardous to humans as well. This family of chemicals, called cyclodienes, found common use as insecticides and termiticides. They are now restricted. Problems of enforcement, however, keep some of it in use by professional pest controllers, though it is not certain how widespread this action is. The chemical liquids or solids used to carry or suspend the active ingredients are also sources of organic gases. They are considered inert, but that refers to their not being an active pest-killing ingredient. Every pesticide label provides a warning and directions for proper use which must be carefully followed. Professional pest control contractors should be evaluated and screened. Their casual but constant misuse of these dangerous products can have serious consequences for those using the interior spaces being serviced. Personal use is more easily controlled, but it too presents hazards.

Eye and respiratory tract irritations and infections, dizziness, headaches, visual and memory impairment are but some of the everyday effects of these chemicals. Some are suspected or known carcinogens. For instance, exposure to high levels of cyclodienes because of misapplication has produced symptoms such as dizziness, muscle twitching, weakness, tingling sensations, and nausea. There is strong evidence that they also cause liver damage, damage to the central nervous system, and cancer.

Organic Gases (Volatile Organic Compounds)

There are literally thousands of sources of organic compounds that give off gases which pollute air in homes and indoor work spaces. This is another area where unwitting designer participation is paramount. For that reason, our discussion on the subject will be more detailed.

Most hydrocarbons are found at very low concentrations but are nonetheless dangerous, whether alone or in combination, particularly through long-term human exposure. Some products are made up of dozens of chemical components, each giving off a different contaminant. As a group they are called volatile organic compounds, or VOCs. It was the NASA Skylab III experiment that opened minds globally to the pervasiveness of VOCs in enclosed environments. They are gassed off (evaporated) from most things around us. It must be kept in mind that most of today's decorative and functional products are made of synthetic materials, which, given the right conditions, emit these gases. Therefore, the building and its

contents become the major source of interior pollution. Paint, cleaning chemicals, insulation, pesticides, carpeting, air fresheners, construction adhesives, toilet bowl fresheners, residues from dry cleaning fluids, copy machine and duplicating solvents, furniture core and finish materials (varnishes, waxes, etc.), aerosol propellants, cosmetics, and a host of other products become unwitting culprits.

In the mid-1980s, the EPA was commissioned by Congress to scientifically monitor the sources and assess the seriousness of air pollution in private homes and public buildings. The residential project was called the TEAM (Total Exposure Assessment Methodology) Study. It took six years to implement the parallel Public Buildings Study. Together they represent the most important in-depth research on the subject to date. Similar scientific results from projects in Denmark, Sweden, Italy, Germany, and Japan reinforce the findings. For the TEAM Study, seven cities in various geographical areas were chosen around the United States as study locations—some for their high outdoor pollution levels (such as Bayonne, NJ, and Los Angeles), and some for their relative absence of outdoor air pollution (like Devils Lake, ND). Samples of indoor (as well as outdoor) air, water, food, and breath were analyzed for the presence of major groups of toxic and carcinogenic chemicals. Prior studies had shown breath sampling adequately predicted the presence of environmental toxins in the blood, urine, hair, and other body cells.[9] Almost 600 subjects were monitored over a period of three years. All tests showed absorption of these intruders into the body. There was a particularly high correlation between the contaminant concentrations measured in breath samples as compared with concentrations of those pollutants in the home. The TEAM Study, and the concurrent study of indoor air pollution in public buildings, uncovered hundreds of VOCs, many eager to do us harm. Among the most pervasive were benzene, perchlorethylene, methylene chloride, and paradichlorobenzene. They were also surprised to find significant amounts of chloroform around hot water sources (showers, washing machines, etc.). Table 3.2 is a partial list of volatile organic compounds found in the air of typical American homes and public buildings during the EPA's two key studies. The scope of such studies is necessarily limited, but the depth of research gives a clear understanding of the pervasiveness involved.

Most of the pollutants covered by Table 3.2 are VOCs, many are known carcinogens or mutagens. In all, more than 500 VOCs were found and measured during the TEAM Study, but the EPA points out that there were many other air pollutants which were present but not monitored for reasons of cost, timing, or practicality.[10] Air samples to monitor VOCs were drawn at the sites and analyzed by means of gas chromatograph/mass spectrometers. The report points out that a typical air sample contained 100 to 200 compounds. Of these, about 50 compounds were unique to that particular sample. In other words, air contamination within a room is highly dependent on the room's contents. It will vary from place to place, but certain pollutants are common to most locations. All locations were heavily polluted, and indoor samples contained more varied pollutants than outdoor samples. The TEAM Study carried out in residential structures, and the Public Buildings Study carried out in schools, hospitals, nursing homes, and office buildings, found that major sources of pollutants were common, interior materials. Rubber and vinyl moldings, linoleum tile, and wiring were found to emit VOCs such as xylene, ethylbenzene, trimethylbenzene, ethyltoluene, decane, undecane, and dodecane. Latex caulk and cove adhesives

emit up to 17 different VOCs. Adhesives, caulking, paint, wall and floor coverings, and such plastic materials as telephone cables emit VOCs at high rates. Methyl chloride is found in spray paints, paint removers, and pesticide bombs. Tobacco smoke is a major source of benzene, styrene, ethylbenzene, xylene, and hundreds of other toxins. A visit to the dry cleaner's can double perchlorethylene and tetrachloroethylene levels in the breath of test subjects. Moth crystals and room deodorizers give off p-dichlorobenzene. Working and living around paint, plastics, service stations, and industrial plants increases exposure to carbon tetrachloride, xylene, styrene, benzene, ethylbenzene, trichloromethane, methyl chloride, trichloroethylene, and tetrachloroethylene. Figure 3.2 illustrates chromatograms showing the graphic "fingerprints" of a few pollutants typically found in residential and public buildings.

New and newly renovated buildings were found to be particularly high in aromatic and aliphatic hydrocarbons, testament to the fact that building and decorative products are major offenders. The pollution levels decay over many months, but always remain above outdoor levels. Regulations have been proposed calling for all new buildings to be massively ventilated for a period of weeks before use. Other proposals in Europe and California call for new and remodeled buildings to be "baked" (at 90° F) and ventilated for weeks to drive off much of the harmful gaseous emissions prior to use.

Health risk assessment by science is in its early stages and there is much to be learned. Very little has been forecast for the mortality rates from VOCs because the subject is broad and highly complex and has yet to be studied in depth. Of the 70,000 or so chemicals used in commerce and industry, less than 2% have been fully tested for human health effects. Over 70% have received no testing at all. Tests on

Table 3.2

Target Compounds Selected by the EPA for Monitoring in Building Interior Studies

Vinylidene chloride	Dibromochloropropane
Chloroform	m-Dichlorobenzene
1,2 Dichloroethane	o-Dichlorobenzene
1,1,1-Trichloroethane	p-Dichlorobenzene
Carbon tetrachloride	Benzene
Trichloroethylene	Styrene
Bromodichloromethane	Ethylbenzene
Dibromodichloromethane	o-Xylene
Tetrachloroethylene	m-Xylene
Chlorobenzene	p-Xylene
Bromoform	1,2-Dibromoethane
n-Decane	Undecane
Dodecane	n-Octane
1,4-Dioxane	1,1,1,2-Tetrachloroethane
a-Pinene	1,1,2,2-Tetrachloroethane
Dibromochloromethane	Ethylmethylbenzene
Toluene	Trimethylbenzene
Dimethylethylbenzene	Naphthalene
Methylnaphthalene	Propylmethylbenzene
n-Propylbenzene	Diethylbenzene
Trichloroethylene	Trichlorofluoromethane
Dichloromethane	Ethyl acetate
m-Hexylbutanoate	2-Ethyl 1-hexanol
n-Hexanol	2-Butyloctanol
n-Dodecanol	n-Nonanal
n-Devanal	Acetone
Acetic acid	Dimethylphenol
Ethylene oxide	2-Methylhexane
2-Methylpentane	3-Methylhexane
3-Methylpentane	Nonane
Tridecane	Methylcyclohexane
Heptane	Tetradecane
2-Methylheptane	Cyclohexane
Pentadecane	4-Methyldecane
2,4-Dimethylhexane	Pentane
Hexane	Eicosane
3-Methylnonane	1,3-Dimethylcyclopentane
2-Ethoxyethylacetate	m-Cresol
n-Butylacetate	m-Ethyltoluene
Particulates	Formaldehyde
Radon	Pesticides
Polynuclear aromatic hydrocarbons (PAHs)	Metals
Carbon monoxide	Nitrogen dioxide
Asbestos	

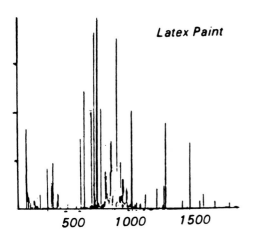

Latex Paint

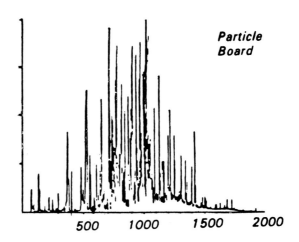

Particle Board

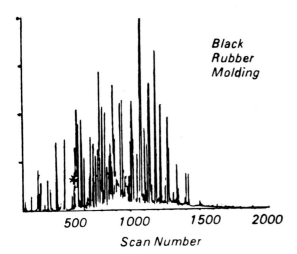

Black Rubber Molding

Scan Number

Figure 3.2: Graphic "fingerprints" of pollutants typically found in residential and public buildings. Source: L. Sheldon, et al, *Indoor Air Quality in Public Buildings: Volume II* (Washington, DC: U.S. Environmental Protection Agency, September 1988), 7.

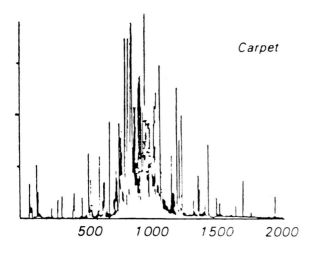

Carpet

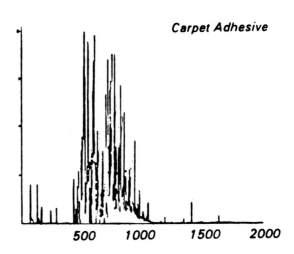

Carpet Adhesive

laboratory animals have uncovered hundreds of suspected human carcinogens, but many do not subscribe to that method of evaluation as being conclusive. Much greater effort is needed in this aspect of environmental study.[11] Researchers have evidence that certain combinations of pollutants may be riskier than others, and that mixtures are probably more important risk factors than individual gases, even at concentrations below the threshold of known neurological effects.[12] Health studies have shown that VOC mixtures at levels similar to those found in homes and offices may cause sensory irritation and behavioral effects such as memory loss. Many studies have attempted to relate environment to mortality. Some current estimates suggest that the total death toll attributed to cancer induced by occupational and pollution hazards in the United States is 120,000 annually. This is considered conservative by many. Studies by the National Cancer Institute (NCI) have correlated high cancer death rates with local industries, such as paper, petrochemical, chemical, shipbuilding, and transportation. These high rates are attributable to polluted water, air, food, and the work environment.

While the assessment of how much human risk there is in long-term exposure to various air pollutants is an inexact exercise because much has yet to be learned, the EPA reports there are two types of health risks associated with continuous exposure to IAP. First, chronic health effects (including cancer) result from long-term exposure (or possibly short-term exposure under certain conditions) to some of these compounds. Chloroform, methyl chloride, perchloroethylene, trichloroethylene, tetrachloroethylene, carbon tetrachloride, and p-dichlorobenzene are animal carcinogens and highly suspect in causing human carcinoma. Benzene is a known human carcinogen. Environmental tobacco smoke and its associated particulate/gaseous

compound combinations are highly suspect in causing lung cancer. Risk assessment for long-duration occupants of private residences, nursing homes, schools, offices, hospitals, and the like is greater indoors than out. That affects homemakers, children, medical staffs, office workers, the sick, the elderly, and most of us who work and live primarily indoors.

Data obtained from the EPA's TEAM Study showed a strong correlation between environmental pollutants and human absorption. This was further defined by the National Adipose Tissue Study. More than 100 environmentally derived toxic chemicals were found in human fatty (adipose) tissue samples. These unwanted invaders came from air, water, food, and work environments. The study provides an insight into the retention of pollutant chemicals in the human body. All cells are subject to retention by these damaging substances; adipose tissue data is simply a convenient indicator of general tissue absorption. Table 3.3 lists a portion of the chemicals found in human tissue.

Other studies show the pervasiveness of toxic chemicals in human blood samples, another indicator of how polluted the human body has become (see Tables 3.4 and 3.5).

In reviewing the preceding data, it must be kept in mind that this is a "short-list" of chemicals found in the subjects. Again, for reasons of economics, timing, or convenience, testing was limited to a select group of chemicals. Many others were present. The subjects' bodies were polluted over long periods of time (years), primarily by exposure to relatively low concentration levels. Damage to cells and metabolic systems are the inevitable result, as are related diseases. There is growing scientific evidence that IAP degrades the immune system over time, gradually making us more susceptible to many diseases, and progressively increasing sensitivity to pollutants.

Table 3.3

National Adipose Tissue Survey of the National Public Health Service
Retention of Select Pollutant Chemicals in the Human Body (% Distribution in Subjects)

Compound	Possible Sources of Exposure	% Distribution in Subjects
styrene	styrofoam cups, carpet backing	100%
1, 4 dichlorobenzene	mothballs, house deodorizers	100%
xylene	gasoline, paints	100%
ethyl phenol	drinking water	100%
OCDD (dioxin)	wood treatment, herbicides, auto exhaust	100%
HxCDD (dioxin)	wood treatment, herbicides, auto exhaust	98%
benzene	gasoline	96%
chorobenzene	drinking water	96%
ethyl benzene	gasoline	96%
DDE	pesticides in produce	93%
toluene	gasoline	91%
PCBs	air, water, food	83%
chloroform	drinking water, wash water	73%
butylbenzylphthalate	plastic products	69%
heptachlor	termite control	67%
DDT	pesticides in food, air	55%

Source: Debra Lynn Dadd, *The Non-Toxic Home and Office,* (Los Angeles: Jeremy P. Tarcher, 1992).

Table 3.4

Select Pesticides Present in Human Blood
% Distribution in 200 Chemically Sensitive Patients

Pesticides in Human Blood	% Distribution
DDT and DDE	62.0%
hexachlorobenzene	57.5%
heptachlorepoxide	54.0%
beta-BHC	34.0%
endosulfan I	34.0%
dieldrin	24.0%
gamma-chlordane	20.0%
heptachlor	12.5%
gamma-BHC (lindane)	9.0%
endrin	5.5%
delta-BHC	4.0%
alpha-BHE	3.5%
mirex	2.5%
endosulfan II	1.5%

Source: David Rousseau, W.J. Rea, Jean Enwright, *Your Home, Your Health and Well-Being* (Berkeley: Hartley & Marks Books [Ten Speed Press], 1988).

Table 3.5

Select Volatile Organic Compounds (VOCs) in Human Blood
% Distribution in 114 Chemically Sensitive Patients

VOCs in the Blood	% Distribution
tetrachloroethylene	83.1%
toluene	63.2%
xylene	59.7%
1, 1, 1-trichloroethane	50.5%
dichloromethane	49.7%
ethylbenzene	39.2%
chloroform	36.9%
benzene	23.4%
styrene	22.0%
dichlorobenzene	10.5%
trichloroethylene	8.6%
trimethylbenzene	3.2%

Source: David Rousseau, W.J. Rea, Jean Enwright, *Your Home, Your Health and Well-Being* (Berkeley: Hartley & Marks Books [Ten Speed Press], 1988).

Table 3.6

Comparisons—Concentrations of Toxic Pollutants, Indoor vs. Outdoor Air, and Human Breath Samples at Test Locations (Los Angeles—Winter and Spring 1984)
Pollutant Concentrations in Air and Human Breath (grams/meter3)*

Pollutant	Winter 1984			Spring 1984		
	Indoor Air	Outdoor Air	Breath	Indoor Air	Outdoor Air	Breath
1, 1, 1-Trichloroethane	96	34	39	44	5.9	23
m, p-Xylene	28	24	3.5	24	9.4	2.8
m, p-Dichlorobenzene	18	2.2	5.0	12	0.8	2.9
Benzene	18	16	8	9.2	3.6	8.8
Tetrachloroethylene	16	10	12	15	2.0	9.1
o-Xylene	13	11	1.0	7.2	2.7	0.7
Ethylbenzene	11	9.7	1.5	7.4	3.0	1.1
Trichloroethylene	7.8	0.8	1.6	6.4	0.1	1.0
n-Octane	5.8	3.9	1.0	4.3	0.7	1.2
n-Decane	5.8	3.0	0.8	3.5	0.7	0.5
n-Undecane	5.2	2.2	0.6	4.2	1.0	0.7
n-Dodecane	2.5	0.7	0.2	2.1	0.7	0.4
a-Pinene	4.1	0.8	1.5	6.5	0.5	1.7
Styrene	3.6	3.8	0.9	1.8	—	—
Chloroform	1.9	0.7	0.6	1.1	0.3	0.8
Carbon Tetrachloride	1.0	0.6	0.2	0.8	0.7	0.2
1, 2-Dichloroethane	0.5	0.2	0.1	0.1	0.06	0.05
p-Dioxane	0.5	0.4	0.2	1.8	0.2	0.05
o-Dichlorobenzene	0.4	0.2	0.1	0.3	0.1	0.04

Source: *Report to Congress on Indoor Air Quality: Volume II;* (Washington, DC: U.S.Environmental Protection Agency, August 1989), 2–32.
* Note: Indoor and outdoor air pollutant figures are averages of arithmetic means of day and night 12-hour samples.

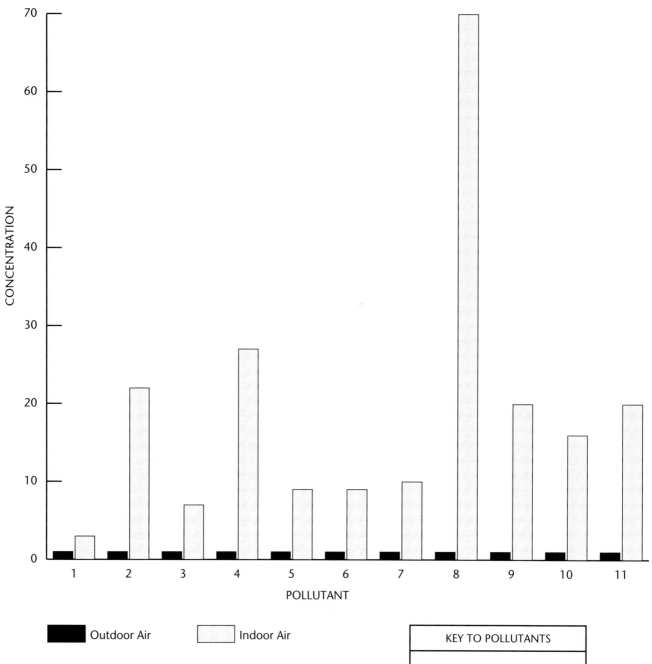

Figure 3.3: Ratio of chemical concentrations of polluted outdoor air to indoor air in homes. Bayonne, NJ; Fall 1981.

	KEY TO POLLUTANTS
1	Chloroform
2	1,1,1-Trichloroethane
3	Benzene
4	Carbon tetrachloride
5	Trichloroethylene
6	Perchloroethylene
7	Styrene
8	m,p-Dichlorobenzene
9	Ethylbenzene
10	Oxylene
11	m,p-Xylene

The second type of health effect is acute, caused by rapid exposure to high pollutant doses. These effects are most commonly eye, nose, and throat irritation, headaches, dizziness, neurotoxic symptoms such as depression, irritability, disorientation, forgetfulness, and general malaise. This group of symptoms is generally characterized as "building related illnesses."

The EPA studies found that concentrations of these chemicals were, in virtually every class, greater indoors than outdoors, and generally much more so. Indoor/outdoor concentration ratios as reported for each compound varied from 2:1 (twice as heavy a dose indoors) to more than 100:1 (100 times stronger concentrations indoors). This was a common thread running through the results of both the housing study and the public building study. Indoor pollution levels were also independent of air quality outdoors. Table 3.6 from the EPA's 1989 *Report to Congress on Indoor Air Quality* shows comparisons between indoor and outdoor air contamination in Los Angeles area homes (considered one of the nation's top problem areas for atmospheric pollution), as well as concentrations in occupant breath samples. The table typically shows greater concentrations indoors of 19 toxic chemicals (there were many more). Figure 3.3 shows ratio comparisons of indoor-to-outdoor air pollution in metropolitan Bayonne/Elizabeth, NJ, for 11 of the many pollutants discovered in homes there. That geographical area is also noted for its heavy smog from local industry. Contrary to conventional wisdom of the time, it became evident from these and many other studies that indoor exposure to pollutants is a greater risk to human health than outdoor exposure. The EPA's main assessment reported to Congress in 1989:

> Based on this analysis, EPA concluded that indoor air pollution represents one of the most important environmental problems

based on population risk. . . . the information available suggests that exposure to indoor air pollutants in non-industrial environments poses a significant health threat to the domestic population.[13]

The conclusion became particularly significant because of the large amounts of time humans dwell indoors in industrialized societies. Of major concern is the fact that the National Institute for Occupational Safety and Health (NIOSH) and most contractors providing building environmental testing services do not use methods sensitive enough to make qualitative and quantitative determinations for the presence of most VOCs. They go undetected in routine building investigations and the problem is thereby underestimated. The sophisticated gas chromatograph/mass spectrometer methods, which can detect very low concentrations of a wide range of gaseous toxins, are expensive and time-consuming to run, and generally not used for routine environmental testing.

Sick Building Syndrome and Building Related Illness

After years of study, the terms "Sick Building Syndrome" (SBS) and "Building Related Illness" (BRI) were coined to tag certain unhealthy building conditions as separate phenomena. NASA's research confirmed some of the suspicions about industrial materials adding to the problem.[14] Sick Building Syndrome describes health and comfort effects that large numbers of building occupants experience. The symptoms appear when the building is entered and disappear when the building is left. Typically, in these cases no specific illness can be identified.

Symptoms generally involve irritation of the eyes, nose, throat, and skin; neurotoxic symptoms, such as mental fatigue and headaches; unspecified hyperreactions, such as runny nose and asthma-like symptoms; as well as complaints about disturbing odors and tastes. Investigations of buildings with affected occupants have not been able to pinpoint any particular cause of the problem since individual pollutants are generally below threshold levels. Conclusions reached usually involve multi-causal factors and mention the additive or synergistic effect of combining various individual pollutants. General environmental conditions, such as lighting, humidity, and temperature, are also thought to have an influence. The indoor environment is concentrated and complex, giving rise to complex cause-effect relationships between human occupants and other local elements. Unhealthy conditions can frequently be improved by increasing room and/or building ventilation to circulate more fresh air, but that has only a palliative effect and does not eliminate the underlying problem.

The term "Building Related Illness" refers to human sickness brought on by exposure to the air in a building, but in this case symptoms of common illnesses can be readily diagnosed. These include fever, infection, and clinical signs of pathology. Hypersensitivity pneumonitis and Legionnaire's Disease are also examples.

Few homes or public buildings are ever related to either Sick Building Syndrome or Building Related Illness, nevertheless they are dangerous to their occupants with a subtlety that beclouds the true hazard. These are the tens of millions of typical homes and public buildings containing low concentration levels of hundreds of toxic gases mixed in with the air we breathe, contaminating our life-support systems. Science has shown chronic, long-term exposure to these conditions to be a significant health risk.

Strategies for Abatement

Because of the complexity of the issue and the variety of pollutant types and sources, clean-up of our interior spaces must be implemented along a broad front. The main courses of remediation advocated by the EPA involve:

1. Removal of pollution sources.

2. Modification of harmful sources to render them harmless, or at least reduce their toxic potential.

3. Ventilation to either displace or dilute offensive air.

4. Cleaning the air by filtration or other means.

Strategies generally involve a combination of these methods, and are influenced by technical factors as well as economic.

Unfortunately, the reality is that clean-up costs generally take precedence over the purity of the resultant environment. The most obvious action involves the *elimination of pollutant sources,* commonly known as source control. The design community is deeply committed to this strategy, and numerous programs have been in the works for many years. For instance, prompted by the attention asbestos received in the 1960s and 1970s, its use has been banned in construction. Major programs were also implemented to strip existing buildings of this dangerous substance. The efforts have largely been successful and, as a result, asbestos contamination is no longer a major issue.

Similar programs have reduced or eliminated the danger of other products as well. The ban on the use of certain pesticides, carpeting on wall surfaces, copy machines, lead paints, toxic aerosol propellants, formaldehyde-containing building insulation, many types of unvented kerosene heaters, and the use of smoking tobacco in select areas has been a good start. New procedures have been offered to prevent the growth of biological agents (dust mites, bacteria, fungus, etc.) in homes and public buildings. Changing filters in ventilation systems, cleaning humidifiers, air ducts, fan coils and air conditioners, cleaning water-damaged carpeting and furniture, and preventing moisture build-up in any confined space are among the recommended maintenance procedures. Radon is controlled by sealing cracks in basements, walls, slabs, and floors, along with other methods.

Most important to this issue is how the architect and interior designer perceive their role as specifiers of products that contain environmentally sensitive materials. Decisions are made by the design community during construction, renovation, and redecorating which either introduce toxic materials to the built environment or exclude them. Other decisions might also be made concerning the use of planter (biological) remediation technology. More will be said about this in Chapter Four.

The *modification of existing products* takes various forms. Product manufacturers have the key involvement, but architects, engineers, and interior designers can influence this remediation issue as well. Building products that contain benzene or formaldehyde have been replaced or modified with other components to meet air quality requirements. This is particularly true of particleboard, plywood, and other common construction materials rich in these dangerous substances. Carpet binders, paints, floor waxes, cleaning materials, air fresheners, and pesticides have been notable areas of improvement.

Another concept of product modification that has been implemented involves the sealing off or isolating of pollutant sources from the occupied areas of buildings through the use of coatings and vapor barriers. These surface modifications can be both decorative and functional, and can be particularly effective in containing pollutants like formaldehyde, pesticides, and radon in their immediate source areas. Nevertheless, it is suspected that eventual leakage will in many cases result in high concentrations of these substances being outgassed to the occupied environments.

Ventilation is another of the important strategies used for the control of high concentrations of carbon dioxide, particulates, combustion by-products from heating and cooking devices, stale air from smoking, as well as VOCs. It is the primary mitigation method in use today. Dilution of indoor pollutants involves the use of two basic techniques in HVAC systems. Both can be quite effective in reducing pollutant levels (particularly at acute concentrations), but have drawbacks and should only be considered as interim solutions until more effective measures have been developed. One method is to eliminate stale air from the enclosed microenvironment by interchanging it with fresh air from the outside. A certain amount of natural exchange is expected, as air goes in and out of a building through leaks, cracks, semi-permeable walls, open windows, and doors. Mechanically induced, however, this method of air exchange can be costly to use in sealed modern buildings because of the large amounts of air that must be handled and the conditioning and reconditioning (cooling, heating, humidifying, and filtration) that is necessary. It is non-selective in the quality of air it draws in and large energy expenditures are involved, making its use counterproductive to energy conservation strategies. Air-to-air heat exchangers are recommended to help reduce the added burden of indoor/outdoor air interchange. However, these add to project cost, so relatively few buildings, and even fewer homes, have them. Another problem is that the fresh air brought into a building is far from pure in most locations.[15] NIOSH estimates most buildings have no gas filtration devices installed, and many of those that are are inoperative—so air handling systems mainly clean air of particulates, but not gases. In those situations, unhealthy air recirculates continuously through the building, picking up more gassed-off toxins as it goes.

More practical are the methods of diluting interior air with clean, conditioned indoor air, thus reducing pollutant concentrations to more manageable levels. This is not easy to accomplish in a cost-effective way, for air movement can be frequent, and generally in fairly large volume. Recycled air must be cleansed and reconditioned, with added power cost. And again there is the problem of inadequate or impractical gas filtration technologies for HVAC systems, in addition to the complications of fresh air placement. Present recommended ventilation rates have been artificially inflated to accommodate the fact that no practical HVAC gas removal methods are available to cope with our highly polluted, energy-efficient buildings. Rates were decreased in the early 1970s in reaction to the energy crisis. But in the late 1980s higher ventilation rates were reestablished (to 20 cubic feet of air exchange per minute) when indoor pollution and health issues were associated with inadequate air circulation.

Ventilation is seldom efficient. Erratic air flow patterns can considerably reduce ventilation rates in pockets of rooms, frequently to levels much lower than 0.1 air changes per hour (ach).[16] Interiors are typically irregular in layouts with partitions, room dividers, arches, closets, hallways, and closures, making them terrible examples of aerodynamic efficiency. The laws governing air flow produce many irregularities and contra forces which restrict efficient circulation and ventilation. In addition, intermittent ventilation cycles can create dead air throughout commercial buildings for long periods, and generally even longer in residential systems. Night cycles are particularly low. Many buildings have occupied areas which are pockets having low ventilation dynamics, and which also exhibit high levels of contamination. In these cases the HVAC system is inadequately designed.

There is also the unfortunate fact that HVAC systems are in many instances the root cause of a variety of biological pollutants and gaseous combustion by-products. Improper inspection and cleaning of humidifiers, filters, cooling systems, air ducts, heaters, flues, and boilers can create a number of environmental problems. These devices and pathways are prime breeding grounds for microbes that thrive on warmth and moisture, which are then distributed through the system to all parts of the building. Although most of the consequences to occupants involve relatively minor occurrences of respiratory disorders, there are occasional outbreaks of such fatal infectious diseases as Legionnaire's Disease and Pontiac Fever. Serious, but less severe, are cases of hypersensitivity pneumonitis and humidifier lung. Heating systems in homes and commercial buildings are also frequent sources of pollutants, such as carbon dioxide, carbon monoxide, nitrogen dioxide, formaldehyde, and sulphur dioxide. They, too, can breed pollutants in humidifiers and duct work. Proper exhaust venting of the heating, clothes drying, and cooking areas is essential to the elimination of local gases before they can circulate. Recent years have seen several court cases brought against hotel chains by guests seriously affected by gas leakage from mechanical rooms into their suites. In many cases, the problems rest with the architectural or mechanical design. Heating systems must be properly housed in rooms or cells so as to provide adequate air circulation, otherwise improper combustion results, with offgassing of carbon monoxide and other undesirable substances.

The removal of carbon dioxide from high-density work and recreational areas is one of the prime concerns of engineers, for this by-product of human metabolism is present at high levels in most buildings. Unfortunately, however, CO_2 monitoring receives an inordinate amount of attention from environmental control contractors and in-house specialists, with not enough attention to gas chromatograph/mass spectrometer testing for the multitude of other low level gases. That is presumably due to the ease with which CO_2 can be detected, the economy and availability of monitoring devices for this compound, the historical awareness of "stale air problems" by HVAC engineers, and the lack of substantial knowledge about other IAP factors. The last comment is not meant to challenge the competence of engineers and technicians in this field, but is a reflection of the complexity of the IAP issue and the incomplete knowledge by the research community.

Because all structures have HVAC systems, ventilation techniques will be a permanent part of indoor air pollution abatement strategies. There are, however, obvious difficulties beyond energy consumption which must nonetheless be addressed. While simple particle matter can be easily removed from the air, gases cannot, and the air remains largely unhealthy when moved to another part of the building or expelled to the outdoor environment. As previously mentioned, bringing polluted outdoor air into the building during air interchange is only a stopgap measure. Critics explain that simply moving polluted air from one part of the ecosystem to another is not a reasonable answer. Collectively, the waste gases from billions of new and existing buildings around the world represent a major source of global pollution. Future strategies must concentrate on designing, building, and maintaining environmentally cleaner buildings. Meanwhile, only source control and air cleaning, the removal and disposal of all types of pollutants from return air in active structures, can satisfy environmental goals.

Effective *air cleaning* is essential to success in indoor air pollution control programs, but it can be difficult to achieve. Filtration—the removal of most solid particles from the air—is a fairly simple matter and can be accomplished with mechanical and electrostatic devices. Organic and inorganic gases, however, are difficult to remove, particularly over long periods of time. Current technology for removing gaseous pollutants involves the use of absorbent and adsorbent materials to catch gases on their external or internal surfaces. Once the carbon, alumina, or other sorbent material has been saturated, further filtration is impaired. It must be frequently replaced or regenerated to remove the toxic materials. This makes for expensive and cumbersome maintenance procedures. Chemical scrubbers, thermocatalytic filters, and other methods of removal are also of limited practicality in their present states of development. Small, table-top utility air cleaners are also of very limited value. They have been tested by *New Shelter* magazine, Lawrence Berkeley Laboratory, and by Consumer Union. The testers by and large considered them useless for removing gases from indoor air.[17] Evaluations of this kind generally deal with environmental tobacco smoke, as it contains such a wide range of gaseous and particulate matter. In order to remove particulates as well as gases in the same HVAC system, multi-stage filtration/air cleaning devices are required.

One of the problems facing engineers, building owners and planners is the high cost of adding advanced air handling and filtration equipment to new construction and to the large inventory of existing buildings. Another technology made public in the past few years could have great potential in this area. The concept has actually been in continuous use for eons, but only recently has its power and effectiveness been understood and appreciated. It involves biological processes, using ornamental plants in large numbers to absorb and degrade gaseous pollutants—air cleaning indoors the natural way. They are used in conjunction with conventional HVAC filtration, helping to take some of the load off of the latter. Studies have demonstrated this biotechnology can be very effective and has several advantages. It requires little or no external energy, using mainly natural sunlight. It utilizes natural photosynthesis and microorganic processes to absorb, degrade, and assimilate organic gases from the surrounding air. It has no waste to dispose of, so the process is self-regenerating (self-cleaning). The technology is readily available, inexpensive, easy to install, and can be used in new and old buildings alike. Photosynthesis is one of the most complex, sophisticated, and powerful processes on earth, whether natural or man-made. We should use it to our advantage. Chapter Four will deal more thoroughly with the details of planter/gas sorption air cleaning systems.

FOUR

Biological Solutions to Indoor Pollution

Only recently have we begun to understand that plants perform many critical functions in the creation and management of our planet's life processes. As a subject of scientific study, plants are highly complex, and to understand their mysteries many scientific disciplines are involved, such as plant physiology, physiological ecology, botanical microbiology, environmental microbiology, and other life sciences. We now know that without plants there would be no animal life on earth, and with the continuous destruction of the earth's greenery, we erode our own life-support systems.

How We Rely on Plants

The truth is, human life depends on plant life. On a physiological level, for example, we eat plants for nourishment. Our digestive systems cannot function without plant enzymes, which along with pancreatic enzymes break down food particles to permit absorption and assimilation. On a medical level, plant extracts and juices have been used for their healing and medicinal properties for centuries. The word *chemical* comes from the Greek word *chemia,* meaning "the juice of a plant."[1] It is estimated that between 25% and 40% of the drugs currently being produced have plant origins. Pharmaceutical companies are scrambling to discover even more before the Amazonian rain forest is decimated. Even on a spiritual level we have close ties with the plant kingdom. A Hopi leader once said: ". . . almost all life will stop unless men come to know that everyone must live in peace and harmony with nature. Only those people who know the secrets of nature, the mother of us all, can overcome the possible destruction of all land and life . . . ."[2]

Air pollution control is one of the many services that plants have provided us. From the simple plants in the sea (phytoplankton) to the more complex plants on land (trees, shrubs, and grasses), nature has given us miniature chemical processing machines capable of drinking in carbon dioxide and other organic gases and expelling oxygen, thereby purifying our atmosphere in the process. Over hundreds of millions of years living organisms have evolved and adapted to their changing environment. Yet the more we tamper with nature's delicate balance, the more we endanger our future. We tend to view the future in the context of man-made technologies alone—the technosphere, as some call it. That kind of thinking brought about our current environmental dilemma,

and now we are charged with the task of restoring a balance. The concepts discussed in this chapter are offered as an important means of accomplishing just that.

In the previous chapter we learned of indoor air pollution's growing presence. This chapter will explain in greater detail some of the attributes of plants and how they can help solve this serious health problem with their unique biochemistry.

The Role of Plants in the Evolution of Planet Earth

The creation of our planet is a subject that evokes controversy and speculation. There are many aspects of it, however, that most scientists agree upon. One is the role of green plants in the refinement of a gaseous atmosphere that covered the primeval globe, over time making it suitable for the evolution of other organisms. Some of those eventually became the oxygen-consuming animal kingdom. It is estimated that 99% of the Earth's atmosphere is of biological origin.[3] In other words, our sky is a product of life on Earth.

The air we breath is composed of a number of elements. Nitrogen is the main constituent, accounting for roughly 76% of the total (by weight). Oxygen accounts for approximately 23%. Various other gases make up the balance in minute proportion—1% of the total.

The global atmosphere was not always that way. The earth was formed about 4.6 billion years ago, enveloped in a dusty and gaseous environment composed chiefly of methane, ammonia, water, and hydrogen. It was not until about 600 million years ago that the oxygen content of the primeval atmosphere reached 1%. At that point aerobic (oxygen-using) respiration by minute organisms living in the seas became more efficient than respiration without

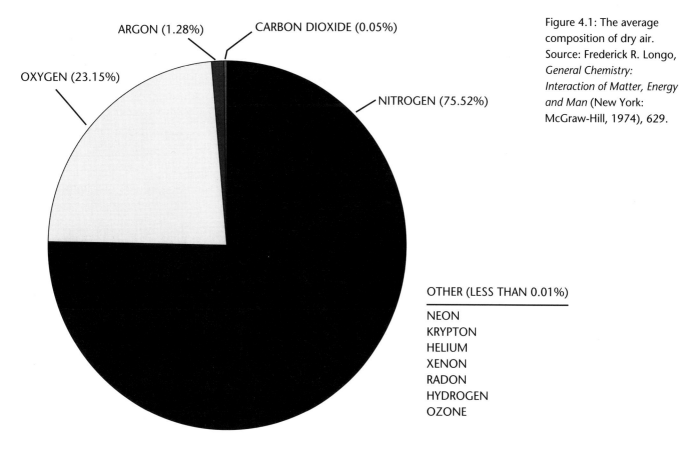

Figure 4.1: The average composition of dry air. Source: Frederick R. Longo, *General Chemistry: Interaction of Matter, Energy and Man* (New York: McGraw-Hill, 1974), 629.

ARGON (1.28%)

CARBON DIOXIDE (0.05%)

OXYGEN (23.15%)

NITROGEN (75.52%)

OTHER (LESS THAN 0.01%)

NEON
KRYPTON
HELIUM
XENON
RADON
HYDROGEN
OZONE

oxygen. Primitive life slowly adapted to the change, and about 400 million years ago the first simple green plants appeared, the first form of life on dry land. These and unicellular plants living in the sea had the unique ability to absorb carbon dioxide from the atmosphere, and in the presence of sunlight and water, convert the sun's radiant energy to another form of potential energy—carbohydrates, starches, and sugars, and then other complex chemicals. By-products of the molecular reaction in green plants are pure oxygen and water vapor, which are given back to the atmosphere. In this way, over a period of hundreds of millions of years, there was a gradual rise in the oxygen level surrounding earth, until it reached its present 23%, sustaining the evolution and survival of larger, more complex organisms like mammals. Our survival is thus derived from the wonderful chemistry of a plant's conversion of light energy to food energy and oxygen. Almost all other human needs revolve around the availability of live and once-live plants, and the carbon (organic) compounds they contain—the result of photosynthesis, the key to all life on earth.[4]

The Process of Photosynthesis

The photochemical process by which green plants are able to draw carbon dioxide and other organic gases from the air in the presence of sunlight and water and convert it internally to chemical carbohydrates is called *photosynthesis*, a word meaning "putting together with light." Photosynthesis is the largest-scale systemic process on earth. It is highly complex with details which extend far beyond our summary here, but the following explanation will help clarify one of life's most important secrets.

To understand the unique abilities of green plants, we have to tap the knowledge of plant physiologists. In basic structure, most plants are made up of leaves, stem, and roots. Leaves are miniature chemical processing factories. Just below the upper surface of a leaf is a barrier of cells containing chloroplasts, which are packets of green chlorophyll, the organic catalysts of photosynthesis. It is within these cells that photosynthesis takes place. The leaf structure also contains pores called *stomata* that are found mostly on the lower leaf surface. These pores permit the passage of carbon dioxide, oxygen, other gases, and water vapor in and out of the plant. The average plant leaf contains between 2,000 and 40,000 stomata in each square centimeter of surface area.

When multiplied by the total leaf area of a plant, it becomes apparent that a plant's absorption apparatus is quite extensive.

Water, too, is essential for all living organisms. Most of the water for plant sustenance comes from the soil surrounding the roots. By means of a highly efficient water transfer system, and as a by-product of the photosynthetic process, water vapor is released to the air through the leaf pores, or stomata. The effect is like that of a semi-continuous suction, from leaves down to roots, causing the roots to draw in a new supply of nutrient-laden moisture from the soil to be distributed throughout the plant. The movement of water from the roots up through the tubular channels in the stem and leaves, through the stomata to the

Figure 4.2: Drawing of leaf cross section.

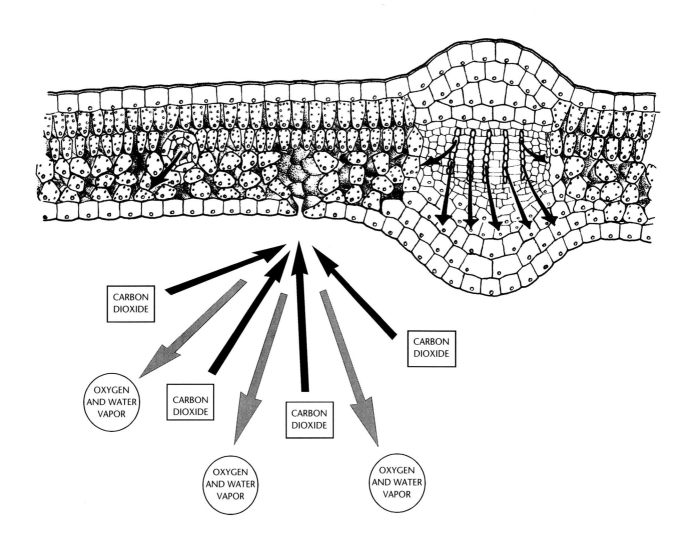

surrounding air is called *transpiration*. One of its varied functions is to stiffen plant tissues. Another is to cool the plant by evaporation from leaf surfaces, in much the same way as does human perspiration. Transpiration also is responsible for distributing nutritional elements throughout the plant. In fact, many of the biological processes of higher plants are strikingly similar to those of our body processes, from the DNA content, to the cellular structure, to the multitude of complex chemical changes constantly taking place.

When *chlorophyll* absorbs sunlight, it excites local electrons which pass electrochemical energy to other molecules. *Chloroplast* cells will have already absorbed some of the moisture and carbon dioxide present outside its walls. That combination promotes a chemical reaction to take place. The energy generated by chlorophyll splits water molecules in the chloroplast into oxygen and hydrogen atoms. In complex, multi-stage reactions, hydrogen atoms combine with carbon dioxide molecules (and with other organic gases present) which the plant has absorbed from the air to make simple carbohydrates, energy-containing sugars (sucrose and glucose), and starch, which are then passed into the stem and carried to various parts of the plant. There they are stored and eventually converted by other metabolic processes into more complex chemical substances such as lipids, nucleic acids, proteins, and other organic molecules used in plant growth. Most of the oxygen atoms freed from water molecules by the photosynthetic reaction are expelled back into the atmosphere through the leaf stomata along with excess water vapor. It is this continuous photochemical process that cleanses the air of unwelcome organic gases and renews it with pure oxygen. The starches and sugars created within the plant are used for the plant's sustenance and growth, eventually

to be used by humans and other animals for their needs and life support.[5] Even carnivores that are exclusively meat eaters consume other animals that feed on plants, and so absorb the chemical nutrients and energy of plants in a second-hand way.

The Role of Plants in Our Ecosystem

Green plants in the sea and on land continuously process enormous amounts of carbon dioxide and other organic gases. The total complex of living organisms—among them plants, insects, microorganisms, and mammals—are referred to as the *biosphere*. Carbon is said to be fixed, or converted, by photosynthesis. The amount of carbon fixation determines the amount of oxygen given back to the global ecosystem. Collective plant activity maintains oxygen in the proper atmospheric balance. Figure 4.3 illustrates the relative contribution by

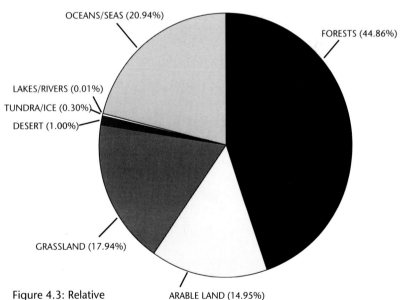

OCEANS/SEAS (20.94%)

FORESTS (44.86%)

LAKES/RIVERS (0.01%)

TUNDRA/ICE (0.30%)

DESERT (1.00%)

GRASSLAND (17.94%)

ARABLE LAND (14.95%)

Figure 4.3: Relative amounts of carbon fixed by green plants on Earth. Source: G.R. Noggle and G.J. Fritz, *Introductory Plant Physiology*, (Englewood Cliffs, NJ: Prentice Hall, 1983), 159.

various components. Land plants account for almost 80% of the carbon fixation on Earth. More than half of that is accomplished in the forested areas of the world, which occupy about 30% of the land surface. Very little is accomplished in extremely cold or extremely hot areas, like tundra and desert.

The main reason for the high productivity of forest communities as a whole is the high rate of carbon fixation in tropical trees and shrubs. They are evergreen and reside in areas where environmental conditions are very conducive to growth and general metabolic functions. This is one of the reasons for the high environmental value placed on the Amazonian Rain Forest. It represents a dense, highly efficient mass of greenery constantly absorbing carbon dioxide and giving off massive amounts of oxygen.

While plants do grow in the water that covers 70% of the earth's surface, they only account for 21% of all carbon fixation. Freshwater lakes and rivers are not very productive in nurturing plant life, and the great depths of the oceans rule out photosynthesis. Algae in phytoplankton living near the surface of deep seas account for most carbon fixation there, using carbon dioxide dissolved in the water as their carbon source.[6] Plants growing in the shallow seas and continental shelf areas are the most productive of the aquatic plants, and fix carbon at rates similar to land plants.

The total amount of carbon fixed annually by terrestrial and aquatic plants is 199 billion metric tons. To put this in perspective, about 3 billion metric tons of carbon are used each year by humans for fuel (coal, natural gas, and petroleum). If we consider that carbon dioxide, the main carbon source for photo-synthesis, makes up only 0.033% (by volume) of the atmosphere, the total quantity of air that the world plant population must "inhale" to get enough carbon dioxide for its needs is staggering to contemplate.

In photosynthesis, for every atom of carbon fixed, two atoms of oxygen are released to the atmosphere. The total annual production of oxygen by green plants on earth is estimated to be 530 billion metric tons. Approximately 30% of the oxygen released is reabsorbed by the plant systems and used in their respiratory processes, thus the net free oxygen production by plants is estimated at 371 billion metric tons annually.

What does all this mean in more practical terms? Living plants might well be considered our planet's respiratory/air filtration system, taking in more air by far than all humans on Earth. The average tree inhales 26 pounds of carbon dioxide annually, and exhales enough oxygen to keep a family of four breathing for a year.[7] Plants alone have the ability to turn the non-living into the living.

Indoor Plants

Plants are mainly used as a form of decoration in building interiors, but the awareness of plants' technical ability to provide important human life-support functions brings a new reason for the use of greenery indoors. From an ecological standpoint, interiorscapes help to replace the biomass lost to construction excavation while improving the air quality in the microenvironments they inhabit. Plants, therefore, have a modifying influence on indoor ecology (also called shelter ecology, closed system ecology, and microenvironmental ecology).

Interiorscaping plants are essentially the same as those found outdoors. Originating in the tropical and subtropical regions of the world, they grew as evergreens, not shedding leaves with the seasonal changes. Interior landscape professionals found that plants had to be conditioned, or acclimatized, in shady outdoor environments to prepare them for their new lives indoors. Light levels indoors are many times lower than in the field, and plant metabolism slows down considerably under these very different conditions. Acclimatization permits the plant to gradually adapt.

Photosynthesis takes place indoors as well, albeit at a reduced level. The large difference in light intensity between indoors and outdoors is somewhat limiting to photosynthetic activity. Scientific research has shown, however, that the photosynthetic system is light-saturated at irradiation levels about 20% of full sunlight values. In other words, strong, subdued light can produce almost the same photosynthetic result as full, daytime sunlight. Nonetheless, plants do grow in the dimmer interior environment with reduced vigor.

NASA Research with Plants as Gas Sorption Filters

Most work in the field of closed system ecology originated in the competing space programs of the United States and the Soviet Union during the Cold War. For that reason, the great preponderance of data available today comes from their reports.

The space programs had a problem that demanded resolution. Because it is impractical to store large quantities of fresh air and water on board on long-duration missions, there was a need for practical systems to purify and recycle used supplies. NASA established research projects designed to mitigate air pollutant hazards in future missions. To find solutions they turned to nature. One of the strategies undertaken involves the use of higher plants as self-regenerating bio-filters for air and water purification. Part of their problem had to do with the fact that any system used on board space vehicles to clean air and water had to

be energy-efficient, with some practical means of disposing of the toxic waste extracted by the filters during long voyages. The problem is not as severe on Earth, where disposal systems can be implemented, but with the limitations of space vehicles, more compact and efficient systems were necessary. Building on the knowledge of plant physiology at the time, the photosynthetic process was enlisted to create food for the voyagers, but also to absorb and degrade carbon dioxide and other unwelcome organic gases from the air and wastewater.

One advantage to using plants as air filters was that the soil system contains millions of microorganisms that also feed on organic and inorganic materials—including trapped gases. Microorganisms have short lives, and can therefore readily adapt to new conditions. This adaptability broadens their appetite for a variety of substances in the soil. A number of early scientific projects focused on plant root/microbial degradation of pollutants in soils and wastewater, particularly toxic chlorinated hydrocarbons. They, too, confirm plants' abilities as purifiers. The internal metabolic processes that destroy toxic materials make the planter/filter system self-regenerating or self-cleaning and able to operate (at reduced levels) in the dark as well. When light levels are reduced, the photosynthetic process may shut down, but the microbial part of the system continues to operate.

Concurrent to the air purification work, studies were undertaken by NASA to cleanse water via root system absorption and biological degradation of the pollutant chemicals. Research was carried out under the direction of Dr. B.C. Wolverton at NASA's Environmental Research Laboratory, National Space Technology Laboratories in Mississippi (now John C. Stennis Space Center). NASA was already years behind the Soviets in this type of life-support research. They had embarked on a similar project much earlier, and had a sophisticated and active biospheric laboratory at Krasnoyarsk. Over a twelve-year period, two or three researchers at a time had been sealed inside their BIOS-3 chamber (an enclosure about the size of a small house) for as long as six months, kept alive by planter-based oxygenation and water purification as well as plant foods. Photosynthesis was the primary life-support system. Medical testing of the subjects afterward reported no adverse health effects from being in close proximity with the plants for such prolonged periods, nor did they find any adverse effects on quality of air, water or food.[8] This research dispelled critics' contentions that plants can endanger human health when in close proximity for long periods, and that plants' biological systems are not powerful enough for this type of human life support. It proved that when used properly, plants can serve us in important ways other than decor or food. One of the striking anomalies that came out of this work was the Soviet's openness in sharing these important results with the world, particularly at a time when the cold war was in its depths. They recognized the significance of their data to our global society.

Meanwhile, NASA struggled with the fundamentals. They were out to discover how and why biological purification systems would work. Most of NASA's early studies were carried out in small, sealed, clear acrylic chambers 0.400 cubic meters in volume containing the subject plant, a fan to circulate air, and a means of controlling temperature and humidity. Grow lights surrounded the chamber to provide necessary illumination. On one side of the chamber, a sealed port permitted test gases to be injected into the enclosed environment and to take air samples. The use of small chambers is a common experimental technique, and such enclosures are found in horticultural and environmental research laboratories throughout the country.[9] For example, the EPA's pollutant emission studies of common building materials were carried out in small chambers during the Public Buildings Study.[10] This technique is necessary because it provides a highly controlled environment in which precise monitoring can take place. Small systems are better able to isolate factors and more clearly define mechanisms at work.

Early bio-system experiments concentrated on relatively high concentrations of formaldehyde, carbon monoxide, and nitrogen dioxide, because they are among the most common indoor pollutants.[11] These screening tests were designed to gauge plants' tolerance to toxic gases and to get a general indication of various species' effectiveness in absorbing gases. Conventional wisdom at the time predicted the quick demise of plants at such high toxin levels. Much of NASA's work was done with civilian uses in mind, as a spin-off from their space studies. It was felt the pollution concerns of enclosed, residential, and work areas on Earth were in many ways similar to those in space. The plant types used in these screening studies were common ornamental varieties of houseplants, such as Scindapsus aureus ("Golden Pothos"), Syngonium podophyllum ("Goosefoot Plant"), and Chlorophytum elatum var. vittatum ("Spider Plant"). Close attention was paid to experimental detail using multiple replications and other accepted scientific procedures. In order to determine the integrity of the chamber, gas measurements were taken in empty chambers and other controls were used, such as plantless potting soil in containers to determine whether the soil itself might be a gas sorbent material. Earlier studies suggested soil did absorb certain quantities of gas.

The plants did not die and, on the contrary, showed a remarkable ability to adapt in their alien test environment. The graphs on the next few pages have been extracted from NASA's early experimental data and illustrate some of the gas sorption characteristics of select plants. These data clearly demonstrate plants' abilities to absorb and assimilate toxic gases other than carbon dioxide, as well as their tolerance of relatively high concentrations of these pollutants (see Figures 4.4, 4.5, and 4.6).

The study went even further, attempting to define the relative efficiency of each plant by measuring its total leaf surface and computing gas sorption per square centimeter.

The data in Table 4.1 show the comparative rates of absorption and assimilation of three toxic gases (formaldehyde, carbon monoxide, and nitrogen dioxide) by three plant types. This information was derived by measuring the plants' leaf surface area and using it as a basis against which gas sorption efficiency is determined. NASA concluded that of those few plants tested, the Chlorophytum elatum

("Spider Plant") was the most efficient. Their other early conclusion was that plants did appear to possess the attributes necessary for effective gas sorption filters, and as a result research was expanded to include other pollutants and a wider range of plant materials. In the expanded studies, a greater variety of houseplants were investigated and pollutant monitoring was accomplished through more sensitive techniques. Gas chromatograph/mass selective detector (GC/MS) analysis provided measurements at much lower contaminant levels and with greater accuracy.

The second phase of experimentation concentrated on formaldehyde contaminants with a wider variety of plants. It was designed to screen for some of the more environmentally effective ornamentals. Aloe vera, philodendrons, and the green spider plant were found to be the best (of those tested) under these specific conditions (see Figure 4.7 and Appendix Table 3.2).

The data in Table 4.2 express the amount of contaminant gas formaldehyde absorbed

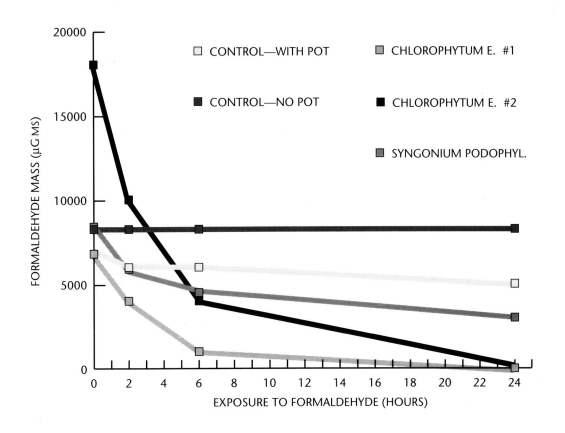

Figure 4.4: Formaldehyde removal by plants/high concentration. Sources: Compiled from B.C. Wolverton, Rebecca C. McDonald and E. A. Watkins, Jr. (NASA, Environmental Research Lab.), *Foliage Plants For Removing Indoor Air Pollutants from Energy-Efficient Homes*, 38(2)(Bronx.NY: Econmic Botony, New York Botanical Garden, 1984), 227; B.C. Wolverton, Rebecca C. McDonald and Hayne H. Mesick (NASA, Environmental Research Lab.), "Foliage Plants for Indoor Removal of the Primary Combustion Gases Carbon Monoxide and Nitrogen Dioxide," *Journal of the Mississippi Academy of Sciences*, Vol. XXX, (1985): 5.

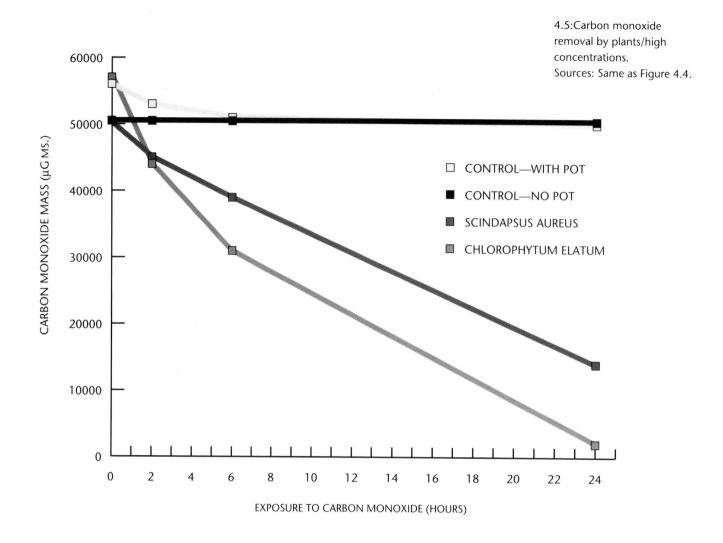

4.5:Carbon monoxide removal by plants/high concentrations.
Sources: Same as Figure 4.4.

- □ CONTROL—WITH POT
- ■ CONTROL—NO POT
- ■ SCINDAPSUS AUREUS
- ■ CHLOROPHYTUM ELATUM

CARBON MONOXIDE MASS (μG MS.)

EXPOSURE TO CARBON MONOXIDE (HOURS)

Table 4.1

Change in Contaminant Mass Expressed as a Function of Leaf Surface Area (Grams of Gas Absorbed/cm^2 of Leaf Surface)

Contaminant Gas	Plant Subject	Reduction in Gas Mass (μg/cm^2 leaf surface) after 6 hours	After 24 hours
Formaldehyde	Scindapsus aureus	0.46μg/cm^2	0.61μg/cm^2
	Syngonium podophyllum	0.50	0.67
	Chlorophytum elatum (v. vitt.)		
	Set 1	0.81	> 0.81
	Set 2	2.27	> 2.74
Carbon Monoxide	Scindapsus aureus	0.98	2.89
	Chlorophytum elatutm (v. vitt.)	2.86	5.86
Nitrogen dioxide	Chlorophytum elatum (v. vitt.)		
	Set 1—soil exposed	3.63	3.63
	Set 2—soil covered	3.29	3.29

by each plant type as a function of leaf surface area. Most efficient for their size were philodendrons, spider plants, and golden pothos. The control using a plantless pot of soil exhibited an absorption rate of 33%, lending credence to researchers' perceptions that the soil system is at least partially responsible for a plant's gas sorption properties.[12]

Experiments with benzene gave similar results. In a 1986 paper, NASA reported highly efficient removal of benzene from test chambers by golden pothos and elephant ear philodendron plants. After 24 hours of filter activity, each plant was able to assimilate 79% and 80% of the benzene respectively. To see what would happen over longer periods, the philodendron testing was extended to 48 hours. During that time it removed 95% of the benzene present (see Figure 4.7). As the studies developed, it became obvious that plants absorb pollutants in varying degrees of efficiency. In other words, one plant might

be a highly efficient formaldehyde sorption system, but not quite as good with benzene or other chemicals. This phenomenon is also encountered when trying to clean air through other techniques. For example, commonly used activated carbon or alumina treated with potassium permanganate are effective as sorbent materials for only a narrow range of gases. Overall, plants exhibit greater tolerance for a wider range of airborne pollutants than any other sorbent system.

NASA began another series of experiments in 1988 in cooperation with the Associated Landscape Contractors of America (ALCA). The objective of this phase of NASA's research was to screen a number of other plant varieties for their efficiency as gas sorption filters. Three gases were chosen for study: benzene, formaldehyde, and trichloroethylene, at both high and low gas concentrations and under a variety of conditions, in order to more closely identify the important absorption mechanisms in

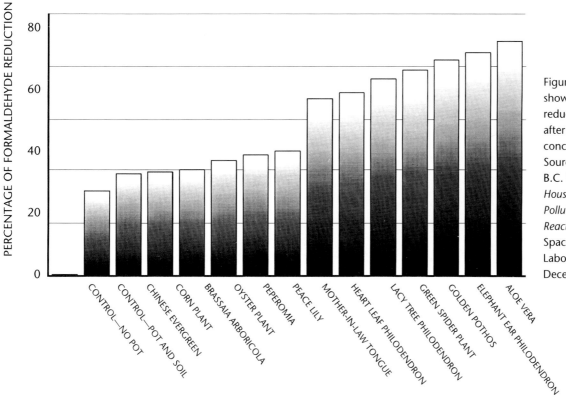

Figure 4.6: Bar graph showing formaldehyde reduction by plants after 24 hrs/high gas concentration.
Source: Derived from, B.C. Wolverton, *Houseplants, Indoor Air Pollutants and Allergic Reactions* (NASA, Nat'l Space Technology Laboratories, MS; December 1986).

Table 4.2

Change in Contaminant Mass Expressed as a Function of Leaf Surface Area
(Formaldehyde Pollutant—Grams of Gas Absorbed / cm² of Leaf Surface in Descending Order of Efficiency)

Contaminant Gas	Plant Subject	Reduction in Gas Mass (µg/cm² leaf surface)	
		after 6 hours	After 24 hours
Formaldehyde	Philodendron oxycardium (heart leaf philodendron)	3.93µg/cm²	4.99µg/cm²
	Philodendron domesticum (elephant ear philodendron)	2.97	4.31
	Low concentration trial	0.47	0.57
	Chlorophytum elatum (v. vittatum) (green spider plant)	2.29	4.15
	Philodendron selloum (lacy tree philodendron)	2.84	3.65
	Aloe vera (aloe vera)	2.18	3.27
	Scindapsus aureus (golden pothos)	2.35	3.26
	Aglonema modestum (chinese evergreen)	1.59	2.31
	Brassaia arboricola (mini schefflera)	——	1.96
	Peperomia obtusifolia (peperomia)	0.96	1.46
	Spathiphyllum clevelandii (peace lily)	1.05	1.41
	Dracaena fragrans ëmassangeanaí 0.72 (corn plant)	1.37	
	Sensevieria trifasciata (mother-in-law tongue)	0.76	1.31
	Tradescantia sillamontana (oyster plant)	0.43	0.67

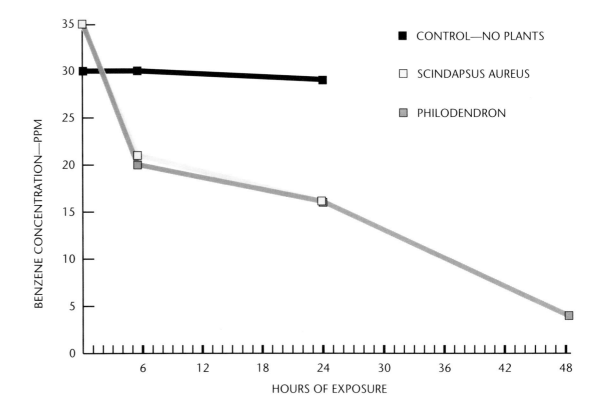

Figure 4.7: Graph showing benzene reduction by plants golden pothos and philodendron.

these systems (see Figures 4.8a, 4.8b and 4.8c). Sensidyne/Gastec air sampling pumps were used with gas detector tubes specific for the gases under test. Other tests for gases used more sensitive GC/MS and GC/FID (gas chromatograph/flame ionization detector) techniques. Appropriate tests were also used to quantify microbial activity.

These experiments, conducted at relatively high gas levels, once again confirmed that plants can act as gas sorption filters. All of the plants tested absorbed at least 47% of the formaldehyde gas in their environment. Mass cane was the most efficient at 70% removal in 24 hours, and ficus the least efficient at 47.4% removal in 24 hours (see Figure 4.8a). Gerbera daisy proved to be the most effective at removing benzene gas at 67.7% removal in 24 hours, and mass cane the least effective at 21.4% in 24 hours (see Figure 4.8b). Trichloroethylene (TCE) was the most difficult of the three gases for the plants to process. At high concentrations of TCE gas, flowering plants proved to be the most effective. Peace lily filtered 50% of the TCE in its chamber in 24 hours, pot mum removed 41.2% of the TCE in 24 hours, and gerbera daisy filtered 35% of the TCE in 24 hours. At 41% removal, marginata was the most effective of the non-flowering plants (see Figure 4.8c). There is no current explanation for the efficiency of flowering plants with TCE pollutants. It should be pointed out that, as other experiments demonstrated, plant sorption activity extends beyond the 24-hour cut-off period of these experiments (see Figure 4.7), and if left in the environment for longer periods, would totally remove the pollutants.[13]

Another series of experiments was carried out with the air pollutants benzene and trichloroethylene at low concentrations. They more typically represent the environmental conditions of most buildings. While these low pollutant level studies cannot be directly related to those studies

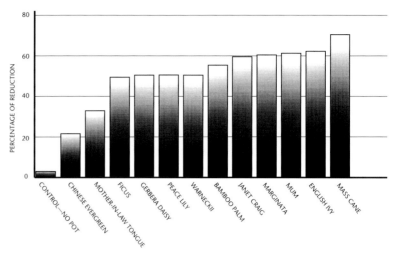

Figure 4.8a: Graph of Table 4.5a, formaldehyde/high concentration.

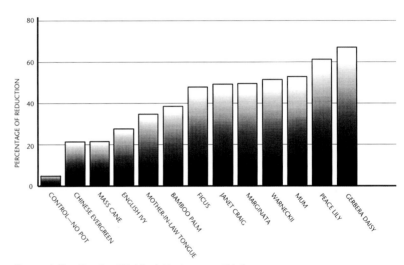

Figure 4.8b: Graph of Table 4.5b, benzene/high concentration.

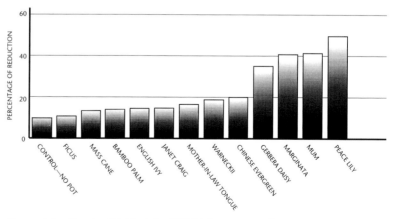

Figure 4.8c: Graph of Table 4.5c, TCE/high concentration

Sources: Derived from B.C. Wolverton, Anne Johnson, Keith Bounds (NASA Environmental Research Lab.), *Interior Landscape Plants for Indoor Air Pollution Abatement* (Stennis Space Center, MS: NASA/Associated Landscape Contractors of America, September 15, 1989), 12; and NASA research data sheets.

using higher levels of pollutants, they clearly demonstrate the gas sorption ability of the plants under investigation. Low concentrations of benzene can be removed efficiently with any of the plants tested. Chinese evergreen was the least effective at almost 50% removal in 24 hours. English ivy was the most effective, removing almost 90% of the gas in 24 hours (see Figure 4.9a). As seen in previous series, trichloroethylene proved to be a more difficult gas to filter.

None of the plants tested was able to remove more than 23% of the gas in 24 hour test periods. Peace lily was the most effective at 23.0% removal in 24 hours, and golden pothos the least effective at 9.2% removal (see Figure 4.9b).

Other experimental data gathered by NASA suggests that over time planter systems increase their efficiency in absorbing and degrading environmental organic gases. The explanation for this

Figure 4.9a: Graph of Table 4.6a showing plant absorption of low benzene concentrations.

Figure 4.9b: Graph of Table 4.6b showing plant absorption of low TCE concentrations.

Source: B.C. Wolverton, Anne Johnson and Keith Bounds (NASA Environmental Research Laboratory), *Interior Landscape Plants For Indoor Air Pollution Abatement,* (Stennis Space Center, MS: NASA/Associated Landscape Contractors of America, September 15, 1989), 12.

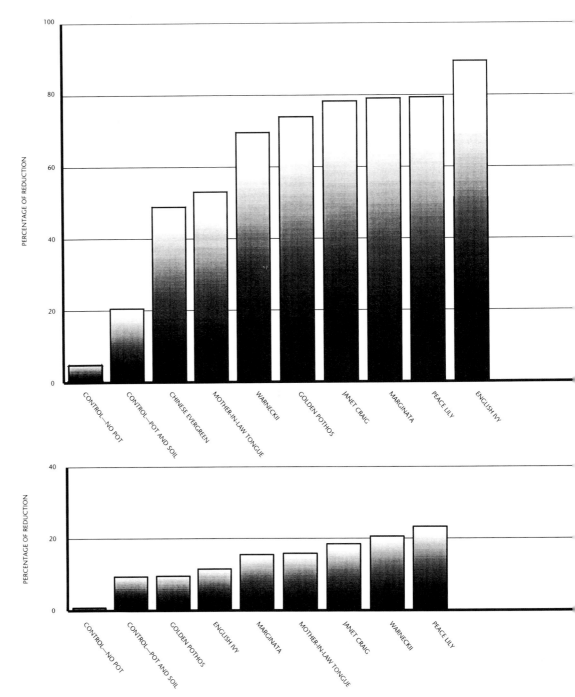

BIOLOGICAL SOLUTIONS TO INDOOR POLLUTION

comes from the earth. Much of a plant's ability to filter gases comes from the soil system that surrounds its roots. Soil contains many types of microorganisms which break down and return organic materials to the ecosystem for reuse. They cause leaves to decay into soil nutrients, and foods are acted on by bacteria in our bodies as part of the human digestive process. Many researchers have used the attributes of microbial systems to effectively degrade organic and inorganic pollutants.[14] NASA studies found that gases trapped in soil are more rapidly biodegraded by microorganisms when in the presence of plant roots. Roots exude an enzyme into the soil which attracts and stimulates microorganisms, thus accelerating microorganic activity. Experimental results imply the longer a plant is exposed to environmental gases, the more it and associated microorganisms adapt to those conditions, thereby more effectively utilizing toxic chemicals as food sources. Air cleaning efficiency is also improved in the process. The genetic adaptability of microorganisms over short as well as long periods of time is well known, and appears to play an important part in planter/gas sorption systems.[15]

This concept is also used commercially as aquaculture, or solar aquatics, to remove toxic chemicals from wastewater in the city of San Diego and other municipalities.[16] These concepts are also the major part of damage control used to clean up oil spills. Microbes are dispersed in the water to feed on petroleum (an organic compound), breaking it down chemically to render it harmless. Basically, the same thing happens around plant roots. Experimental results from NASA's extended duration tests are illustrated in Table 4.3. It shows the increased benzene removal ability of a Chinese evergreen plant after 24 hours of exposure and after six weeks of exposure, as measured by percent of gas removed and by soil bacterial counts (an indicator of

microorganic activity). Approximately 48% of the gas was removed in the first 24-hour period, while six weeks later, after additional exposure to the pollutants, the planter system increased its sorption ability considerably by removing almost 86% during a 24-hour period. They also show a significant increase in bacteria count during that period, suggesting the plant microbial system was adapting to its severe environmental challenge by increasing the number of microbes, just as our own immune systems manufacture antibodies to counter toxic invasion.

There has been concern over the years in some scientific and medical circles that these soil and leaf bacteria may possibly be airborne and harmful to humans. A 1982 study at the University of Michigan Allergy Research Laboratory dismissed that concern, and demonstrated that decorative houseplants are not an allergen contributor. The study found dozens of microorganisms in the air of private houses, but found the same ones in the air outside those houses. It was concluded that most were not related to the interior plants, but had been brought indoors by air transfer and tracking on shoes. They carefully monitored the air around houseplants and found no significant difference in fungus bacterial levels during periods of mild disturbance, such as during watering or from air drafts. The most prevalent fungus spores found indoors were Cladosporium, Alternaria, Penicillium, Epicoccum, and Aspergillus (in that order), accounting for about 30% of the total. The same order of prevalence was found indoors and out. The study's main conclusion is that common decorative interior landscape plants are not important sources of air pollution from allergens and do not constitute a health hazard.[17]

The researchers did express concern, however, over the prospect of chronically overdamp soil acting as a breeding ground for potentially unhealthy fungi (molds) or other microorganisms. That may have some

Table 4.3

Benzene Removal in a Sealed Experimental Chamber Over a 6 Week Period
(Chinese Evergreen Plant—Mass Removal and Bacterial Count After 24-hour Exposures)

	Percent Removed	Soil Bacterial Count (cfµ/g)
First 24-hour exposure	47.6	3.1 x 104
Another 24-hour exposure six weeks later	85.8	5.1 x 104

Source: B. C. Wolverton, Anne Johnson and Keith Bounds, *Interior Landscape Plants For Indoor Air Pollution Abatement*, (John C. Stennis Space Center, MS: NASA/Associated Landscape Contractors of America Cooperative Study, Sept. 15, 1989).

validity, but any potential problems in this regard have more to do with planter maintenance practices (irrigation quality) than with the basic issue of plant use. Decorative plants have been used indoors for many hundreds of years, if not longer, and except for isolated cases with hypersensitive occupants, inappropriate plant species, or heavy-handed irrigation, they have not posed a threat to human health. Irrigation methods have been refined to minimize the prospect of overwatering. Advanced, automated precision micro-irrigation (APM) systems that provide highly controlled watering regimens are now available for a wide variety of interior landscape installations.[18] They provide a safer, more cost-effective way of maintaining interiorscapes. That technology is the subject of the second part of this book.

Other scientists have expressed concern about trace (very small amounts) chemicals that are known to be given off by plants under certain conditions, such as terpenes, ethylene, and other products of plant metabolism called ***metabolites***. We know that some plants, like poison ivy and poison oak, are very toxic. Indoor plants, however, are non-toxic and are grown under relatively low light conditions, so their metabolic rates are therefore lower than plants grown outdoors under full-intensity light. The volatile organic compounds that may be gassed off from indoor plants are considerably reduced, and many are reabsorbed by the plant system. NASA's studies have shown airborne metabolites

from interior plants to be negligible.[19] The EPA, in its report *Indoor Air Assessment: Indoor Biological Pollutants* (1991), also treats the toxic potential of plants as a non-issue.[20] More detail about this subject will follow in later discussions.

Advanced Biological Systems for Indoor Air Pollution Control

One of NASA's important contributions to this science has been the development of activated carbon/plant root/microbial gas sorption systems, or bioreactors. The HVAC industry has various forms of air cleaners under continuous development. Airborne particulate matter is the easiest to extract from the air and effective filtration methods are in current use. Gaseous pollutants, however, are among the most difficult to remove from the air, and practical solutions have yet to be demonstrated. Concepts have been either too expensive to consider, too pollutant-specific (effective with only a narrow range of chemicals), not adaptable to retrofit installations, too energy intensive, or just not efficient enough. Building on nature's photosynthetic and microbial systems, NASA combined activated carbon with soil media to trap airborne pollutants in an effort to develop more efficient biosystems. This provides a "feeding ground" for plant roots and soil bacteria. The pollution entrapment rate is increased by accelerating the passage of air through the system with subterranean fans pulling air through the granular growing medium. Their studies of such systems demonstrate considerably greater efficiency over the use of unaided plants. Gaseous pollutants, such as trichloroethylene (TCE), which is difficult for unaided plants to filter, can be effectively adsorbed and degraded by these bioreactors. NASA's studies were conducted using a small bioreactor operating within an enclosed chamber. The flow of air around and through the planter system was contained within the enclosure. As seen in Figure 4.10, relatively high concentrations of trichloroethylene in enclosed chambers can be reduced to negligible levels in a matter of a couple of hours. The same studies show benzene concentrations can also be eliminated from enclosed chambers much faster than with planter systems alone. Figure 4.11 shows equivalent efficiencies at much lower benzene and TCE pollutant concentrations, in the range closer to that found in building interiors.

Comparing the two sets of data, it appears that the rate of TCE elimination is more rapid at higher concentrations—testimony to the efficiency of the system. One of the benefits of bioreactors is the added ability to filter some of the more common air pollutants, such as smoke particulates, combustion gases, viral bacteria, dust and pollen particles, and possibly even radon. Other research has demonstrated the activated carbon/plant root/microbial system's ability to absorb and assimilate radon from wastewater.[21] NASA feels the bioreactor should show similar tendencies with airborne radiation, particularly radon-infected dust. No known studies have been performed to date to confirm this. These advanced bio-filters can be used as freestanding systems or integrated with more conventional HVAC systems. NASA suggests that air conditioning flow be directed through and past planter/filter beds for

removal of pollutants before passing into return air ducts.

A 1991 study by Dr. John R. Porter, a microbiologist working under contract to NASA, further broadens our knowledge of the mechanisms involved in plant adaptation to alien environments.[22]

Using a dieffenbachia plant (Dieffenbachia amoena) as the subject in small chamber tests, with toluene and benzene as the organic pollutant gases, physiological changes in the plant were monitored as gas concentrations and light intensities were varied. The light levels used in the series were typical of those found in interiorscape settings. Industry sources report only 30 to 200 foot-candles of light fall upon the average indoor plant installation.[23] Low-light studies were performed by Porter at 30 to 50 foot-candles. Other studies were carried out at higher light levels of 100 to 200 foot-candles, relatively dim illumination compared with outdoor exposures. In each experimental sequence, photosynthesis, respiration, photorespiration, stomatal conductance, and percent gaseous pollutant removal were all measured and reported. It was concluded from this series that at low light intensities, soil microorganism activity and soil/root absorption and adsorption accounted for about 70% of the total pollutant removal. At higher light intensities, plant leaves were doing 80% to 85% of the removal. These findings lend weighty evidence that the plant's metabolic system was active in absorbing pollutant gases within the enclosed chamber, and not merely adsorption by potting soil or by other plant tissue, as some detractors continue to suggest. It also reconfirms earlier conclusions that air cleaning activity continues in dark or dim environments, although at reduced levels. Photosynthesis ceases in the dark for most plants, but soil microorganic activity continues.

The Porter studies also addressed the question of whether plants, while adapting to toxic environments, tend to give off toxic

Figure 4.10: Graph showing removal of benzene and TCE by activated carbon/planter system—high gas concentration. Source: B.C. Wolverton, Anne Johnson and Keith Bounds, *Interior Landscape Plants for Indoor Air Pollution Abatement,* (John C. Stennis Space Center, MS: NASA/Associated Landscape Contractors of America Cooperative Study, Sept. 15, 1989).

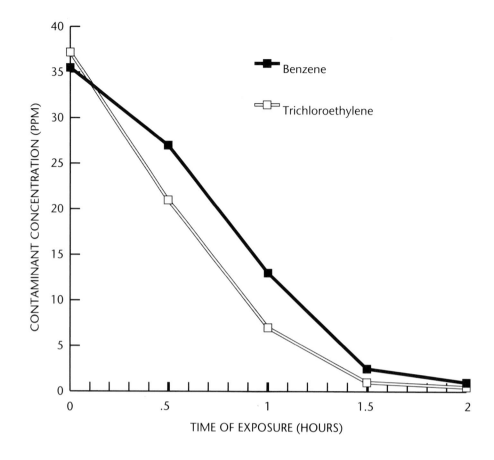

Figure 4.11: Graph showing removal of benzene and TCE by activated carbon/planter system—low gas concentration. Source: B. C. Wolverton, Anne Johnson and Keith Bounds, *Interior Landscape Plants for Indoor Air Pollution Abatement,* (John C. Stennis Space Center, MS: NASA/Associated Landscape Contractors of America Cooperative Study, Sept. 15, 1989).

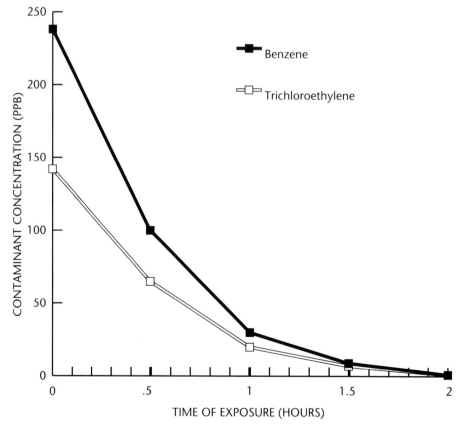

substances of their own, further aggravating the polluted atmosphere. Again, because plants' internal processes are extensive and highly complex, they have the potential to generate chemical emissions as waste, or metabolites, common in all plants and animals. During the toluene and benzene absorption studies, because of abnormal environmental conditions, the chamber was monitored for off-gassed metabolites by means of GC/MS analysis. No abnormal gaseous emissions were detected other than those normally found around dieffenbachia plants, confirming earlier studies by NASA and others.[24] While more research is needed in this area, current scientific evidence indicates that common, decorative tropical plants of the types investigated by NASA are benign and pose no threat as sources of toxic emissions when exposed to air pollutants at typical and elevated indoor concentrations.

To facilitate larger-scale studies, in 1987 NASA constructed a research laboratory named the "Biohome." Its function was to incorporate the latest technology in the field of bio-regenerative systems for indoor air and waste water treatment, and provide a living and work environment for researchers. About the size of a small apartment, it was completely sealed from the outside environment and equipped to provide a fully functional habitat for one person. Biohome was NASA's version of the Russian Bios-3 chamber. The heart of the structure was a network of bioregenerative systems which provided reclaimed waste water and potable water, as well as edible plant products and purified air. When first completed, the interior environment of Biohome was hostile to human occupancy. Its construction materials off-gassed so many toxins that one's eyes burned and respiratory discomfort was experienced by those who entered. Mass spectrometer/gas chromatograph analysis of the air at that time indicated high levels of volatile organic chemicals, confirming suspicions. After ornamental plants were installed in the unit, pollutant levels were

reduced and after three days, follow-up testing showed that most of the VOCs had been removed by the greenery, making the structure habitable.[25]

Aside from some work being done in NASA's CELSS Project (Controlled Ecological Life Support Systems), most research in the field is now being carried out by Wolverton Environmental Services in Picayune, Mississippi. Their work continues with bio-regenerating systems for waste water and indoor air purification. They have done some interesting work with azaleas, showing among other things the plant's capacity to absorb formaldehyde gas efficiently under a variety of conditions.[26] The sorption studies extended for as long as 45 days and focused on activity in dark environments as well. The latter produced surprisingly good results. Other studies by Wolverton validated the importance of soil bacteria in these biosystems and demonstrated the excellent gas sorption characteristics of the plant dieffenbachia.

In another experimental series, Wolverton investigated the capacity of orchids, succulents, and bromeliads to absorb pollutant gases in the dark. This class of plants has a different metabolic timetable. Instead of having their stomata open during the daylight hours, as most plants do, they open them at night, providing gas sorption properties during that period when no light is available. These plants are native to hot, dry climates, and some are jungle tree-dwellers (epiphytic). Biological evolution has apparently provided this property to conserve moisture during the heat of the day. It was anticipated that these plant types could be intermixed with normal plant species to provide gas sorption properties during the dark hours, thus evening out an interiorscape installation's filtration efficiency curve. The plant varieties used in this series of experiments were dendrobium and phalaenopsis orchids, and aechmea fasciata (urn plant), cryptanthus "Elaine," guzmania "Cherry," and Neoregelia perfecta tricolor bromeliads. The studies confirmed the dark-cycle filtration ability of these plant varieties. The dendrobium orchid was a particularly efficient performer with most of the contaminant gases.[27] About two thirds of the plant's adsorptive capacity was attributed to its soil microorganisms.

In a 1992 paper Wolverton presented to the International Conference on Life Support and Biospherics, he listed the following plants as being among the most efficient gas sorption filters for specific pollutants: Boston fern for removing formaldehyde; Lady palm (Rhapis excelsa) for chloroform and ammonia; Dwarf date palm (Phoenix roebelenii) for xylene; and Kimberley queen fern (Nephrolepis obliterata) for ethyl alcohol.[28] In a 1993 paper presented to the Mississippi Academy of Sciences, Dr. Wolverton concluded low-light-requiring interior plants were able to remove significant quantities of formaldehyde, xylene, and ammonia from sealed chambers. Over 30 varieties of ornamental plants were tested and Boston fern (Nephrolepis exaltata "Bostoniensis"), Pot mum (Chrysanthemum morifolium), and Dwarf date palm (Phoenix roebelenii) were most effective in removing formaldehyde. The Dwarf date palm was most effective in removing xylene, and the Lady palm most effective for removing ammonia.[29]

Wolverton has extended his research into advanced bio-systems for residential and commercial buildings. In one implementation, a building's wastewater is filtered, then introduced into a bed of decorative plants to allow microbial interaction and eventual water purification. Air purification takes place at the same time through photosynthesis and microbial activity. A commercial system has been installed at the Northeast Mississippi Community College for prototype testing. The building has been occupied since 1993, and while no scientific monitoring has yet

been done, indoor environmental quality is considered good.

This field of study has attracted other inquiring minds. In Germany a group of biochemists and microbiologists have recently duplicated and expanded on the early NASA studies. Their goal was to try to validate the active role plants can play in indoor air pollution control. Under carefully controlled conditions, radioactive tracer elements were introduced into a microenvironment containing the test plants (spider plants), and subsequently followed and monitored through the many biochemical reactions that make up a plant's metabolic functions. They found conclusive evidence, as had Wolverton and Porter before them, that a green plant's photosynthetic and metabolic activity are two of the main routes for gaseous pollutants to be adsorbed and degraded. To exclude the factor of soil microorganisms, the test plants were grown hydroponically (without soil). They concluded that plants are in fact a sink (eliminator) for at least formaldehyde, the only pollutant they studied.[30]

Some work in the field is being done at other research centers around the world. Pennsylvania State University has researched plants' ability to tolerate an ozone-rich indoor environment. The University of Toronto has been active in developing bioreactor modules for commercial buildings, using plants as the functional air cleaning element. Space scientists on both sides of the ocean have gained an abiding respect for the power and reliability of plants.[31] In June of 1992, U.S. and Russian space scientists joined forces in a media event to urge the use of biological indoor air cleaning systems as a tool to help improve air quality as well as for the prevention of disease. NASA biotechnology is expected to spur greater activity in the movement toward more effective indoor ecology. Working in conjunction with conventional HVAC techniques, their concepts are destined to become among the more important strategies in future indoor air pollution abatement and health risk management.

The EPA's Position on Biological Remediation Techniques

The U.S. Environmental Protection Agency has taken a rather benign position concerning the use of living plants for remediation of indoor air quality problems. They now recognize the role of plants as air purifiers in the grand ecosystem, yet voice skepticism over concepts using plants for the same purpose indoors. Many in the scientific community have advocated using plants for healthier shelter environments. Nevertheless, the EPA resists any serious effort by the government to validate or build on scientific achievement in this field.

Their mind-set comes from the HVAC industry which gave it roots. It naturally gravitates toward electro-mechanical solutions. The EPA's present position is more open on the subject, however, than at any other time. As expressed in a 1993 letter to the author:

> "The information available on the use of houseplants to clean indoor air has been evaluated by our office and the EPA Office of Research and Development. We agree that houseplants have the ability to metabolize chemicals . . . we do not have concerns about the use of houseplants as an adjunct to source control and ventilation."[32]

The EPA's current posture on the issue is the result of serious reconsideration by the agency over the past several years. Early positions were not as open-minded. As a matter of fact, at one point the Indoor Air Office gave clear notice they doubted plants' ability to absorb any gaseous pollutants except carbon dioxide, despite an impressive collection of existing scientific research validating the concept.[33] This early position proved to be embarrassing to the office. They had no persuasive science on which to base their argument. Commercial building tests involve the installation of plants in offices and public buildings to measure pollutant levels before and after. Until these tests have been performed successfully, the EPA will not publicly endorse the use of plants for indoor air pollution control service. Such tests, however, are expensive and difficult to stage successfully because of the many variables involved which must be controlled. Not many in the private sector possess the funding or expertise to run definitive tests in buildings.

Meanwhile, enough positive scientific evidence exists about the powerful, natural tools at our disposal to disregard the EPA's position on the matter and advance the use of plants and planter-based air cleaning technologies in buildings. The stakes are too great to put any promising solutions on hold.

The Economic Advantages

There is another powerful reason to use bio-remediation systems in houses and public buildings. It has to do with energy-efficiency and cost-effectiveness. We know the importance of saving fuel reserves and reducing toxic emissions from power generating plants. We also understand the needs of the homeowner and building manager in budgeting funds allocated to overhead. In the midst of all this lies a federal policy instituted by the EPA to improve indoor air quality, which is proving counterproductive economically and seriously impacting other environmental strategies. Ventilation of buildings is a key factor in the EPA's indoor air quality program. Electromechanical air handling equipment, however, costs money and energy to run. In 1989 ASHRAE reversed itself concerning air exchange rates in buildings (ASHRAE 62-89). During the mid-1970s they had called for a significant reduction of air flow and interchange in buildings in response to the fuel crisis earlier in the decade. The reversal came about later when energy-efficient buildings caused health problems among occupants because not enough air was circulating to exhaust toxin build-up. The EPA's current policy tends to increase energy costs and deplete fuel reserves.

Greater air exchange rates create other problems. Ventilation simply moves toxic air from one part of the built environment to another, or outside to the global environment. Gases still remain to be dealt with and neutralized. To understand the gravity of the problem, one simply has to stand on the roof of a large building near its exhaust ducts. The noxious fumes are intolerable. Outdoor pollution levels suffer from such strategies, as do disease prevention and energy conservation strategies. Such practices mean the large office building is permitted to belch its wastes into the air breathed by its neighbors. It means that the thousands of homes in an urban community are permitted to evacuate their toxic indoor wastes to the outdoors where they, too, can pollute their neighbors' space, and drift to surrounding areas. It also means that large countries can emit enormous quantities of indoor gaseous chemicals to an already badly polluted biosphere, causing pathogenic harm over a wide area of the globe. With exploding population growth, the problem multiplies at an enormous rate. Just as factory emissions are controlled, so too must residential and commercial microenvironments, for collectively, they are an even greater threat.

Air cleaning is the strategy seen by many as a more effective and ecologically correct strategy for long-term use. It sinks toxins from shelter microenvironments as well as from the global atmosphere. In fact, such cleansing reduces the need for outdoor air infusion and for maintaining artificially high ventilation rates. It reduces energy consumption, for less outdoor air requires less preconditioning expense and air handling blowers can be slowed. With energy-efficient air cleaning methods, home and public building power costs would be lower and the environmental impact of power stations would be reduced. Billions of dollars and millions of barrels of fuel oil could be saved annually. Air cleaning, along with source reduction, are the only responsible strategies. Plants and advanced bio-reactor systems can help.

Ventilation systems are expected to remove all pollutants, but because of real-life building dynamics, they don't. TEAM and other studies showed us that. Present recommended ventilation rates have been artificially inflated to accommodate the fact that no practical HVAC gas filtration methods are available to cope with energy-efficient built environments. Secondly, many, if not most buildings are operated at lower than recommended ventilation rates. The EPA's Public Buildings Study found some as low as 0.14 ach (air changes per hour), with night-time levels lower than average. Improper HVAC system design, degraded system operation, improper diffuser or damper adjustments, friction losses, complex space configurations, and furnishings further reduce room ventilation rates. Irregular air flow patterns can considerably reduce ventilation rates in pockets of rooms, frequently to levels much lower than 0.1 ach.[34] Interiors are typically erratic in layout with partitions, room dividers, arches, closets, hallways, and closures, making them probably the worst examples of aerodynamic design.

The laws governing air flow produce many irregularities and contra forces which restrict efficient circulation and ventilation. In addition, intermittent ventilation cycles induce dead air throughout commercial buildings for long periods, and in residential systems generally even more. Night cycles are low as well. The point is, real-life building ventilation dynamics are highly variable and cannot be relied upon to remove pollutants completely. In the absence of effective gas filtration methods, most toxins are recirculated back to occupied rooms. This is particularly true of residential structures, which typically use closed-loop ventilation systems with no mechanically induced indoor/outdoor air interchange. NIOSH maintains that relatively few buildings have any artificial means of removing gases from circulating air. Data from the EPA's TEAM and Public Buildings Studies showed high and pervasive VOC presence in the buildings randomly tested, in spite of typical ventilation rates. There have to be other systems operating in concert with HVAC equipment to clean the air. Again, planter filtration systems help fill that void.

Planter systems for cleaner indoor air are expected to be an important supplement to other air quality improvement techniques, and as their technology matures, will prove to be one of the least expensive, most effective means of eliminating indoor air pollutants. In the next chapter we will discuss the practical aspects of how plants can be used in residential and commercial interiors to utilize their air cleaning attributes.

FIVE

Designing for a Healthier User Environment

Designers must take advantage of the wealth of information currently available on the causes and effects of indoor air pollution to responsibly fulfill their obligations to clients and to the public. While much of what is available is incomplete—for science has only a moderate grasp of the problem and solutions, and much more is yet to be learned—that should not stop design professionals from incorporating what we do know into current projects. We know that some of the problems are caused by the carelessness of home owners and public building occupants and management. The designer can't do much about that except to make it easier for habitat users to act in an environmentally responsible manner. Yet designers do have a great deal of influence in the specification of systems and materials that will surround building occupants and quantifiably alter their environment and affect their health.

General Building Design Considerations

Interior landscape design is generally the province of the interior landscape architect or interior landscape contractor (interiorscaper). Architects and interior designers should nevertheless be aware of the options available so that they can be integrated into the overall project design. Many projects will find informed architects and interior designers teamed with uninformed interior landscape architects and interiorscapers. The informed practitioners should always dominate decision making for environmental design matters. Unfortunately, it is common practice to leave interiorscape-related details to the latter stages of design, or even to the latter stages of construction. Because of the increasing complexity of interior landscape use, such practices are no longer acceptable. Early planning is mission-critical for a well-conceived, decorative, cost-effective, and environmentally viable installation. If the technical properties of plants are to be properly utilized, they must be carefully integrated into the project from the beginning when all factors are under scrutiny.

Appropriate building design for indoor air quality encompasses such considerations as HVAC systems, building envelope and structural design, and spacial layout of interior activity areas and their relationship to potential indoor and outdoor pollutant sources. If indoor air quality is to be optimized, these components must be designed to work within the constraints of other factors, such as overall building performance, structural integrity, economic viability, comfort, and safety.

HVAC engineers and architects typically provide the professional support needed on the design team. As we will see, the interior designer is deeply involved as well. To provide a full measure of environmental integrity, interior landscape architects and interior irrigation specialists are also called upon. Ultimately, the environmental integrity of a project depends to a large extent on the expertise, talent, cooperation, and coordination of these professionals.

HVAC design criteria serve to ensure that the indoor atmosphere can be conditioned to provide thermally comfortable air throughout the occupied zone of a building. Just as important are the indoor air quality goals which may be prescribed in building codes or standards. According to the EPA, HVAC-related environmental design goals are achieved by supplying adequate outdoor ventilation air, properly distributing the outdoor air throughout the occupied zones, and taking other steps to ensure that indoor air contains no residual pollutants. They advise that HVAC system design must balance ventilation with indoor source emissions and the quality of neighborhood outdoor air. Consideration of indoor pollutant sources starts with consulting project architects and the owner to learn of the planned use of spaces and materials used in the construction, decoration, and furnishing of the building. Every effort must be made to avoid placing air intakes near outside pollutant sources, like exhaust vents. Pretreating ventilation air may be necessary before it can be mixed with stale indoor air.[1]

In addition to meeting criteria for durability, structural integrity, functional utility, and ease of maintenance, the structural materials used in construction should also meet low pollutant emission criteria. It's best to choose carefully in the design stages in order to avoid costly removal later. Building envelopes may be designed to minimize infiltration and exfiltration of air for energy conservation reasons and to prevent the encroachment of radon gases. Adequate outdoor air ventilation must be designed into the building structure, and can be provided by natural means (open windows and vents) or mechanical means. Roof designs must minimize water accumulation and leakage to reduce biological contamination and structural damage.

When designing the interior space, adequate floor space for occupant activities should be considered. In addition, the space must meet the necessary aesthetic, acoustic, light, and privacy requirements while maintaining occupant exposure to indoor pollutants at tolerable levels. Care must be taken in the selection and placement of moveable partitions and other furnishings, which can be pollutant sources themselves, or can retard effective air flow patterns. It is strongly recommended that the elements of shelter ecology should also be incorporated into the project. This provides the means to support plant growth for ornamentation and for their natural air cleaning qualities.

To provide clean indoor air to occupants, protect their health, ensure their comfort, and maintain their productivity the designer needs to consider the ongoing maintenance requirements of the occupied spaces and HVAC system. Cleaning and maintenance can in and of themselves create indoor air pollution. Planning for environmentally effective space therefore requires that the long-term building environment be free of dust, microorganisms, and pests. These can be conflicting factors, for the pesticides that control pests can pollute the microenvironment more than the problem they serve to control. Materials should be chosen that are easy to clean and do not trap dust and dirt. The growth of microorganisms—affected by the humidity inside the building—should be limited to prevent fungal and bacterial growth. HVAC ducts are particularly vulnerable to the growth of microorganisms and system design should incorporate maintenance ports. These are small doors in air conditioning ducts which allow access to the inside for inspection and cleaning.

Planter air cleaning systems should be equipped with automated, precision micro-irrigation systems to control soil moisture levels and to improve the economic viability of the bio-system. If properly designed, automatic irrigation systems can save as much as 30% to 60% on plant leasing and maintenance contracts, and can pay for themselves in about one year. They also allow the copious use of plants for decorative effect and environmental integrity without increasing the maintenance cost burden. These subjects will be covered in more detail in following chapters.

EPA Strategies for Indoor Air Pollution Abatement

The EPA has categorized its basic recommendations for the control of indoor air pollution into four groups, the first two of which the design professional can be especially active in implementing:[2]

1. Engineering and operational control strategies to mitigate or prevent indoor air problems.

2. Appropriate building design and maintenance to control indoor air pollution.

3. Appropriate methods of diagnosing indoor air quality problems.

4. Regulations and other administrative control of indoor air quality.

Source Substitution and Removal

Source control is one of the strategies the design professional must address. It generally involves existing buildings or facilities where hazardous materials, appliances, and furnishings are already in place. The EPA suggests various ways of handling the problem, the first of which involves **source substitution** or complete **removal**. This involves the removal of an indoor air pollutant source and its replacement with another, safer product. For example, many cooking ranges and other combustion appliances were manufactured without regard for environmental integrity, particularly the older ones which may leak hazardous gases or are not vented properly. In this case, replacement is generally necessary. Carpeting and furniture are frequent offenders which, when found to be dangerous, must be substituted for a safer product. Building materials such as pressed wood products, foam insulation containing formaldehyde, bricks and concrete containing radon, and asbestos and uncontrolled glass fiber products must be painstakingly removed. Consumer and commercial products are also generally suspect. Ozone and solvent emissions from copy and addressing machines, cleaning fluids from dry cleaned clothing, as well as low-level emissions from paints, wall coverings, paneling, cleaning chemicals, and personal care products are all sources of unwanted pollutants. Even the soil around building foundations frequently contains dangerous gases which penetrate the building, also calling for removal and replacement. Restricting tobacco smoking in common areas is an important aspect of this strategy. Poorly designed HVAC systems may have pockets where harmful microorganisms can spawn, contaminate the air, and circulate throughout the building. These must be found and modified or replaced. There are times when a product is removed and it may be necessary to sacrifice the function of the material unless a substitute is found. Consequently, decisions to remove and find substitutions for pollutant sources may require careful balancing of economic, functional, and health concerns.

Lists of safe and unsafe products are available for the concerned designer's use. One such guide is *Environmental by Design: Volume I—Interiors.*[3] This is billed as a source book of environmentally-aware material choices and is the most comprehensive I have come across. It is also a good guidebook for designers having strong environmental sensitivities, for it considers not only the hazard products can pose through long-term use and exposure, but also the dangers to installers and the environmental impact of the manufacturing process. Adherence to some of the ideas in this book may save building owners, designers, contractors, and occupants considerable grief and cost as the building progresses through various stages of use. Following are some typical recommendations from that source (see Table 5.1).

The list of materials and products in Table 5.1 is far from comprehensive. It should also be kept in mind that many of the products listed may compromise other attributes important to a project. For example, some may sacrifice durability, color availability, or other properties for environmental reasons. Product choices must be weighed against the various factors involved. Wherever possible, environmentally correct products and procedures should be used. Remember that many of the recommended products are not totally safe as far as health risks are concerned. They are merely the best available choices at this time.

Encapsulation and Confinement

There are times when it will be impossible or impractical to remove or replace pollutant sources. Encapsulation or confinement of the source should then be considered. **Encapsulation** of hazardous products can be accomplished with suitable coatings or

Table 5.1

Partial List of Common Pollution Sources and Substitution Products

Pollutant Sources	Substitution Products
Concrete colorants (many contain heavy metals)	Chromix admixtures (L.M. Schofield Co.)
Caulking compounds (solvent-based types like urethane, neoprene, polysulfides, and butyls)	A.F.M. caulking compound (A.F.M. Enterprises, Inc.) Dyno flex (A.F.M. Enterprises) Lithochrome Colorcaulk Sealants (L.M. Schofield)
Wall coverings (embossed/printed, vinyls, printed papers, etc.)	Designwall acoustical wall paneling (Homasote Co.) Nova Cork (Homasote) 440 Sound-a-sote (Homasote) Guard Contract Wallcovering (Columbus Coated Fabrics) Genon Contract Wall Coverings (GenCorp Polymer Products)
Surface finishes (paints, varnishes, stains, sealers—contain biocides, solvents, other petrochemicals, and heavy metals)	No. 320 Room White Paint (Auro Organic Paints) No. 321 Emulsion Wall Paint (Auro Organic Paints) No. 360 Plant Pigments for Wall Glazing Biofa White Wall Paint (Biofa Naturfarben GmbH [Germany]; imported by Bau, Inc.) Biofa White Priming Paint (Biofa Naturfar ben GmbH) No. 400 Dubro Natural Resin Wall Paint (Livos Plant Chemistry/USA) Safecoat All-Purpose Enamel (A.F.M. Enterprises) Safecoat Paint (A.F.M. Enterprises) Regal Interior Latex Paint (Color Your World [Toronto]) Envirospray Enamel Spray Paint (Environmental Technology, Inc.) Envirolac 2200 Satin Acrylic Lacquer (Mills Paint & Wallcoverings [British Columbia])
Furniture (domestic and office—ureaformaldehyde and phenolformaldehyde binders, glue, high-pressure laminates, low-pressure laminates, acrylics, solvents, polyurethane foam, etc.)	Gesika Storage Wall (Gesika Furniture, Inc. [Mississauga, ON]) Ethospace Office Furniture Systems (Herman Miller, Inc.) Action Office Furniture System (Herman Miller) Reff System Z (Knoll North America Corp.) Nienkamper Office Furniture (Nienkamper Furniture & Accessories [Scarborough, ON]) 9000 Series Office Furniture (Steelcase Inc.)
Upholstery textiles (synthetics [petrochemicals], solvents, trichloroethane, and formaldehyde finishes, etc.)	Guilford Upholstery Fabrics (Guilford of Maine, Inc.) Natural fiber fabrics with safe dyes and finishes
Carpeting (petrochemicals, solvents, latex, pesticides, other finishes)	Powerbond RS (Collins & Aikman) Crossley woven nylon carpet (Crossley Carpet Mills, Ltd.) Natural fiber carpets

Source: Kim Leclair and David Rousseau, *Environmental by Design—Vol. I: Interiors* (Point Roberts, WA: H&M Publishers, 1992).

films, or by or by building an impervious wall around the source. Proper *confinement* of certain pollutant sources can considerably improve the safety of an installation. Prime examples of this are heating systems in public buildings. Mechanical rooms must be able to seal off any leaking gases or be able to vent them to the outside. Equally important is the "breathing room," necessary for the proper combustion of fuels. Combustion heaters must have a lot of air space around them to provide enough oxygen for complete combustion. If not designed properly, carbon monoxide and other unwanted by-products will result. Hundreds of liability cases have been brought to court in recent years from just such occurrences. Making sure appliances are working properly is an operational and management facet of source control.

Modification

Pollution source *modification* is practiced by manufacturers when they are made aware of environmental problems with their products. Feedback from designers and consumers is important for manufacturers who are unaware of problems, or for those who may have to be pressured by the marketplace to act in a more environmentally responsible fashion. Products can also be modified on-site when necessary, as witnessed in certain cases of encapsulation. One example of this is the effort by the lumber industry in recent years to reduce the formaldehyde content in flakeboard, chipboard, wall panels, and other decorative and structural building materials. These changes were instigated by federal codes and consumer pressure. Also, air coolants such as chlorofluorocarbons are being replaced with compounds known to be more environmentally friendly.

Ventilation

At the core of the EPA's IAQ program is the previously discussed tactic of ventilation control, a strategy that depends on designers, builders, homeowners, and building managers to implement. While it is not possible to eliminate all toxic pollutants from our built environments, *ventilation* can be used to help remove much of the hazard, particularly during acute periods of exposure. The reason for its importance lies in the fact that inadequate ventilation is the cause of many indoor air-related health complaints. This strategy involves using outside air to dilute indoor concentrations of air pollutants. The success of this approach to indoor air quality is obviously based on the presence of a relatively clean outdoor atmosphere. Also necessary are the proper mechanisms for exchanging air between the building exterior and interior, as well as the efficient distribution of this mixed air throughout the structure.

While they may be necessary for short-term objectives, these are concepts that fall somewhat short in actual practice. For example, the EPA reported in 1989 that more than 100 million Americans live in areas where air pollution levels exceed federal standards.[4] That's about 40% of the population. The dumping of indoor pollutants to the atmosphere through interchange makes matters worse. The strategy also neglects residential environments in large measure. Few houses are currently built—or, realistically, will be built—with expensive air interchange/heat exchanger equipment. Instead, most houses rely on natural infiltration of air through walls, cracks, window and door seams, as well as appliance exhaust fans to evacuate heat and fumes. EPA studies of residential structures show a median value of only 0.5 air changes per hour (ach) from a broad range of sources.[5] This means there are millions of houses below that level which have very inefficient air exchange characteristics. These studies also showed that with current ventilation pathways, gaseous toxins remain pervasive in the average home.[6] Residential HVAC systems simply recirculate bad air, filtering out only dust, pollen, and other coarse particulates. Commercial buildings show higher ventilation rates because many are fitted with air exchange equipment, but NIOSH and other agencies note that most are ineffective and underutilized.

Studies also show a broad range of air exchange values within commercial buildings. This demonstrates the pervasiveness of dead air pockets in the average building and the high variability in ventilation rates among the different building areas. A study of 38 commercial buildings showed variations within buildings of 0.3 to 4.2 air changes per hour (ach).[7] Another study of 14 commercial buildings showed the same type of variability from one area to the next (0.29 to 1.73 ach for each building studied).[8]

Then there is the question of energy consumption. At a time when energy conservation programs are being implemented, the EPA ventilation strategy imposes extra fuel burdens on building operation. For these and other reasons, it would be foolish to rely on current ventilation standards as a long-term strategy.

Because air handling is an integral function in virtually all buildings, the questions relating to indoor air quality bring new emphasis to planning and design. Tightly sealed, energy-efficient houses and public buildings must be modified to accommodate greater indoor/outdoor air interchange. Part of this involves the use of local ventilation systems—generally, exhaust fans in the vicinity of pollutant sources. This strategy helps to remove toxins before they can circulate to other areas.

Another technique is to automate the removal of toxins from the building when built-in sensors indicate a problem. Carbon dioxide and carbon monoxide sensors are the most common. Probably the most important aspects of ventilation techniques involve the type of HVAC equipment used and the design of air flow patterns and

rates. ASHRAE indoor air quality standards upon which new building codes are being written assume that ventilated air is perfectly mixed into the areas of occupancy. We have just discussed the variability of air flow within a building, so we know this is a questionable assumption. Careful design, however, can reduce this variability to manageable limits. Much of this involves the strategic placement of air registers and damper controls in large buildings.

It also involves the floor plan design. Open plan space permits unimpeded flow of air and is much more efficient. Most building designs, however, require partitioned space. It must be kept in mind that partitioning retards efficient air flow and must be used judiciously. Air flow characteristics within each partitioned cell should be planned with care.

Air Cleaning

The EPA considers air cleaning to be important in the improvement of indoor air quality. *Air cleaning* involves the physical or chemical removal of pollutants from the indoor air, and is a process that must be incorporated into a project during the design stages. Different technologies are used for different air cleaning tasks. Most devices are HVAC-related and are for the purpose of removing particulate matter like dust, mites, and pollen from the air. The type of technology required is determined by the nature of a project and its intended use. The best source of information currently available on particulate filters comes from the Association of Heating, Refrigeration and Air Conditioning Engineers (ASHRAE) in Atlanta, Georgia.

Gas or vapor sorption is one type of air cleaning. Its purpose is to remove gaseous pollutants from the indoor air by physical or chemical sorption (absorption and adsorption processes). Activated carbon, silica, and alumina are the sorbent materials generally incorporated into these air cleaners. Some are very selective and to rid the air of a broad spectrum of gases, multiple stages would have to be designed into the system, each acting on a specific group of gases. Provisions would also need to be made for regular maintenance of the sorbent system, as efficiencies vary with the amount of gases already absorbed (or adsorbed). These materials can become clogged after relatively short operating periods, making them ineffective until replaced or reconstituted. Because of the hundreds of gases found in the average indoor environment, this process can become quite complicated. ASHRAE is the best source of information for gas sorption air cleaners.

Biological air cleaners such as plants offer another solution for removing not only gases from indoor air, but also particulate matter and airborne microorganisms like viruses as well. Plants are a readily available, inexpensive tool with the added benefit of easy implementation. American, Soviet, Danish, and other city planners advocate the use of landscaping as a strategy for neighborhood air pollution abatement.[9] A similar situation will no doubt exist some day for natural, indoor air pollution control.

While much has yet to be learned, enough expertise is currently available to institute meaningful projects involving shelter ecology. When used indoors, plants replace some of our globe's life-support greenery lost to building excavation, thereby helping to restore an ecological balance. Aside from being scavengers of air pollutants, plants improve the aesthetics of our habitats, provide comfortable humidity levels, have important noise abatement properties,[10] improve employee productivity, and provide relief from emotional and physiological stress.[11] That's an impressive array of attributes. New policies for home and commercial building design should be developed incorporating planter-based air

cleaning systems—from simple installations of unaided potted plants scattered throughout an interior, to more effective installations incorporating heavy concentrations of greenery and the most advanced bio-technical concepts in the field.

NASA's Vision for the Improvement of Indoor Air Quality

The grand concept for making buildings environmentally safe with biological systems was developed by NASA during the last decade. It envisions a unique forced-air system using large beds of ornamental plants as reactors to absorb and metabolize pollutants from constantly recirculating air. Stale air would pass over and through these reactors, be purified, then flow back to other areas of the building. In its most complex form, NASA's plan involves recycling wastewater from the building as well, using the planter's aquaculture attributes. NASA's implementation simply harnesses nature's tools for improving our sheltered environments.

At the other end of the spectrum, simple bioreactors can have design elements like those of Figure 5.2, which shows one of NASA's early prototypes developed for civilian use. It is designed for single plant support, and incorporates a subterranean exhaust fan which circulates air through the planter system, to be acted on by leaves and root/microbial components. Activated carbon is used as part of the growing media. The carbon adsorbs gaseous molecules and the resident colony of microbes then feed on them, destroying them in the process. The carbon bed is a "feeding ground" or "killing field" for the microorganisms. The result is that the microorganisms eliminate toxins from the atmosphere. The self-contained exhaust system draws stale air through the planter at an accelerated rate, greatly speeding up the purification process. Cleaner air is thus returned to the room environment.

Between these two extremes lies the practical implementation of NASA's vision. Planter beds large enough to process a prescribed quantity of air can be built into homes and public buildings using the concepts just described. Because technical planter use involves interior design, interior landscaping, architecture, interior irrigation, and engineering expertise, all of these disciplines should be included in task forces dedicated to designing environmentally advanced projects.

Figure 5.1: An illustration of NASA's early ideas for whole building bio-filtration systems. Illustration from *Spinoff 1988* (page 95) showing Wolverton's concept in a large building. Source: NASA.

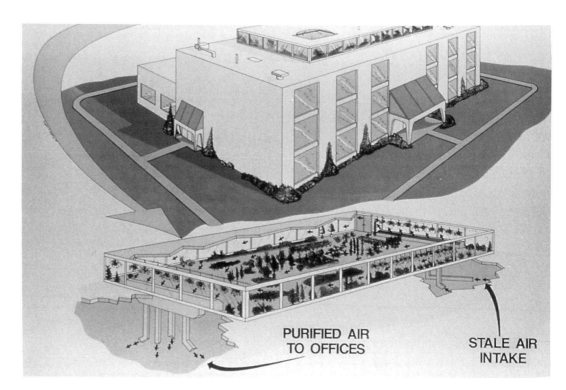

PURIFIED AIR TO OFFICES

STALE AIR INTAKE

Figure 5.2: Illustration of a small reactor from *Spinoff 1988* (page 95). Source: NASA.

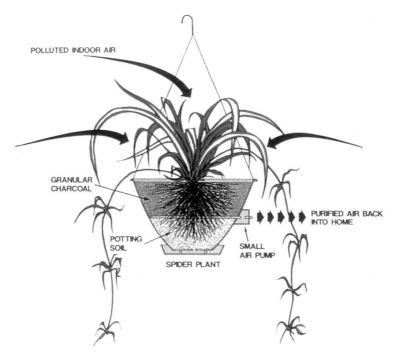

POLLUTED INDOOR AIR

GRANULAR CHARCOAL

POTTING SOIL

SPIDER PLANT

SMALL AIR PUMP

PURIFIED AIR BACK INTO HOME

Implementing NASA's Recommendations

Selecting the Plants

Based on their experimental data, NASA reached certain conclusions about the way tropical foliage plants should be used in residential and business settings. While the early guidelines are being revised as greater understanding is achieved, they nevertheless serve as a starting point. At this stage of development, there is no simple answer to the question, How many and what kind of plants do I use to help purify the air in my projects? NASA simplified the process of choosing the most efficient plants to use by recommending those that performed best in their experimental series. The list was first published in 1991 by Plants for Clean Air Council (a division of Associated Landscape Contractors of America), and includes the following varieties, not necessarily in order of effectiveness (see Table 5.2). Keep in mind that this biotechnology should be used in conjunction with other EPA strategies for a comprehensive indoor air quality program.

We know that EPA studies show the average residential or commercial interior contains literally hundreds of pollutants, so it is impractical to say that one type of plant is best in all situations. NASA research indicates that most interior landscape plants can process most pollutant gases, but with varying degrees of effectiveness. This qualification is true of chemical and electromechanical systems as well. For example, when HVAC air cleaners are designed, major variations and multi-stages are necessary to optimize them for the diverse range of gases likely to be encountered. As a practical matter, none have attained that ideal because of the complexity involved. In biological systems, while the degree of efficiency for any gas may vary from one plant to another, it is expected that most gases would ultimately be absorbed by the planter system. Yet the absorption rate of any given plant species increases significantly as multiples are used to purify the microenvironment containing them. The greater determining factors, then, appear to be the *number* of plants in a room being brought to bear on the air quality problem, their deployment, as well as air circulation rates and patterns in the microenvironment.

Supplementing Nature with Technology

A biological pollution abatement system can be augmented by using NASA's activated carbon/subterranean fan technique to accelerate pollutant absorption and adsorption, as well as create a situation more conducive to microbial activity. Microbial activity in the activated carbon

Table 5.2

Tropical Plants Recommended by NASA for Indoor Air Pollution Abatement

Azalea	Mother-in-law's tongue
Dieffenbachia	English ivy
Philodendron	Marginata
Spider plant	Janet Craig
Golden pothos	Gerbera daisy
Bamboo palm	Warnekeii
Corn plant	Peace lily
Chrysanthemum	

Source: *Plant Tips for Commercial and Residential Environments*, (Falls Church, VA: Foliage for Clean Air Council, 1991).

breaks down trapped pollutants, and with root absorption, is constantly regenerating and cleansing the system—overcoming one of the major drawbacks of other activated carbon filters. Some carbon filters are laced with permanganate or other compounds to increase their effectiveness with narrow classes of gas. They tend to lose their effectiveness quickly as their pores fill with gas, requiring frequent replacement or rejuvenation.

The bio-system would be further improved by linking it with the building's HVAC system, positioning planters in air streams (either individually or congregated into filter beds), and exhausting air from the planter/filter to the room environment or to air return plenums in the building to be further filtered by HVAC devices. NASA studies showed the effluent from these bio-filters to be essentially benign; that is, the return air was non-toxic. A coordinated, multi-stage system such as this can reduce much of the HVAC filtration load, as well as its energy requirements. Plant filters require very little energy application to function and are self-cleaning. Aside from lower energy requirements, indoor/outdoor air interchange rates could be reduced. Mechanical filtration and humidification systems could be smaller and less expensive to install as well.

Advanced planter/gas sorption filters have the potential to absorb and degrade not just organic and inorganic gases, but also dust, pollen, and other particulates, the many constituents of tobacco smoke, as well as airborne biological pollutants, including those causing infectious diseases. NASA's research into water-borne radon abatement by planter/microbial systems predicts the possible absorption of airborne radon as well.[12]

Making It Work

One aspect of the EPA's position on plant use is its contention that HVAC ventilation will exhaust pollutants before biological air cleaners can do much good. TEAM and other indoor air quality studies have shown that conventional systems are not working well in the typical home or office where investigators found a wide range of pollutants. Therefore, we are left with no choice but to conclude that inadequate and/or dysfunctional HVAC systems cannot do the entire job. Even top drawer ventilation systems will eventually fail to provide relief for want of properly trained or diligent maintenance technicians, or because periodic budget constraints force procedural changes. It is unrealistic to expect consistent results out of building equipment or the people that operate and maintain them. There has to be a "safety net" in place to take up the slack, and this is where plants figure in the equation by assisting in the destruction of remaining toxins.

NASA's early rule of thumb recommended the use of at least one tropical foliage plant for each 100 square feet of room area. (Although NASA's original recommendation called for one plant per 100 square feet, better air cleaning results would be obtained by using at least three plants per 100 square feet.) This assumes average ceiling heights of 8 feet, average plant size (8" to 10" pots), average absorptive materials like furnishings in the room, average air circulation rates, and adequate lighting.

As the efficiency of any type of filter is dependent on the rate of air flow around and through it, plants should be placed as close to air streams as possible. Heating and air conditioning systems run intermittently, so forced air circulation within a building is not constant. Unaided plants cannot draw air to themselves as HVAC filters do, nor can they move about to capture pollutants. Instead, gases inevitably find their way to them, either by means of drafts or by natural gas expansion. The laws of physics tell us that gases expand to fill their containers. If that container is the microenvironment of a room or suite of rooms, air and pollutant gases expand to fill every corner. If a few plants happen to be in the room absorbing toxins in their vicinity, natural gas expansion will bring pollutants to them for continuous processing. This process is slow, however. Placing plants in air streams accelerates this activity.

As simple functional additions to an interior design plants could be used as individual, unaided greenery or in the form of flowering plants of specific varieties. A more practical design for the use of unaided plants in a home or business should have most of them grouped in planter boxes, either on the floor, elevated, or on planter shelves. If possible, these should be placed near existing air ducts. In an even more effective system, supplementary HVAC air ducts would be installed by the massed greenery. Supply and return registers should be placed on opposite sides of the planter so that the draft passes through the bio-mass (see Figure 5.3). Registers could also be located over and under planters for the same result. In this case it might be more efficient to position the planter box or shelf slightly away from the wall, so air can circulate behind the plants as well.

If the project has the luxury of advanced system design, dedicated forced-air ducts as part of a recirculating system can be incorporated into partitions to provide air flow only to the nearby planters. If such is the case, smaller fans can be utilized in the dedicated draft units, and these can be operated by the home or building's master control system. Independent timing cycles should also be used. For normal conditions, periodic fan operation should be spaced throughout the day, possibly for about ten minutes or so every half-hour or hour. The frequency of the cycle would depend on the severity of the environmental conditions. In the case of new buildings or newly decorated buildings, more frequent cycles

would be called for. The same would be appropriate for other abnormal environmental situations. For example, offices and homes are frequently repainted. If solvent-based paints are to be used and noxious odors will be prevalent for a period of time, the forced-air component of the system should be operated on a more frequent schedule. If environmental testing of the living or work space uncovers high levels of pollutants or low levels of large numbers of pollutants as a normal condition, frequent air flow cycles would be called for as well. Remember that closed systems of this type do not dump polluted air to the outside; they recirculate bad air through the unit until it is clean. The greater the circulation rate and frequency, the quicker this happens.

Another aspect of advanced bioreactor design is the use of activated carbon in the

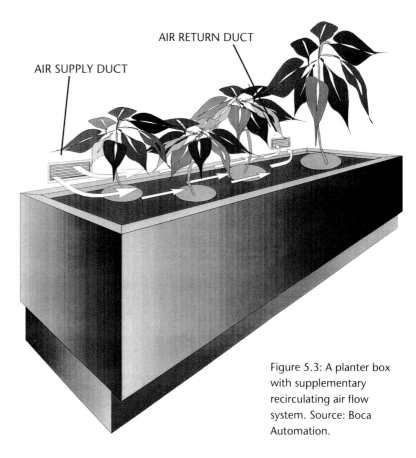

AIR RETURN DUCT

AIR SUPPLY DUCT

Figure 5.3: A planter box with supplementary recirculating air flow system. Source: Boca Automation.

soil system to improve its pollutant adsorbing ability. This involves a thick layer of large particle, activated carbon installed over the soil layer. It should not contain carbon dust. Plant roots grow into both layers.

A further complexity to the design of advanced systems is the nature of the soil mixture used. A wide variety of formulations are used in the industry to grow interior plants. One of the attributes of soil mixes is that they are either relatively inert (mostly Perlite, Vermiculite, etc.) or highly active with respect to resident microorganisms. As we've learned from the NASA studies, soil microbes perform an important function in bioreactors. The determining factors are not only the quantity of bacteria, but also the type. Certain strains are more effective than others. It is best to consult with someone who is knowledgeable in this area for the type to use for your particular purpose.

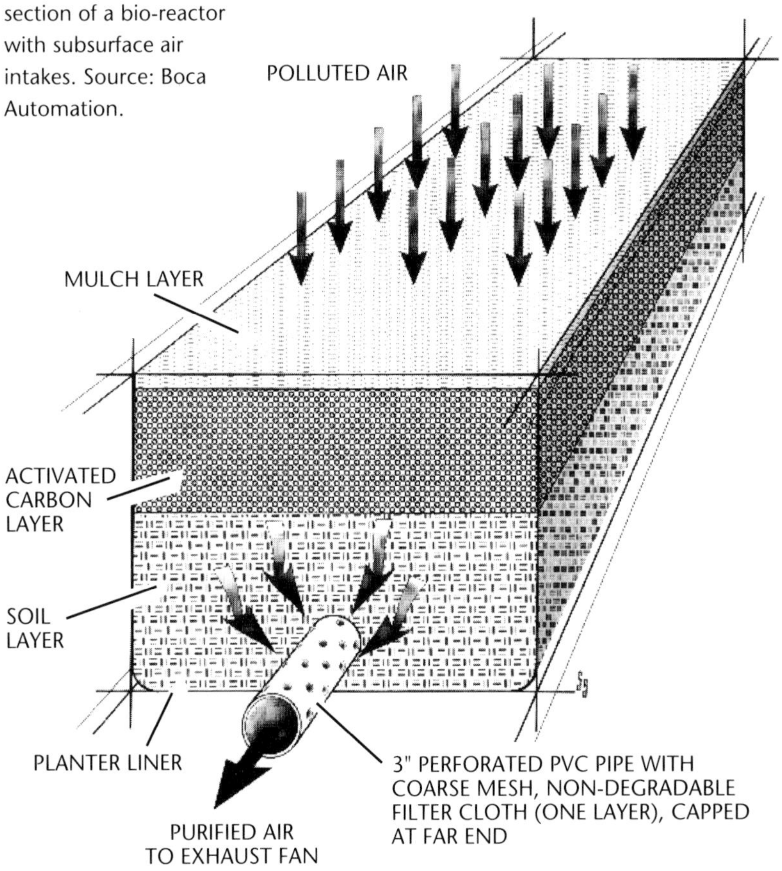

The subterranean exhaust system that NASA recommends for activated carbon/planter air cleaners (planter/bioreactors) provides a local air stream from built-in exhaust fans which introduce polluted air to the planter/filter at a highly effective rate and with better placement. This greatly improves filter efficiency. The dedicated, recirculating forced-air strategy discussed above can be designed into soil layers to be used in a subsurface mode. This also involves the use of exhaust fans configured with the suction side rather than the blower side connected to input ports in the soil (see Figure 5.4).

Supplementary lighting may be called for to ensure enough illumination for the plants' growth needs. Higher light levels promote greater photosynthetic activity, and thus more efficient air cleaning. Lights can provide accent duty for decor, as well as energize biological air cleaning systems. They can be activated by master building control systems, or by dedicated lighting controllers. Proper bulb types for plant growth should be sought, but not necessarily the traditional grow bulbs, as their color may not be suitable for interior decorating. Use of fluorescent or halogen bulbs in bullet reflectors is frequently the better course to take.

One of the disadvantages of these techniques is that plants tend to dry more rapidly with greater air circulation—enough to endanger their health if not watered frequently. Irrigation schedules would have to be increased. By manual irrigation means, the additional attention can considerably increase the maintenance cost burden, particularly under commercial leasing/maintenance contracts. Advanced, micro-irrigation systems solve this problem through automation, easily implementing additional watering cycles without additional cost. This important support technology will be discussed in following chapters.

Figure 5.4: Cross section of a bio-reactor with subsurface air intakes. Source: Boca Automation.

POLLUTED AIR

MULCH LAYER

ACTIVATED CARBON LAYER

SOIL LAYER

PLANTER LINER

PURIFIED AIR TO EXHAUST FAN

3" PERFORATED PVC PIPE WITH COARSE MESH, NON-DEGRADABLE FILTER CLOTH (ONE LAYER), CAPPED AT FAR END

If the prospect of designing planter/bio-reactors seems intimidating, there is an easier way. Bio-reactor modules that have all the essential elements built into them are already available. They can be dropped into preframed supports in building projects and connected to an exhaust system. Other units are available which have fans integrated into the module for easy installation. Bio-reactor modules are also available with automated precision micro-irrigation (APM) support systems. Sources for these products can be found in the Appendix.

More bio-systems should be designed into work spaces, such as office suites. The tendency today is to design extensive plantings into building lobbies and atria for a decorative effect with little thought to tenant space. Work spaces, restaurant dining rooms, classrooms, and the like are where most occupants can be found for long periods in commercial and institutional buildings. That is where the greatest impact can be made on employee satisfaction issues and on the reduction of health risks.

SIX

Interiorscaping

When decorative plants are used in buildings for the purpose of controlling indoor air pollution, a number of disciplines are involved in planning, selection, installation, and care—not only of the plants themselves, but also of the equipment specified. Interiorscapes in commercial buildings and in the common areas of large residential buildings particularly demand the attention of professionals from various fields. In this chapter we will discuss the interiorscape industry and its major players, their particular responsibilities, and how their specific jobs intersect.

An Industry Profile

The interiorscaping industry hardly existed in the early 1970s. At that time interiorscaping pioneers learned to nurture and adapt plant species which had thrived outdoors for millions of years to grow in indoor environments under adverse conditions. Everett Conklin is one of those early heroes of the business, and from the efforts of nurserymen and interiorscapers like him came a new area of expertise, a new era of interior plant use, and a new industry. As one measure of tropical plant use indoors, wholesale value of foliage plants for indoor or patio use increased from $20 million of use in 1970 to $487 million in 1994.[1]

The conditions these early interiorscapers found in buildings were so different from outdoor horticulture that plants commonly went into shock and died. The technology of the time was steeped in agricultural methodology, and much of it did not easily apply to indoor plant culture. Interiorscaping techniques had to be developed by trial and error. Methods are still being developed, for the industry is young and much has yet to be learned.

By and large, the interiorscaping branch of the landscape industry is made up of small companies, most of them family-owned businesses. Because the capital investment required to enter this field is very small, we see a broad diversity of practitioners. Some are part-timers such as homemakers, college students, and others using their spare time to make a few dollars. Most, however, are full-time businesses manned primarily by owners trained and experienced in the techniques of interior plant horticulture, and staffed with hired employees possessing varying degrees of knowledge and experience.

The results of a study conducted by *Western Landscaping News* showed that the average gross dollar volume earned by interior landscape contractors (interiorscapers) in 1982 was $53.1 thousand, with 35% showing less than $10 thousand, and 74% with less than $50 thousand gross dollar volume annually. Of the top 25 in the industry, the median concern did $5 million in 1991. In relation to other types of American industries, no interiorscaping businesses would be considered truly sizable.

The business of interiorscaping may not be huge, but it is definitely growing. For the past decade or so we have seen a movement toward consolidation in the industry. Large corporations like Rentokil and Orkin have franchised hundreds of small interiorscape contractors under their respective banners. This has provided needed capital and a measure of stability to an industry in short supply of both. Rentokil is the largest by far with annual sales of about $60 million nation-wide. Foliage Design Systems is second largest at about $14 million annually.[2] However, this was generated by about 800 franchises, each averaging roughly $75 thousand in gross sales.

The interiorscape business is very labor-intensive and requires a great deal of manual work. There is a lot of digging, climbing of ladders and retaining walls, and hauling around of heavy plants as well as watering paraphernalia involved. For these reasons, the industry is also young in age, with most of the employees being in the statistical age bracket of 18 to 24. The industry hires a large number of part-time employees to help out during peak periods, and virtually all are young.

The *WLN* study also pointed out that interiorscape installation and maintenance employees are the lowest paid in the general landscape industry with an average hourly wage of $4.29 in 1982. This has risen somewhat since, but it is not surprising that the interiorscape business also had the highest rate of employee turnover.[3] Such high turnover rates are expensive and counterproductive, and are very hard on the reputation of interiorscape firms. It is difficult to maintain a high quality level of service with new, partially trained maintenance technicians. The industry recognizes that it takes about a year to train a new employee to be a fully accomplished manual watering plant-care technician. There are many difficulties in doing so because of the nature of the job.[4] The industry is doing a good job of organizing training programs through its trade organizations, an innovation which should do much to raise standards.

Working against the interiorscaping business, however, is that the 18 to 24 age group upon which it relies so heavily is shrinking as evidenced by demographic trends. The U.S. Bureau of the Census forecast that by the year 1995, this critical age group will have dwindled to 9.2% of the population, from the 13.3% position it held in 1980 (See Table 6.1). That will occur at a time when the need for plant usage indoors will be greater than ever, and the need for trained plant-care technicians acute. The low pay scales and routine, difficult work will make it hard to attract competent employees in a highly competitive job market. A possible crisis situation is expected to face the industry. New technology, such as the automated plant-care systems now available for interior plantscapes, will help solve many of these personnel problems for the interior landscape industry, as they reduce the need for extensive training in the critical area of irrigation, reduce significantly the physical labor involved, and permit more efficient utilization of available labor. This subject will be discussed in more detail in following chapters.

Another great handicap of the interiorscape industry is that because casual attitudes about plant use prevail among construction, design, and real estate professionals, plant specialists are traditionally called in at the "tail end" of a project. Much of the time, interior landscape planning is done almost as an afterthought, particularly in small- to medium-sized projects. This is changing, but slowly. Even in large building projects and in upscale residential construction,

Table 6.1

United States Population (in Millions)

Year	Total U.S. Population	Population Ages 18-24	Percent of Population
1970	205,052	23,714	12.1
1980	227,757	28,492	13.3
1985	239,283	28,741	12.0
1990 (proj.)	249,657	25,794	10.3
1995 (proj.)	257,559	23,702	9.2
2000 (proj.)	267,955	24,601	9.2

Source: Current Population Reports, Series P-25, Nos. 870,952*, 985, U.S. Bureau of the Census.
*Used middle series projections.

seldom are plant cultural and maintenance details considered at the drawing board. This usually leads to a compromised job, and frequently the installation reflects it, either initially or after a period of time. How, for example, can a plantscape contractor do a proper job of irrigating a bed of plants by manual means or otherwise if proper drainage had not been planned for or hose bibbs not made available at reasonable locations? The problems increase in magnitude when one arrives at the site and finds that the planter bed has already been back-filled with debris and common soil which cannot come close to resembling quality growing media. Also, by the latter stages the interior lighting will have been specified, and frequently with no consideration of the plantscape's supplementary lighting needs. Perhaps window treatments were chosen that further lower ambient room light. Interior irrigation systems are frequently not considered in the early stages because they, too, are plant-related, and receive only casual attention. None of these are unusual scenarios. What is seldom realized is that these systems sometimes require tubing and piping to be incorporated into partitions and concrete slabs during construction. To do otherwise may seriously increase installation costs and undermine the effectiveness of the system operation, as well as increase planter maintenance fees the building owner and his tenants must pay over many, many years. In some cases these are minor problems, but in most they are significant. Leaving plant considerations to chance is a disservice to the building owner, the plantscape designer, the interior plantscape contractor who would install the plant stock, but most of all, to the interiorscape maintenance contractor who will be charged with taking care of the less-than-ideal installation. When the installation starts to look bad, recriminations start. In many of these situations the complications can be chalked up to a lack of proper planning at the design stage. The resulting conditions cannot be overcome by the front-line contractor.

The author has experienced many bad installations that could have been thriving examples of interior landscapes had the proper elements been included in the project at the appropriate time. For instance, many shopping mall promenades are being designed with large planter boxes embracing all manner of foliage and iron grate-covered planter pits in which large trees grow. In too many of these projects the planters have not been provided with electrical service for lighting and local irrigation control, nor have provisions been made for a simple water supply line from a central source, with a spigot at the planter for a hose connection. If one were to observe what the technician must go through to maintain the greenery in situations like this one, the irresponsibility of the poor planning becomes apparent. These problems could have been avoided if the design and specification work had been done more diligently. Many maintenance people (usually young women) have to climb tall ladders with heavy watering tanks strapped to their backs in order to take care of planters high up on the walls or in the rafters. A building comes to mind where planter boxes were designed into the edge of a narrow sixth-floor ledge, just under the skylight of an atrium court. The trailing plants have to be manually watered twice a week by an acrobatic plant technician tethered to the end of a safety cable to prevent a fall to the atrium floor far below. Automatic precision micro-irrigation systems could easily solve maintenance problems like these. The recent tendency to use the "team approach" in large projects is helping to alleviate problems such as these by bringing a broader base of plant-oriented expertise to the design team.

Landscape Architects

The landscape architect creates large and small topographical settings by using natural and man-made materials interspersed with live plantings to create a specific design effect. Most landscape architects specialize in outdoor settings, but the popularity of live plantscapes in building interiors has inspired a widening corps of practitioners to extend their specialty to include interior work. Some prefer to concentrate only on interior landscape design projects and have honed their training and experience to that end.[5]

It is important that interiorscape projects be designed and managed by professionals with the proper training. There is a great deal of difference between the environmental and cultural factors of plants growing indoors and those thriving in outdoor settings. This factor will be stressed repeatedly in this book for it cannot be over emphasized. Without proper understanding of the special needs of indoor horticulture, the firm responsible for plantings—whether they specialize in landscape architecture or interiorscaping—cannot hope to do an acceptable job of planning, designing, installing, or maintaining even a simple interior landscape installation. A competent interior landscape architect will have been properly trained to deal with land contours, soil composition, drainage systems, rocks and boulders, retaining walls, paving materials, walkways, accent lighting, irrigation, waterfalls and fountains, and, of course, with tropical foliage plants.

Interior landscape architects take the general space plan developed by the building architect and provide the topographical design. They begin by specifying the plant materials, a task which clearly requires a fairly high degree of indoor horticultural knowledge in order to be done successfully. Once the plant types are selected, the landscape architect proceeds by deciding on their locations. Plant placement must be considered in an overall aesthetic plan that provides an interior ambiance appropriate to the project. Plant and planter locations should be both functional and attractive while also serving to fulfill the vision of the building owner. It is crucial that the landscape architect's involvement in the project begin in the early design stages.

Plants are selected carefully according to the specific needs of the indoor environment, the anticipated maintenance situation, and the aesthetic the owner wants to achieve. A plant's size, shape, and color determine how well it might fit into the design scheme from an aesthetic standpoint. Other important factors the interior landscape architect considers are the growth habits and requirements of the plants (both above and below ground), how well they might adapt to the interior environment being developed, and their functional effectiveness in indoor air pollution control. Designers have to look at the amount of available light coming through the windows or skylight, and how the quantities and qualities of that light change over the course of the day—or, for that matter, over the course of the year. Temperature levels can drastically affect the plants, particularly when they are located near sources of heat and air conditioning. Soil type and drainage do as well, as does the quality of plant-care services that would be maintaining the installation. All in all, plants are selected for their hardiness in a variety of environmental conditions. Specimens can be purchased from wholesale nurseries.

In many cases the plantscape design work is done far in advance of the building construction, when it is not possible to accurately determine what the area in question will be like. Many assumptions have to be made under these circumstances.

Interior landscape architects frequently provide for the maintenance needs of the greenery by planning the supplementary lighting and irrigation systems, hiring interiorscape maintenance contractors, and collaborating with lighting and interior irrigation specialists. Residential projects seldom require the services of "interior" landscape architects, with the exception of condominium lobbies and clubhouse interiors in upscale developments. The outdoor environments of many communities, however, are extensively planned by landscape architects.

Interiorscapers

The contractor known as an interiorscaper or interior plantscaper is considered by many to be the nucleus of the interior landscape industry. Interiorscapers are generally experienced plant people well trained in their specialized field of plant horticulture in indoor environments. In many projects, particularly small- to medium-sized installations, he or she is called on to do it all—and most interiorscape projects in this country fit that category.

At the low end are the few potted plants a homeowner or office manager may want to have installed to dress up their home or place of business. Frequently plants are rented under a lease/maintenance contract, rather than being sold to customers. At the other end of the spectrum are the major office building, department store, restaurant, and shopping mall projects that require hundreds or possibly thousands of plants to achieve broad area coverage. Interiorscapers buy stock from wholesale nurseries for installation in their projects, while some of the larger plantscape companies own and operate nurseries. Other companies also maintain a kind of holding facility where they keep a small stock of plants for current or future contracts, or for rejuvenation of sickly specimens.

Interiorscapers would normally be hired for projects on a bid basis, to install and/or maintain plant stock. Some interiorscapers involve themselves in irrigation design and installation, but those are few. Sometimes they are asked to design the plantscape, particularly in small- to medium-sized projects. Large interiorscape companies also do some of the landscape design work normally relegated to the landscape architect. Yet the average interiorscaper does it all—from designing, leasing, or selling the plants, to installing them and guaranteeing their maintenance. When a project is installed, the interiorscaper can frequently obtain a separate maintenance contract. These are normally written for one-year periods, but they can also be renewed. Contract maintenance fees can be as low as $25 per month for contractors working on very small installations, to as much as tens of thousands of dollars billed monthly for major projects. In actual practice, however, interiorscapers generally find themselves in projects for only a couple of years.

Some contractors specialize in only a phase or two of the business, such as maintenance or design, but most are full-service companies. Many will concentrate only on commercial work, preferring the large projects available in restaurants, banks, office buildings, and the like. Still others prefer the more personal atmosphere of the residential markets and will sell or lease potted plants to the home or apartment owner and possibly take care of them as well, especially in cases where the client is away a good deal of the time. Because of the trend toward greater numbers of home businesses, more interiorscape contractors recognize this as a market of growing importance.

The benefits of automation to the interiorscaper can be considerable, but open-mindedness is coming slowly. Most interiorscapers are still suspicious of

automatic plant care systems for fear that automation will cause them to lose business. Nothing could be further from the truth. Automation does not *replace* the experienced interiorscaper, for no responsible supplier of automated plant-care systems would promote his or her products without strongly recommending that they be used in conjunction with competent plant-care specialists. As interiorscapers become increasingly familiar with the techniques of advanced interior irrigation, they will no doubt learn how they can use them to their benefit.

Tropical Foliage Nurseries

Hundreds of wholesale nurseries, most of them relatively small, grow tropical foliage plants for interior decorative uses. Most tropical foliage originates in Florida, California, or Texas. The largest supplier of tropical plants to the interiorscape trade does about $12 million a year in gross volume (wholesale), with about $6 million of that going to the trade for indoor installations. Most nurseries supply both outdoor and interior plant stock, but will tend to concentrate on one or the other. They also concentrate on specific plant varieties. The production of plants for interior applications is a specialized and more involved process because the plants must be conditioned for low-light environments prior to shipment. There are canopied fields around the country dedicated to conditioned, or acclimatized, plants. They are nurtured under shade cloth of varying densities to get them used to their final destination. Not all nurseries are willing to invest in this extra treatment. The tropical foliage industry has done an excellent job of adapting the hundreds of varieties of plants to the unnatural conditions of building interiors, and in catering to the special needs of the interiorscaper and retailer. In many projects, particularly the major ones, interiorscapers take a shopping tour of the nurseries months and even years before delivery, to select in advance those plants considered most suitable. The nursery would then acclimatize them gradually to the specific conditions expected to be found at the final destination.

Irrigation Contractors

Few contractors are trained in the specialized field of interior irrigation. It is so new that not many have had the opportunity to install systems in building interiors. Irrigation contractors are primarily local companies that design and install outdoor irrigation systems for homes and recreation areas, as well as for commercial and institutional buildings. Most installations are relatively simple, and therefore don't require much planning, but large public parks, golf courses, residential communities, and office parks require extensive coverage, and the irrigation systems can get quite complex. These jobs are generally obtained on a bid basis, and frequently a systems maintenance contract is negotiated for long-term troubleshooting and repair. For shopping malls, lobbies, and other common areas inside of public buildings irrigation contractors bid on installations of drip or sprinkler systems.

Large planter boxes in public areas of buildings that require heavy watering can sometimes be automatically irrigated with outdoor-type systems. Mirage Brand[6] precision micro-irrigation (APM) systems are designed for use in furnished areas of the building that are sensitive to precise irrigation control, such as the private living quarters of a home or apartment, office suites, or restaurant dining rooms. The technology as well as the design and installation of these systems is quite different from the "garden variety" system and requires specialized training and experience. Expertise in outdoor irrigation is of little value in most interior situations, and now that more comprehensive technology is available, we will find many irrigation contractors learning this specialty to become full-service companies. The development of automated precision systems establishes an entirely new area of expertise that will allow other contractors to specialize in interior work. The market for irrigation services has been broadened considerably. This subject will be discussed more fully in later chapters.

SEVEN

Types of Plants Used in Interiorscaping

For anyone dealing with interior design involving live plants, it helps to have some knowledge of the varieties available, how they are used, and what it takes to keep them alive. In this chapter we will discuss the different varieties of plants used to decorate and purify the air in residential and commercial interiors. It is my hope that the following sections will provide an overview of plant types, as the details are best left to the experts in the field. There are many excellent books on the subject of horticulture, and I highly recommend the reader become more knowledgeable through further study.

Houseplants versus Interiorscaping Plants

By and large there is no difference between those familiar objects called houseplants and the plants used by professionals for interiorscaping commercial projects. The plant varieties are generally the same, except that larger, more mature plants are usually used in commercial landscaping. Homeowners also tend to use more flowering varieties of plants than do the professionals. There are practical reasons for these differences. Concerning the question of size, the pros learned a long time ago that it is easier and less costly to care for larger plants. Plants in larger pots do not dry out as fast, and therefore require less frequent care. Besides, they also look better and provide more apparent value. While virtually all interiorscapers use potted flowering plants from time to time in their projects, they perceive their decorative value to be very short-lived, particularly when compared to potted foliage plants. In a survey by *Interiorscape Magazine* it was discovered that 45% of the respondents had to replace flowering plants every two weeks because of their short floral display, thereby creating high maintenance costs. For this reason, potted flowers find only limited use by the professionals. More common is the use of cut, dried, or artificial flowers on a regular basis to liven up small furnished areas.[1]

Tropical Foliage Plants

Most of the species used in interior decoration are classified as tropical foliage plants. These are not special varieties created by nature for our comfort and enjoyment indoors. Their natural habitat was the tropical and sub-tropical regions of Central and South America, Africa, Asia, the Far East, and the South Pacific. One can visualize them growing in the shade of rain forests and jungles, near rivers and streams, or perhaps fed from underground rivulets beneath a canopy of dense trees. Still others called the dry, sandy desert regions home. While their original living conditions were varied, they all have one thing in common: They spent a long time getting used to their specific outdoor environment and have adapted accordingly.

Figure 7.1: Bamboo palm in its natural environment.

Modern man has used this quality of adaptation to increase the usefulness of foliage plants, bringing many into indoor settings as well as new outdoor environments. Not all species have been able to survive the change, however, and only those which are most adaptable can be used by the homeowner or interiorscaper. The differences in environmental conditions found outdoors and indoors are great indeed. The light levels in building interiors are much lower, and this drastically changes the growth habits and biological needs of the plants, mainly in terms of moisture and nutritional requirements. To put the difference in perspective, plants growing outdoors are exposed to 8,000 to 10,000 foot-candles of light on a bright summer day. If those plants were then moved indoors, into a home or office, for example, they would find typically only 30 to 200 foot-candles of light.[2] Little wonder that a plant in those circumstances would experience shock. A plant that is transported from one environment to another always faces the possibility of deteriorating, sometimes with fatal results, but more frequently only temporarily. The delicate balances within their systems are easily upset. These stresses occur mainly from changes in light intensity and available water, both at the roots and airborne moisture for absorption by the leaves. The movement of the plant could be as slight as repositioning it within a house or office, or it could be a major shift, such as moving it from favorable outdoor growing conditions to unfavorable, alien interior settings. Any change prompts some degree of shock, but drastic environmental shifts could kill it.

Acclimatization

Nurserymen have found a way to reduce plant shock. *Acclimatization* is the adaptation of the plant during growth in the field or greenhouse to conditions closer to those which the plant will face when finally installed indoors. The refined techniques now used to acclimatize plants account in large part for the success interiorscapers have had in installing and maintaining them indoors. Those nurseries that specialize in producing indoor foliage plants grow them in shadehouses. These are simply areas in their outdoor fields that have been fitted with translucent cloth canopies that allow only a portion of the sun's rays through. The plants beneath are shaded to the degree required by the particular plant, its size, and shipping schedule. Some small houseplants are grown almost exclusively in shadehouses or greenhouses, as they are shipped while young. Larger plants are generally started under full sun for the early years of their existence, and then gradually grown under deeper and deeper shade conditions. By the time they are ready to ship, they are used to the lighting conditions under which they will be grown in the building interior.

As mentioned in a previous chapter, it is common practice in large building projects (when the plant materials have been specified well in advance of the building's completion) for interiorscapers to visit various nurseries six to nine months prior to delivery and pick out the particular plants they want for the job. The tagged plants, trees, and smaller foliage varieties are then conditioned in dense shadehouses up until the time of shipment to ensure that they will not encounter undue shock from completely unfamiliar lighting levels. An excellent discussion about the technology of acclimatization can be found in the book *Interior Plantscaping* by Richard L. Gaines.[3]

Nursery Irrigation

Irrigation of the containerized plants is done in the nurseries once or a few times daily depending on the plants, time of year, and other factors. Many water using different types of sprinkler systems. *Mist*

Figure 7.2: Exterior view
of shadehouses.

Figure 7.3: Interior view
of shadehouses.

systems are frequently used in greenhouses, mostly on smaller plants. Increasing numbers of growers are using *drip and trickle* irrigation in the fields and greenhouses as these are more water conservative and efficient. The drip and trickle techniques direct water carefully to the root zones so it reaches the soil where it will do the plants the most good. This technique also helps to reduce fungus and other leaf-borne diseases. Outdoor installation requires much more water than indoor because of the faster growth rate of the plants and the environmentally harsh conditions under which they find themselves. Outside, watering is done fully and frequently. Wind, bright sunlight, and heat tend to dry the plants quickly, and the lost moisture must be replenished often to prevent the plants from wilting. These watering techniques will be discussed in more detail in a later chapter.

Nursery Soil

It is difficult to be specific about the soil used to grow tropical foliage plants because the soil types vary widely. There are a number of *soil mixes* recommended for potted plants. Some of the supplying nurseries use the best soil mix for the varieties they grow, but many do not. An unfortunately large portion of the foliage industry chooses soil for convenience and cost-efficiency over horticultural merit. One will find large numbers of plants shipped in what is mostly sand, with little humus or loam to be found in the pots. Such plants are more difficult to maintain because the soil is virtually unable to hold moisture and nutrients. It takes natural humus and loam, or artificial soil additives, to provide needed absorption properties. It is highly recommended that poor soil be replaced by a mix specified for that plant variety. The use of proper soil is one of the most important factors in achieving efficient plant irrigation, whether it is by manual

means or automatic. This cannot be stressed strongly enough. One way to assure overall quality is to buy plant stock from reputable nurseries.

Plant Sizes

Plants for indoor use vary in size from the smallest cactus to the largest palm tree. They are grown at the nursery in plastic containers called grow pots, grow containers, or production containers. All varieties of plants are sold in many different stages of growth—from young to mature—and will therefore be found in various sizes. Plant sizes are usually specified by *container volume or diameter*, and sometimes by *plant height*. There is a correlation between pot size by diameter and the trade's designations of pot size by volume (see Table 7.1).

Plants are chosen for size by the interior landscape designer according to the area they will occupy and their eventual size and

Table 7.1

Container Sizes by Diameter and Volume

Container Diameter (in inches)	Container Volume (in gallons)
6	1
8	2
10	3
12	4
14	7
17	10
22	20
23	30
28	45 (taller than 30 inches)
32	65
38	95
42	100

Source: Wholesale Price List (Delray Beach, FL: Tropical Ornaments, Inc., 1985).

shape once they become more mature. It would be a poor looking plantscape indeed if after a year or two the plants were so tall that they appeared ungainly and unkempt. In addition to size, the designer considers the plant's color, shape, texture, growth habit, normal moisture and lighting requirements, and tolerance to disease, pests, and abuse. These factors are compared with those prevalent in the installation environment and a number of different plant types are chosen to meet the project objectives.

Plant Varieties

The varieties of plants chosen for use in interior decorating run into the hundreds. They are specified by using either their common names or their botanical (scientific) names, and sometimes by both. For example, the common spider plant is known scientifically as Chlorophytum comosum. The Norfolk Island Pine Tree is known scientifically as Araucaria heterophylla. Is it any wonder that the common names are generally the ones used to identify them? Some of the names are tongue-twisters and the professionals have developed nicknames for them. The Spathiphyllum wallisii is known simply as a "Spath." The Dracaena deremensis var. "Janet Craig" is known affectionately as a "Janet Craig," and so on.

There are a number of plant families that have become very popular with the decorating trades. These are Aralia, Aglaonemas, Dieffenbachia, Dracaenas, Palms, Schefflera, Spathiphyllum, Ficus, Ferns, Bromeliads, Philodendron, and others. Within each of these major classifications there are several, if not many, subclassifications. Following is a list of the foliage plants most commonly found in the catalogs of major suppliers to this industry. It is by no means a complete list of plants used in the interior landscape business, but

it is representative of the more popular types. More complete coverage of plant types can be found in good books on houseplants and interiorscaping. Comprehensive plant lists are also published by *Interiorscape Magazine*, Associated Landscape Contractors of America (ALCA), and by major interiorscape firms. Many of those sources include plant photos.

One of the major influences in the rapid rise of landscaped interiors has been the tropical foliage industry's development of techniques for adapting a large number of plant species to the specialized conditions of indoor cultivation, as well as breeding new strains for this use. Their production capacity has increased, as has their awareness of market needs, making environmental interiorscaping even more viable an option for the control of indoor pollution.

The following list of plants has been culled from NASA's experimental data, as well as from research carried out since 1989 when the NASA program ceased. Keep in mind that only a relatively small number of plant varieties have been subjected to the environmental stress testing that determines their gas sorption profile, and the range of pollutants studied has been confined to a few of the more common ones. Many other plant varieties may give superior results under similar conditions, but at this stage we cannot wait for exhaustive screening studies to further define the myriad conditions that exist. What is presented here is the current state of the art. Those plants listed below are known to have effective sorption characteristics under common pollutant conditions (see Table 7.3). If the nature of an air quality problem is known, then a plant variety can be matched to the need. However, in most cases a smattering of different varieties should be used.

Table 7.2

A Partial List of Popular Plants for Interior Use

Common Variety	Scientific or Common Name	Common Heights
Aglaonema	Abijan	6" to 14"
	Commutatum	6" to 14"
	(Emerald Beauty)	6" to 14"
	(Silver Queen)	6" to 14"
Aralia (Polyscias)	Fruticosa (Ming Aralia)	12" to 10'
	Elegantissima	12" to 8'
Araucaria	(Norfolk Island Pine)	5' to 15'
Caladium	Lindenii	18" to 30"
Cissus	Rhoicissus rhombidea (Ellen Danica)	1' to 2' (cascades)
	Rhoicissus rhomoidea (Grape Ivy)	1' to 2' (cascades)
	(Fiona)	1' to 2' (cascades)
	Mandaiana	1' to 2' (cascades)
	Tetrastigma	1' to 2' (cascades)
Crotons	(Norma)	8" to 8'
	(Petra)	8" to 8'
Cycads	Circinalis (Queen Sago)	30" to 10'
	Revoluta (King Sago)	30" to 10'
	Zamia Furfuracea (Cardboard Palm)	20" to 4'
Dieffenbachia	Camilla (Dumbcane)	12" to 30"
	(Tropic Snow)	30" to 42"
	(Aurora)	25" to 40"
	Perfection Compacta	20" to 36"
Dracaenas	Deremensis 'Janet Craig' (Janet Craig)	18" to 48"
	Marginata (Madagascar Dragon Tree)	5' to 20'
	Fragrans Cane (Corn or Cane Plant)	4' to 18'
	Massangeana Cane (Corn or Cane Plant)	4' to 18'
	Reflexa (Pleomele)	36" to 16'
	Warneckii (Striped Dracaena)	30" to 48"
	Yucca elephantipes (Joshua Tree)	12" to 8'
Ferns	Bostoniensis (Boston Fern)	6" to 24"
	Whitmanii (Feather Fern)	6" to 18"
	Platycerium bifurcatum (Stag horn)	6" to 18"

Common Variety	Scientific or Common Name	Common Heights
Ficus	Benjamina (bush form)	2' to 8'
	Benjamina (tree form)	5' to 24'
	Nitida	5' to 24'
	Pandurata (Lyrata)	3' to 9'
	Elastica Decora (Rubber Plant)	3' to 9'
Ivy	Hedera helix (English Ivy)	1' to 3'
	Hedera canariensis (Canary Ivy)	1' to 3'
Palms	Areca	5' to 22'
	Chamaedorea Erumpens (Bamboo Palm)	3' to 14'
	Chamaedorea Sifrizii (Bamboo Palm)	3' to 14'
	Caryota Mitis (Fishtail Palm)	3' to 25'
	Howea fosterana (Kentia)	3' to 12'
	Phoenix Roebelenii (Dwarf Date Palm)	2' to 15'
	Beaucarnea Recurvata (Ponytail Palm)	2' to 20'
	Rhapis Excelsa (Lady Palm)	3' to 10'
Philodendrons	(Angel Wing)	1' to 3'
	Cordatum	1' to 3'
	Domesticum (Elephant's Ear)	1' to 5'
	(Emerald Queen)	1' to 3'
	(Marble Queen)	1' to 3'
	Pertusum (Split Leaf)	1' to 3'
	(Pluto)	1' to 3'
	Scandens (Sweetheart Plant)	1' to 3'
	Selloum (Lacy Tree)	1' to 8'
Pothos	(Golden)	1' to 3'
	(Large Leaf)	1' to 3'
Sansevieria	Laurenti (Snake Plant)	18" to 42"
Scheffleras	Arboricola (Dwarf Schefflera)	3' to 10'
	Brassaia actinophylla (Umbrella Tree)	5' to 22'
Spathiphyllum	Deneve #1	18" to 3'
	Floribunda	18" to 3'
	Mauna Loa (Peace Lily)	3' to 6'
	Tasson	15" to 18"
	Variegata "Mini"	15" to 18"
	Wallisii (Peace Lily)	15" to 3'

Sources: Various wholesale nursery catalogs; *Plant Source '85, Interiorscape Magazine TPIE Show Issue, 1985*, p.59; *Interior Planting in Large Buildings,* (Halsted Press, 1980); *Interior Plantscapes*, (Prentice Hall, 1987).

Table 7.3

Commonly Available Ornamental Plants for Indoor Air Pollution Abatement

Plant Variety	Tested Effective with these Pollutants
Azalea	Formaldehyde
Dieffenbachia (exotica compacta)	Formaldehyde, xylene, toluene
Philodendron (Philodendron selloum—'lace tree') (Philodendron oxycardium—'heart leaf') (Philodendron domesticum—'elephant ear')	Formaldehyde
Green spider plant (Chlorophytum elatum 'vittatum') (Chlorophytum comosum 'vittatum')	Formaldehyde, carbon monoxide, nitrogen dioxide, xylene
Golden pothos (Scindapsus aureus)	Formaldehyde, carbon monoxide, benzene
Bamboo palm (Chamaedorea elegans) (Chamaedorea seifritzii)	Formaldehyde
Corn plant (Dracaena fragrans 'massangeana')	Formaldehyde, xylene
Chrysanthemum (Chrysanthemum morifolium)	Formaldehyde, benzene, trichloroethylene, ammonia
Mother-in-law's tongue (Sansevieria trifasciata) (Sansevieria laurentii)	Formaldehyde
English ivy (Hedera helix)	Formaldehyde, benzene, trichloroethylene
Janet Craig (Dracaena deremensis 'Janet Craig')	Formaldehyde, benzene
Peace lily (Spathiphyllum 'Clevelandii') (Spathiphyllum 'Mauna Loa')	Formaldehyde, benzene, trichloroethylene, xylene, ethyl alcohol, acetone, methyl alcohol, ammonia
Boston fern (Nephrolepis exaltata 'Bostoniensis')	Formaldehyde
Dwarf date palm (Phoenix roebelenii)	Formaldehyde, xylene
Kimberly queen fern (Nephrolepis obliterata)	Formaldehyde, xylene, ethyl alcohol
Weeping fig (Ficus benjamina)	Formaldehyde, xylene, benzene
Goose foot plant (Syngonium podophyllum)	Formaldehyde
Aloe vera (Aloe vera)	Formaldehyde
Chinese evergreen (Aglonema modestum)	Formaldehyde
Bromeliad (Cryptanthus 'Elaine') (Aechmea fasciata) (Guzmania 'Cherry')	Formaldehyde
Orchid (Phalaenopsis) (Dendrobium)	Formaldehyde, xylene, acetone, methyl alcohol, ethyl acetate, ammonia
Marginata (Dracaena marginata)	Benzene, trichloroethylene, xylene
Gerbera daisy (Gerbera Jamesonii)	Benzene, trichloroethylene
Warneckii (Dracaena warneckii)	Benzene, trichloroethylene
Lady palm (Rhapis excelsa)	Ammonia, chloroform
Liriope spicata	Ammonia
Anthurium andraeanum	Ammonia, xylene
Homalomena	Ammonia, xylene

One of the interesting results of NASA studies and those of Wolverton Environmental Services is the revelation that certain types of plants are more effective in dark environments than in the light. Most notably these are in the orchid and bromeliad families. Evolution has conditioned them to open their pores to accept air intake in the evening, when the environment is cooler and there is less moisture loss from heat-induced evaporation. That's not surprising, for these are species from climates where days are hot and dry, and where cool nights provide condensation and moisture for the plants. That attribute can be useful in augmenting the gas sorption efficiency of interiorscapes. By including them in the plant mix, the bioreactor would improve its round-the-clock service, providing air cleaning at night at a higher level than would ordinarily be obtained. Bromeliads may be the better choice between the two classes of plants, because orchids require higher temperatures and humidity levels than most plants, and the average business environment may not be suitable. Nevertheless, all green plants clean air to some degree in the dark, so the bioreactor works at all times. With most varieties the root zone is the more active mechanism under dark conditions, for microbes that destroy pollutant molecules in the soil do not appear to be light-dependent. In considering these factors, factor in that the HVAC system in commercial buildings is relatively inactive at night, when the tenant businesses are idle. This means that there is less air cleaning being done by mechanical systems during the dark hours. Meanwhile, pollution sources are ever-active and continuously off-gas their emissions to the atmosphere. Dark period air cleaning can be improved with the installation of these specialized plant varieties. The extensive list in Table 7.3 makes available quite a variety of plant types, colors, textures, and shapes for interesting decorative schemes. At the same time, their technical attributes can be brought to bear on indoor air quality problems.

EIGHT

Plant Biology and Other Growth Factors

Plants are living organisms, and as such require certain conditions to keep them alive and sustain their growth. There are many growth factors that must be considered in the placement and maintenance of plants in an interior environment, all of which must be understood by the designer, interiorscaper, and irrigation specialist for them to be effective in their work. Overseeing all of this are the real estate owners and managers who must understand the complexity of the situation and hire only qualified people knowledgeable in their specialty. As we've discussed before, too often the interior landscape plant stock as well as its critical growth, maintenance, and environmental needs are taken for granted. Designers have more control than they realize over factors affecting the ultimate success of plants in their new home.

Design Considerations

Following are a few examples of factors designers can influence to affect plant growth:

- Placement of planter locations in proper relation to natural lighting.

- Use of automatic, artificial lighting systems to supplement natural light.

- Proper design of glazing, particularly in large window areas to assure recommended lighting levels can be maintained (plants are frequently "baked" in strong-sunlight locations).

- Proper design of built-in planter boxes with adequate drainage provisions.

- Incorporation of effective irrigation systems into planter locations.

- Assuring the specification and installation of proper soil mixes.

- Location of planters relative to traffic patterns.

To neglect plant needs and other related considerations in the final building design, either by choice or by ignorance of the biological principals involved, is a disservice to the project's integrity and the financial interests of the building owners. Once the project has been completed, it is usually too late to right the wrongs. Building management may then wonder why their project looks awful despite the big numbers on the plant-maintenance contract. Often this has to do with poor initial planning, which is totally avoidable.

It has been mentioned that learning something about plant growth is an essential part of the educational process for architects, interior designers, building managers, and other specialists. Anyone dealing with plants must understand their biological needs to some extent. It is certainly not necessary to become an expert on this horticultural subject, but just as the architect and engineer study the stress or light-transmission characteristics of building materials, or as the interior designer is informed about the special characteristics of textile materials, woods, and surface finishes, so too should they have some understanding of live plants, a more vulnerable design material they use in their work.

Plant Growth Cycle

A plant's basic requirements for growth are air, water, nutrients, and a suitable environment that includes sufficient light, proper temperature, and protection for the plant's leaves and roots. Since a plant cannot gather its own food, it absorbs the chemical substances it needs from its immediate surroundings—the atmosphere and soil—and makes its own from carbon dioxide and water. In the leaves, through complex photochemistry and biochemistry, it manufactures sugars with the help of energy from absorbed sunlight. This process is called *photosynthesis*. The broad, flat shape of the leaf is nature's design for an efficient, miniature food manufacturing plant. It provides a large surface area for the absorption of sunlight and for gases to diffuse in and out through many tiny pores. While food is manufactured, carbon dioxide is absorbed by the leaf from the air and diffuses with water brought into the leaf from the roots by way of the stem. The green substance in the leaves, called *chlorophyll*, is able to chemically generate the sugar food substances when activated by sunlight. A by-product of this process is the release of oxygen into the air. The sugar is circulated throughout the plant to be either used for plant growth or to be stored as starch.

That sugar used for plant sustenance and growth goes through a process called *respiration*. Chemically, it is the oxidation of manufactured food to release its energy

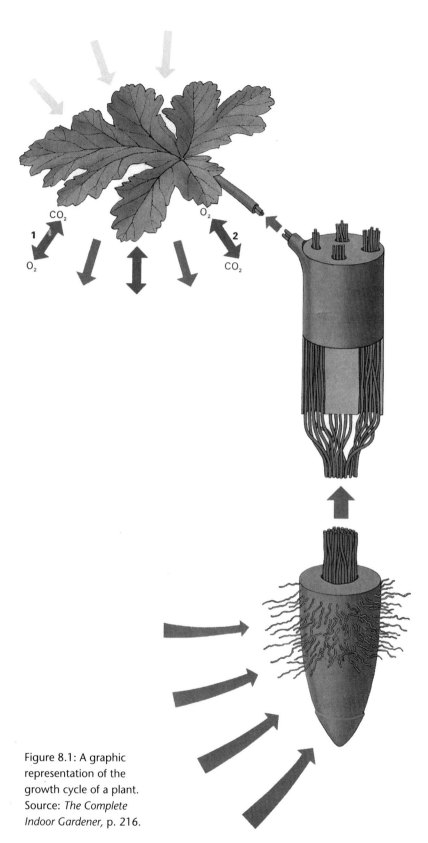

CO_2

1

O_2

O_2

CO_2

2

Figure 8.1: A graphic
representation of the
growth cycle of a plant.
Source: *The Complete
Indoor Gardener,* p. 216.

and promote cell division, absorption of minerals, and other necessary biological functions. During respiration, oxygen is absorbed from the air by the leaf to enter into the chemical reaction, while a small amount is also available from the photosynthetic process. Carbon dioxide is the by-product of respiration, and is subsequently released into the atmosphere through the leaves. It is then again available to be absorbed by the plant to further photosynthesis, completing the cycle.

Water that was brought up from the roots passes out of the leaf through the pores. That process is called **transpiration.** It is a form of sweating, much like animals do. As the water is evaporated away, it has a cooling effect, like it does on our skin, but it also creates a tiny vacuum or suction throughout the plant, right down to the roots. This generates a "pull" on the moisture in the soil, causing it to be drawn into the root system for circulation through the plant.

Water also migrates into the roots by the process of **osmosis.** The absorbed water carries with it dissolved mineral salts and other nutrients that are necessary for the plant's sustenance and growth. High temperatures, a dry atmosphere around the plant, and drafts from open windows, air conditioning, and heating systems and environmental bioreactors will increase the rate of transpiration, releasing more water than normal through the leaves into the atmosphere. This lost water must be replaced by the plant, so it is essential that enough moisture be available in the soil at the root zone for replenishment to take place. In hot weather, it is necessary to water the plant more frequently. In colder weather, or when the ambient humidity is higher, transpiration slows down and less water is released from the leaves. There is less need to replenish the moisture in the soil, so the plant watering schedule can be reduced.[1]

Roots need to breathe in order to remain healthy and functional. The spaces between soil particles, called **pores** or **interstices,** must contain oxygen as well as moisture. That means the soil should not become waterlogged, because in this condition water fills the pores around the roots and drives out the oxygen. The roots will soon drown and rot, causing them to be dysfunctional, and the plant will die. The opposite happens when water is given off by the leaves faster than the roots can replace it. In this case the soil dries out and the plant wilts because the leaves lack the moisture that is normally in the stem and is responsible for much of their turgidity, or stiffness.[2]

Nature has provided a balance between the roots, their ability to absorb water and nourishment, and the top growth that the plant system propagates. This balance is known as the "root/shoot ratio." If there are more roots than the amount of top growth requires, the top grows out quickly to catch up. This is what happens when branches are pruned back or broken. In the case of plants in interior environments, much less light acts on the leaves and the photosynthetic and transpirational processes are slowed considerably, with the result that less food is produced and less top growth occurs. This, in turn, reduces the plant's need for a highly developed root system, as moisture and nutritional requirements are kept at a lower level. This is all relative, however, and those indoor plants growing in brighter light do so more vigorously, both topside and at the root level. The other side of this story is that if the top growth is much larger in volume than the root system, hampering its ability to gather enough moisture and soluble salts, then the top growth starts to die back, generally dropping leaves and drying up branches in order to compensate. This happens not only when the root system is not mature enough, but also when the roots become damaged from mechanical

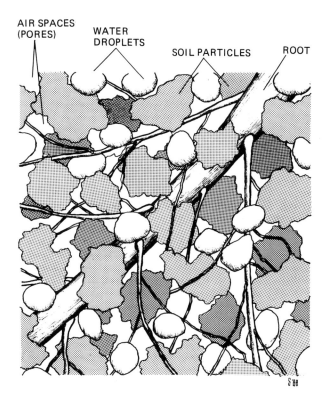

AIR SPACES (PORES)   WATER DROPLETS   SOIL PARTICLES   ROOT

Figure 8.2: Soil particles and the pores between them containing water and air.

mistreatment or from the soil being oversaturated with water, as well as when the soil is permitted to become too dry. That is why proper irrigation is important. It must provide the right amount of moisture at the root level without depleting the soil of its oxygen.

Soil Moisture

Water-borne nutrients are absorbed into the plant system by the roots. Soil moisture, therefore, is paramount in a plant's biological process. The general moisture requirement of the various plant varieties used in interiorscaping is commonly found in books on the subject, and there are many. Moisture-related specifics are usually simplified as **dry**, **moist**, and **wet**. The largest category by far into which most plants fit is moist. Of the 204 plant varieties listed in Ortho Books' *Mini-Encyclopedia of House Plants*, 157 of them carry the watering recommendation of "keep evenly moist."[3] In the book *Interior Plantscapes* by George H. Manaker, of the 74 plant types delineated by variety and requirements, 60 carry the "keep soil moist" recommendation.[4] Likewise, in the book *Interior Plantscaping* by Richard L. Gaines, of the 54 plant types delineated by variety and requirements, 49 carry the "keep soil moist" recommendation.[5] Most experts in the field contend that more plants are destroyed by heavy-handed manual watering than by any other means. Such practices eventually saturate the soil and the plant's root system rots. The new Mirage™[6] series of automated precision micro-irrigation systems (APM) come closest of all techniques to maintaining even levels of soil moisture. We will discuss this subject in more detail later in relation to interiorscape watering practices.

Light

Light acting on a plant's leaves is a key ingredient in the process of photosynthesis, and a necessary one for its life, growth, and development. The subject of light is a complex issue, and should be considered in the context of interrelated factors of intensity, duration, and quality.

Intensity is the amount of light that acts on the plant's leaves, and the photosynthetic process reacts in direct proportion to the intensity of the light—the greater the amount of light, the greater the amount of food manufactured by the plant. Intensity is measured by photoelectric light meters, and the units of measurement are called *foot-candles.* Plants growing outdoors under field conditions are typically exposed to 10,000 to 16,000 foot-candles of sunlight in Florida, Texas, and California, which are the main source states. Compare this with the typical light intensity of 30 to 200 foot-candles found in offices.[7] There is little wonder that the plants must go through a long acclimatization period before they can be used indoors. Otherwise, the shock would

be too great. Once installed in interior settings, the greenery must be bathed in at least minimum levels of light to survive. If plants are to be sustained at their original size and vigor the light levels should be somewhat greater, and even greater if they are to really thrive. Minimum interior light levels will vary with the plant and how it was raised prior to installation. Note that flowering plants need brighter light than most foliage varieties.

The time in which light acts on the plant is called the lighting *duration.* Plants grow better when illumination is sustained for long, continuous periods of time. This is frequently difficult in interior settings, for natural sunlight comes through windows and skylights at varying intensities during the course of the day. Effective intensity levels may be available for only very short periods in many interior locations and supplementary lighting may be called for.

There is an interrelationship between intensity and duration. The question of how long light of a given intensity must act on a plant each day is a complex one. There are a number of factors that influence the response, but plant species appears to be the predominant one. The general rule of thumb used by the trade to cover most situations dictates that the plant must have at least 12 hours of exposure to lighting of at least 50 to 100 foot-candles in intensity. Most interiorscaping plants will fit that mold. Those classified as high-light-level plants, however, will not.

Moisture requirements are generally specified in relation to lighting conditions, as the two are also strongly interrelated. The more light a plant receives, the more water it needs to sustain its life processes. Any listing of moisture recommendations is contingent on the plant receiving recommended lighting conditions as well.

The *quality* of light is another important factor that needs to be considered when dealing with plants. Quality has to do with

Table 8.1

Plant Categories and Recommended Lighting Levels

Plant Category	Minimum* Light Level	Recommended* Light Level
Low light	50fc	75-150 fc
Medium light	75-100 fc	200+ fc
High light	200 fc	500 fc
Very high light	500 fc	1000+ f

Source: Richard L. Gaines, *Interior Plantscaping* (New York: Architectural Record Books, 1977), 70.
*Light levels as measured in footcandles, at 12 hours per day exposure.

the color, or wavelength, of the radiant light energy that is received by the plant, either from the sun or from artificial light sources. The radiant energy spectrum contains a narrow band of wavelengths that represent visible light to our eye. It is within this band that plants also get radiant energy to help their growth. Reddish and bluish visible light are the most effective in the horticultural life processes. Sunlight is rich in these energy wavelengths, but its light quality does change as it passes through the atmosphere on its way to the earth. There is the least change around high noon, accounting for the fact that light rays are strongest at that time. The greatest changes occur early and late in the day because the energy must pass through a longer atmospheric barrier before it reaches earth. Sunlight at the earth's surface is redder during the early morning and late afternoon hours, and bluer around midday. The sunlight is also altered as it passes into the interior of a building, picking up the color cast of the walls, curtains, or windows (glazing), or reflecting off surrounding interior surfaces. So the sunlight that finally reaches the interior planters is generally quite different than that found outside. Aside from being much less intense, its quality is not as effective from a plant growth standpoint.

Light quality is an even more important issue when dealing with artificial sources used to supplement natural lighting. The quality varies with the type of bulb used, and the differences can be quite large. Incandescent as well as a wide variety of fluorescent and other sources are used over planters. Special bulbs are made to stimulate plant growth, but research has shown them to be no more effective than standard lamps, and very poor as contributors to general room lighting. As a result, they are not used much by designers. The main choices of professionals are high-intensity discharge lamps (mercury vapor, high-pressure sodium, etc.) and halogen and fluorescent "cool-white" lamps, which have a high blue content that is beneficial to plant growth. The other attractions of fluorescent lamps are that they are energy-efficient and also good for general room illumination, serving a dual purpose quite well.[8]

Nutrients

When we speak about nutrients we are talking about chemical salts dissolved in soil moisture, which are then absorbed into the plant's system to be distributed for food production and other biological processes. These chemical salts are referred to as *fertilizers*. Although many different elements are available to the plant, those containing nitrogen, phosphorus, and potassium are considered the most important primary nutrients. Smaller amounts of calcium, magnesium, sulphur, iron, and other trace elements are also provided in a well-balanced fertilizer, but plant species differ in their need of these various components.

Fertilizers can be added to the soil as dry chemicals to be subsequently dissolved by irrigation water, or they can be dissolved prior to watering. Automated irrigation provides the opportunity to water and feed plants through a central system, for fertilizer can be either injected into the stream or reservoirs can hold irrigation water laced with fertilizer. Slow-release fertilizers are commonly used in interiorscape maintenance. These are dry materials manufactured with a coating that allows the chemical nutrients to be released into the soil at a very slow rate over a long period of time. Interior plants don't require large doses of nutrients for the same reasons that moisture requirements decrease when they are brought indoors. Very dilute solutions can be fed to plants regularly through APM systems or slow-release fertilizers can be used in the soil.

Atmospheric Conditions

A plant's immediate environment has much to do with its health. The **temperature, circulation,** and **quality** of the air, as well as local humidity are some of the important atmospheric factors that affect a plant's health. In some circles this is known as the plant's **microclimate** or **microenvironment** —the close environment as opposed to the larger, more universal environment in which the plant resides. Because most plants used for interiorscaping are of the tropical variety, they naturally prefer warmer temperatures. However, they are more tolerant to relatively short, cool periods than people realize. Most plants prefer a temperature range of 65° to 75°

Fahrenheit, with slightly lower temperatures at night.[9] Many interior environments are more severe than that, and plants are commonly subjected to baking or near-freezing temperatures. The areas behind large windows bathed in direct sunlight during the midday hours can become quite warm in both summer and winter. Temperatures in these areas can reach well over 100 degrees Fahrenheit. At the other end of the thermal scale, building interiors in cold climates can become fairly frigid at times, particularly next to windows and when the heat is turned down at night or on weekends. Plants have a difficult time coping with these extremes, and they can become damaged, sometimes fatally.

Circulation of air around plants is desirable, so long as it is not excessive. Often fixed or freestanding planters are placed close to air conditioning and heating ducts where air currents can be quite strong. This can have a drying effect on the plant. It also can elevate or lower the plant's temperature to a dangerous level. These

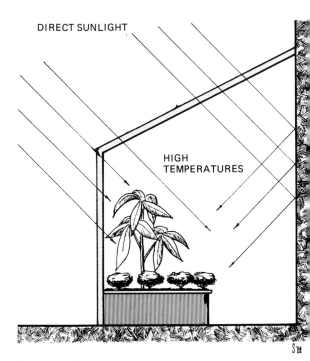

Figure 8.3: Heated planter area behind large windows.

conditions are particularly prevalent with biological air cleaners mentioned in earlier discussions.

Air quality is difficult for the designer or builder to control for it involves a wide variety of polluting sources. The major source of air contamination which could have an adverse effect on interior plant growth is in the air of the neighborhood itself. Heavily industrialized areas carry strong pollutants which are injurious to humans and to vegetation. Construction and decorative materials, as well as activities within a building, contribute additional contaminants. Most plants have a way of tolerating bad air, but similar to humans, there is a limit and the side effects can be serious.

Humidity is another important factor in plant growth. Most plants prefer a relative humidity on the high side, and run into problems when the interiors of homes and commercial buildings are dried by non-humidified heating systems. Moisture can be artificially introduced into the air at or near plants to help them along. Irrigation practices should include dampening the surface soil or mulch around the plants so that evaporation will increase the humidity in the leaves. Automated irrigation systems are quite effective in providing this extra moisture on a continuous basis. Those systems that spray water on the leaves should generally be avoided indoors, however, as they can lead to fungus and other leaf-borne diseases. This problem is particularly troublesome when air circulation around the plants is poor. Plants are frequently grouped close together to promote greater humidity levels, and by placing them near water landscape elements like artificial ponds, waterfalls, fountains, and streams, they can benefit from these higher-humidity locations. The transpiration mechanism of plants (which gives off moisture) helps humidify dry rooms.

The Growing Medium

The quality of the growing medium can be as important to the irrigation practices used in an installation as any other factor. Plants need something to sink their roots into which will in turn provide them with support as well as nourishment, air, and moisture. That is the function of the *growing medium*. To refer to it simply as soil would be misleading, for although it is the most important type of growing medium, there are other effective media which cannot be classed as soil.

Soil is a term which cannot be clearly defined. Roughly described, it is the relatively thin layer of loose material around the earth, composed of mineral

Figure 8.4: Plants around artificial pool/waterfall.

elements from weathered rocks, dead and living organic matter, air, and water. It is constantly undergoing change from the effects of weather, chemical processes, microbial processes, vegetation, and human activity. There is no precise point at which the loose material becomes soil. As a rule of thumb, however, if it supports vegetation it is considered soil.[10]

Natural soil, which comes from the ground, varies widely in its composition due to factors determined by local geology. In its natural state it is seldom well suited for use in potting plants. Without modification, its properties of moisture and air retention, as well as its drainage, pH, and nutrient content are usually not conducive to good plant growth. Soils that have a high clay content tend to compact into a heavy mass that has very small pores, thereby excluding air and hampering drainage. This type of soil easily becomes oversaturated with water.

Coarse, sandy soils, on the other hand, are very open and loose, with large pores in which lots of oxygen—but little else—can be harbored. It drains too well, for water tends to pass through without much moisture retention. Nutrients are carried through the soil with the water, and the roots have little chance to benefit from their presence. Fine-grained, sandy soils, however, are known to exhibit slow moisture transfer characteristics. Therefore, sandy soils are not generally considered very fertile. From an irrigation standpoint, they increase the watering frequency considerably because of their fast drying characteristics.

Soils containing a predominance of silt drain poorly and are also poor growing media.

Loam, the medium used for potting, is a soil composition made up of sand, silt, and clay, along with other soil modifiers. Depending on its source, it generally contains these soil elements in incorrect proportions for a well-balanced growing medium. Natural loams are therefore modified with various organic and inorganic materials to change their

characteristics and make them suitable for the growth of plants in containers or for those directly planted in indoor beds.

One will find almost as many growing media recipes as there are plant varieties, but the most common revolve around the use of equal amounts of coarse sand, garden loam or topsoil, and sphagnum peat moss. Sand is the ingredient that keeps the mix from packing tightly, and therefore promotes better drainage and oxygen retention. Peat moss is an organic ingredient that also promotes drainage and aeration, but other important contributions stem from its ability to absorb large quantities of water and water-borne nutrients, improving the water retention and fertility characteristics of the mix. Because of its fibrous nature, it also improves the wicking ability of the soil, that is, the movement of moisture along narrow air spaces by capillary action. This promotes better water distribution in the planter. Wicking is a particularly important property in micro-irrigation systems, which will be covered in greater detail later in this book. Garden loam and topsoil contain clay and silt particles that also hold water and nutrients. Sand is sometimes replaced in a potting mix with perlite or polystyrene foam beads. Peat moss is frequently replaced with vermiculite, composted leaf mold, or tree bark particles. Other additives such as charcoal and lime are used to control soil acidity and toxicity. Bone meal and other organic materials are used in many cases to improve soil fertility. Proportions of all these elements are changed to accommodate the special needs of some plant varieties. Some of the newer mixes delete the garden soil (loam) content altogether to produce a lightweight medium commonly referred to as "soil-less." This type of growing medium has advantages for anyone who must grow, handle, or transport the potted plant, but some do not provide a sturdy support for the plant (particularly the larger varieties) and toppling sometimes occurs. Peat-Lite, U.C. (University of California), and Jiffy-Mix are common soil-less media.

Virtually all plants used in interiorscaping are shipped from wholesale nurseries either balled and burlapped or, more commonly, in containers filled with growing medium. Do not assume that the medium is good quality and will promote healthy plant growth. Sometimes, nurseries indiscriminately use soil from their back lots to fill containers. Poor soil in a container should be replaced with the proper mix as soon as possible. Since South Florida is the major area of wholesale plant production, those plants that are substandard tend to be shipped in very sandy soil. The poor moisture retention exhibited by these plants makes frequent and proper irrigation critical. This can lead to very high maintenance costs if manual irrigation is used. Automated irrigation systems can relieve most of that extra burden, making the best of these bad situations. Fortunately, most growers are responsible, and interiorscapers and architects are advised to seek them out and deal exclusively with them.

Another pitfall in the specification of soil media is the casual attention that built-in planter beds and pits receive during building construction. All too often the soil at the construction site becomes the bedding soil for costly ornamental plants, which were grown to that stage with great care and at great expense. Placing them in poor sub-soil laced with harmful construction debris could have expensive and long-lasting implications for the building owner and managers. The informed and responsible architect or project overseer will ensure that proper growing media are specified for built-ins, and along with horticultural advisers and contractors, that these specifications be followed during installation. Once plants begin to take root in poor soil locations, it is usually too late to do anything about the damage that will result. The die is then cast for problems over long periods of time.

The *acidity* of the soil, as measured by its pH, is a factor that the interiorscaper must always take into consideration. Most indoor plants prefer soil on the slightly acidic side (sour), and the pH must be monitored from time to time to check on the drift that normally occurs. Water-borne minerals accumulate in and on the soil, reaching acid levels that can be detrimental to the plants. High concentrations of mineral salts can actually chemically burn plant roots. Horticulturists recommend the regular flushing of these salts from the container by running large quantities of water through them. In many types of installations, however, this is not practical, and the plants can deteriorate over a period of time from sour soil. Manual irrigation maximizes the build-up of these soluble mineral salts in the soil, for it takes much more water to irrigate by this method. The greater the amount of water passing through the soil (with the exception of actual flushings), the greater the mineral deposit left behind (fertilizer salts as well as unwanted mineral salts). Automated, micro-irrigation techniques use much less water in the proper irrigation of containerized plants, and will therefore deposit harmful salts at a much slower rate. Also, less fertilizer is wasted because water drainoff can be virtually eliminated.

Pests and Diseases

One of the important jobs of the interiorscape maintenance technician is to inspect the foliage for pests and diseases. One might hear about *slugs* and *thrips, mealybugs, scale,* and *fungus.* Any of these or other afflictions can be dangerous to the plant if left unchecked. There are countermeasures that can usually be taken to eliminate the problems, and these are among the tasks of the maintenance personnel. Inspection, diagnosis, and treatment are carried out by the competent technician.

NINE

Interiorscape Irrigation:
Manual versus Automatic

In previous chapters we discussed the increasing use of live potted and bedded plants in the interiors of buildings, as well as the developing technologies which can transform an inanimate structure into one of functional usefulness that does things for us, making our lives and jobs easier and less costly to perform. The automation of plant care in building interiors is the latest innovation along these lines, creating a new climate in our real estate markets where buildings can be designed and built with prolific use of indoor plants in mind for commercial, economic, and health reasons. From time immemorial, plants have been watered by hand, with the exception, of course, of rain. With the advent of automatic sprinkler systems, lawns and gardens around buildings could be cared for more conveniently and economically. Yet until fairly recently, improvements in techniques were only a minor aspect of indoor horticultural maintenance.

Options

Now that we are closing in on the twenty-first century, we find interior plant care methods hardly more advanced than they were centuries ago. For at least 20 years, irrigation contractors have installed outdoor technologies in noncritical interior plant locations. Sprinkler systems were first used in promenade areas of shopping malls and in large planter beds of office building lobbies, as well as other common areas. Soon after, drip or trickle irrigation systems were also designed into some of these nonsensitive interior locations. Because of technology limitations, the rest of the building interior was relegated to manual plant care. In most commercial buildings, the majority of decorative plants housed in the structure are in the upper floors, where hundreds or even thousands of potted plants grace corporate office suites, lounges, restaurants, banks, and so on. That's also where the building occupants are. This foliage receives highly labor-intensive weekly maintenance, incurring untold millions of dollars in plant maintenance fees throughout the corporate community. One attempt at reducing labor costs in recent years was the development of commercial-grade, self-watering containers. They provide the first real element of easier plant care for the critical furnished areas of homes and commercial buildings, and are being used to some extent today by interiorscape maintenance contractors. Widespread use, however, has been retarded by a number of inherent limitations. For a long time a void existed for more complete, advanced plant care technology. That technology is now available in automated precision micro-irrigation (APM) systems which promise to revolutionize interior plant care just as automated sprinkler systems did for outdoor landscape care.

Manual Plant Care Techniques

Decorative plants have always been watered and cared for by hand. This is almost universally true of interior plant care, even today in the age of high-technology. While outdoor irrigation practices were transformed by automation, commercial indoor technology was virtually non-existent until several years ago. It can be safely estimated that about 98% of all containerized and direct-bedded plants used indoors are still being fully maintained by manual labor.

Manual plant care takes a number of forms, with watering as only one facet of it. The work is done by interiorscape maintenance technicians who are trained in the horticulture of indoor ornamental plants with particular emphasis on the aspects of their maintenance. Through the considerable labor and knowledge of these professionals, the greenery is generally cared for on a weekly schedule, although many companies have lengthened their routines to 10-day cycles. The most time-consuming part of their work involves the irrigation, or watering, of the plants. Industry sources estimate that 25% to 50% of on-site maintenance time is involved with watering. It is also the most physically demanding part of the interiorscape maintenance technician's work. Irrigation is the main reason for weekly maintenance visits to a client's location. The other plant care tasks can be accomplished in two- to four-week cycles, depending on the nature of the installation.[1]

Hand watering is done in most cases by means of a watering can or other container that is filled at the closest faucet. The source's convenience depends on how concerned and diligent the architect was in designing the installation. Water is transported to the planter location and carried from plant to plant, being poured onto the soil surface. This is referred to as *overhead watering*. Water is heavy, with each gallon weighing 8.34 pounds, and the physical strain on field personnel who are constantly carrying water-filled containers weighing from six to thirty pounds is considerable. In complex installations they must frequently climb ladders with the watering equipment or in other ways perform gymnastics around planter beds.

To alleviate some of the strain, devices called *watering machines* have been developed. These are sealed water containers mounted on wheels or casters. Some types use built-in pumps to generate a flow from the container to the planters, while others pressurize the water vessel to create the flow. In either case, hoses that carry water to the plants are connected to the container. A convenient hand-operated valve at the end of the hose permits the operator to control the flow. Wands and other handle extensions facilitate watering beyond arm's length. Extensively used in the trade, these machines have reduced the labor involved

Figure 9.1: Watering machines.

in refilling water cans. Watering machines are also very heavy, however. Commonly available models are built to hold between seven and forty-four gallons of water. That represents 367 pounds of water in the larger units, plus the weight of the unit when it is empty, which is usually about 145 pounds. The total is then a hefty 512 pounds, which must be wheeled around the client's complex and afterward reloaded onto a truck or van, only to have the entire process repeated at the next maintenance stop. The smallest of the units holds seven gallons (58 pounds) of water, in addition to its empty weight of 38 pounds.[2] This makes for a still considerable 96 pounds when full. Despite the physical strain, watering machines are a help in that they reduce the number of trips to the faucet.

Where possible, properly designed interiorscape installations provide for a source of water and an electrical outlet in close proximity to the planter boxes. The water source is almost invariably a hose bibb connection to the building's cold water line. It should be located no farther than about 40 feet from the most extreme point in a planter, otherwise long, heavy, unwieldy hoses must be employed. Hose bibbs, therefore, are most practically located in the planter boxes or beds, along with an electrical outlet for lighting, water pumping, and general utility use. More often than not, water and electrical service are not provided in convenient places by designers, even for large or critical planters that require an unusual amount of irrigation. This magnifies the burden on the plant-care technician, for the time, inconvenience, and physical exertion are increased considerably—as is the cost. The money saved in the elimination of hardware from the original installation is spent year after year in higher, ever-increasing maintenance expenses.

Freestanding containerized plants are placed by the interiorscaper or interior designer where they complement the

decorating scheme, but their needs, and those of the maintenance technician, are seldom provided for in the building plan. Irrigation of freestanding planters is almost always done by means of watering cans or machines. In the furnished areas of buildings, such as in private homes, corporate office suites, bank lobbies, hotel suites, lounges, restaurant dining areas, and waiting rooms, great care must be exercised to prevent splashing or drain-off from the bottom of containers. Accidents frequently occur when technicians get careless, wetting and soiling carpeting, furniture, moldings, and wall coverings. Overhead potted planters are particularly bothersome and difficult to judge, so they cause frequent problems. Self- watering containers are used in some of these situations, but they too must be refilled manually on a regular reduced schedule.

The frequency with which a containerized plant is manually watered depends on many factors. The most important of these are:

- Plant species

- Plant size and current state of activity or dormancy

- Composition of the growing medium

- Room temperature

- Ambient humidity levels

- Air drafts passing the plant

- Amount and quality of light it receives

- Presence or absence of surface mulch

- Size, shape, and composition of the container

That's a complex menu, and one that points to the variety of conditions that are normally encountered from plant to plant. Common manual irrigation practices call for an indoor plant to dry out for a period of time to allow oxygen into the root zone.

Once this happens, the soil should be thoroughly soaked until run-off occurs from the bottom of the container. The soil at this point is saturated with water, displacing the life-giving oxygen. Well-drained soil will pass most of the water through the container quickly. Sandy soil will pass it through too quickly, while heavy clay soil will pass it too slowly. Soil that has been dried out too much will have shrunk from the walls of the container and the water application will drain down this space quickly and without much benefit to the plant. Run-off in this case will be excessive.

For these and other reasons, the instructions for watering given the homeowner are not usually the same as those given to professionals; those techniques would not be commercially feasible. Firstly, the drainage underneath planter boxes and pits is always suspect, and usually inadequate. One cannot pour large amounts of water into a plant to soak it thoroughly. The run-off would most likely ruin something, making a mess in the process. This can also happen with freestanding and hanging container plants in offices, homes, and restaurants. The maintenance technician is not able to move most of them to a faucet because of the size, weight, and quantity of the plants. Keep in mind that ornamental plants used in commercial interiorscapes are generally larger than those used by the homeowner. Medium-sized plants in 14" pots (7-gallon size) weigh about 50 pounds. Larger plants weigh 225 to 275 pounds (30-gallon, 23" containers) to over 1000 pounds (95-gallon, 38" containers).[3]

The commonly suggested watering frequency is also impractical for the interiorscaper. Technicians cannot be available to service each plant when it reaches its proper time for irrigation. Instead, clients must be serviced on a regular, frequent schedule, regardless of the condition of the plants. Weekly maintenance cycles are most frequently used so as to avoid excessive water stress.

When maintenance technicians arrive on the scene each week, they find plants in various states of dehydration. They must quickly determine how much moisture each plant needs. There are a number of techniques used to judge the condition of soil moisture in each plant. Some technicians simply use a finger to feel for moisture, others probe into the soil with a stick, while many use a moisture meter. These simple tests indicate how much watering is required at that time.

Judgement is involved here, and because of the nature of the job, it is not easy to train good personnel. It takes a good deal of time for a trainee to become proficient in his or her task, as there is always the tendency to underwater or overwater. Industry managers concede that it usually takes the better part of a year to fully train a maintenance technician in the art of manual irrigation.[4] That is a long, expensive road littered with plant replacements and frustrated, discontented clients. Company profits are at stake. The large turnover that interiorscapers commonly experience leads to constant hiring and training. Maintenance labor is a major problem for them, and the irrigation aspects of the job are the principal part of it.

There are many other facets of interiorscape maintenance besides irrigation. One of the most important is the inspection of plants for pests and diseases. This means getting close to the plant and carefully examining the top and bottom of the leaves, the stems, and soil for signs of improper lighting, nutrition, watering, or insect infestations and disease. This inspection must be done about every two to four weeks to detect any changes in the plant's condition. It is not an easy task; the work is hard on the eyes, particularly in poorly lit areas, and the kneeling and bending is physically demanding. If any signs of trouble are detected, the technician must take quick corrective action to prevent further deterioration of the plant's health. In the cases of insect infestations or disease, this generally involves application of an insecticide or herbicide by spraying or simply wiping it on the affected area. Occasionally the plant-care chemicals are applied systemically, that is, through the root system carried by the irrigation water.

Another of the tasks relegated to the maintenance technician is that of fertilizing the plants. This is done manually by dissolving a small amount of soluble plant food in the irrigation water and applying the dilute solution during the weekly maintenance visits. Another way of doing it is by means of the newer, slow-release fertilizers which are mixed into the potting soil. Through water hydrolysis or soil bacterial action, they release and diffuse their nourishing chemistry into the soil slowly over long periods of time. This means that they don't have to be replenished often, and fertilization thus becomes an easy task for the interiorscaper. There are a number of forms of slow-release nutrients, the most common being coated globules, tablets, and briquettes. Because of the much slower metabolic rate of plants grown indoors, fertilization rates are greatly reduced, so this is not one of the high-frequency tasks of maintenance technicians.

Rotating the plants is another important maintenance function. The plants are gradually rotated over a period of time so that all leaves are given even exposure to the lighting. This helps the plant grow fuller and develop a more symmetrical shape.

During the course of maintenance visits, it is also necessary to clean and sometimes polish the plant leaves. Cleaning is done by wiping off dust and other particles from the leaves, not just for aesthetics but so that the pores of the leaves do not become clogged with dirt. Leaf polishing is done by applying a chemical specifically suited to that purpose. Nevertheless, some of these remedies tend to clog the plant's pores, and many interiorscapers do not follow this practice for that reason.

Plants also need to be replaced periodically when they appear wan or have become diseased. Sometimes they can be moved temporarily, in order to rejuvenate the plant in a better growing environment. In order to make commercial interiorscapes fresh and healthy, however, plant replacement may be a common and frequent necessity, particularly where flowering varieties are involved.

The manual plant care process requires a solid knowledge of the subject, good eyes, and a great deal of stamina. Each plant is scrutinized individually and decisions are made by the maintenance technician as to its general condition, moisture requirements, type of corrective actions needed, and so forth. So, in addition to the physical burden of the job, the technician is subjected to mental stress as well. Any improvement in plant care techniques that relieves some of these burdens and stresses for the employee should be seriously considered by the interiorscape contractor. Changes in irrigation methods can be the most effective way of alleviating worker discontent, particularly through the use of automatic systems.

Moisture Meters

Many interiorscapers use moisture meters to judge the amount of moisture in soil. The meter's reading indicates whether the plant needs watering at the time of measurement. Moisture meters are easy-to-use precision instruments that rely on moisture probes to generate small electrical currents when placed in damp soil. The amount of current generated is in proportion to the wetness or dryness of the soil, and is read from a meter attached to the probe. The greater the degree of soil moisture, the higher the

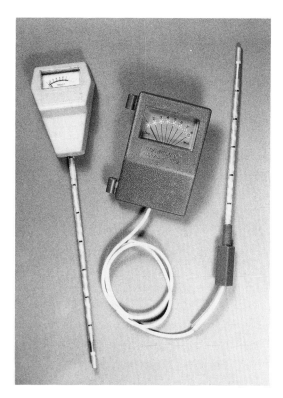

Figure 9.2: Two types of moisture meters.

meter reading. There are a number of brands and designs of moisture meters on the market, most very inexpensive. Many have the meter and probe as an integral, one-piece unit. Others are made in a two-piece configuration in which they are connected by a wire. The latter type is more convenient as the meter can be held in one hand where it is easily seen while the probe is inserted into the dark recesses of a planter. For this reason, the two-piece style has become more popular with professionals.

Because of the differences in design from one brand to another, readings cannot be compared except in broad terms. Low numbers on the meter represent dry soil readings, while the higher numbers indicate when the soil is on the damp or wet side. There is usually little attempt to calibrate the meters, as that type of accuracy is of lesser interest to the maintenance technician.

Most technicians learn after a while that the mineral salt content in soil can affect the accuracy of the meter readings. As salts build up in the soil over a period of time, they increase the value of moisture readings. In other words, soil on the dry side with a high salt content can read the same as salt-free, damp soil. Experienced maintenance technicians are able to recognize the difference between these two conditions, however. When the soil should be leached (rinsed) of these salts, corrective action is taken.

Self-Watering Containers

One of the more recent attempts to reduce the labor in interior landscape maintenance was the introduction of the self-watering container. It is the first easy-care maintenance system developed specifically for interior foliage plant installations. Originating in Europe where they have gained more popularity than in the United States, these devices are variations on the old household technique of using a braided or woven fabric wick to transfer water from a tray or other source through the bottom of the container to the underside of the root ball. This process is also called wicking. The movement of water upwards through the narrow pores of the fibrous wick and the subsurface soil happens by means of naturally occuring capillary action. This technique is called subirrigation by some, as the moisture diffusion runs upward rather than downward as in overhead watering.

Self-watering containers are frequently referred to as automatic devices or systems. This is a misnomer, for their effectiveness lasts only a short while, at which time the maintenance technician must replenish the water supply. As unattended irrigation systems go, self-watering containers are not in the same class as fully automated, drip/trickle, or APM systems.

Self-watering containers are either double-walled or divided into two parts, one containing a water reservoir section and the other a planter section into which the foliage is directly planted. The containers are made of sturdy plastic and the outer shell is available in a selection of decorative colors. Woven or braided wicks, made from non-degrading fibrous materials (such as nylon or fiberglas) are interfaced between the reservoir and the soil section in order to transfer water between the two. The water reserve is mostly under the planter, but in at least two designs it also wraps around the sides of the container. A filler hole or tube is provided for convenient refilling. In some designs the wick is wrapped around the filler tube, which then performs a dual function. Gauges and sight glasses are provided in most models to indicate the level of water remaining in the reservoir.

At least two planter designs use a wickless system featuring a sensor that is inserted into the soil to detect the moisture level. The soil is in limited direct contact with the water reserve. The sensor is a porous ceramic element which allows air to penetrate the tube to which it is attached whenever the soil becomes dry. This has the effect of decreasing the vacuum in the reservoir chamber, exerting a slight air pressure against the water surface. That, in turn, renews capillary transfer of water through the soil mass at the bottom of the container (see Figure 9.4).

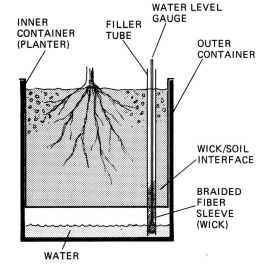

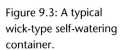

Figure 9.3: A typical wick-type self-watering container.

Another type uses elongated plastic reservoirs which are buried in planter areas directly beneath the foliage. Moisture diffuses up from the reservoirs through capillary action to the root levels, and a filler tube rises to the surface. These independent reservoirs can be interconnected with tubes to make an extensive underground network.

Among the main benefits of using self-watering containers, the foremost is their ability to reduce the labor involved in the plant care cycle. This ability to reduce the number of manual waterings results in a potential savings of time and money. Maintenance cycles can be reduced from once per week to every two to four weeks. Most self-watering units are able to sustain a continuous watering period of between two to eight weeks. This, however, depends on the size of the reservoir, the size and species of the plant, the number of plants coexisting in the same container, and the rate of transpiration of the plants as determined by their growth cycle and local environmental conditions. The composition and texture of the growing medium are also factors. As the plant grows larger, the reservoir must be refilled more frequently. Another benefit is that with the time saved using self-watering containers, maintenance technicians can concentrate on the other aspects of plant care. These containers tend to offer a greater degree of consistency in the quality of plant care as well, particularly when a novice is at work or during periods of technician change, vacation, or building shut-down. The plants benefit from consistent watering as the containers maintain a fairly even moisture level, thereby reducing water stress. In addition, plants can be fertilized simply by dissolving nutrients in the irrigation water. Aeration of the root system is also more efficient because the soil is not compacted as it can be with overhead watering.

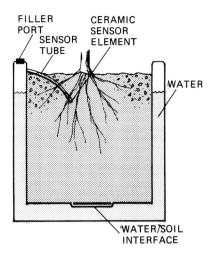

Figure 9.4: A sensor-type self-watering container.

Notwithstanding the benefits, the use of self-watering containers is not widespread. There are a number of deficiencies in the concept that keep it from gaining greater acceptance in the market. One has to do with the decorative aspects of the containers. Many designers find the plastic containers inelegant. Then there is the problem of color obsolescence when the decorating scheme of the interior location changes in a few years. The planter color is fixed, as is its shape. They are also larger and bulkier than plain containers because of their integral water reservoir. The interiorscaper objects to the fact that in most types, foliage must be grown directly in the self-watering planter and cannot be kept in the nursery container, as is the preferred technique. Plant rotation and replacement are made more difficult as well. Most of the drier-soil plants cannot be used with these systems because they would be overwatered. Contractors also feel that the purchase price of self-watering containers is prohibitive, especially when large numbers of plants are involved, and containers must be replaced with larger ones when plants outgrow them. Another objection is that capillarity draws water up only so far, and the surface layers of the planter remain fairly dry, confusing maintenance personnel. As mineral salts build up on the underside of the root ball, they restrict proper capillary action and slow down moisture diffusion. This problem is particularly troublesome with regard to moisture sensing devices. The porous ceramic element in the sensor tends to clog with soil particles and mineral salt build-up after a period of time, and this changes the monitoring characteristics of the system, thereby reducing its accuracy. There is a decided drift in soil moisture level during this period caused by sensor malfunction. The heavy weight of the water-filled containers makes them difficult to use in overhead installations. The buried reservoir type of self-watering devices has caused problems when sturdy roots grow down to the system level and engulf the reservoirs and tubing, causing breaks, leaks, and difficulties in removing plants. Others contend that the containers don't save maintenance time because the technician must refill the reservoirs anyway, and the frequency of filling increases as the plant grows.[5] But the biggest disadvantage mentioned by maintenance contractors has to do with the accuracy of the irrigation. They feel that the watering control varies with too many conditions, namely the soil composition, the mineral content, and the size of the plant. They feel they can't count on the planter to do what it was installed to do, and it is therefore too risky for commercial use.

One of the unspoken factors that prevents greater use of self-watering containers is the concern on the part of interiorscapers that self-watering technology will replace them, or in other ways reduce their ability to make a living. Part of this is not without foundation, for some clients installing self-watering containers will try to do it on their own. Many have the unfortunate perception that watering is the only real concern in plant care. Others hire amateurs to do the supplementary maintenance work and risk the quality of care given the installation. Some will hire contractors that specialize in outdoor lawn and garden maintenance services to look in on their ornamental interior plants. As mentioned previously, that would be a risky course of action since outdoor specialties are so different from those concerning interiors.

In addition, a very real concern for the interiorscaper is the fact that he or she must reduce maintenance charges on contracts involving self-watering containers as their labor content is reduced. The client expects some savings from the self-care features of the system, and contractors are frequently reluctant to offer them. Some of this resistance is justified. As just mentioned, real savings through the use of self-watering containers are sometimes minimal or possibly non-existent. Contractors will frequently avoid being put in this position by simply not using the self-watering containers.

In situations where real labor savings are gained, however, the interiorscaper's business can actually increase in volume. For example, whenever the contractor is able to reduce the maintenance cycle from once per week to once every two or possibly three weeks (which can be safely done in many installations), many more accounts can be covered by the same field staff. Significant savings can also accrue from greatly reduced plant replacement and training costs. Some of these savings should rightfully be passed on to the customer. By doing so it makes the interiorscaper more competitive.

Regardless of the difficulties, self-watering containers do present some real advantages to the contractor and home-owner. They present a viable supplement to other technologies and can be used to advantage where competing systems are not feasible. Therefore, they will continue to have a place in the industry and to be used in limited applications.

Automated Techniques for Plant Care

The use of fully automated plant care techniques is the industry's attempt to reduce interiorscape maintenance labor to minimum levels without sacrificing high efficiency. The impetus for this development has come from the commercial real estate industry. Managers look for ways to operate their buildings more conveniently and cost-effectively on the inside as well as out. Automatic sprinkler systems have been used for many years to take care of the exterior landscape. Because they have saved real estate managers enormous sums of money in landscape maintenance costs, ways of doing the same in their property interiors are constantly being sought. The priorities here depend on whether the interiorscape is a major feature of the building, such as in shopping malls and lobbies of top-drawer office buildings, or merely a minor decorative feature. As solutions develop in the marketplace, it appears that we are heading toward a future of fully automatic interior plant care systems, which will be supplemented wherever necessary by other techniques like self-watering containers.

There are five irrigation technologies that are used in building interiors which can be fully automated:

1. Sprinkler systems

2. Drip/trickle systems

3. Subterranean systems

4. Hydroponic systems

5. Mirage™ precision micro-irrigation (APM) systems

All but hydroponics and APM systems were first developed for outdoor agricultural irrigation. The various types of irrigation technologies used in building interiors are diagramatically represented in Figure 9.5.

A few years ago irrigation contractors were asked to install their systems in large planter boxes and beds in the lobbies of office buildings and the promenades of shopping malls. The only systems available to them were sprinkler and drip/trickle irrigation technologies developed for outdoor landscape maintenance and agricultural production. It has taken some time for the irrigation industry to refine its thinking and techniques for coping with many of the more delicate situations indoors. For the most part, the industry has not yet caught up with the demands of this new market. Concept and equipment limitations have hampered efforts to satisfy a broad range of interior plantscape needs. Sprinkler and drip/trickle irrigation technologies are predicated on the use of large amounts of water spread over large areas and distributed for long periods of time. Outdoor soil dries out rapidly from sun, wind, and plant absorption, thereby requiring a hefty system to keep up with its moisture demands. Indoor plantscape requirements are very different. Much smaller quantities of water must be distributed more precisely and with a greater degree of safety. This is particularly true of the furnished areas of buildings, and outdoor irrigation technology is not sophisticated enough to handle these more refined demands. Irrigation contractors shudder when they think of their sprinkler or drip systems being applied to living or family rooms, or in the lushly furnished offices of an executive suite. These are simply not practical options in these cases. As a consequence, the technology used in Mirage automated precision micro-irrigation systems was developed to successfully cope with *all* automatic irrigation situations indoors. It is the first fully-automatic system developed specifically for interior applications.

Figure 9.5: Types of
irrigation used in
building interiors.

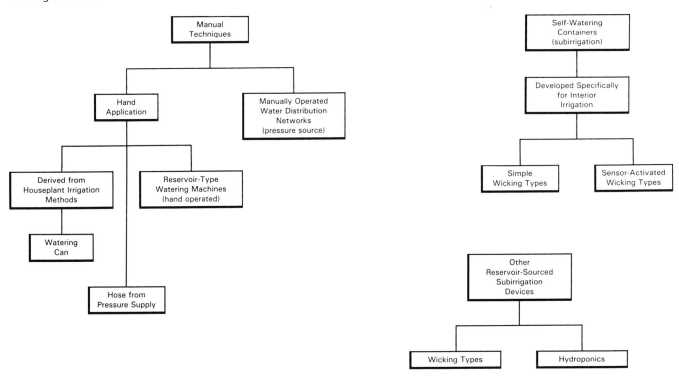

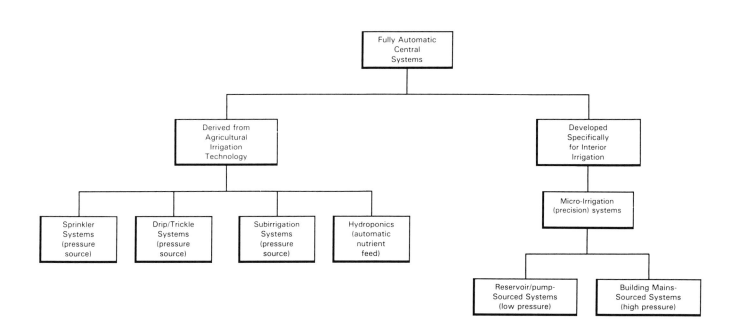

There are several features common to all automatic irrigation systems. First of all, there must be a water source. This is sometimes a well, pond, or stream from which water is pumped. Interior installations are more often sourced from city water supplies. Pumps and city water provide the pressure needed to generate a flow. When easy access to city water mains is not available, holding tanks or reservoirs are used. Next there must be a network of tubing or pipes through which the water can flow from the source to plant locations. In the water distribution network, there must be flow and sometimes pressure-control devices that vary flow rates and direction to meet installation needs. Finally, in automatic systems there must be timing devices to regulate the period between watering cycles and the length of time that flow is permitted. These timing devices are also controllers, for they activate and deactivate pumps and solenoid valves at the properly timed intervals.

Automated interior plant care is in its very early stages, and the field of automatic interior irrigation is in a rapid state of flux. Some refer to it as auto-interigation—a new area of expertise.

Now that automatic irrigation systems are available for total building coverage, their possible applications have multiplied many times over and their versatility will provide the impetus for developers, as well as corporate office and building managers, to use them in their major projects. Large restaurant and hotel chains can reduce interior plant maintenance costs by tens and hundreds of thousands of dollars each year in their many locations. Builders of housing units have a new high-tech amenity available to increase the convenience, functionality, and futuristic image of their products. Even "smart" homes will prove to be more saleable. The social and commercial implications of these developments are many, and they will present themselves more clearly in the years to come. Automated irrigation systems will be discussed in greater detail in Chapter Ten.

TEN

Interiorscape Irrigation:
Fully Automatic Techniques

Having quickly described the general characteristics of automatic systems in the previous chapter, we will now delve into some of the details that differentiate them so that a clearer understanding can be gained of their uses, advantages, and disadvantages. Again, the fully automatic irrigation technologies that have been used inside of buildings are: sprinkler systems, drip/trickle systems, subterranean systems, hydroponics, and Mirage™¹ precision micro-irrigation systems. As a group these technologies comprise the field of auto-interigation (automatic interior irrigation). All of them will be discussed in some depth in this and following chapters.

Sprinkler Systems

This is the most prominent of the various systems involving fully automated irrigation. It is the first that comes to mind when the subject is mentioned, probably because sprinkler systems are the most common method of automatic irrigation used outdoors. Sprinklers were developed many years ago for the purpose of field irrigation to aid in agricultural production. The majority of field systems is still operated manually, but recent years have seen the slow shift to automatic control.

Sprinkler systems were soon found to be invaluable in maintaining landscapes, particularly on golf courses, college campuses, and around commercial buildings. These applications were more suitable for automatic control, as many zones were usually involved and operation was frequently scheduled for more than once per day. Soon homeowners were offered the benefits of automatic sprinkling for their properties, using the same technology and some of the same equipment that had been developed for heavier-duty landscape maintenance jobs. In many areas of the country today, such as parts of Florida, Texas, Arizona, and California, it is rare to find homes being built without a lawn and garden sprinkler system.

About 20 years ago, irrigation contractors began installing sprinkler systems in building interiors because many architects, real estate owners and managers wanted to experiment with them. Prior to that they had been used only in rare project applications, but interest in sprinkler systems for interiors has grown in recent years. The applications chosen were almost invariably non-critical areas in shopping malls, office buildings, and institutional structures. Built-in planter boxes and pits in building promenades, as well as tiled or paved lobbies and atria, were the main areas of concern for the designers and managers.

These were the areas with the highest maintenance costs, and they presented other problems as well. Although they generally contained many hundreds of plants, these areas were not as demanding from an applications standpoint. Knowing that sprinkler systems broadcast relatively large amounts of water over large surfaces but were not considered reliably safe, these planters were a reasonable target for automated irrigation. In most cases, the early installations were offshoots of the outdoor landscape sprinkler system. They were separate branches of the system, devoted specifically to the interior zone to be watered. These interior branches were usually set up to have independent flow duration and flow rate control, and in some cases zone pressure was regulated as well. Automation of these more complex sprinkler systems made sense, as manual control placed greater labor and heightened diligence demands on maintenance employees. More recently, independent systems were designed for the interiors of large, commercial buildings where the added cost and control could be justified. Residential indoor installations have been used over the years—mainly in upscale housing—in coarse planter areas like atria and large planter boxes and beds, safely away from the furnished living quarters.

When used indoors, sprinkler systems are normally sourced from city water mains. On occasion well water is also used. A filter at the source prevents the small orifices throughout the system from becoming clogged by dirt. Automated installations have an electromechanical or solid-state timer/controller which switches on the system at predetermined times and for predetermined watering periods. The timer/controller operates a pump or solenoid valve at the appropriate times to achieve that result. In more complex installations, various zones (or stations, as they are sometimes called) of the building are established as branches to a common system. The controller permits flow to each zone in sequence by activating remote, zone-control solenoid valves which are either electrically or hydraulically operated. Because of the lesser water flow requirements of interior installations, flow and pressure control devices are frequently used to reduce either one or the other hydraulic element. The water distribution network is a series of interconnected pipes and tubes leading from the water source to the locations of the planters. Pipe sizes in indoor applications can generally be kept fairly small (½" to 1½" in diameter), and the pipe materials normally used are copper, iron, PVC, or polyethylene plastic (called "poly" tubing). Sprinkler heads and other emitting devices are connected into the piping at the appropriate locations and spray or dribble water at and around the plants. Sprinkler systems are normally operated in the pressure range of 45 to 80 psi (pounds per square inch) outdoors, and about 25 to 55 psi indoors. Higher pressures promote greater flow rates, which are generally not required indoors.

There are many types of emitters available for sprinkler systems—literally scores of different configurations. *Emitters* are those small devices which control the application of the water to the plants. The types of emitters most commonly used in sprinkler systems are sprinkler heads, which spray water in a predetermined pattern toward the plants at and over the foliage, stems, branches and surface of the ground. The spray patterns are generally full-circle, half-circle, quarter-circle, and strip (a very narrow stream). There are other types of heads used in these systems that do not spray at all. Shrub bubbler heads, for instance, simply dribble water onto the ground in the immediate area of the head. The water distribution pattern is tight, and capillary action in the soil is relied upon for moisture diffusion to other parts of the planter. If the bubbler heads are grouped close enough together, then fairly even coverage of an area can be obtained.

Sprinkler heads and other emitters are positioned in the installation to cover the area in need of irrigation. The types used are selected according to what is to be accomplished at their location. Sprinkler heads are meant primarily for broad-area coverage of crops and turf. Some sprinkler heads are capable of spraying water great distances (50 or 60 feet) to achieve maximum coverage. Indoor applications of

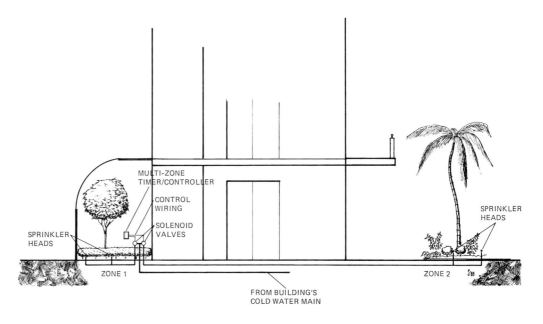

these systems are very different. Seldom will an interiorscape planter be so large in area as to require broad-area sprinkling. Sprinkler heads can then be use in planter boxes and pits:

1. If their flow rates are reduced down to manageable levels by adjustment at the head itself.

2. By lowering the system water pressure.

3. By selecting heads with low flow rates.

4. All of the above.

Many interiorscapers don't like to work with sprinkler systems because of the poor control over spray patterns. Mischievous tampering with the spray heads by children and vandals frequently causes hazardous conditions. One common result is that floors become slippery when wet, particularly the tile and marble floors found in most shopping malls and office building lobbies (see Figure 10.3). Some building managers will not permit the usage of sprinkler systems in their facilities for fear of the liabilities.

The length of time a sprinkler system is permitted to operate indoors depends on a number of factors, but the most important determinants are the plant's moisture requirements at the time of irrigation, the soil composition, and the type of time switch used for the installation. Sprinkling

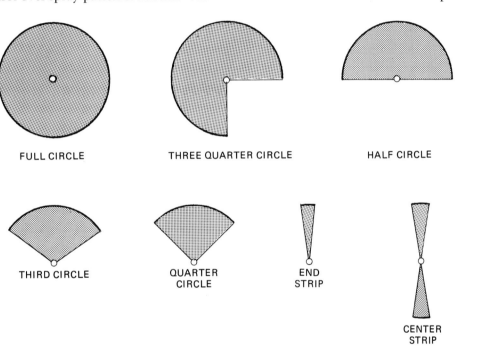

FULL CIRCLE　　THREE QUARTER CIRCLE　　HALF CIRCLE

THIRD CIRCLE　　QUARTER CIRCLE　　END STRIP　　CENTER STRIP

Figure 10.2: Spray patterns available.

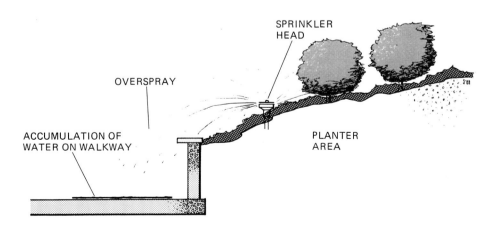

SPRINKLER HEAD

OVERSPRAY

ACCUMULATION OF WATER ON WALKWAY

PLANTER AREA

Figure 10.3: Indoor sprinkler overspraying onto floor.

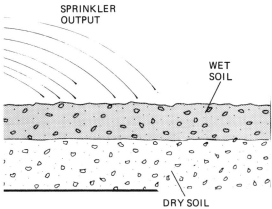

or 7-day clock cycles. Timers (also called time switches or controllers) for sprinkler applications are usually coarse-incremented, meaning their on-off cycles are set in increments of 3 to 15 minutes. The minimum time of system operation is important in interior work, for one of the dangers of any type of irrigation here is the tendency to overwater. The time switches made for commercial irrigation systems are of the electromechanical, electronic, and combination (hybrid) types. The more expensive timing devices permit sprinkler operation down to 1 minute in duration, however most are designed with 3 to 15 minute minimum "on" periods. Too often indoor sprinkler installations are operated for longer than necessary—a habit carried over from outdoor work.

is very inefficient and indiscriminate; it wets everything in its path, including most of the ground in the planted area. Much of the moisture evaporates from the spray before ever reaching the ground. Further, water absorption by the soil is a slow process, taking time for the moisture to penetrate the depths. Water from sprinkler irrigation tends to move laterally in the soil and is slow to sink because it is held up against gravity by soil capillarity (see Figure 10.4 and Table 10.1).[2]

Figure 10.4 and Table 10.1 clearly demonstrate the long periods of time required for sprinkler watering to penetrate the deepest levels of ornamental plant root masses. With turf grasses this is not a problem, for the roots are only a few inches below the surface. But upright plants must be sprinkled for extended periods in order to be properly irrigated.

Timers are used to determine the interval between sprinkler operations and the duration of watering. They use 24-hour

Relatively long irrigation cycles are generally necessary, however, because sprinkler systems are the least efficient of all automatic irrigation methods. They broadcast water over a larger area than required, wasting a lot in the process. Support soil, found in planter boxes between the plants, absorbs most of the water unnecessarily. The root zones are the only really important areas that need water, and they are frequently neglected by sprinklers.

Another reason why sprinkler systems require long irrigation periods has to do with the compacting of the surface soil. As it is moistened by the water spray over a period of time the surface soil becomes compacted. The compacted soil takes longer to penetrate, so more water has to be

Table 10.1

Time Required in Minutes for Sprinkler Water to Penetrate Various Soil Types

Soil Depth	Coarse Sand	Sandy Loam	Clay Loam
12 inches	15 min.	30 min.	60 min.
24 inches	—	60 min.	—
30 inches	40 min.	—	—
48 inches	60 min.	—	—

applied in order to ensure proper wetting at the root zones. The problem is further compounded in planters filled with improperly formulated soil mixes. Heavy clay soil is difficult to penetrate, and the surfaces of fine-textured, sandy soils are frequently very difficult to irrigate when dry because they are too dense. While coarse sand does accept water easily, fine sand dries out rapidly and surface tensions must be overcome before it can be rewet. That takes time and frequently a lot of water. Using more closely spaced irrigation cycles helps to keep the surface soil from drying out, but indoors that can easily lead to saturation unless cycles are kept short and flow rates low. Uncovered surface soil promotes moisture evaporation, drying the plant more quickly. The use of mulch also helps to keep surface soil damp but many materials such as cypress bark and peat moss absorb a great deal of the irrigation water, keeping it from the root zone. More water is usually needed to overcome this effect. This is particularly true of sprinkler systems using spray heads. It can be prevented by using bubbler heads, which provide a more concentrated application of water close to root zones.

Some professionals strongly recommend against the use of sprinkler systems for interiorscapes. Their objections could stem from the fact that spraying the leaves of foliage plants often leads to fungus diseases and the ultimate demise of the plants. Interior plant installations are particularly vulnerable to such health problems for several reasons. Overwatering with an automatic sprinkler system is easy to do. The water is sprayed over a broad area for a relatively long period of time. Much of it lays on the soil or mulch surface and becomes a continuous source of evaporation, creating a highly humid atmosphere for the plant leaves. In addition, the water is sprayed directly on the leaves by the irrigation system. Now introduce the factor of low air circulation in some planter locations, creating a stagnant, overly moist microclimate. Fungus diseases easily breed under such conditions and many professionals have faced the problem often enough to want to avoid use of automatic sprinklers. Some misinformed practitioners tend to categorize all automated systems in the same negative way without taking their differences into consideration. Drip and micro-irrigation technologies are more precise in their water placement, and seldom foster such problems.

With proper design and installation, sprinkler systems can prevent some of these plant diseases. If it is possible to direct the spray from sprinkler heads under the leaf canopy of the plants, only the soil will be wetted. If the sprinkler head has a flow adjustment, it should be turned down so that less water issues during each watering cycle. That, of course, also reduces the coverage of each head and so more will be necessary. Shortening the irrigation time will also help.

Sometimes bubbler heads can be used near each plant to dribble water onto the ground above the root zones. There are basically two types of bubbler heads: one that emits a gentle stream of water, generally in several directions, and the other that trickles water down the riser on which the head is mounted (see Figure 10.5).

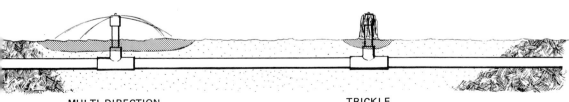

Figure 10.5: Two types of bubbler heads.

MULTI-DIRECTION,
STREAM TYPE

TRICKLE
TYPE

Because of superior flow control, bubbler heads can overcome many of the plant disease problems common to sprinkler systems and should be used as frequently as possible indoors. Bubblers designed for very low flow rates are available, down to 0.25 gallon per minute. That's pretty stingy for sprinkler technology, which more commonly operates at 1 to 8 gallons per minute per head.[3] By operating a sprinkler system equipped with bubbler heads for short periods, much better control is provided. If the bubbler heads are used properly, planter boxes can be irrigated with a reasonable degree of assurance that the bed will not be saturated. If necessary, multiple cycles can be used daily.

Proper drainage of the planter boxes is critical when automated sprinkler systems are used. Because of the poor control over moisture distribution, soil pockets can easily become oversaturated, promoting heavy drainage from the planter subsurface. This is more acute when plants are left in their nursery containers—the preferred practice of interiorscapers. The design of planter boxes is too often flawed, creating a potentially messy and frequently damaging situation. The preferred planter box design calls for the installation of a wide perforated pipe under the box to drain water away from the area. The pipe is surrounded by a few inches of coarse, crushed rock to complete the drainage bed. A woven soil mat (generally made of polypropylene) is laid over the crushed rock, and the support soil or growing medium filled in above it (see Figure 10.6).

Providing proper drainage for freestanding potted plants irrigated by an automatic sprinkler system can be a difficult thing. Too often all that is provided in a planter box to catch drainage is a heavy plastic liner (see Figure 10.7). That may suffice for some situations, but with sprinkler systems one can never be terribly confident of the system's flow rate and control. Not only would water placement be a problem, but the flow rates are so great that the pots would soon be flooded. Saucers placed under the containers would not be adequate to handle the drain-off. In furnished areas of a building this could be a serious problem. Particularly distressing is a leak in the piping, fittings, or emitters, with water subsequently spewing out while the system is on. With inherently high flow rates, that could be disastrous in these critical residential, corporate, retail, and food service areas.

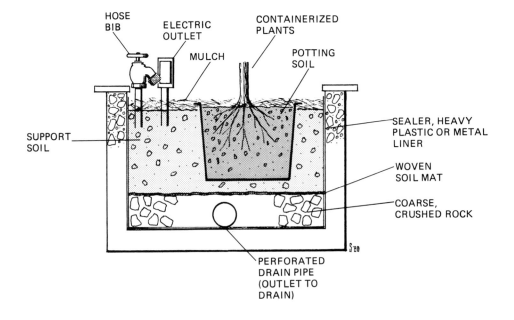

Figure 10.6: Properly designed planter box.

HOSE BIB

ELECTRIC OUTLET

CONTAINERIZED PLANTS

MULCH

POTTING SOIL

SUPPORT SOIL

SEALER, HEAVY PLASTIC OR METAL LINER

WOVEN SOIL MAT

COARSE, CRUSHED ROCK

PERFORATED DRAIN PIPE (OUTLET TO DRAIN)

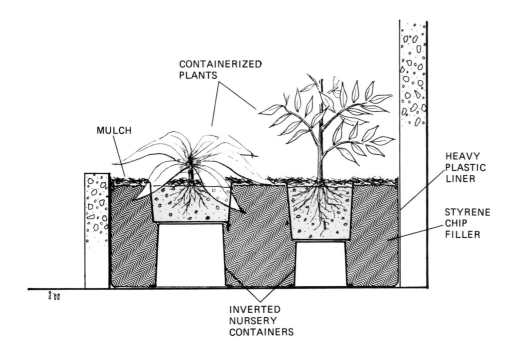

CONTAINERIZED PLANTS

MULCH

HEAVY PLASTIC LINER

STYRENE CHIP FILLER

INVERTED NURSERY CONTAINERS

Sprinkler systems are the coarsest form of automatic irrigation and must be used with caution in interior settings. They are mostly suitable for open areas in building lobbies, promenades, and atria where planter boxes and pits are at a safe distance from furnished portions of the building. Sprinkler equipment is too unrefined, water distribution too voluminous and uncontrolled, and the duration of operation too long for widespread use in building interiors. For those reasons it will remain the major method of irrigation in outdoor landscape and agricultural applications, seeing decreasing usage indoors as more appropriate technology gains favor.

Drip/Trickle Systems

Another common form of irrigation that is frequently automated is the drip system, sometimes called trickle irrigation. It, too, was developed for outdoor plantings in agricultural production, later finding applications in greenhouse horticulture, and more recently in building interiors. Because of the inefficiencies inherent in sprinkler irrigation, better methods were sought by farmers and nurserymen to reduce water utilization. Water conservation became imperative in many areas of the world and sprinkler irrigation was an expensive tool. The solution of dripping water into the soil around plants is generally credited to the Germans, who around 1860 buried clay pipes with loose joints. Water was permitted to drip from these openings and saturate the soil around crops. In the mid-1930s, Australian farmers overcame the agricultural consequences of a drought by drilling holes in galvanized pipe laid on top of the surface soil to irrigate their peach orchards. The slow drip of the system efficiently wetted the ground around the precious trees. At about the same time, an Israeli engineer developed a way of slowly applying water to plants under low pressure by passing it through a tiny coil that extended the water's path yet allowed it to issue from a relatively large opening. This method opened the door for modern drip irrigation technology, which has become an important alternative means of irrigating plants.[4]

The technology has been refined many times and in many ways since, but the concept remains the same. It is based on the highly controlled flow of water applied directly to the root zone of each plant by means of specially designed emitters. These small devices reduce the system's pressure by passing water through a long and complex internal labyrinth, the pathway the water takes just before being introduced to the planter soil. Because of the long flow path, internal friction, and turbulence, the water trickles out of the emitter at a very slow rate. Other concepts are used as well, but the labyrinth type predominates.

While drip systems represent a type of overhead watering, they differ greatly from sprinkler irrigation. Water is given to the plant in a highly localized manner at the surface above the root zone, relying on gravity and capillary action for the moisture to diffuse throughout the root zone (see Figure 10.8). For this reason its effectiveness depends highly on the soil texture and composition. Proper use of drip irrigation keeps the soil in an evenly moist condition, preventing wide fluctuations from overly wet to dry. When these systems are automated, they can provide a slow, regular irrigation regimen, very well suited to the needs of ornamental plants as well as crops. Less water is used, making this type of irrigation highly efficient.

The key elements in drip technology are the emitters, which come in many different types and flow rates. Emitters are plugged into a network of water distribution tubing that is generally polyethylene plastic ("poly") tubing interconnected with control valves. In automated systems sourced by a city water supply, the control valves are electrically or hydraulically operated solenoid types. They are connected to sprinkler system timer/controllers which turn them on at preprogrammed times and for predetermined durations (see Figure 10.9). Because of the

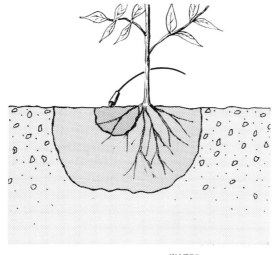

Figure 10.8: Moisture diffusing throughout the root zone from a drip emitter.

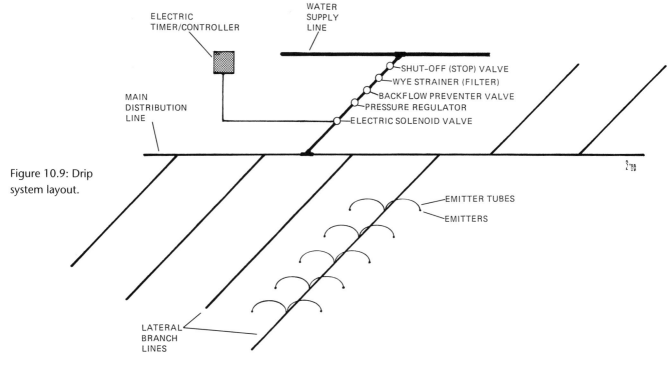

ELECTRIC TIMER/CONTROLLER

WATER SUPPLY LINE

SHUT-OFF (STOP) VALVE
WYE STRAINER (FILTER)
BACKFLOW PREVENTER VALVE
PRESSURE REGULATOR
ELECTRIC SOLENOID VALVE

MAIN DISTRIBUTION LINE

EMITTER TUBES
EMITTERS

Figure 10.9: Drip system layout.

LATERAL BRANCH LINES

very slow flow rates, operating times are extended, sometimes running longer than sprinkler system irrigation periods. Most emitter designs rely on a long and complex path for the water to squeeze through on its way from the water supply tubing (under modest pressure) to the plant. This labyrinth reduces water pressure down to manageable levels, dropping flow rates considerably. These systems are designed primarily for outdoor use. Some cover large farm areas with many topographical variations. Water pressures change over these different grade levels, as does emitter output. Uphill flows can reduce emitter input pressures and flow rates considerably. Downhill flows can conversely increase pressures and flow rates. Installations with long and complex pipe and tubing layouts are also subject to severe pressure losses because of surface friction along the tubing walls and through valves and fittings. Emitters at the outer extremities experience less input pressure than those closer to the water source. Systems engineers have gotten around these problems by designing pressure compensating emitters and intermediate flow devices. They automatically adjust for variations in input pressure, usually in the range of 5 to 55 psi. Certain brands are not recommended for input pressures above 40 psi and must be used with pressure-dropping regulators. Some emitters connect directly to the water supply tubing while others are connected by means of a small-bore emitter tube (see Figure 10.10). The latter arrangement seems to be the more prevalent as it is the most flexible from a layout standpoint.

The type of emitter used determines whether the installation would be called a drip system or trickle system. The difference is slight and only a matter of definition. Most emitters are of the drip type and are commonly available with flow rates in the range of 0.25 to 2.0 gallons per hour (GPH). For comparison, remember that sprinkler emitters are rated in units of gallons per minute (GPM). Soaker hoses and tubes are used in some systems. Although they are not labyrinth-type emitters, they do emit water at a slow rate to a localized area of soil. Some drip system manufacturers also offer miniature spray and misting heads to be used in conjunction with standard drip emitters. Their use, however, would no longer constitute drip irrigation technology.

Most tubing and piping used in drip systems are plastic, usually "poly" tubing and some PVC pipe. These are used not only for their economy, but also for ease of installation. Holes are punched into the poly tubing water supply line, and emitter tubes or pressure-compensating connectors are simply plugged into them (see Figure 10.10). These connections are crude but normally adequate because of the nature of drip system usage; outdoor installations can tolerate occasional leaks. Interior installations usually require more secure connections. System pressures are frequently

Figure 10.10: Five types of emitters: trickle type, soaker line, in-line types, direct-connected types, and those on an emitter tube.

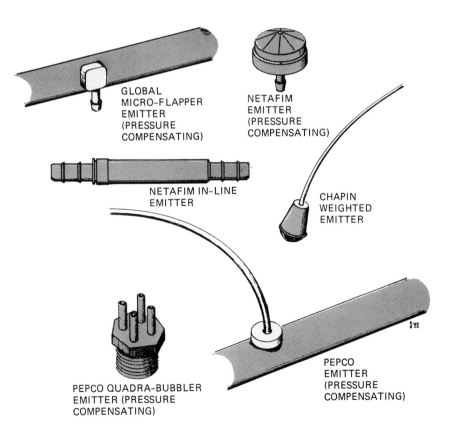

GLOBAL MICRO-FLAPPER EMITTER (PRESSURE COMPENSATING)

NETAFIM EMITTER (PRESSURE COMPENSATING)

NETAFIM IN-LINE EMITTER

CHAPIN WEIGHTED EMITTER

PEPCO QUADRA-BUBBLER EMITTER (PRESSURE COMPENSATING)

PEPCO EMITTER (PRESSURE COMPENSATING)

reduced to 15 to 35 psi indoors to provide a better measure of safety. At any rate, irrigation volume can be reduced indoors because of lower plant transpiration rates.

The problems usually associated with drip irrigation have to do with clogging of the very small ports through which water is distributed and emitted. Dirt, debris, insects, and mineral salts get into the system and possibly block the small openings in the equipment. Emitter labyrinths have very small passages, and it doesn't take much to cause a blockage. Because emitters are frequently placed on the surface of the ground and occasionally buried, soil comes into direct contact with them. The emitter design must be efficient enough to minimize clogging. Also, leaks frequently occur from rodents chewing on the "poly" tubing. They seem to have a liking for that kind of plastic and can cause extensive damage at times. Drip systems have also been criticized for being too sensitive to soil composition and moisture content. Because they rely on capillary action for water distribution, they don't work very well when the soil has accidentally dried out. Capillarity diminishes rapidly in arid soil, yet frequent waterings prevent that from happening. Poor growing media also reduce capillary efficiency. Close attention should be kept on this aspect as well.

Within the past twenty years, irrigation contractors have installed drip systems in greenhouse nurseries where they assist in containerized crop production. More recently, installations have been made in interior landscape settings, almost exclusively in the common areas of buildings that had previously been the exclusive domain of modified sprinkler systems. These built-in planter boxes and pits are far enough away from furnished areas as not to raise concern about leaks, rodent attacks, etc. The use of drip systems in interiorscape irrigation is a relatively recent phenomenon, and the concept is being adopted slowly by the interior landscape industry. The delay stems in part from inadequate training, but mostly from misinformation about automated interior plant care. Much of the prejudice comes from bad experiences some contractors have had with systems involving sprinkler technology and from long-established dogma peculiar to manual irrigation. The most common cause of sprinkler malfunction was bad design and/or installation by firms inexperienced in interior work, or the fact that sprinkler technology is not the best choice for most interiorscape maintenance. Some interiorscape maintenance contractors believe they'll lose business to automated technology, yet those who are more astute are embracing these new methods. The impetus for automated service systems is, of course, coming from the owners and managers of commercial buildings, who seek to increase efficiency.[5]

Drip systems applied indoors are usually designed with water supply input devices similar to those used in sprinkler systems such as shut-off valves, backflow preventers, screen filters, and pressure regulators. Branches are installed into planter boxes and pits, with appropriate drip, trickle, or soaker emitters used in the planting areas. Many interiorscape contractors prefer drip systems over sprinklers in building common areas because of the accident liability created by wet floors. When large interiorscapes must be serviced, the systems are designed into the structure of new buildings from the drawing board stages and piping can then be incorporated into the structural framework. The same applies to extensive renovation work. Piping or tubing stubs are brought up into the planter boxes during construction, ready for finishing connections at a later stage (see Figure 10.11).

Sometimes complex layouts are necessary, and several branches or zones

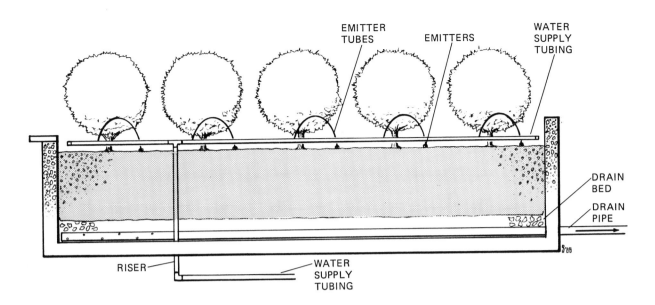

EMITTER TUBES   EMITTERS   WATER SUPPLY TUBING

DRAIN BED

DRAIN PIPE

RISER   WATER SUPPLY TUBING

must be incorporated into the plan. These zones can be automatically turned on by the controller, or one zone at a time can be activated for sequential watering schemes.

Because drip irrigation systems for building interiors are frequently designed by contractors and engineering firms whose training and experience is steeped in outdoor irrigation technology, there is still a tendency to provide for much more water than is necessary. Pipes are too large, emitters are too coarse, and watering times are too long. It should be remembered that 15 minutes worth of watering with a 0.25 gallon per hour drip emitter (the smallest available) will provide a plant with 8 ounces of water at the root zone. For most small containerized plants indoors, one watering a day with that output is more than sufficient, and frequently too much. Irrigation cycles can be reduced to every two or three days if necessary.

New problems are introduced when there is a great disparity in the sizes and water requirements of the plants being serviced simultaneously by the same system. Larger capacity emitters would be used for the bigger plants and lesser capacity for the smaller ones, but the balancing of irrigation durations and emitter sizes could be a difficult task. If the

plants are direct-planted in the soil (out of containers), then somewhat larger volumes may be required, as the surrounding soil absorbs a lot of moisture and cuts irrigation efficiency. It is up to the interiorscape maintenance contractor to undo some of the design excesses and bring the watering pattern to levels more suitable for indoor

Figure 10.11: Planter box with drip system tubing installed.

Figure 10.12: Drip system in use in multi-purpose building.

horticulture. Unfortunately, most interiorscapers don't know how to work with these automated systems yet. For that reason, many automated installations are being misused. Time, further experience, and training will overcome many of these problems.

Be warned that serious leaks can occur with indoor drip systems, which were made for outdoor use where conditions are not as critical. Connections are coarse and many times unreliable, animals (particularly vermin) tend to chew on the "poly" tubing, maintenance technicians accidentally pull joints apart, and vandals have a habit of cutting the highly exposed emitter tubes. With openings in the water distribution tubing, the relatively long watering periods give plenty of time for unwanted leaks to make a mess of things. It is imperative that proper drainage is provided under the containers or planter box so that runoff can be evacuated. One of the major disadvantages of indoor drip systems is that there is too much equipment that is vulnerable to water damage. Therefore, these systems must be designed, installed, used, and maintained with care.

Although drip irrigation is well suited to indoor planter boxes and pits in the common areas of buildings, it is not acceptable for most furnished interior areas. System pressurization lasts for long periods, the water distribution system is unpleasant to look at, and the integrity of the fittings is suspect. For those reasons, they are not very suitable for the interiors of houses, furnished office suites, shops, restaurant dining rooms, banks, clubhouses, or the many other indoor settings where live, potted plants are used to complement interior decor.

Drip systems can be used successfully for containerized plants on terraces, patios, and pool decks, in commercial as well as residential applications. These outdoor settings generally require greater quantities of water more precisely placed than

sprinklers are capable of providing. Drip technology is able to meet those needs. Irrigation cycles are longer outdoors because of the greater moisture requirements, and in many cases the drip equipment can simply be branched off from most convenient lawn sprinkler lines. Independent timing and control would, of course, require a separate branch for the drip system.

Automated drip irrigation is seeing increasing use not only in farm and nursery applications, but in interiorscape maintenance as well. Indoors, automated drip systems are shaping up to be the preferred technology for large planters in the common areas of commercial buildings. They are capable of providing a convenience and cost-efficiency suitable to real estate executives, and their labor-saving, water-saving, and horticultural benefits are starting to be understood by the interior plantscape industry. The limitations inherent in drip systems, however, will keep them relegated mainly to patios and gardens of residential units. Sensitive, furnished portions of building interiors will be increasingly serviced by the newer, more precise irrigation technologies.

Subterranean Systems

A variation of drip irrigation that can be automated and used on occasion for the watering of interiorscapes is subterranean irrigation, or *subirrigation* as it is frequently called. This is the application of water underground near the root zone, and sometimes even below it. In theory this is a very efficient way to water, for the moisture is applied directly to the roots. There are many different types of subterranean systems, yet each configuration does essentially the same thing. They are similar to soaker hoses in that they emit water at a very slow rate along their entire length into the surrounding soil near the root zone, with water distribution running along the tubing axis. While self-watering containers and buried reservoir systems are considered forms of subirrigation, as the water is diffused into the growing medium from below, these techniques are really semi-automated (as discussed in Chapter Nine). Here we will discuss only those technologies that can be fully automated—in other words, flow devices rather than wicking devices.

Subterranean systems generally function with emitters that are tubes within tubes. The simplest versions are the early types, which were normally home-made. Garden hoses or "poly" tubing were punched or drilled with small holes along their length and then slipped into a heavy fabric tube or hose (see Figure 10.13). The resultant structure would be connected to a sprinkler line or faucet and buried near the plants in need of irrigation. Water flowing through the interior hose would seep out from the pores of the fabric casing into the soil. The fabric tube then serves not only as a large-area emitter surface, but also as a kind of filter to keep the holes in the interior hose from becoming clogged with dirt. These types of systems, also referred to as ooze pipes, are generally used at low pressure in order to provide low flow rates and to avoid channeling and bursting of the soft plastic tubing.

Another version is constructed from a perforated interior hose fitted inside a porous clay drainpipe. Water from the interior pipe slowly seeps through the outer ceramic casing into the surrounding soil. Microporous synthetic or rubber casing can also be used to slowly exude water, while some types are simply made from perforated plastic pipes or hoses which are directly buried in the ground. In-line drip emitters—those having emitters in series along the length of pipe—installed at regularly spaced intervals in a "poly" tube are a type of system that is also effective (see Figure 10.14). Yet another type of subterranean system is designed with tiny

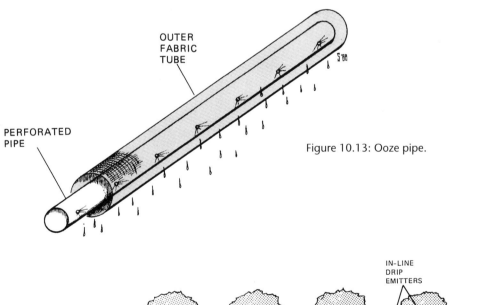

OUTER FABRIC TUBE

PERFORATED PIPE

Figure 10.13: Ooze pipe.

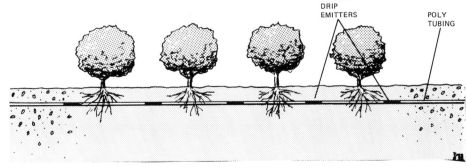

IN-LINE DRIP EMITTERS

POLY TUBING

Figure 10.14: In-line drip emitter system buried in soil near plants.

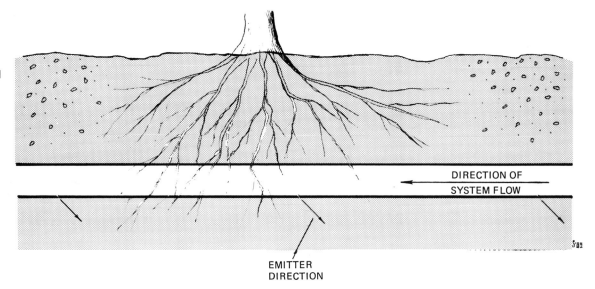

Figure 10.15: Laser Soaker Line™ buried under turf.

DIRECTION OF
SYSTEM FLOW

EMITTER
DIRECTION

holes laser-drilled into "poly" tubing at a reverse angle to the direction of flow (see Figure 10.15). In some models the holes are spaced 6 inches apart, in others, 12 inches apart. Each configuration does essentially the same thing underground. They are similar to soaker hoses in that they emit water at a very slow rate along their entire length into the soil surrounding the root zone.

Subterranean systems are frequently automated by connecting the water supply tubing to a means of interrupting flow. This is generally a solenoid valve operated by an electromechanical or electronic sprinkler controller at timed intervals. The controller supplies power at intervals to open the valve and permit water flow.

These systems are sometimes used to irrigate interiorscapes, particularly long, narrow planter boxes that fit the natural configuration of the tubing lines. When subterranean irrigation is used, the foliage must be direct-rooted into the planter soil. On occasion the tubing is circled around the root line of trees and large ornamental bushes. While the buried tubing makes the plantscape aesthetically pleasing, the hidden lines can be problematic when maintenance technicians have to dig out plants. The tubing gets in their way and frequently gets damaged. Another

drawback is that it is difficult to monitor the condition of the soil when tubing has been deeply buried. Most of the moisture is under the roots and the maintenance technician must check often and carefully to be sure the deep soil is not so saturated that it poses a danger to the plants' health. Once again, it is essential that proper drainage be designed into the planter boxes. Roots, which tend to grow around the submerged tubing, also can easily break connections and/or choke the emitter holes. Large plants can be particularly damaging. Once this happens, it is difficult to maintain the system without causing extensive damage to plant roots. But perhaps the main factor that keeps subterranean irrigation from gaining wide application in interiorscape projects is that it cannot be used with smaller containerized plants—the mainstay of the industry. Water placement is not localized enough for potted plants, so water would be absorbed into the support soil rather than the growing medium. Since there is little interface between them, the moisture cannot be diffused to the root zone. Obviously, this type of irrigation system cannot easily be used with free-standing potted plants. That eliminates application in most furnished, decorated interiors.

Hydroponics

Hydroponics is quite different from other horticultural concepts in that plants are grown without soil in a medium that is essentially inert and used primarily as a means of support for the plant. The soil substitutes are normally materials like gravel, pebbles, pearl chips, coarse sand, vermiculite, perlite, or even coal. A nutrient solution of a balanced fertilizer mix is fed to the plants daily by manual or automatic means. Plant roots grow into the crevices and pores between the medium's particles and aggregates, seeking out the moisture and nutrients. The major part of the nutrient solution is allowed to drain to below the root level to avoid rot. This type of hydroculture is sometimes called soil-less gardening or water-gardening. As an active concept it has been around for centuries, but was popularized in this century by agricultural concerns. They have found that vegetables, flowers, and fruits can be grown more quickly and with greater yields through hydroponics than by conventional farming. Less acreage is required; weed, insect, and disease problems are minimized; less water is used; chemical pollution is minimized; and because most of this type of growing is done within a greenhouse, crops can be produced year-round.

Europeans have used hydroponics to a large extent in their interiorscaping industries to grow flowering and tropical foliage plants in indoor settings. The technology, having been developed primarily for use in sheltered areas, lent itself quite readily to decorative, rather than productive applications. The equipment used for this is similar to that of the self-watering containers discussed earlier. The Luwasa System, which is the prime European hydroculture brand, features a growing medium of expanded clay pellets which draw the nutrient solution up to the root levels by capillary action. The plant resides in a container mounted near the surface of the planter box surrounded by clay pellets. The reserve liquid lies in the

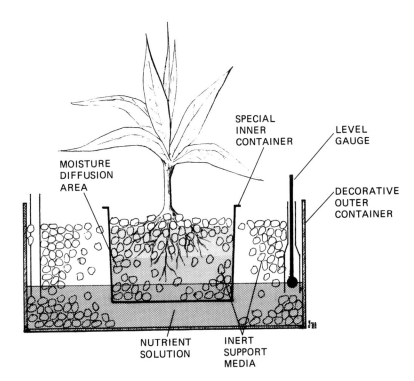

bottom of the container, wetting the growing medium, and ready to diffuse toward the plant—much like the capillary diffusion of self-watering containers. The reservoirs are refilled every 3 to 7 weeks. These systems are not automated, and to our knowledge no attempts have been made to make them so in commercial interiorscape installations. Most of the automation associated with hydroponic systems has been applied in do-it-yourself home gardening projects and in agricultural greenhouse settings. Small pumps are fitted to inject nutrient solution every day or so.

Hydroponic systems have not achieved much popularity in this country for application in interior landscapes, and are not expected to do so because of the strong competing technologies available. The weak marketing effort behind these systems is an additional hindrance. Hydroponics has the additional drawback of requiring large, specialized containers which restrict the designer's options in placement, shape, color, and texture—a negative attribute shared by self-watering containers. Automated precision micro-irrigation (APM) systems overcome these design and technical problems.

Figure 10.16: Hydroponic unit.

147

Mirage™ Automated Precision Micro-Irrigation Systems

Mirage II™ and Mirage III™ precision micro-irrigation systems are the first fully automatic technologies developed specifically for the watering of containerized plants in the interiors of buildings.[6] More refined than drip irrigation or sprinkler irrigation, the Mirage™ APM systems are very precise in their placement of water and control overflow rates, and are designed to be at the exceedingly low levels required by indoor plant culture. They are characterized by very short irrigation cycles that last only seconds and by a variety of flow control devices. APM systems allow us to fully automate the watering of potted plants in the critical, furnished areas of our homes, restaurants, hotels, and offices—all the places where it would be too risky to install drip systems and impossible to contemplate the use of sprinklers. Decorative plants throughout the entire building can now be serviced by automated plant care, and special containers aren't required. Large planters in common areas can be irrigated with the same system as small potted plants in the decorated shops and suites elsewhere in the building.

In short, Mirage II™ and Mirage III™ automatic precision micro-irrigation systems provide the most advantages in both commercial and residential settings. Because of the precise flow control and placement of water, drain-off (overflow) from containers is eliminated. Standby irrigation water is contained in tubes within the room environment, so the water temperature at the time of irrigation cycles is essentially the same as that of the room and the plants. This is a plus because water that is too hot or too cold can damage plants, as occurs frequently with manual irrigation. Also, fertilizer and other systemic chemicals can sometimes be dissolved in the irrigation water for automatic feed to the plants. Because APM systems keep soil moist at all times, irrigation water is not wasted wetting out dried growing media. Therefore, less water is required, plants are not subjected to water stress, and mineral salt build-up is reduced. Comprehensive systems can be designed to service large planter boxes in common areas at the same time as freestanding potted plants in furnished areas. Special containers are not required.

Mirage™ and related systems (Aqua/Trends™ and EnvironMate™ Systems)[7] have been developed around new concepts, yet they incorporate some of the better features of preceding methods. These new systems promise to be the leading technology for widespread use in interiorscaping. As with self-watering containers and automated drip systems (when they can be applied to interior landscapes), APM systems are capable of providing a great deal of convenience and plant care consistency, as well as saving much manual labor, time, and money. Because Mirage™ systems are fully automated and applicable to the entire building, they provide unprecedented convenience and cost-effectiveness. Mirage™ APM system technology solves many interior management problems for the homeowner, corporate office manager, restaurateur, retailer, and the real estate executive.

When APM systems are used in commercial interior landscapes, for example—whether with large groupings of plants in shopping malls and office building lobbies, or scattered potted plants in corporate office suites and restaurants— most, if not all watering is eliminated from the maintenance contractor's list of responsibilities. This does not mean that automated systems can or should totally

Figures 10.17: Applications of APM systems in restaurants and shopping malls.

Figures 10.18:
Applications of APM
systems in offices and
commercial buildings.

Figures 10.19:
Applications of APM
systems in private
residences.

Figures 10.20:
Applications of APM
systems in hotels.

replace human plant care. The industry generally recognizes that between 25% to 50% of on-site maintenance time is taken by manual irrigation and it is the primary reason that maintenance cycles are scheduled once a week. While watering is the most time-consuming chore contractors perform, there are many plant care tasks other than irrigation that must be attended to. Without the need to water, however, maintenance cycles can be extended to once every two or three weeks. Using two-week maintenance cycles as our example, labor content can be reduced by 75%. Two visits per month would then be required instead of four. That saves 50% in maintenance visits, as well as materials, travel, and fringe expenses. Further, consider that 50% of the on-site time is

Figure 10.21: Outdoor applications of Mirage™ systems.

reduced during each of those two visits because no manual irrigation would be required. That saves another 25% of the monthly labor cost total (50% of the remaining 50%). Total labor saving through automated irrigation is therefore 75% (50% by virtue of half the visits, and 25% by virtue of shorter visit), plus 50% savings in other pertinent maintenance cost elements. Plant replacement costs are also reduced considerably. Irrigation is more reliable and consistent, so fewer plants are lost. Lighter physical exertion and greater concentration on the other forms of plant care increase interiorscape employee satisfaction and reduce labor turnover. New employee training is a long, expensive proposition, and automation reduces the need for much of it. Customer satisfaction is improved because fewer visits are required by plant-care personnel and the quality and consistency of the maintenance is at a higher level. Unlike manual irrigation, precision irrigation wastes virtually no water, so fertilizer is saved because it doesn't go down the drain in run-off. In total, the savings for the contractor can be considerable. If the contractor passes some of these savings along, the customer can realize reductions of 30% to 60% on interiorscape maintenance contracts. Experience has demonstrated that Mirage™ systems can typically pay for themselves in a year or less.

These systems are so versatile that they can be used to service virtually every containerized plant in a building interior—no matter how remote or delicately placed. Its broadest applications are possible in new and renovated construction, where water distribution networks can be designed into the building structure and conveniently installed while partitions are open. Retrofit installations can generally be made, but these cannot be done as easily or as inexpensively.

Some unorthodox uses have surfaced over the years. For example, homeowners have been known to design a watering station into their homes to provide pets with fresh water several times daily. In these instances, emitters are mounted on pet bowls rather than plant pots.

Mirage™ automated precision micro-irrigation systems represent the newest concept in fully automated interior plant care and building automation. The technology is very different from sprinkler and drip systems, and is specifically designed for interior applications with its very low flow requirements, as well as its critical aesthetic and reliability specifications. It is the most suitable of all technologies for broad application in building interiors and is expected to ultimately become the standard of the industry. In the following chapters we will discuss the technology of Mirage™ APM systems in detail, explaining how they differ from preceding methods, how they function, and how they are designed into buildings, installed, and used.

ELEVEN

The Concepts of Automated Precision Micro-Irrigation Systems

Mirage II™ and Mirage III™ automated precision micro-irrigation systems or APM systems are different from preceding technologies in a number of ways, all having to do with refining the methods by which water is delivered to plants, the quantities of water involved, and the techniques of installation. The technology is designed specifically for the irrigation of potted plants in the furnished interior areas of buildings—the most critical application for any irrigation system. However, because the technology is highly refined, these systems can also be used in other areas of the building where sprinkler and drip systems might normally be installed, as well as outside for patio and balcony applications. This allows containerized plants in the common and furnished interior portions of a building, as well as in some outdoor areas, to be maintained by the same automatic irrigation system.

The Creation of APM Systems

The technology of Mirage™ APM systems was originally developed by Aqua/Trends (predecessor to Boca Automation, Inc.) in response to the need for better ways of caring for interior foliage plants in the South Florida Gold Coast. Many home and condominium owners are away from their dwellings a large part of the year, and their potted houseplants suffer from neglect or well-meaning but ineffective "plant-sitters." From these beginnings, more sophisticated systems were developed to service the more heavy-duty requirements of commercial interiorscape installations. Many versions had to be designed to meet the needs of a broad variety of interior applications. What they all have in common, however, is the use of what is known as *pulse-flow* technology, which reduces watering cycles to seconds, rather than minutes or hours as in other systems. That, coupled with the use of frequent, periodic watering cycles, adjustable mini-valves at each plant, and other flow control devices, makes for a system of the highest refinement and flexibility, capable of watering small, dry-loving plants on the same system as plants requiring much more water. APM systems can be used on different building levels, so that multi-floor installations are easy to service. Of equal importance indoors, APM systems installations can be almost completely hidden, sparing the aesthetics of decor. They provide a degree of versatility and convenience never before available to the homeowner, interiorscaper, and property or facilities manager.

The Pulse-Flow Concept

In order to accommodate the much smaller quantities of water required by ornamental plants indoors, particularly those in containers, the concepts of short-interval watering were developed. We call this *pulse-flow* technology, the flow of short pulses of water—seconds in duration—used repeatedly at fairly short intervals. The resulting irrigation pattern provides a high degree of accuracy and flexibility, offering the greatest benefit to the plants. Most people believe that indoor plants must be allowed to dry out for an extended period before the next watering is applied. This idea has become so prevalent from manual irrigation practices that most consumers, plant shops, and even interior plantscapers still believe that it constitutes the only valid regimen for interior plant care. This is simply not true, but confirmation was not available until serious technical development in the area got underway. Following are some excerpts from various publications on the subject. As expected, most relate only to manual irrigation techniques, and some even warn against use of automated systems.

"When you do water your plants, do so thoroughly, so that the water reaches all parts of the pot. But do not give so much water every time that some always drains from the bottom of the pot, or valuable nutrients will be washed away."[1] (True for manual irrigation, but only partially true for automatic irrigation.)

"Happily, none of the vagueness of the 'how often' question beclouds the 'how much' question. Whenever a plant needs watering, it must be watered thoroughly—until water drains out of the holes at the bottom of the pot."[2] (True for one type of manual irrigation, but false for automatic irrigation.)

"Feel the soil to a depth of one inch below the surface; if it's dry to the touch, add tepid water to the soil surface. Continue until you see water seeping from the drainage hole. Allow the plant to drain (either into a sink or drainage saucer) for at least ten minutes. . . . When the top inch of soil again becomes dry to the touch (a few days to a few weeks, depending on the pot size and plant type), repeat this procedure."[3] (True for one type of manual irrigation, but false for automatic irrigation.)

"The first and most important rule when watering any plant is: water it thoroughly. Thorough watering means to saturate the soil from top to bottom."[4] (True for one type of manual irrigation, but false for automatic irrigation.)

"It is always recommended that plant watering be done manually, not by automatic watering systems."[5] (False)

"Basically, the movement of water in soil is vertical and not lateral. Because of this, it has always been a rule of thumb to water well when watering." (False)

"Do not shallow-water plants. Frequent light sprinklings are usually injurious in that the surface of the soil remains moist, while the strata below remain dry. It is better to lengthen the period between waterings and then water the plant well than it is to water frequently only the topsoil surface."[6] (The first sentence is particularly true for sprinkler irrigation. The second is true for sprinkler irrigation, but false for APM systems.)

"The growing medium should be watered when it needs it, not according to a predetermined schedule."[7] (Can be done either way with manual or APM irrigation.)

"Plants require a constant supply of water to maintain their normal processes." (True)

"Apply a sufficient quantity of water to thoroughly wet the growing medium from top to bottom with some draining from the growing container. Small quantities of water applied at frequent intervals will not disperse evenly throughout the entire mass of growing medium."[8] (True for manual irrigation, but false for APM irrigation.)

These passages reflect the conventional wisdom of the day, yet they contain several inconsistencies and inaccuracies. Nevertheless, it is typical of the information given homeowners as well as the training given interior landscape professionals. These rules of thumb (and in some cases, old wives tales) have led to much confusion about irrigation practices, but now that automated techniques are available, the rules have changed. The advice presented above is solely oriented toward manual irrigation, and must be accepted in that context.

It is more realistic to consider that the tropical foliage plant varieties used indoors are, to a large extent, native to habitats where growing conditions are always moist, like the rainforest, for example, where the forest floors are damp at all times. One author puts it well:

> The amount of water a given plant needs is determined by the conditions it found in its natural habitat. A plant which in nature grows by a waterfall, where it is continually bathed by the spray, or in a tropical jungle where rain is a daily occurrence, will need constant moisture and, without it, may dry up and die. But even with a moisture-loving plant, the word is 'moist,' not 'soggy'.[9]

Most plants flourish under these conditions, and it is not until we get them into our homes or offices that the dry-wet-dry syndrome begins. Even the tropical foliage nurseries that produce these plants water the containerized foliage at least once a day through drip, mist, or sprinkler irrigation. The potting soil is never allowed to dry out. It is always kept evenly moist, meaning that the soil is kept consistently as close to the proper moisture level as possible and not permitted to experience broad fluctuations from wet to dry. Horticultural recommendations call for most plants to be kept evenly moist (see *The Encyclopedia of Houseplants* in the Appendix).

If Mother Nature can do it, and if the large wholesale nurseries do it, we know that we can, too. It's just a matter of having the right means available to accomplish it conveniently—which is where APM systems come into the picture.

Years ago, before automated plant care was an option, the tendency was to manually overirrigate potted plants to the point where they were dangerously overwatered. Life-giving oxygen was thus displaced from the soil mass, and gardeners found that by letting the plants dry out for a time, the oxygen was then able to reenter the soil. This technique, however, promotes broad swings in moisture levels which can have adverse effects on the plant. Excessive dryness can create a form of shock called *water stress* in the plant. Some of the cells actually die off, stunting growth. It is too easy for the careless or inexperienced maintenance technician to overlook a plant during a maintenance visit, promoting moisture starvation in portions of the root system. The resultant shock, if severe, could actually kill the plant.

Partial drying also creates problems when the soil is irrigated. Remember that enough water must be introduced to rewet the soil, mulch, etc. This is not as easy as it sounds. Surface tensions must be overcome before the moisture can penetrate the grains and fibers of organic matter in the growing mix. The use of *surface-active agents* (*surfactants*) in the irrigation water helps to break down these tensions and promote wetting. Household detergents are a form of surface-active agent, and they do in a wash what other surfactants accomplish in planter soil by promoting wetting as part of their job. Fine sand and peat moss fibers are particularly difficult to rewet when dry. By spreading irrigation cycles out over one or two week periods, the surface soil can become particularly dry. During the next irrigation, much of the water will simply filter through the soil or run off the surface

without much benefit. Some of this drains to the saucer, or worse, onto the carpet or tile floor. In order to keep planter soil in an evenly moist condition with a proper balance of moisture and aeration, small-dose applications of water would have to be made at frequent intervals to at least replace the small quantities of moisture lost to plant intake and evaporation between waterings. To do this manually is not only inconvenient but requires an attention to detail that few could tolerate. Given the technology we have available to us these days, it is simply not practical for most homeowners or professional interiorscapers to follow such a demanding schedule.

Oxygen can permeate the root area before being displaced again at the next dousing. Some plant authorities advocate that small plants should be placed in large pots of water until they are fully saturated. Large plants are to be inundated with water until the excess drains out of the bottom holes (see Figure 11.1). Most specimen plants are large and sometimes ponderous, and it is impractical to move them often. In this case heavy manual watering must be done in-place. Can you imagine careless or inexperienced attendants trying to do that in a furnished living room, restaurant, or office suite?

During the course of a day, moisture is lost through transpiration and by evaporation from the surface of the planter soil (see Figure 11.2). The loss is slow, therefore its replacement should be slow. Studies show that only fractions of an ounce of water are lost to the soil and atmosphere of most small containerized plants. Even some larger plants do not require much more indoors. The technology of APM systems is based on the principal of providing small doses of water at frequent intervals to replace only the moisture lost and to evenly maintain the level of soil moisture best suited to that particular plant. With this scheme there is no need to douse-and-purge, for oxygen is always in sufficient

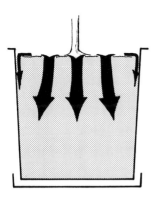 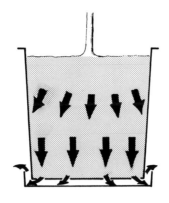

Figure 11.1: Plants being fed large amounts and small doses of water.

LARGE DOSES OF WATER APPLIED AT INFREQUENT INTERVALS DRAINS THROUGH RAPIDLY AND INEFFICIENTLY—SOMETIMES CAUSING DAMAGING OVERFLOW.

SMALL DOSES OF WATER APPLIED AT FREQUENT INTERVALS DIFFUSES SLOWLY THROUGH THE SOIL MASS BEFORE THE NEXT DOSE IS APPLIED.

quantity around the roots. The soil is never permitted to become dry, nor is it permitted to become saturated. Rather, it maintains a good balance of moisture and oxygen at all times. The application of small doses of water permits slow diffusion into the soil before the next watering. Because soil particles are always somewhat moist, the problem of constantly breaking surface tensions to rewet them does not exist, and less water is required. And because large quantities of water are never used, runoff problems become a thing of the past, making carpet and other floor coverings less vulnerable to damage.

In pulse-flow technology, irrigation cycles are measured in terms of ounces of water per 10 seconds, reflecting the small quantities issued during each cycle and the very short cycles used. Compare this with the gallons per minute unit used to measure

Figure 11.2: Plant losing moisture through evaporation and transpiration.

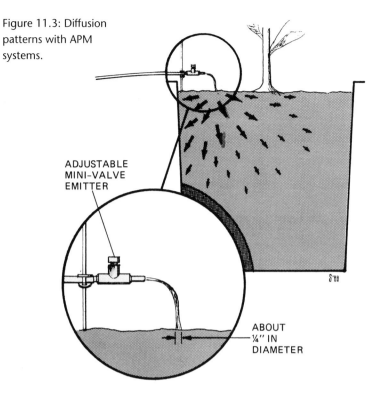

Figure 11.3: Diffusion patterns with APM systems.

ADJUSTABLE MINI-VALVE EMITTER

ABOUT ¼" IN DIAMETER

emission in sprinkler systems and gallons per hour with drip systems.

Pulse-flow techniques permit operating cycles typically only 10 or 15 seconds in duration, generally feeding only a fraction of an ounce of water to each plant. For very small plants that is enough, but for larger plants irrigation cycles must be repeated once or twice more each day. By turning down the adjustable emitters on the smaller plants, even potted cacti and other dry-loving varieties can tolerate multiple irrigation cycles. In a given installation, irrigation cycles can be repeated as many times as necessary to give all of the plants being serviced their prescribed amounts. However, there is seldom a need for more than two or three cycles per day. *One of the most important things to remember about automated precision micro-irrigation systems is that they are designed to constantly maintain an optimum level of moisture in a planter, rather than to wet out dried planter soil.* By automating this delicate watering technique, we not only

provide the best irrigation regimen for plant health, but are able to do it with an accuracy, consistency, and convenience only dreamed of by manual irrigation practitioners. Because of the methods involved, automation is a necessity with micro-irrigation systems used in this way.

Boca Automation's APM systems were designed to be highly flexible in their ability to control the small amounts of water fed during the irrigation cycle. In addition to the variability of flow adjustment at each plant and the use of multiple cycles daily, the length of the irrigation cycle can also be easily varied to provide more or less water during each operating period. The duration of the basic irrigation cycle for interior plants is 10 or 15 seconds. Provisions are made at the control center so that the duration of flow can easily be doubled to 20 or 30 seconds whenever necessary. These multiple controls give the system a high degree of flexibility and enable it to cope with the moisture needs of most combinations of plants on a common installation.

Moisture Diffusion Patterns

The emitter most commonly used in APM systems is a small adjustable valve that sends a narrow stream of water to the surface of the soil above the root zone. That stream directly impinges upon an area no larger than 1/4" in diameter. The mechanisms found in APM systems are similar to those found in drip irrigation in that from that small irrigated section, the moisture must diffuse throughout the entire planter (see Figure 11.3).

Capillary action and gravity are relied on to diffuse moisture throughout a root area from a point of concentration. The efficiency of this diffusion is therefore highly dependent on the composition of the planter media, which is soil in most cases.

A well-balanced planter mix will promote efficient capillary transfer. Capillary action is aided by very small spaces, or pores, between soil particles or fibers. Larger pores aid in soil aeration and drainage, but small ones promote capillarity. This is one of the reasons for good moisture diffusion in clay, which has very small pores. Conversely, the drainage characteristics of clay are poor because of the tiny pores. Fibrous materials in the soil tend to aid capillarity because they have microscopic pores between individual fibers, and even smaller ones in the amorphous regions between their long-chain molecules. In fiber technology, these pores are frequently called **interstices**. They are relatively long and very narrow, and run in the direction of the fiber axis. Water seeps into these pores, swelling the structure. It then travels along the length of the fibers in a highly efficient, natural wicking action, following the elongated pores as if they were railroad tracks. They are, in fact, microscopic aqueducts. This is the reason why wicks are made of narrow woven, twisted, and braided fibrous materials. They exhibit a high degree of capillarity along their axis and readily transfer water from one end to the other. Natural fibrous materials used as soil modifiers in horticulture, such as sphagnum peat moss, composted wood chips, straw-filled manure, ground fir, and redwood and cypress bark, exhibit these properties and enhance the wicking properties of the soil, making it easier to diffuse moisture throughout the entire area of a planter. The use of a properly formulated growing medium in interior landscape work cannot be overemphasized. It is one of the major factors contributing to irrigation efficiency, regardless of the methods used. It is particularly important with drip and APM systems as well as self-watering containers that rely so heavily on the capillary diffusion of moisture.

Moisture Diffusion Studies

Moisture diffusion in a properly formulated soil mix runs laterally as well as vertically. There are many in the horticultural businesses who maintain that irrigation water is simply pulled down by gravity and does not have a chance to fan out laterally. While this is essentially true of coarse sandy soils, it does not describe the diffusion patterns in well-balanced mixes.

Through our development work with APM systems, we know that the water supplied to the small surface area of potted plants diffuses well throughout the soil mass and maintains even moisture levels. In order to define and record what was happening in planters serviced by APM systems, a detailed study was made in the late 1980s of the diffusion patterns. It spanned a period of about 9 months, and recorded literally thousands of moisture readings under closely controlled conditions. Although the reader will be spared from the voluminous data resulting from this study, Figure 11.8 illustrates typical variations found from one level to the next.

Although Figure 11.8 is a simplistic summary of the sets of readings taken at two points in time, it nevertheless illustrates the types of readings typically found at various times of the diffusion cycle. Note that only the small areas of soil just below the watering points become very moist, and that it happens immediately after a watering. The heavy pockets of moisture dissipate to other areas and are absorbed by the plant during the 12-hour period following watering. Surface levels show low to modest amounts of moisture, with gradual increases toward the lower levels. The moisture at any location in the planter (except watering points) stays fairly constant throughout the entire diffusion cycle. This supports the contention that the

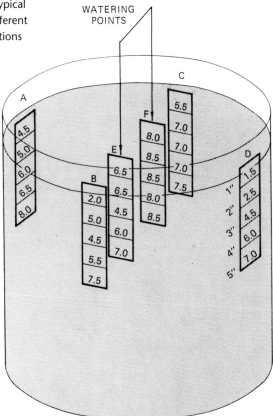

Figure 11.8: Typical readings at different container positions and levels.

WATERING POINTS

WATERING POINTS

IMMEDIATELY AFTER WATERING

12 HOURS AFTER WATERING

plant absorbs enough moisture from the last watering to keep the soil mass at a relatively constant dampness level. Because the three inches or so just below the surface are in a lightly damp state, they contain large amounts of oxygen available for plant use. There is never any inundation of these crucial layers with water, as there would be with manual irrigation. Furthermore, compaction of the top soil layers does not occur from this type of overhead watering as it does with manual and sprinkler irrigation. With properly adjusted systems, the lower levels never become waterlogged, and there is no excess to drain from the bottom of the container. The full moisture diffusion cycle shows a very slight increase in dampness at any level just after watering, and then declining again slightly over the next twelve hours, until the next gentle watering again replenishes the mass (see Figure 11.9).

In taking the thousands of readings for this study, it was noted that meter reaction was strongly influenced by the soil composition in a given subsurface location, and additionally by the proximity to a root mass. The homogeneity of the planter mix used in the study was found to be less than ideal, and pockets of soil were encountered that diffused and retained moisture better than others. For example, Position D exhibited particularly poor diffusion properties (see Figure 11.8). The subsurface areas around roots were found to be better moisture absorbers than outlying sectors. This was particularly true of finely divided root systems having many root hairs. Moisture tends to diffuse into those areas more readily because its fibrous nature promotes better wicking activity. Pockets of root/soil mass may exhibit higher moisture readings than other sections devoid of roots, regardless of their depth.

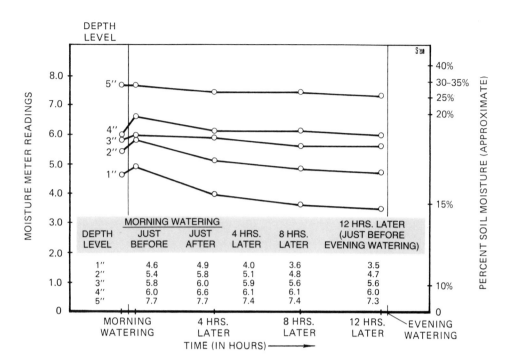

Figure 11.9: A moisture diffusion cycle—moisture readings vs. time at various levels.

DEPTH LEVEL

MOISTURE METER READINGS

PERCENT SOIL MOISTURE (APPROXIMATE)

DEPTH LEVEL	MORNING WATERING		4 HRS. LATER	8 HRS. LATER	12 HRS. LATER (JUST BEFORE EVENING WATERING)
	JUST BEFORE	JUST AFTER			
1"	4.6	4.9	4.0	3.6	3.5
2"	5.4	5.8	5.1	4.8	4.7
3"	5.8	6.0	5.9	5.6	5.6
4"	6.0	6.6	6.1	6.1	6.0
5"	7.7	7.7	7.4	7.4	7.3

MORNING WATERING — 4 HRS. LATER — 8 HRS. LATER — 12 HRS. LATER — EVENING WATERING

TIME (IN HOURS) ———→

APM systems were shown to require less water for a given plant than manual irrigation because of their gentle application at frequent intervals. The technique prevents soil drying yet allows thorough diffusion of moisture before the next watering cycle. As an added bonus, it also eliminates wasteful run-off. Because less water is used, fertilizer requirements are reduced and mineral salt build-up in the soil—largely a result of the amount of water and water-borne fertilizer used over a period of time—is slowed considerably. It is not altogether eliminated, however, as the studies showed. A dwarfed corn plant in the study showed the white accumulations of mineral salts on its soil surface six or seven inches from the emitter. Its presence there clearly demonstrated lateral movement of moisture in the soil (see Figure 11.15). The study also determined that moisture is depleted at higher levels by day than at night.

Although further experimentation is necessary to fully define these mechanisms, the initial series of moisture diffusion studies have demonstrated conclusively that APM systems are capable of maintaining

Figure 11.15: Surface of a dwarfed corn plant with salt accumulations.

moisture levels in planter soils in a remarkably accurate manner. The gentle watering cycles permit slow diffusion of moisture throughout the root ball, and keep the plant system at evenly moist levels at all times—something that manual irrigation can accomplish only at great inconvenience and expense.

Mulches and Moisture Retention

During the course of the diffusion studies, average moisture levels in the test planter were slowly declining due to the hot weather passing through the area. When using APM systems, the normal course of action taken under such circumstances would be to adjust the emitter valve for slightly greater flow, or to switch the system into its longer operating cycle. For example, one would switch from 10 seconds of operation to 20 seconds, the latter being the system's "high gear." In the above-mentioned case, however, the 20-second watering period was already being used, and so a top dressing of sphagnum peat moss was added to reduce surface evaporation, a probable cause of the moisture loss. A 3/4" layer of peat moss was spread across the planter surface and moisture level readings were continually measured for several months after the change. The downward trend did, in fact, reverse, confirming the use of mulch to be quite effective in reducing moisture loss from surface evaporation.

The effect is not as dramatic as it would be outdoors, where direct sun would cause very rapid surface drying. Indoors the effects are more subtle, but they do nevertheless alter the irrigation schedule. In one portion of the study it took about two months under the micro-irrigation system regimen of 2.25 ounces of water every twelve hours for subsurface moisture to return to earlier levels in a large plant. This study was carried out in South Florida during a period when that area was experiencing its hottest summer on record. Although the house in which the test plants were contained was air conditioned, it was still warmer than normal, and plant transpiration had naturally increased. The curve of soil moisture indices illustrated in Figure 11.16 graphically portrays the turnaround.

In this chapter we have discussed the concepts behind automated precision micro-irrigation (APM) systems, and how this new technology is different from those methods that preceded it. Chapter Twelve will describe the operating equipment and technical systems that were developed to implement these new concepts of plant care.

Figure 11.16: Soil moisture indices over a five-month period before and after adding a peat moss top dressing.

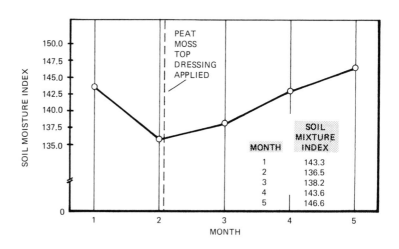

Table 11.2A

Integrated moisture meter readings one month before mulch was added.

Depth	Condition**				
	1	2	3	4	5
1"	3.4	4.6	4.1	3.9	3.5
2"	4.9	5.9	5.4	4.8	4.6
3"	6.1	6.6	5.6	5.6	5.5
4"	6.5	7.0	6.7	6.4	5.9
5"	6.9	7.6	7.4	7.4	7.0

Soil Moisture Index= 143.3***

Table 11.2B

Integrated moisture meter readings just before mulch was added.

Depth	Condition**				
	1	2	3	4	5
1"	3.4	4.6	4.1	3.3	2.8
2"	4.4	5.6	5.0	4.9	4.1
3"	5.2	5.8	5.7	5.3	4.9
4"	5.9	6.5	6.4	6.4	5.5
5"	7.2	7.9	7.4	7.3	6.9

Soil Moisture Index= 136.5***

Table 11.2C

Integrated moisture meter readings one month after mulch was added.

Depth	Condition**				
	1	2	3	4	5
1"	3.1	4.6	3.7	3.4	3.1
2"	4.9	5.9	5.0	4.4	4.6
3"	5.3	6.6	5.9	5.4	5.4
4"	5.7	6.8	6.3	6.1	5.8
5"	6.9	7.7	7.4	7.1	7.1

Soil Moisture Index= 138.2***

Table 11.2D

Integrated moisture meter readings two months after mulch was added.

Depth	Condition**				
	1	2	3	4	5
1"	4.6	4.9	4.0	3.6	3.5
2"	5.4	5.8	5.1	4.8	4.7
3"	5.8	6.0	5.9	5.6	5.6
4"	6.0	6.6	6.1	6.1	6.0
5"	7.7	7.7	7.4	7.4	7.3

Soil Moisture Index= 143.6***

Table 11.2E

Integrated moisture meter readings three months after mulch was added.

Depth	Condition**				
	1	2	3	4	5
1"	4.1	4.8	4.9	4.4	3.7
2"	4.1	6.1	5.3	4.9	5.0
3"	5.5	6.3	5.9	5.6	5.6
4"	6.4	6.9	6.5	6.1	6.0
5"	7.6	7.9	7.8	7.6	7.6

Soil Moisture Index= 146.6***

Table 11.2: Summary of moisture diffusion studies (integrated readings—depth/location/moisture level matrix*)

* Readings from all locations at a given depth level were totaled and averaged.

** Conditions Key

1= Readings just before morning watering.

2= Readings just after morning watering.

3= Readings 4 hours after morning watering.

4= Readings 8 hours after morning watering.

5= Readings 12 hours after morning watering, just before evening watering.

*** Soil moisture index is the sum total of all integrated readings on a given day, and indicates the soil moisture retention level at that time.

TWELVE

The Equipment of Automated Precision Micro-Irrigation Systems

The equipment supplied by Boca Automation for automated precision micro-irrigation systems is quite varied, as many different system configurations are necessary to meet a broad variety of installation needs. Some elements are similar to those used in drip and sprinkler systems, but most are different. The need for specialized control systems and water distribution networks was fostered by the unique and demanding requirements of indoor applications, particularly in the context of its broadest uses. As we have learned in previous chapters, tropical plants used in interior decor require relatively small amounts of water. That means smaller tubing and pipe sizes can be used in the water distribution network. In order to achieve the highest degree of control over the flow and placement of water, as well as to minimize the risk of serious leaks, the pulse-flow concept was developed.

The Basics

The pulse-flow concept is characterized by very short watering cycles occurring at fairly frequent intervals. That, in turn, necessitated the development of specialized controllers capable of providing low flow rates and extremely short operating cycles. The rigorous aesthetic requirements of having to install these systems into highly sensitive, furnished areas of building interiors—like living and dining rooms, executive office suites, restaurant dining rooms, and all the other conceivable nooks and crannies of a decorated building—made system leak-resistance extremely important. Outdoors, a leak, whether major or minor, generally matters little. Indoors, of course, such accidents can have very costly consequences. The very short periods of pressurization used in APM system technology make it highly improbable that large amounts of water could leak from a system of this type. The flow in these systems possesses nothing close to the magnitude which might be encountered with drip or sprinkler systems. Nevertheless, during the course of the system's development, tubing and fittings had to be chosen carefully to assure complete system integrity to prevent accidents. Some of the specifications had to meet building codes, for many of these systems are integrated into the framework and partitions of a building, and local codes take jurisdiction over such installations through normal inspections and testing. These and other considerations made this new technology unique in many ways. This chapter will delve into the details of APM systems and equipment, and provide the reader with an understanding of the elements that make the system work.

As with all other automatic irrigation systems, there must be a:

1. Source of water.

2. Means of delivering the water to planter locations.

3. Device somewhere between the two to cause flow to start and stop.

4. Timing and control device to cause the activating device to start or stop, open or close.

These elements are usually widely separated and must therefore be remotely controlled.

The source is generally city water, when it can be accessed, or pump-drawn water from a well or reservoir of some kind. Irrigation systems for building interiors tap into the city water at a cold water pipe running through the structure (cold water mains). Pump systems used in interior irrigation draw water from an exterior well or from a reservoir installed somewhere in the building.

The means of delivering water to planter locations is always a tubing or piping network leading from the water source to the various plant locations. This network can be simple or complex, short or extremely long depending on the nature of the installation. Indoors, this could mean a ten-foot stretch of tubing to water a couple of potted plants on an office work station, or a run of several hundred feet to service the entire building floor, or the many and diverse variations in-between.

Electrically operated solenoid valves are placed at appropriate locations in the tubing line to interrupt the flow of mains-sourced systems. This is true indoors or out. Water flows through the tubing network only when the solenoid valve is open. Electrically operated pumps are used in the other types of systems to create a flow of water. Water flows through the system only when the pump is operating.

Electromechanical or electronic time-switch/controllers are used to control the action of the solenoid valves and pumps. They time the period between operations and the length of time the system is activated watering plants. They are called controllers because they provide and shut down power to the activating devices at the proper times.

These capsule explanations present only a simplistic view of the technology involved. Other devices are used as well, but those described above are the essentials for automated systems. Other elements of APM systems will be mentioned as we go through detailed discussions in the balance of the chapter.

Categories of APM Systems

High-pressure and low-pressure systems are the major divisions of APM technology. They are different in the ways they deliver water to the tubing network. Other than that, they are essentially similar. Each of these major divisions is, in turn, subdivided into a number of other categories according to use. There are various degrees of usage and wear-and-tear (duty ratings) for each, for example. Combined, APM systems are capable of servicing a broad variety of installation configurations. The equipment used for each has its own peculiarities. Although APM technology was designed mainly for critical interior applications, it finds non-critical indoor uses and some outdoor uses as well. The equipment used for each had to be designed with its particular usage in mind. An illustration of the various configurations of APM systems can be found in Figure 12.1.

High-Pressure Systems

High-pressure systems, in the context of this technology, are sourced by the building's cold water lines, which generally are sourced from the local water supply. Occasionally, a building may have its own well and pump system to furnish its needs. Input pressures to buildings are most commonly in the range of 55 to 75 psi (pounds per square inch). Many local building codes require a reducing pressure regulator in the input line if pressure exceeds 80 psi. This is to protect plumbing fittings and appliances, which are subject to excessive wear or damage by high water pressures.[1] The pressure to which the equipment is subjected fluctuates throughout the day. For example, most city water systems are most heavily used in the morning when people are getting ready for work, and in the evening when they are

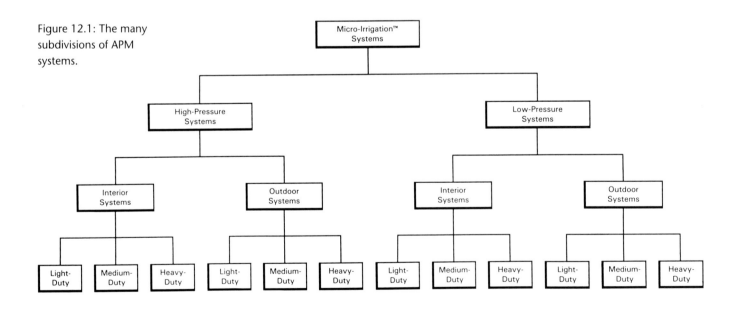

Figure 12.1: The many subdivisions of APM systems.

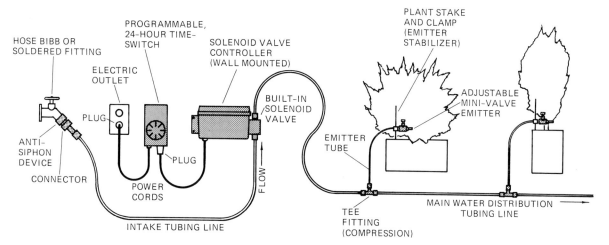

HOSE BIBB OR
SOLDERED FITTING

ELECTRIC
OUTLET

PROGRAMMABLE,
24-HOUR TIME-
SWITCH

SOLENOID VALVE
CONTROLLER
(WALL MOUNTED)

BUILT-IN
SOLENOID
VALVE

PLANT STAKE
AND CLAMP
(EMITTER
STABILIZER)

ADJUSTABLE
MINI-VALVE
EMITTER

PLUG

ANTI-
SIPHON
DEVICE

CONNECTOR

PLUG

POWER
CORDS

FLOW

EMITTER
TUBE

INTAKE TUBING LINE

TEE
FITTING
(COMPRESSION)

MAIN WATER DISTRIBUTION
TUBING LINE

Figure 12.2: High-pressure APM system.

showering or running washing machines and dishwashers. Summer weekends create heavy demand on local water systems as lawn sprinkler systems are operated more frequently and people wash their cars. Sometimes local industry creates heavy, fluctuating demand which also affects pressure in residential and commercial buildings. Building and zoning codes are meant to control system aberrations such as these, but the reality is that they don't always work.

The general configuration of high-pressure APM systems is shown in Figure 12.2. The system is connected to a cold water line by means of a hose bibb (faucet) as shown in the illustration, or by means of a soldered or compression fitting installed in a pipe junction. The irrigation system becomes another branch of the plumbing, but under independent control. Following the connection, a shut-off valve is installed in order to be able to shut down the irrigation branch in emergencies, for repair, or for maintenance of the system. Sometimes the connection and shut-off valve are one and the same, such as with the hose bibb shown in the illustration. Other times an in-line globe valve is used.

Many plumbing codes call for an anti-siphon device installed between an auxiliary water branch (such as an irrigation system) and the city water supply. These measures are taken to prevent accidental pollution of the local water system. A filter of some kind is always used in the inlet group to remove dirt and other contaminants from the water supply. It is generally installed just after the connection to reduce wear on all system parts and prevent clogging of small orifices. Contaminants are ever-present in the water supply, so don't take chances. In smaller systems, a screen filter is integral to the input fitting of the solenoid valve, so no additional filtration is necessary. Filters must be cleaned regularly to maintain normal operation.

In most installations it is necessary to reduce system water pressure down to lower levels. Pressure reducers or pressure regulators are sometimes introduced after the filter unit, but in most instances they are installed just after the solenoid valve. The type of pressure regulator will, in large measure, determine its location. Integral screen filters can be found in some of these devices as well.

Next comes an electrically operated solenoid valve which controls the flow of water through the system at timed intervals and durations. Solenoid valves are open-and-shut types of devices, with no other flow regulation involved. They open to allow water to pass through for very short durations, and then shut down for long intervals to keep water from flowing through the system. The timing and control of the solenoid valve is accomplished by means of time switches and solenoid controllers. In Boca Automation's APM systems, most models have solenoid valves mounted in the controller for a compact, easy-to-install unit. Most APM controllers are plug-in devices. The power cord plugs into a 24-hour timer (time switch) which activates it according to the time schedule programmed for the system. The timer determines only when the system comes on, not when it shuts off. That is determined by the solenoid valve controller, which permits the valve to open for only very short periods of time.

Downstream from the solenoid valve is where the water distribution takes place through a network of tubing, fittings, and flow-control devices that direct water to the individual plants. Throughout the network there are connections to small-diameter tubing. It is this tubing that carries water to individual potted plants. At the end of these tubes are fitted miniature adjustable-valve emitters that can be turned down for very low flow rates or can be opened up for more volume. The emitter assembly is held in place by a stabilizer stake which is anchored in the potting soil.

The system is considered "high-pressure" because it operates essentially under water pressures of 20 to 50 psi. While that level of pressure seems modest when compared with truly high-pressure hydraulic systems operating at a few hundred pounds of pressure, compared to the pump-operated versions of APM systems, these pressures are considerably higher. For those reasons, tubing connections must be more secure and fittings should be chosen accordingly.

High-pressure APM systems are used in a broad variety of installations, servicing just a few plants or hundreds of them, indoors or out. Because of the higher pressures involved, they are capable of moving greater amounts of water into the far reaches of a building. The low-pressure systems are limited in that regard. To implement a high-pressure installation, easy access must be available to the building's water line. As this is not always the case, there are situations where low-pressure versions must be substituted.

Low-Pressure Systems

The low-pressure versions of APM systems use a plastic reservoir as their water source. Pumps are used to draw water and deliver it throughout the tubing network at a pressure of 3 to 15 psi. Some models reach as high as 30 psi, but those are exceptions. The water distribution network used in low-pressure systems is basically the same as that used for high-pressure configurations, except that tubing connections are not as critical. Boca Automation's APM systems use units called pump/reservoir modules (see Figure 12.3).

Figure 12.3: Low-pressure APM system.

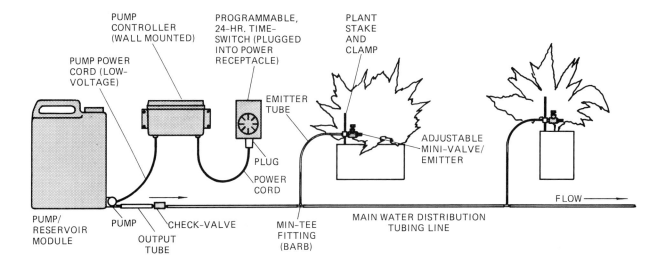

These are integrated devices, with a small pump built into the water container for convenience and economy.

The pump is powered by a controller designed for the purpose, and wires interconnect the two. The pump controller is powered by a 24-hour time switch which is programmed to turn it on at predetermined intervals (usually one to three times per day). Here, again, the 24-hour timer determines only when the system comes on. It is the controller that determines for how long the system is permitted to operate. That duration is normally 10 to 30 seconds. Some of Boca Automation's models have a 24-hour timer integrated into the pump or solenoid valve controller, thereby cutting down on equipment.

Low-pressure versions of this technology are used whenever convenient connections to a water line are not feasible for high-pressure systems. Also, some designers could choose to specify low-pressure systems in certain critical interior areas where the safest type of installation is desired. The greatly reduced pressures of these versions recommends them for such situations, though their irrigation capacity is limited.

Because some attention is required to refill reservoirs, these low-pressure systems cannot be classified as fully automatic. However, techniques are available for automatically refilling reservoirs, thus extending the capabilities of low-pressure installations.

Sequence of Operation

High- and low-pressure APM systems operate on basically the same sequence. It is illustrated graphically in Figure 12.4. The 24-hour time switch runs continuously. At a preset time of day (typically once, twice, or three times per day), it switches the output power on and applies it to the pump or solenoid valve controller. The controller then applies power to the pump or solenoid valve for a mere 10 to 30 seconds, causing water to flow through the distribution tubing network for that short period of time. Water reaches plant locations and passes through emitter tubes, and from the emitters to the planter soil. Emitters are preadjusted for the proper amount of flow for each plant (each has its own emitter). When the system stops, pressure is released from the tubing and remains essentially near zero until the next activation many hours later. ***This provides an important measure of safety for the interior environment. Total pressurization of these systems is no more than about 40 seconds per day in duration.*** Occasional leaks are not to be feared as they are with other technologies. Low-pressure APM systems are the safest kind of irrigation, as flow rates are lower and minimal water pressure puts the least strain on connecting joints. High-pressure versions can achieve this same level of safety through proper design and careful installation.

Figure 12.4: Graphic representation of a sequence of operation of APM systems.

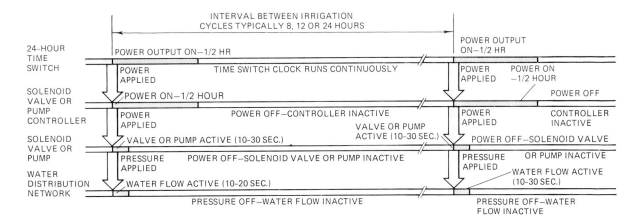

Control Centers

The group of equipment around the source of water is considered the control center. In the case of Mirage II™ and Mirage III™ high-pressure systems, the control center typically involves the actual connection to a cold water line, the shut-off valve, filter, pressure regulator, timer, solenoid valve controller, and water distribution manifold. In the case of low-pressure systems, it involves a pump/reservoir module, the timer, and pump controller. The control center is the heart of the system, providing water and the means for its overall control. Downstream, there are other control devices that perform more subtle chores.

Timers

There are many variations of timers used in APM systems to accommodate different installation needs. There are simple, inexpensive, utilitarian units, while other models lend a more decorative and professional appearance to the installation. Some models simply plug into a wall outlet, others are wired into an electrical junction

box. In most cases, pump or solenoid valve controllers plug directly into the timer. This provides an easy, versatile means of interconnection which can be executed even by the layperson. Neater, more professional-looking installations can be made by using a timer that has all its electrical connections hidden in a junction box. This way, input as well as output power wiring are kept out of view. This procedure is somewhat more difficult, and requires the services of an electrician.

Timers can also be housed in weatherproof cases for outdoor use (Figure 12.5) or for use in damp interior locations, such as a planter box. Light- and heavy-duty models of all varieties are available; their intended use dictates which is the practical choice. The timers used in most current versions of APM systems are simple, electromechanical, 24-hour time switches. Timers are capable of turning the system on as many as twelve times per day. In most installations, however, only two or three waterings daily are necessary.

Boca Automation uses another means of timing for its systems. It is a programmable timer/controller based on X-10 (carrier-frequency, remote control) technology that transmits control signals through the building's electrical power wiring to remote locations, where various APM systems can be activated once or twice daily. This schedule is sufficient for most light- to medium-duty installations. The important feature of this system configuration is that any number of satellite APM systems scattered throughout the building can be controlled remotely as a group from a central location. The concept will be discussed again in following chapters on design, installation, and interfacing with other technologies, particularly home and building automation control systems.

In some models, timers have been designed into the digital control circuits. That makes for a compact control center.

Figure 12.5: All-weather timer.

The configuration has other advantages as well, such as a lower cost. There are, however, good reasons for choosing separate timers and controllers. One has to do with the fact that an independent timer can be used to control supplementary lighting for planters and other accessories at the same time it is operating automated irrigation equipment. That subject will also be dealt with later in the book.

Solenoid Valve Controllers

The purpose of the solenoid valve controller is to provide a timed application of power to the activating element of the system. In keeping with the concepts of APM system technology, the controller activates the system electronically for very short periods, generally 10 to 20 seconds indoors, and occasionally up to 30 or 40 seconds outdoors (in patio and terrace installations, for instance). One of the advantages of low-duty cycles—that is, cycles with very short operating periods and very long dormant periods—is that because of the minimal operating times, electronic and electro-mechanical devices involved (such as pumps and solenoid valves) last a remarkably long time.

Boca Automation has developed a broad variety of controllers to meet a wide range of Mirage II™ and Mirage III™ System installation needs. In virtually every model, the solenoid valve is mounted as an integral part of the controller case, making a compact, easy-to-install unit. Most models are designed for indoor use where conditions are dry, but a few are housed in all-weather cases for outdoor and unusually damp indoor settings. The size and durability of the unit determines the type of duty it can withstand. Light-duty solenoid valve controllers are capable of servicing only small interiorscapes, with relatively few plants (in general, up to 12 or 15). Medium-duty units have heavier electronic equipment and valves to feed water through larger tubing networks, servicing a greater number of plants (up to about 50). Heavy-duty solenoid valve controllers are larger and sturdier. They are able to feed irrigation water into large-diameter tubing and piping, configured in more extensive and complex arrangements. As many as 200 plants can be serviced by some of these larger units. For even more extensive and complex interiorscapes, multiple systems can be installed to care for a single zone. Multi-zone models are also available. Most solenoid valve and pump controllers in Boca Automation's catalog are designed with multiple safety features to prevent accidents.

With a few exceptions, solenoid valve controllers are simply plugged into electromechanical or electronic time switches to provide 115 volts AC (alternating current) input power at programmed, recurring intervals. A couple

Figure 12.6: Different types of solenoid valve controllers.

of models are wired into receptacle boxes for hard-wired connections to time switches. Still other models have timers integrated into the controller's electronic circuits. All controllers that are wall-mounted are considered by many building codes as a type of specialty appliance because they are not integrated in the building structure. The variations provide a broad degree of versatility in meeting installation needs.

Most models have switches to conveniently change irrigation cycle timing. For example, with a simple throw of a switch, the duration of each operating cycle can be changed from 10 to 20 seconds, or from 15 to 30 seconds. Also built into these units is a remote-control port (jack) into which can be plugged a long, manual-control cord or a radio-controlled activator. These allow the operator to turn the system on manually for very short periods while adjusting emitters at remote plant locations. The utility of such an arrangement will become more apparent later when we discuss system installation and start-up.

Pump Controllers

In the same way that solenoid valve controllers activate electrical valves, pump controllers power small pumps and time their operation for very short periods, generally 10 to 20 seconds in interior

applications and 15 to 30 seconds in outdoor systems. The input power cords of these devices are simply plugged into electro-mechanical or electronic time switches (timers) to provide 115 volts AC (alternating current), while output power cords connect to the terminals of pump/reservoir modules. Power output of these units is a safe, 12-volt DC (direct current). On rare occasions, pumps are integrated into the controller for special purposes. Other models provide timers integrated into the controller itself for a compact, space-saving unit. The size and ruggedness of a pump controller has to do with its duty requirements. Larger pumps servicing extensive and complex plantscapes require a heavy-duty controller, while smaller pumps can get by with light-duty controllers. Most models are made for indoor use, but a few are housed in all-weather cases for outdoor use or for indoors in damp locations. Pump controllers are wall-mounted, and these, too, are considered a type of specialty appliance.

All pump controllers provided by Boca Automation have a switch for convenient control of watering cycle duration (10 or 20 seconds for most indoor uses, and 15 or 30 seconds outdoors). They also feature a remote control port for convenient manual operation of the unit from remote locations while setting up.

Pump/Reservoir Modules

These are plastic containers of 2¼-gallon to 32-gallon capacity with self-contained pumps. Functioning as water sources, they are used in conjunction with electronic pump controllers. Actually, the size of the reservoir can be much larger than 32 gallons for special applications. Within some of these containers are mounted submersible pumps of various duty ratings. In other models, pumps are mounted on the outer wall of the reservoir. In all cases, the pump connects to a controller appropriate to its

Figure 12.7: Pump controller with low voltage power cord.

size and duty rating by means of a low-voltage electric power cord. Most of these pumps are operated by application of 12 volts DC (direct current) for short periods of time, in keeping with the pulse-flow concept of APM systems technology. The pumps used in these low-pressure systems are small in size (some miniature), and provide water flow at very low pressures, generally below 12 psi. A few units reach 30 psi for special needs, particularly where plants are at different levels, such as an upstairs/downstairs installation or with hanging planters.

Small, 2¼-gallon pump/reservoirs are inexpensive units capable of caring for up to about 10 or 12 plants. Also available are 5-, 10-, 20-, and 32-gallon pump/reservoir modules to accommodate the needs of larger or drier (as one would find outdoors) installations. Patio installations, for example, require the use of 20- or 32-gallon reservoirs in order to dispense relatively large volumes of water for reasonably long periods of time without refilling. At least six weeks of continuous operation is sought when designing any low-pressure installation.

Figure 12.8: Pump/reservoir modules.

Tubing and Pipes

Tubing and pipes make up the distribution network that carries water from the control center or source location throughout the building area that is to be serviced. This subject can be quite complex and bewildering due to the fact that there is more than one convention determining product sizing. The first is rooted in the nomenclature of the plumbing industry, where pipes are sized by describing their inside diameter. The second comes from the instrumentation and control segments of industry where small-diameter tubing of various descriptions is commonly used. That tubing is sized by describing the outside diameter. The third comes from various industries using hoses as part of a multitude of mechanical devices. Hoses are sized by describing their inside diameter. Installations of APM systems sometimes use a combination of relatively small-diameter tubing, hose, and pipe. Most systems, however, require only tubing. The nomenclature involved should be understood, for it will also be an important factor when we consider fittings, flow-control devices, and accessories later in this chapter. It is something that anyone dealing with APM systems at the design and/or installation levels must work with closely.

The flexible tubing, hoses, and much of the pipe used in the installation of APM systems are plastic, with some metal pipe used on occasion. The reasons for the use of plastics are mainly because of the:

1. Economy of the product

2. Ease of use

3. Growing scarcity of copper pipe and tubing

Copper pipe and tubing are slower to install, thus increasing installation labor costs. Generally cut with a hacksaw or tubing-cutter, deburred, fluxed, and then soldered ("sweat") into fitting sockets, the process is time-consuming and not cost-effective. Flexible plastic tubing, on the other hand, can be cut quickly with utility knives and cutters and connected by means of easy-to-use compression and slip-on barb fittings. It can be bent into fairly tight curves, saving some of the time and cost of installing angle fittings. Plastic pipe is cut with a hacksaw or tubing-cutter, deburred, cleaned, and solvent-welded into fitting sockets. Hose products are used in small quantity for interconnecting manifolds with tubing networks and will not receive much attention in the following discussion. It is recommended that flow velocities in plastic tubing and pipe be kept below 5 feet per second.

Various types of plastics are used in the manufacture of flexible tubing. The main ones adopted for APM system installations are:

• polyethylene (otherwise referred to as PE or "poly" tubing)

• polyvinyl chloride (PVC)

• polybutylene (PB)

Various types of plastic piping are also used, such as:

• polyvinyl chloride (PVC)

• polybutylene (PB)

• chlorinated polyvinyl chloride (CPVC)

Copper is the only type of metallic pipe or tubing used in APM system installations, although that could change if the shortage of copper becomes more acute in this country. It is used mainly where building codes restrict the use of plastics, such as in some union-intensive states where the use of labor-saving materials is closely regulated.

Flexible tubing is manufactured in sizes as small as 1/8"OD (outside diameter), 3/16"OD, and 1/4"OD. These small sizes are commonly called "capillary tubes." Larger tubes are sized in increments of 3/8"OD, 1/2"OD, 5/8"OD, up to 1" or more. Table 12.1 shows a breakdown of flexible tube types and sizes most commonly used in this technology.

Table 12.1

Flexible Tubing Used in APM Systems

Material	Nominal Tubing Size
Polyethylene (PE)	1/4" OD
	3/8" OD
	1/2" OD
Polyvinyl Choride (PVC)	3/16" OD
	1/4" OD
	9/32" OD
	1/2" OD
Polybutylene (PB)*	1/8" ID
	1/4" ID
	1/2" ID

*PB tubing is generally sized by describing inside diameter because the manufacturers cater mostly to plumbing trades accustomed to this nomenclature.

The pipe sizes most commonly used in APM systems are 1/2"ID and 3/4"ID. Table 12.2 details pipe sizes and types.

The relationship between inside and outside tubing and pipe diameters is important because it determines wall thickness, which, in turn, may determine the maximum water pressure to which the product can be subjected. The inside diameter also determines the flow rates and pressure losses water encounters from internal friction. The plastic composition also bears on these factors, as some plastics are slicker than others. Outside and inside tubing diameters also determine the types of fittings that can be used, particularly when dealing with compression types. The subject will be discussed in detail in the next section. Table 12.3 shows the relationship between inside and outside diameters among the commonly used products.

Table 12.2

Pipes Used in APM Systems

Material	Nominal Pipe Size*
Polyvinyl Chloride (PVC)-Sch40	1/2" ID
	3/4" ID
Polybutylene (PB)	1/2" ID
	3/4" ID
Chlorinated Polyvinyl Chloride (CPVC)	1/2"ID
	3/4" ID
Copper—Type L (medium)	1/2" ID
	3/4" ID

*Pipes are also sized by inside diameter because most are used by the plumbing and landscaping irrigation trades accustomed to this nomenclature.

Table 12.3

Tubing and Pipe Diameters and Other Specifications (Common Products Used in Water Distribution Networks).

Tubing or Pipe Description	Nominal Size	Actual Outside Diameter	Actual Inside Diameter	Actual Wall Thickness	Rated Friction Loss/100 ft. at 2 GPM	Color
Polyvinyl Chloride (PVC)	3/16" OD	0.21"	0.165"	0.0225"	N/A	clear
	9/32"OD	0.29"	0.160"	0.065	N/A	black
Sch40	1/2" ID	0.840"	0.620"	0.109"	1.3 psi	white
Polyethylene (PE)	1/4" OD	0.25"	0.16"	0.045"	N/A	black/natural
	3/8" OD	0.375"	0.25"	0.0625"	N/A	black/natural
Polybutylene (PB)	1/8" ID	0.25"	0.126"	0.062"	N/A	grey/blue
	1/4" ID	0.375"	0.25"	0.0625"	N/A	grey/blue
	3/8" ID	0.500"	0.366"	0.067"	20.5 psi	grey/blue
	1/2" ID	0.625	0.491"	0.067"	4.9 psi	grey/blue
	3/4" ID	0.875	0.705"	0.085"	0.9 psi	grey/blue
Copper—Type L	1/2" ID	0.625"	0.545"	0.080"	3.8 psi	copper
	3/4" ID	0.875"	0.785"	0.090"	0.8 psi	copper

There are industry standards for pipe sizes, but such is not the case with small-diameter flexible tubing. It is subject to variations in size from manufacturer to manufacturer, as well as from any given source. This can cause serious problems when it comes to properly connecting them into a network by means of tubing fittings. Disconnections can occur, causing leaks. It is strongly recommended that all tubing and fittings be obtained from the same reputable source of supply. They will have been pretested for compatibility, and purchased only from reliable manufacturers. It cannot be stressed enough how much grief can be avoided by adhering to this advice.

Tubing colors are also important in APM technology. Small-diameter, clear PVC tubing is used in room interiors where it might be visible. Clear tubing easily blends in with the surrounding colors and makes the installation less obtrusive. One of the problems with it, however, is that algae tends to build up in the tubes when they are near windows or other bright, sunlit areas. In that case, black, gray, or opaque tubing of another color should be used to shield the water from algae-promoting rays. This problem is relatively minor, but can cause disruptions in service when the algae clogs small orifices and tubing lines. It usually manifests itself in low-pressure systems that carry dissolved fertilizers in the irrigation water. Tubing that is hidden under carpeting, furniture, or in partitions can be any color. When used outdoors, where it is subject to weathering and exposed to sunlight, tubing is easily degraded unless it has been protected by pigmentation or chemical modifiers that absorb or screen out ultra-violet rays. Tubing products suitable for outdoor use are generally black or gray, as the dark pigmentation helps protect the plastic. Laser Soaker Line™[2] is a special type of plastic tubing made to dispense water along its length, in the manner of a soaker hose.

Tiny holes are drilled every 6 or 12 inches by means of a controlled laser beam. Its size is slightly over 1/4"OD. Laser Soaker Line™ finds specialized applications in APM systems that will be discussed in Chapter 14.

Fittings

Fittings used to connect tubes, hoses, and pipes in APM systems cover a broad variety of types, materials, and sizes, each designed for a specific application. The main categories of types are:

•barb

•compression

•threaded

•soldered

•solvent-welded

•combination

Barb and compression fittings are the ones that are most used in APM technology.

Barb fittings are the easiest to use, but are also considered the least secure. Tubing is simply slipped onto a leg of a fitting, with friction generally relied on to hold the connection securely. Friction is usually not enough, so the legs of most barb fittings are manufactured with ribs and/or notches to grab the softer plastic tubing as securely as possible (see Figure 12.9).

These fittings are made of plastic, copper, or brass. In the manufacture of plastic barbs, nylon, ABS, acetal, PVC, and high-density polyethylene are the most common compositions used. A broad range of fittings can connect tubing from smallest to largest sizes.

Whenever higher water pressures are encountered, clamps are used to secure tubing to barbed fittings. Some crimp over the connection with a special tool, while others exert spring tension or are tightened down with screw adjustments. It is very important that the right type of clamp or crimp ring be used. Most modern building codes permit polybutylene tubing to be

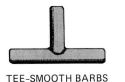
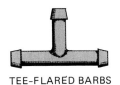

TEE-SMOOTH BARBS   TEE-FLARED BARBS   ELL-RIDGED BARBS   STRAIGHT CONNECTOR-NOTCHED BARBS

Figure 12.9: Several types of barb fittings.

MALE ADAPTER-RIDGED BARB   ELL-RIDGED BARBS   MALE ADAPTER-BEADED BARB

used in plumbing systems with barb fitting connections. The stipulation, however, is that authorized fittings (copper or brass) be used and that properly applied crimp rings secure the connections.

In applications where lower water pressures are encountered, barbed connections can be secured with adhesives, selected for their holding power as well as their degree of fitting/tubing interface, or compatibility with the materials being bonded.

Compression fittings are made to exert a clamping action on the tubing after it is slipped into the fitting socket. The clamping effect is accomplished by tightening down a nut, either by hand or wrench depending on the type. The nut crimps a gripping collar onto the softer tubing, just enough to hold securely. Properly designed plastic compression fittings are available that require only a hand tightening to provide secure connections (see Figure 12.10). Various means of clamping down and gripping the tubing are designed into the products, with each manufacturer having its own method. Some types work better than others with a given type of tubing, therefore the proper fitting must be selected. These fittings are rated to withstand hydraulic pressures of at least two hundred psi, so secure clamping is critical. Keep in mind,

however, that APM systems operate in a pressure range well below maximum ratings.

Compression fittings can be made of plastic or brass and can connect dissimilar materials. For example, plastic fittings can be used to interconnect various plastic tubes, as well as aluminum or copper. Brass fittings can also interconnect copper, as well as plastic tubing. The types of plastics used are similar to the materials that are injection molded into barb fittings. With most compression fittings, soft, flexible tubing must first be supported by a brass insert to prevent wall collapse when the nut is tightened. Many sizes of compression fittings are available to accommodate a tubing range of about 1/8"OD (outside diameter) to 3/4"OD. Most compression fittings are sized according to the outside diameter of the tubing lines they are to connect. Some manufacturers that deal with industries used to pipe sizes (inner diameter specifications) will naturally market their products sized with that nomenclature. Such is the case with plumbing or irrigation-oriented product lines. When crossing fields of technology, dual sizing methods will be encountered. That is frequently the case in products used for APM systems, where parts have been borrowed from varied technologies. Boca

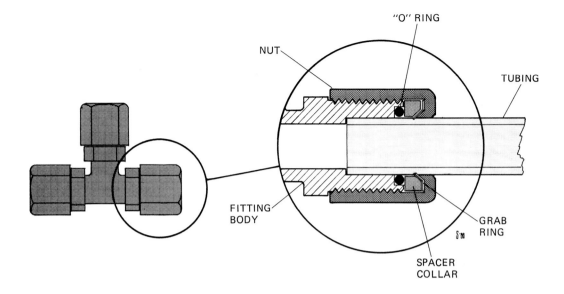

Figure 12.10: Typical compression fitting.

NUT

"O" RING

TUBING

FITTING BODY

SPACER COLLAR

GRAB RING

Automation has attempted to simplify the situation by cataloging parts under a common nomenclature of OD and ID specs.

Threaded fittings used in APM system installations are generally hybrids, combining one or more legs (or branches) that are threaded with a standard pipe or hose thread, and the other (or others) a compression, slip, or barb connector. Such fittings are commonly used to interconnect a pipe system with a tubing system; for example, connecting flexible tubing to a PVC sprinkler pipe. Threaded fittings are also used to adapt between fitting types. A tee fitting might have a center branch molded with a pipe thread, onto which is screwed another fitting having a barb connector for small-bore tubes.

Pipe threads are either male or female. Male fittings have their threads on the outer circumference, while female fittings have their threads on the inner circumference (see Figure 12.11). Threaded fittings are made of plastic or brass. The better quality plastic fittings are molded from the harder materials, such as nylon, ABS, or acetal. There are many types of threaded fittings to fit a wide variety of requirements.

Soldered fittings, or "sweat" fittings, are used only infrequently in APM technology. They are mainly used to connect an automatic plant care system to a building's water line. A tee fitting is soldered into the water line and a branch is extended from it to the irrigation system controls. Soldered fittings are made of copper and brass.

Solvent-welded fittings, used mainly in sprinkler system pipe, provide a quick means of connection. The bond is permanent, and when done properly, is water tight. Solvent-welded fittings are also referred to as "slip" fittings. The pipe is simply slipped into fitting sockets after appropriate solvent has been applied to the two surfaces to be connected. It actually dissolves some of the fitting and pipe-surface plastic, and when dried, rehardens the joint. These fittings are made of PVC and are used with PVC pipe. In APM systems, these inexpensive materials are used primarily outdoors in patio systems and indoors in planter boxes and other non-critical areas as manifolds, distributing water to many plants in the same area.

There are many varieties and configurations of fittings, each having its own nomenclature. The illustrations shown in Appendix B depict the various types used in installations of this technology. As you'll see in that summary, the list is quite extensive. Of course, only some are applied in each installation.

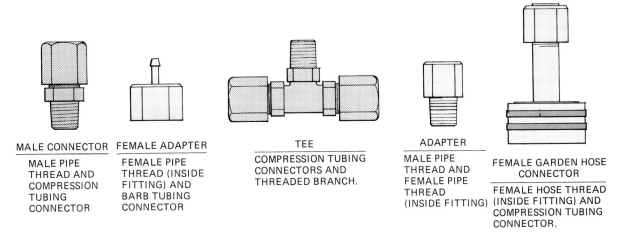

MALE CONNECTOR

MALE PIPE
THREAD AND
COMPRESSION
TUBING
CONNECTOR

FEMALE ADAPTER

FEMALE PIPE
THREAD (INSIDE
FITTING) AND
BARB TUBING
CONNECTOR

TEE

COMPRESSION TUBING
CONNECTORS AND
THREADED BRANCH.

ADAPTER

MALE PIPE
THREAD AND
FEMALE PIPE
THREAD
(INSIDE FITTING)

FEMALE GARDEN HOSE
CONNECTOR

FEMALE HOSE THREAD
(INSIDE FITTING) AND
COMPRESSION TUBING
CONNECTOR.

Fitting Specifications

Fittings are specified by type and by the sizes of tubing or pipe that they interconnect, as well as by the way each end connects. Take tee fittings, for example. They are unique in that they can accommodate three connections. The straight part of a tee fitting is called the **run**. The leg off to the side is called the **branch** (see Figure 12.12). Such a fitting is specified by listing the sizes of the two ends of the run first, followed by the size of the branch.

For example, ⅜"OD (outer diameter) tube x ⅜"OD tube x ¼"OD tube could be the specification for a compression fitting. The ⅜" legs are connected to the main tubing, providing flow straight through the fitting (the run). The ¼" leg connects to a smaller side branch line. In another example we have a ¼"OD barb x ¼"OD barb x ¼"MPT. In this case, the run consists of barb fittings that slip into ¼"OD tubing, while the branch is a ¼" male pipe thread that would screw into an adapter fitting of some sort, providing connection to another part. The same size and type connectors all around a tee fitting of ¼" compression, for example, would simply be specified as a ¼" compression tee, or ¼" union tee-compression type. Similar expressions would be used for other types of fittings. Elbows with ¼" compression fittings on both ends would be called a ¼" ell

compression fitting and would be suitable for interconnecting 1/4"OD tubing. All compression fittings are specified in terms of the outside diameter of the tubing to which they connect. Barb fittings are sized according to outside diameters by some sources, and according to inside diameters by others. The larger fittings generally specify the latter, as that terminology is common in the plumbing markets they usually service. Careful attention must always be paid to the tubing and pipe diameters (outside and inside) so as to be able to choose the proper fitting.

The sizing of pipe threads is fairly straightforward. Male pipe thread sizes are designated XX" MPT (male pipe tapered thread) or XX" MNPT (male national pipe tapered thread). An example of the spec for a male pipe thread would read 1/2"MPT, possibly referring to the branch of a tee fitting or one end of an elbow fitting or male adapter (see Appendix B). Female pipe

Figure 12.11: Five typical threaded fittings.

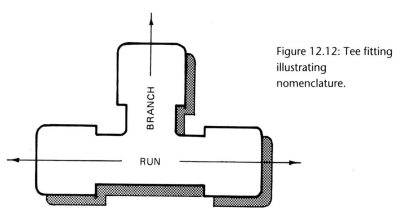

Figure 12.12: Tee fitting illustrating nomenclature.

thread specifications are similar. They are designated as XX" FPT or XX" FNPT. Alternate designations for pipe threads are sometimes encountered as Mipt or Fipt (male iron pipe thread or female iron pipe thread). Keep in mind that threaded pipes (generally iron) are not used in this type of work—only fittings (plastic and brass) and connectors that use pipe threads.

Flow Control Devices

As implied by their name, these devices control the flow in the water distribution networks of APM systems. Among them are shut-off valves, backflow preventers, check valves, vacuum breakers, flow reducers, and pressure regulators. They will be quickly and simply described in this section, along with their functional task.

Shut-off or *stop valves* are used in high-pressure systems at the irrigation branch input, or connection, to the building's cold water line. Its purpose is to disconnect the irrigation branch from the rest of the plumbing in case of trouble or disuse. These are generally globe-type valves, referring to the configuration of the moving part of the valve that cuts off flow. Shut-off valves are placed in-line with various means of connection—some with threaded fittings,

some with barb fittings, and some with compression or soldered fittings.

Check valves are small devices installed in-line at various critical locations in the water distribution system to permit flow only in one direction. Although there are several types of check valves in common use, the only ones used in APM systems are spring-loaded types. They employ a spring to close off flow through the device when the forward-motivating pressure has been released (pump stops or solenoid valve closes). Forward pressure opens the check valve for flow, but when that has ceased, the spring closes it against backward (or reverse) flow, or any additional forward flow. Water can thus flow in one direction and only when sufficient pressure is applied (see Figure 12.13). Check valves are the hydraulic equivalent of diodes used in electronics.

In installations where tubing runs at various levels, without check valve control water drains by gravity to the lowest levels when pressure is released. Plants at the bottom of the installation will continue to get drainoff even after system shut-down. Overwatering results, unless a check valve in the tubing line prevents it. Check valves also prevent unwanted forward flow when the system is dormant. Figure 12.14 is a

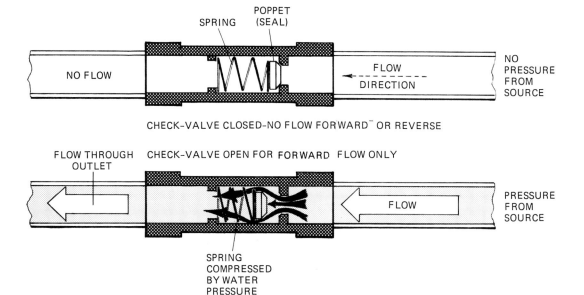

Figure 12.13: Check valve operation.

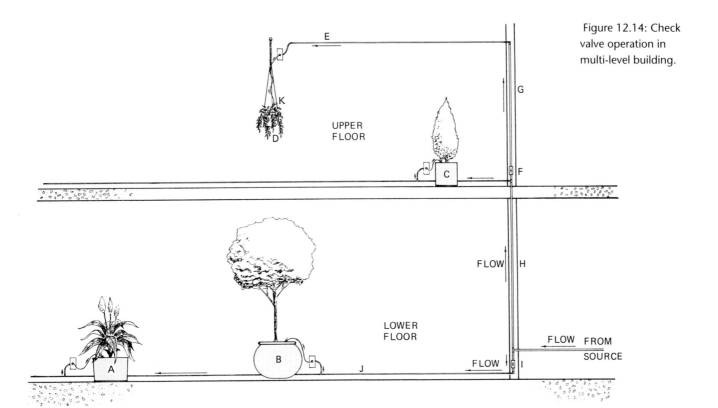

fairly complex example of how check valves can closely control the flow of water to make it do what is desired, when it is desired.

Imagine the figure without check valves at positions F, I, and K. It is unimpeded during the brief operating cycle in which water flows to the plants only through tubing. In reaching up to the ceiling of the second floor, a distance of perhaps 16 or 18 feet, the water flows against gravity, being pushed by the pressure behind it. As the irrigation cycle is completed, water pressure drops to nearly zero within the tubing network. That permits the forces of gravity to take over. Water filling the portions of tubing at E are most subject to movement as that is the highest point in the system. From E the water will drain forward, down into the hanging planter at D. At the same time, some of the water from E and all of it filling the riser tube (two floors of it) will drain backward down the tube into planter C and also further down into planters A and B. Remember, unless it is prevented from doing so, water tends to flow to the lowest

point in the system. The result is flooded planters, and possibly flooring as well. Another unwelcome result is that the entire tubing system will have been purged of water. That means it must be refilled during the next operating cycle before anything can reach the planters.

To solve these problems, we find ways to foil Mother Nature. Check valves, when properly chosen, placed, and oriented, can hold water against the forces of gravity. In this example we would install spring-loaded check valves at strategic positions in the tubing network. One would be placed at position I, oriented with its one-way flow path pointing down. That permits flow to the plants being serviced on the lower floor, yet prevents backdrain into those plants after pressure has been released. Another check valve would be installed at position F. That is just above the branch servicing grounded planters on the upper floor. Its orientation has the one-way flow path pointing upward, so water can flow through it to point E and beyond. Being above it, that check valve can effectively prevent

183

backdrain into planter C. A miniature check valve is placed in the small tubing line leading down the macramé hanger to planter D. Its one-way orientation is down, so that water can flow to the plant, yet the spring tension will sufficiently hold backflow from the planter when pressurization has ceased.

These functions also serve to keep water trapped in the tubing lines between watering cycles. That concept is very important in APM systems, as empty tubing must be refilled during the next operating cycle before it can irrigate anything. Air must also be purged from the tubes as they refill. This takes time, and as operating times are very short in this technology, it is possible that the system could spend all of

its operating cycle simply refilling tubes—unless we design check valves into the network at critical locations to prevent this from happening.

Other gravity-flow problems are frequently encountered that are simpler to solve, but they, too, would utilize check valve flow controls. Figure 12.15 illustrates a common problem. Decorative plants are frequently placed on different levels in the same room. As water tends to seek its own level by means of the natural laws of physics, any water in the highest tubing would tend to drain down to the lowest point, including into the lower planter. That again causes overwatering of plants in the lower levels and the probable underwatering of others at the upper levels. By installing a miniature check valve in the small tubing line at position C, water would be permitted to flow to planter B, yet its gravitational backflow would be blocked from planter B to planter A. The use of check valves will be discussed further in the chapter covering systems design.

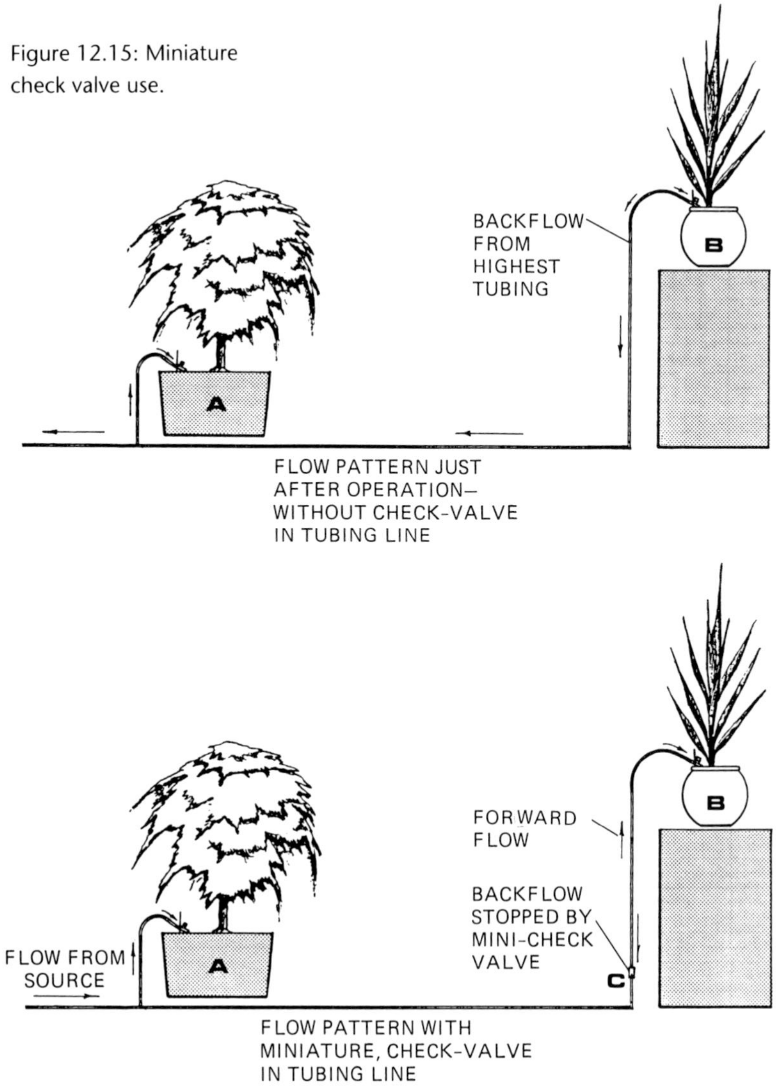

Another type of flow control device used in APM system installations is called a **vacuum breaker** or **backflow preventer**. It is a type of check valve used in high-pressure systems to prevent water in the irrigation tubing from being sucked back into the building's main water supply, thereby preventing possible contamination. This might be particularly important if fertilizer injection was being used or if dirt was allowed to enter the tubing lines through emitters. This protection is most often mandated by local building codes, which call for such devices to be placed in the system at the connection between the main water supply and the irrigation branch. We have all seen outdoor hose connections fitted with little cylinders on the hose bibb outlet. Those are backflow preventers. The hose connectors are just one type. Others connect in-line with other pipe fittings. Some versions are meant to be subjected to

Figure 12.15: Miniature check valve use.

BACKFLOW FROM HIGHEST TUBING

A

FLOW PATTERN JUST AFTER OPERATION— WITHOUT CHECK-VALVE IN TUBING LINE

B

FORWARD FLOW

BACKFLOW STOPPED BY MINI-CHECK VALVE

FLOW FROM SOURCE

A

C

FLOW PATTERN WITH MINIATURE, CHECK-VALVE IN TUBING LINE

B

constant high pressure; others are for use at intermittent pressure. These factors determine their heft and construction, as well as their position in the water distribution network.

Flow reducers are small natural rubber or synthetic rubber discs that fit into other flow control devices (such as solenoid valves) to lower the flow rate of the system. Because interior plants need relatively small amounts of water for their sustenance, the supply lines are frequently oversized for the need at hand and permit too much water to flow. Supplementary controls, such as flow reducers, bring flow rates down to more manageable levels. Some types are designed to maintain a constant flow rate through broad fluctuations of input pressure. These pressure-compensating types are desirable in APM system installations.

Water pressure regulators are also used to bring pressure and flow rates down to manageable levels. Keeping in mind that with all other factors being equal, the higher the system water pressure, the greater the flow rate. This concept is illustrated in Figure 12.17. In other words, as water pressure increases, so does the flow.

Although the figure demonstrates this

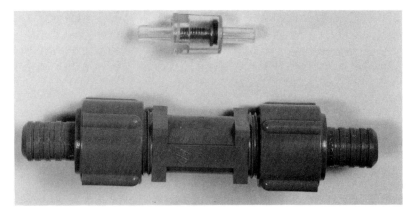

relationship in 1/2"ID (interior diameter) tubing, it follows essentially the same with other tubing sizes and types, but at different levels. The input water pressure from building supply lines is in the range of 55 to 75 psi for most city water systems. That supplies the motivating force for quite a bit of water to flow through the system. Even by reducing the time of flow down to very short periods, as we do in APM technology, the volume is frequently not restricted enough. Flow reducers can be used in some cases, and pressure regulators in others.

There are basically two types of pressure regulators: adjustable and fixed. The adjustable type permits the regulation of input pressures to provide a range of output pressures. The more common types permit

Figure 12.16: Two commonly used check valves.

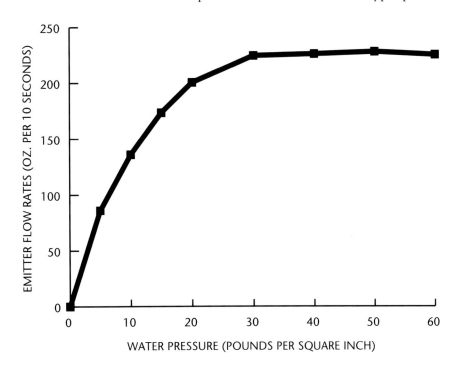

Figure 12.17: Pressure/flow relationship in 1/2" PB tubing.

an input pressure as high as 300 psi, and output pressures can be regulated between 25 and 75 psi. The fixed regulators are preset at the factory for output pressures of 6, 10, 13, 15, 20, 25, 30, 35, and 45 psi.

Emitters

Emitters issue the flow of water to plants. Some are adjustable, some fixed in flow rates. *Adjustable* emitters permit the fine-tuning of the volume of water going to individual potted plants. Boca Automation's APM systems use a miniature, adjustable valve as the emitter in most installations (see Figure 12.18). It permits very fine adjustments to be made at the plant location so that during each operating cycle, the plant can receive as little as a few drops of water or as much as several ounces.

The actual range of flow rates with any emitter will depend on the water pressure and flow rate of the system at the emitter location. That is not the same as input (or source) water pressure. Many things happen to the water in going from the irrigation branch input to the emitter locations, particularly in extensive installations. Every foot of tubing the water goes through creates a drag on it due to friction along the tubing walls and intermolecular friction within the fluid itself. Every bend and fitting connection does the same. The result is a gradual reduction in flow rate; the farther down the line the water goes, the lower the rate. Each active outlet along the way reduces it even more. The data in Table 12.4 illustrate the range of flow rates from adjustable, mini-valve/emitters at various pressure levels. It gives a clear indication of the precision watering capability in this technology. As little as 2 drops of water can be dispensed during a 10-second operating cycle. That makes the system useful for maintaining dry-loving plants. By adjusting the same emitter to its fully-open condition, as much as 10.5 ounces can be made to flow during a 10-second irrigation cycle (at 65 psi), making it useful for large plants in need of more generous doses of water. Most decorative, containerized plants require adjustment on the low end of the range.

Another type of emitter used in APM systems is the *Laser Soaker Line™*, previously described in the section on subterranean systems in Chapter Ten, and in this chapter, under tubing. Its use in this

Figure 12.18: Boca Automation's miniature adjustable valve/emitter.

Table 12.4

Emitter Profile—Flow Rates From Boca Automation's Adjustable Mini-Valve Emitters at Various Pressure Levels

Water Pressure	Flow Rates		
	Emitter Almost Closed	Emitter About 1/2 Open	Emitter Fully Open
3.3 psi	2 drops/10 seconds	N/A	4.0oz/10 seconds
10 psi	2 drops/10 seconds	1.5oz/10 seconds	4.0oz/10 seconds
20 psi	2 drops/10 seconds	2.0oz/10 seconds	5.5oz/10 seconds
30 psi	2 drops/10 seconds	2.5oz/10 seconds	7.0oz/10 seconds
40 psi	2 drops/10 secondss	3.0oz/10 seconds	7.7oz/10 seconds
50 psi	2 drops/10 seconds	3.5oz/10 seconds	8.6oz/10 seconds
55 psi	2 drops/10 seconds	3.5oz/10 seconds	9.2oz/10 seconds
65 psi	2 drops/10 seconds	N/A	10.5oz/10 seconds

Source: Boca Automation, Inc.

technology occurs mainly in planter boxes where the plants are grown directly in the ground and are fairly close together. It is also used to form a loop around the base of trees and other large plants to distribute water more evenly in their containers (see Figure 12.19). In APM systems, Laser Soaker Line™ is generally used in conjunction with an adjustable, in-line valve to vary flow rates. With this regulation, it is capable of a wide flow range (see Table 12.5).

A third type of emitter used with APM systems is called a **fountain plate**. Fountain plates are installed in the wall next to a planter and are fed through a water distribution line installed within the wall partition. The stream of water traverses the space between wall and plant container in the manner of a small fountain, without the use of a tubing conduit. It has many applications in heavily trafficked public areas indoors and out (see Figure 12.20), particularly where vandals are likely to destroy tubing lines.

Accessories

Manifolds

Water distribution manifolds are an important accessory in irrigating interior

planter boxes with APM technology, as well as outdoors in patio installations. They provide a multiple connection for emitter tubes—those short, small-diameter tubes reaching the plant and fitted with adjustable, mini-valve/emitters (see Figure 12.21). Manifolds are available factory-prepared to save time and labor, but they can also be assembled on-site using 1/2" PVC sprinkler pipe, tees, elbows, and special connectors called quad outlets, which

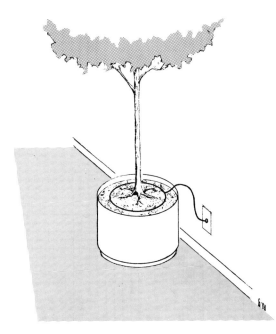

Figure 12.19: Laser Soaker tubing used around the root system of large plants.

Table 12.5

Emitter Profile—Flow Rates From Laser Soaker Line™ at Variable Pressures (6" Hole Spacing)

Water Pressure	Flow Rate per Foot	
	Oz./20 Sec.	Oz./10 Sec.
5 psi	0.833 oz./ft.	0.417 oz./ft.
10 psi	1.25 oz./ft.	0.625 oz./ft.
20 psi	1.75 oz./ft.	0.875 oz./ft.
30 psi	2.08 oz./ft.	1.042 oz./ft.
40 psi	2.33 oz./ft.	1.167 oz./ft.
50 psi	2.58 oz./ft.	1.292 oz./ft.
55 psi	2.58 oz./ft.	1.292 oz./ft.

Source: Boca Automation, Inc.

Figure 12.20: Fountain plate in use.

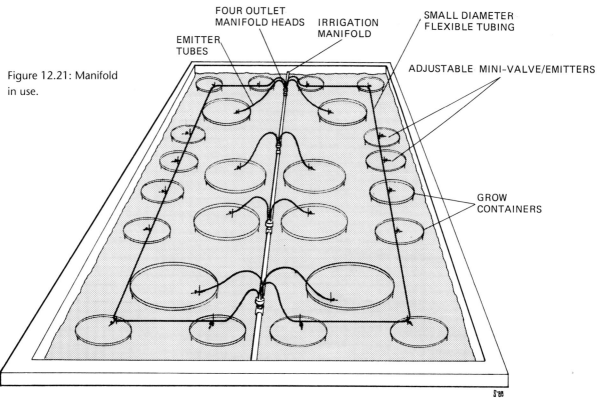

FOUR OUTLET
MANIFOLD HEADS   IRRIGATION
MANIFOLD

EMITTER
TUBES

SMALL DIAMETER
FLEXIBLE TUBING

ADJUSTABLE MINI-VALVE/EMITTERS

GROW
CONTAINERS

Figure 12.21: Manifold
in use.

Figure 12.22: Special
irrigation receptacle in
use (left), and plugged
(right).

accept up to four tubing lines (slipped onto barbed nipples). These will be discussed more fully later in this book.

Irrigation Receptacles

Special irrigation receptacles have been developed to provide convenient access to water distribution lines running within wall partitions in APM systems installed as part of the building infrastructure (integrated). They are installed in wall partitions much the same way that TV antenna plates or phone jacks are installed. Connections are made to the water distribution tubing lines threaded through the interior of the wall. Into these special irrigation receptacles are plugged small emitter-tube assemblies that are routed to the potted plants on the floor and furniture nearby (see Figure 12.22).

Generally at least one irrigation receptacle is installed on each wall for convenient access to all plants in a room. If necessary, receptacles can be installed in ceiling panels, movable partitions, work stations, kitchen counter tops, and vanity tops. Inactive receptacles are simply plugged until needed. Irrigation receptacles need not be placed wherever plants will be located. Emitter tubes can be installed to carry water as far as 50 feet from the receptacle, hidden around the perimeter of rooms. A small receptacle can service as many as 10 to 12 plants.

Emitter Stabilizers

Emitter stabilizers are used to hold emitters in place in the plant container. It is a plastic stake that is poked into the soil and holds small emitter tubing in a notch at the top.

Packaged Systems

Boca Automation offers a variety of pre-packaged APM systems that contain all of the equipment, fittings, and accessories needed to meet a variety of installation requirements. In most cases, installations must be customized by purchasing equipment and parts individually, but packaged kits make it easier to purchase system components. Everything in them is preselected for compatibility, making them a convenient choice for the do-it-yourselfer.

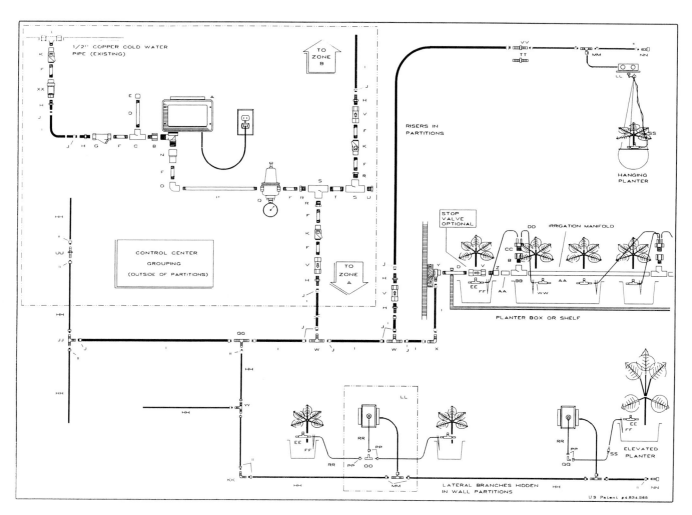

Figure 12.23: Typical tubing layouts using barb insert fittings with crimp rings.

THIRTEEN

Automated Precision Micro-Irrigation in Various Building Types

Until recently, interiorscapers, interior designers, architects, real estate owners and managers, as well as homeowners, thought of technical aids mainly in terms of systems for landscape plants outdoors and in open, public areas of building interiors. Only agricultural and landscape irrigation systems have been available for use indoors, and the adaptations have lacked control, as well as the aesthetic sophistication required to meet the special needs of furnished, residential, and commercial areas. Automated precision micro-irrigation (APM) systems now provide the basic technology and aesthetic attributes around which comprehensive, automated plant-care installations can be designed. The technology is also available for installation in existing buildings, where the limitations may stem from practical installation and cost considerations. Combined with other technologies when necessary, the ideal of complete interior coverage can be realized. This chapter will discuss how particular spaces can benefit from this state-of-the-art building and facility management technology.

Commercial Buildings and Facilities

It is within commercial sectors that automated building management systems have the greatest economic impact. That is particularly true of APM systems for interiors. Outdoor sprinklers have permitted the design of extensive and beautiful landscaping around commercial and institutional buildings, minimizing concern about the cost and bother of manual irrigation for turf and foliage plantings. Most extensive landscaping, in fact, would not have been possible to maintain cost-effectively today were it not for automatic sprinkler systems. In a similar way, much of the beauty and commercial benefit of indoor plantings has been passed over for lack of a viable maintenance technology. Sprinkler and drip systems have been applied to planters in open common areas, giving many projects the impetus needed to make these interior landscapes practical. Most other areas of the building have been neglected, however, because of the absence of practical means to cope with their special demands. APM systems fill that void.

Because of the wide variety of spaces involved, commercial buildings and facilities present many challenges to the designer of interior irrigation systems. The one thing all spaces have in common is the need for a hidden, highly controlled system for dispensing water to scattered plants, most of which are housed in small containers. In some cases, one technology can't do it all, and so combinations must be installed. This is particularly true of retrofit (add-on) projects, where the cost of installing some of the hidden tubing for a central system may be prohibitive, and non-automatic technologies (such as self-watering containers) must then be utilized to care for a portion of the installation.

Because of its advanced attributes, APM systems can be the main source of irrigation for most commercial projects; in many situations, nothing else is needed for complete building coverage. In other cases, independent systems can be installed in a needy portion of a building to service a restaurant, bank, office, fitness center, or other specialized area. Building developers who want to take full advantage of automatic interior irrigation would have an integrated version of APM systems designed into the project. That provides coverage for all public areas as well as all furnished tenant areas. The illustration in Figure 13.1 shows one way APM systems can be integrated into the structure of a building with branches reaching every corner, if needed.

Boca Automation calls these integrated versions Mirage III Systems™.[1] They feature special irrigation receptacles installed on the surface of walls, ceilings, and cabinets of rooms, much like television antenna plates or phone jacks, to provide convenient access to irrigation water distribution lines threaded through wall and ceiling spaces. Into these receptacles are plugged emitter tube assemblies, small-diameter tubing which is routed to potted plants on the floor and furniture of the room. An adjustable mini-valve emitter is provided at each plant for fine flow control. Figure 13.2 illustrates how an integrated APM system might be laid out on each floor of a commercial (or residential) building. Extensions from this basic layout can generally be made to reach portions of another floor or exterior areas, such as decks, patios, and balconies. Branches can also be designed to care for planters in open public areas of the building.

Office Buildings

Office buildings harbor very diverse plant care requirements. Because there are many types of this commercial real estate, the

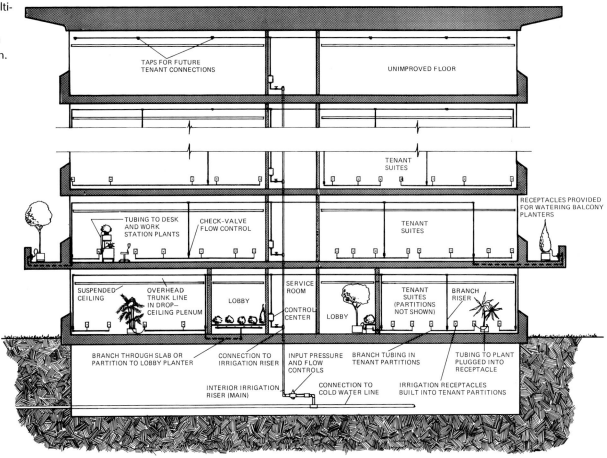

Figure 13.1: A multistory building showing irrigation system distribution.

TAPS FOR FUTURE TENANT CONNECTIONS

UNIMPROVED FLOOR

TENANT SUITES

TENANT SUITES

RECEPTACLES PROVIDED FOR WATERING BALCONY PLANTERS

TUBING TO DESK AND WORK STATION PLANTS

CHECK-VALVE FLOW CONTROL

SUSPENDED CEILING

OVERHEAD TRUNK LINE IN DROP-CEILING PLENUM

LOBBY

SERVICE ROOM

CONTROL CENTER

LOBBY

TENANT SUITES (PARTITIONS NOT SHOWN)

BRANCH RISER

BRANCH THROUGH SLAB OR PARTITION TO LOBBY PLANTER

CONNECTION TO IRRIGATION RISER

INPUT PRESSURE AND FLOW CONTROLS

BRANCH TUBING IN TENANT PARTITIONS

TUBING TO PLANT PLUGGED INTO RECEPTACLE

INTERIOR IRRIGATION RISER (MAIN)

CONNECTION TO COLD WATER LINE

IRRIGATION RECEPTACLES BUILT INTO TENANT PARTITIONS

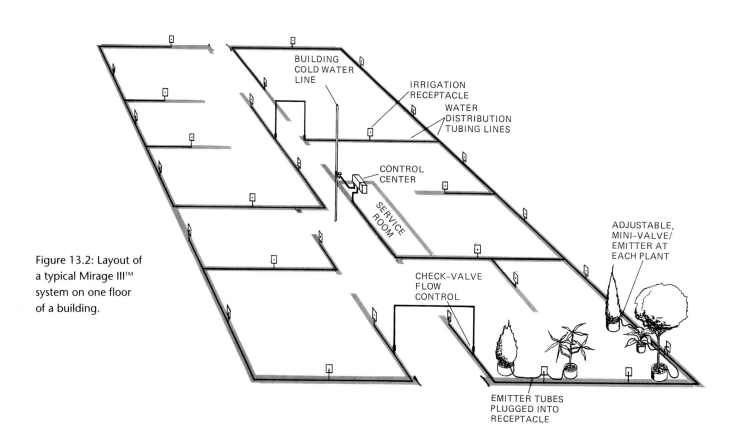

Figure 13.2: Layout of a typical Mirage III™ system on one floor of a building.

BUILDING COLD WATER LINE

IRRIGATION RECEPTACLE

WATER DISTRIBUTION TUBING LINES

CONTROL CENTER

SERVICE ROOM

ADJUSTABLE, MINI-VALVE/ EMITTER AT EACH PLANT

CHECK-VALVE FLOW CONTROL

EMITTER TUBES PLUGGED INTO RECEPTACLE

192   AUTOMATED PRECISION MICRO-IRRIGATION IN VARIOUS BUILDING TYPES ramifications are extensive. All office buildings have an entryway and foyer or lobby/reception area. Not all of these public areas have plants. Many are stark to the point of being uninviting, devoid of any warmth or human appeal. Others are constructed with built-in planters to give a natural, softer look to the building's "greeting place," beautifying the space and providing the tenants or visitors with a welcome, relaxed feeling as they come in the main entrance. Some architects go further, and design extensively verdant public areas that carry traffic through the building or provide rest or dining areas. Many of these are atria and promenades. Planter boxes and pits are used extensively with freestanding containerized plants rounding out the interior landscape. The more enlightened architects, developers, interior landscapers, and property/facilities managers have been specifying some form of plant care automation for these installations to provide a cost-effective management tool as well as to help assure the preservation of interiorscape beauty.

Reliable plant maintenance services are not always at hand. Because sprinkler, subterranean, and various configurations of drip systems were the only technologies available until recently, they were the ones most specified. From a practical standpoint, these versions of auto-interigation can be quite acceptable for many common area planters, but only if they are designed, installed, and used properly. These installations are primarily standard irrigation systems with slight variations to accommodate the interior setting. The source is either city water or a proprietary well. Simpler systems are merely branches of the outdoor sprinkler network, generally set up as a separate timed zone to keep the irrigation cycle as short as is practical with the timer available.

More complex installations in large buildings have their own interior systems.

Controls are installed outdoors or in a core area of the building, with pipe running underground from there to the planter locations. At the input there is a shut-off valve, a backflow preventer, a filter, a pressure regulator, a solenoid valve, and a time-clock/controller. At the output end of the system can be found sprinkler heads, drip emitters, bubbler heads, or subterranean emitters, such as ooze pipes. In the more complex system designs, the latter is a multi-zone type able to control a number of irrigation zones sequentially. Because of the large volumes of water coursing through these systems, properly drained planter boxes are a necessary preventative measure. In spite of their shortcomings, these automated, agriculturally based systems are capable of considerable labor savings.[2] Their use is still the exception rather than the rule in commercial building projects, but the application rate is increasing as more architects and interior landscapers become more comfortable with their design, use, and benefits.

Aside from common areas, many spaces in commercial buildings have been neglected because refined technologies for furnished area service were not available. That has changed with the advent of APM systems, and the building owner or manager now has the option to provide automated plant care to tenants—a cost-saving amenity for the tenant that also yields a profit for building management. In times of slack commercial real estate markets, this gives the more progressive developer a leg-up on competition. In many large office buildings, most of the decorative plants are not in the first-floor lobby but are upstairs in the furnished suites. That is where most of the technical assistance is needed for their maintenance. APM systems can now provide service in small office facilities or modern office skyscrapers.

The most cost-effective way of incorporating APM systems into buildings of this type is to integrate them into the framework during construction. The source is usually the city water supply, with a special irrigation branch (or branches) tapped off of the main water line. Multi-story buildings are accommodated by installing a separate, independent system on each floor of the building (see Figure 13.1). (The details of this arrangement will be discussed more fully in the chapters on design and installation.) The controls are installed in the core area of each floor and tubing distributed from there through the partitions of the individual office suites, or restaurants, shops, etc. Control can frequently be integrated with the building's computerized energy-management system so that time switches are not necessary to energize the individual APM system branches.

Construction of office buildings is mostly done on speculation, with only part of the building leased prior to completion. During periods of over-construction and excess real estate inventory, banks and other construction lenders require larger portions of the building to be pre-leased before they will grant loans. Under the best of circumstances, seldom does a new building face more than 50% or 60% occupancy when it is completed. For these reasons, some developers are reluctant to expend the capital for automation or tenant amenities of any kind that might have to wait years for initial use. Partial installations of automated plant-care systems are made in these instances.

Low-cost *skeleton* installations are made in building areas that will be vacant. These consist of control centers (timers, solenoid valve controllers, and input fittings) and a roughed-in piping network of main lines installed overhead in what will become the drop-ceiling plenum (see Figure 13.3). These pipes are fitted with plugged outlets for later connection to tubing networks to service office suites when they are finally

constructed in the vacant space. Other vacant areas of the building are handled in much the same way. For example, those that would eventually house banks, shops, restaurants, or any commercial establishment likely to use live plants in their decor would benefit by having an automated irrigation system available for their use.

Pre-leased areas would be designed with APM systems integrated into their partitions, with special irrigation receptacles mounted on walls, floors, ceilings, and/or built-in cabinetry of the rooms, ready to plug into with emitter tubing that would run to the various container plants nearby. Keeping in mind that decorative plants do not have to be placed next to, or even near the irrigation receptacles, the tenant space can be designed and constructed without knowledge of final decorator schemes and still realize the full benefit from the system. Plants can be placed anywhere and can be moved at any time.

Building developers may pre-install APM systems into their projects and offer automated plant care to tenants as an option with additional monthly charges added to the lease arrangement. In turn, the tenant benefits from a potential savings of between 30% to 60% on the cost of contract plant care services. Need for contractor visits can be extended from every week or 10 days to every two, or even three weeks. That's quite a savings in labor for the contractor, and a good bit of this should be passed on to the customer. Unfortunately, many interiorscapers are still hostile to all manner of modern irrigation techniques, and will offer excuses for not being able to extend their maintenance cycles in spite of advanced expertise to the contrary.

Nevertheless, enlightened, cooperative interiorscapers can always be found who will work with automated systems. They enhance their professional image by being able to work with state-of-the-art plant care

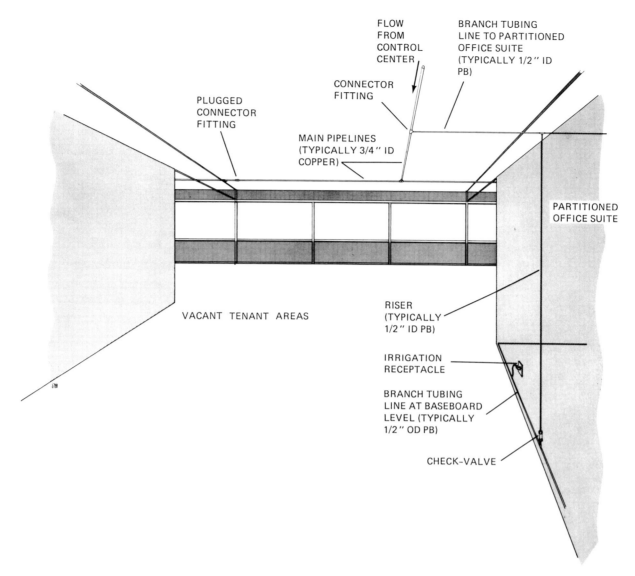

PLUGGED
CONNECTOR
FITTING

FLOW
FROM
CONTROL
CENTER

CONNECTOR
FITTING

BRANCH TUBING
LINE TO PARTITIONED
OFFICE SUITE
(TYPICALLY 1/2" ID
PB)

MAIN PIPELINES
(TYPICALLY 3/4" ID
COPPER)

PARTITIONED
OFFICE SUITE

VACANT TENANT AREAS

RISER
(TYPICALLY
1/2" ID PB)

IRRIGATION
RECEPTACLE

BRANCH TUBING
LINE AT BASEBOARD
LEVEL (TYPICALLY
1/2" OD PB)

CHECK-VALVE

Figure 13.3: Skeleton installation in vacant areas of a building.

systems. Some developers have provided supplementary plant care services for their tenants by hiring interior landscape people to work in-house. The building services can then include plant leasing and maintenance along with other amenities. Building management companies and building maintenance contractors can do the same for their clients. APM systems make these complementary real estate services practical.

Another plan for including APM systems in commercial projects involves the building owner charging the first tenant a one-time charge for the cost of installation in that office suite. The tenant can recoup his/her investment through monthly savings on maintenance contracts, generally during the first year or so. The overall savings during the course of a five-year lease can be significant. The savings over the next five-year lease can be even more significant, as the cost was already amortized during the first five years.

Tenants realize other benefits as well. For an office manager working on a fixed budget, more plants can be installed and maintained for the same amount of money, improving the decor, augmenting the corporate image, and providing an environment more suitable for employee efficiency, health, and satisfaction. Conversely, when a fixed number of plants is suitable, the cost of leasing and care is reduced. The corporate office manager and company executives will also find:

- Fewer interruptions by plantscape technicians.

- More consistent plant care as less skill is required.

- No deterioration when the contractor misses appointments due to employee illness, vacation, or turnover.

- Less office mess from the inevitable spillage manual irrigation engenders.

- The tenant's corporate image is also enhanced by high-tech facility management techniques.

Not all tenants would opt for the new amenity. Where pre-installed, however, it would already be in place to offer the service to new tenants when space turn-over occurs. Most office space turns over many times during its useful lifetime, and each tenant has a different set of needs. The automated plant irrigation systems would be useful to some, but of only marginal interest to others. Having it in place provides the building with versatility and a market appeal that less sophisticated structures lack. The inclusion of technology increases the value of the building, as with any other investment in capital equipment. By leasing the equipment or paying for the initial installation up-front, tenants are buying systems for the owner, and in doing so, are adding to the value and marketability of the building. Tenants, then, augment net worth for project investors.

An important benefit of integral APM systems is that comprehensive interior irrigation systems can be designed to care not only for the tenant suites, but also for common areas—portions of the building normally relegated to sprinkler and drip irrigation. The new technologies can accomplish these other chores better than the old. Because most of the system is upstairs in the main part of the building,

the common areas are then secondary irrigation zones. They can be branched off from the main system for their role in automated building maintenance. Lobbies, atrium balconies, dining and relaxation areas, elevator landings, hallways, promenades, and passageways are just some of the common areas that are targets for interior plantscaping and automated care. Coverage of the building's administrative and sales offices are other important applications for the developer.

Partial building coverage is also sometimes considered. There are projects designed with highlight areas that are the center of attention—usually well-decorated with plants and frequently fitted with accent lighting. Smaller zone systems can be considered for these applications, providing limited area coverage. Sometimes only one or two tenants in a small office building may require automated plant care. The developer could decide to install integrated systems only in those select suites to accommodate the tenants. Sometimes the responsibility for installation would be left up to the tenant, subject, of course, to approval by building management.

APM systems can also be retrofit into office buildings, but installation costs are slightly higher because of the greater difficulty in threading tubing networks from one area to another. Retrofits are technically feasible and in most cases, practical. An advantage in office buildings is that most are designed with drop ceilings, providing an overhead plenum that is easily accessed. Since each installation is different, they must be evaluated on a case-by-case basis.

There are many outdoor uses for APM systems in office building projects. Many are designed with balconies off of the upper floors or patios extending from the main floor, and frequently they are landscaped with potted trees and bushes. It is difficult to water foliage with conventional irrigation systems under those conditions. Again, the

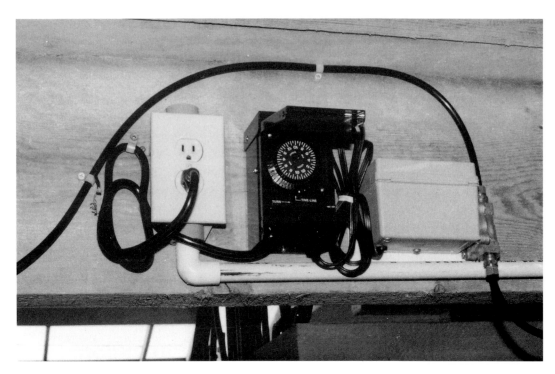

new technology is well suited for this purpose because of its precise placement of water and low flow rates. Hanging planters, sometimes used overhead in covered walkways between buildings and in canopied entryways, can also be serviced by APM systems.

The number of foliage plants and trees being installed in large commercial buildings without the benefit of modern irrigation is staggering. These installations will suffer from high maintenance costs and occasional plantscape deterioration due to inadequate manual care. It must be remembered that with technical aids available, manual irrigation is the least reliable of all methods.[3]

Corporate Offices

Corporate office managers handle the use of plants in a multitude of ways. Plants are becoming more appreciated for their ability to enhance decor by providing a more natural and relaxing workplace, and more recently industrial psychologists and space researchers have found an increase in employee efficiency and health benefits as well. Most office managers hire an interiorscaper to do the office landscaping and to also take care of the plants. This is generally under a lease/maintenance contract, but sometimes the office owns the plants and contracts for maintenance only. In many cases, it is the interior designer who specifies the use of plants to complement the newly established decor.

Containerized foliage plants are used in a multitude of ways in entryways, reception areas, hallways, executive and sales offices, display rooms, conference and boardrooms, open work areas, lunch rooms, relaxation areas, fitness rooms, and rest rooms. They hang from ceilings and beams, are placed on filing cabinets, desks, work stations, bookcases, partitions, wall units, coffee and end tables, kitchen countertops, and on the floor near furniture. Such diverse settings for potted plants create many challenges for the installation of maintenance technology. The vast majority of potted plants are still manually watered, and the labor expended in this endeavor collectively is enormous. APM systems are able to reduce effort and cost to minimal levels, but the practicality in any given situation will depend on the ease of installation. Sprinkler and drip systems could get messy in these settings, so they are not viable options. APM systems can make up the major portion of a plant-care installation, supplemented with self-watering plant containers wherever needed.

In buildings that have already been fitted with an integral automatic plant care system, there is usually a connection nearby that can be tapped into to route tubing to the office suite for irrigation service. Tubing can frequently be plugged into wall-mounted irrigation receptacles at the perimeter of an open workroom and passed under carpeting to workstations where it can connect to another small, hidden network of tubing that distributes the water throughout. In some of the newer office buildings, floors have been raised several inches above the concrete floor slab, creating a floor plenum used for service wiring and, of course, tubing runs. This arrangement produces a high degree of flexibility as well, because laterally run tubing is only semi-permanent and can be removed and rerouted when the floor plan is changed. In those situations where tubing runs are not practical, freestanding, self-watering containers can frequently be used to supplement the main irrigation system. Self-watering containers are most useful with, for example, floor-standing planters.

Most modern offices, however, have connection points located in the space above the suspended ceiling. Large, overhead spaces are used for routing air conditioning and heating ducts, wiring, plumbing, and a multitude of other things. That overhead plenum also provides the convenient opportunity to retrofit APM systems. Tubing and fittings are installed into that space, and dropped down into office partitions to be further distributed to other locations (see Figure 13.5). In such cases, the control center on the floor occupied by the office suite will regulate flow to it and neighboring suites.

Figure 13.5: APM system connections to a typical office suite.

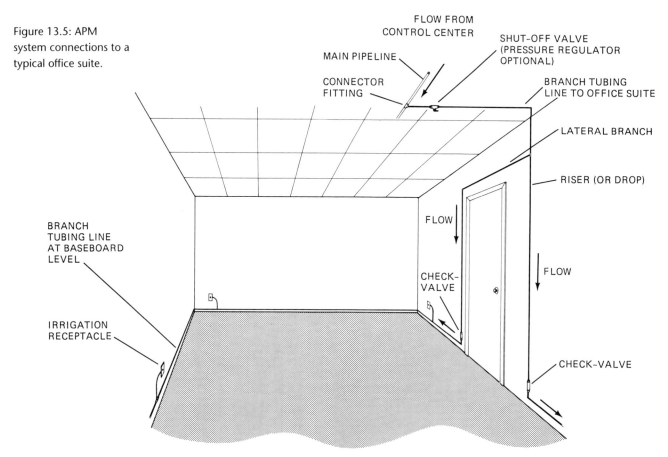

FLOW FROM CONTROL CENTER

MAIN PIPELINE

SHUT-OFF VALVE (PRESSURE REGULATOR OPTIONAL)

CONNECTOR FITTING

BRANCH TUBING LINE TO OFFICE SUITE

LATERAL BRANCH

RISER (OR DROP)

BRANCH TUBING LINE AT BASEBOARD LEVEL

FLOW

FLOW

IRRIGATION RECEPTACLE

CHECK-VALVE

CHECK-VALVE

Emitter tube assemblies are plugged into the special irrigation receptacles and routed to wherever the potted greenery happens to be. This works well in enclosed offices but becomes more of a problem in open-plan work spaces. Those applications are handled in other ways (see Chapter 15). Hanging planters are frequently used around offices, and can easily be serviced by APM systems installed overhead through suspended ceiling plenums. The precise control of this technology prevents overflow problems common to manual watering service.

There are times when it will not be practical to route tubing across flooring. Then, self-watering containers become the technology of choice to care for isolated plants away from room perimeters. Tiled floors are a typical example. While APM systems are technically capable of servicing planters positioned like this, the tubing installation is best accomplished before the concrete floor slab has been poured. Irrigation receptacles can be installed in the floor at planter locations. To retrofit would be much more difficult and expensive. Systems of this type can be added more easily when floors are renovated.

There are also occasions when passing tubing under carpeting to work stations in open plan areas is not practical. This is particularly true where commercial carpeting is used, as it is cemented to the concrete floor surface. One solution is to install small, inexpensive, low-pressure APM systems into the structure of the workstation furniture to service the plants on and around it (see Figure 13.6). Each of these units is independent of the main building system and would be capable of servicing all plants on workstations up to four modules in size. Tubing is threaded through the furniture frames from one location to another.

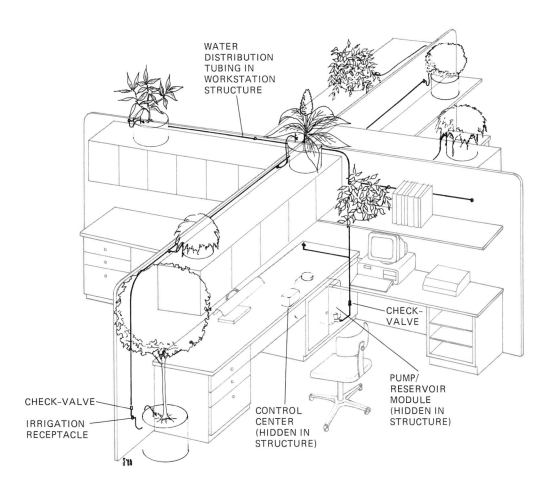

WATER DISTRIBUTION TUBING IN WORKSTATION STRUCTURE

CHECK-VALVE

CHECK-VALVE

IRRIGATION RECEPTACLE

CONTROL CENTER (HIDDEN IN STRUCTURE)

PUMP/ RESERVOIR MODULE (HIDDEN IN STRUCTURE)

Figure 13.6: A multiple workstation with small plants being serviced by a built-in APM system.

The equipment can be installed prior to furniture delivery by the dealer or by the office furniture manufacturer. Irrigation receptacles can be mounted on desk, cabinet, and partition surfaces for neat, convenient installations. Techniques are available to provide safe, leak-free systems. In this way all work station plants can be watered automatically without overflow and with only infrequent attention.

Many designers and managers have concerns about mingling hydraulic, data, and electrical services. Of course, this is done all the time with plumbing and electrical building systems. All hidden tubing and connections in APM systems must meet local building codes. However, nagging doubts can be addressed by encasing irrigation tubing runs in waterproof, flexible conduits.

Another practical technique in offices is the use of X-10 carrier-frequency remote-control systems to time the interval between operating cycles. They are simple, inexpensive energy-management systems that inject electronic control signals into the office's electrical wiring. Receiving modules are plugged into power receptacles wherever lights or other devices are to be switched. They are also capable of controlling many satellite APM systems. These inexpensive units are installed where needed around the office suite.

Hospitality Buildings and Facilities

Hotels

There are profound changes taking over the hotel segment of the hospitality industry. We see some of the following trends nationwide. (The following list has been edited for relevance to this discussion.)

- A significant increase in the variety and diversity of facilities, including all-suite hotels, new mid-priced developments, concierge floors, and convention and airport hotels.

- Public spaces must be more impressive than in the past. Hotels are incorporating atria, expansive spaces, and upgrading furniture to create a stronger image.

- Variety in room design and amenities focuses on the needs of business travelers, 25% of which are now women.

- An emphasis on basic physical comfort with an aesthetically pleasing, tastefully decorated visual environment.[4]

Live planters are a part of these trends, and automated plant care techniques are inevitably following in their wake. Some in the industry look at the strategy of using plants in hospitality settings as the creation of a serene oasis within the frenetic exterior environment.

In many ways hotels are similar to office buildings with respect to the application of APM systems. All hotels have a lobby or a foyer to greet visitors. Many modern hotel lobbies are quite expansive. In some, a major atrium serves the multiple purposes of lobby, elevator landings, food service areas, lounges, art and commercial showcases, as well as access passageways to shops and guest rooms. Most lobbies, large and small, are planted with live foliage—some very profusely. Combinations of in situ (built-in) planters and freestanding containerized planters are normally used. Long, narrow planter boxes are common decorative elements in the large atria common to the Hyatt chain and others. They are used extensively to line atrium balconies on each floor, with their vine-like plants trailing foliage over the edges of balcony facades, cascading into the atrium and giving the appearance of hanging gardens.

This is one of the images that architect John Portman has stamped indelibly onto the American commercial landscape.

Planters of this type require precise irrigation to prevent overflow onto balcony carpeting and to the facade and atrium floor below. Because of the sensitivity of this type of planter box, manual plant care is highly demanding and expensive. Common automated irrigation technologies, such as sprinkler and drip/trickle, are much too coarse and indiscriminate in their application of water to use in most of these demanding settings. APM systems, however, are precise and controlled enough to service such planters effectively.

Figure 13.7: Modern hotel atrium.

Figure 13.8: A typical APM system installation in a hotel lobby.

FROM CONTROL CENTER

WATER DISTRIBUTION TUBING LINES (HIDDEN WITHIN STRUCTURE)

CHECK–VALVE

IRRIGATION RECEPTACLE

There are outdoor installations of potted plants around hotels that could also benefit from automated systems. These are usually around the pool, on sun decks, in tiki bars, and the like. Whenever potted plants are near a sprinklered lawn, a branch can be run to the deck and fitted with drip system elements to service them. When this is not possible, APM systems would be the better choice, run from a nearby hose bibb or other water line connection.

Areas such as hallways, entryways, elevator landings, covered walkways, snack centers, restaurants, lounges, shops, administrative offices, and the front desk are often decorated with freestanding potted plants. The greenery is used to break up the starkness of long hallways or elevator landings, or to add warmth to spaces where guests like to linger. These plants can be serviced by branches of the central system (with irrigation receptacles) when properly designed for them. These images call to mind the old Victorian hotels decorated with the ubiquitous potted palms in the lobby and lounge. Even then hoteliers recognized the value of live plants in softening the environment and making the place seem more hospitable. In fact, the hospitality industry was the first to make extensive use of live plants in interior environments. Other commercial industries have seen similar benefits and have followed their lead.

While plants have almost always been prevalent in exterior and common areas, the average guest room was deprived of them until recently. With the advent of the suite hotel concept, in which buildings are designed with mostly guest suites rather than just single rooms, the use of live potted plants in rooms has gained popularity. The reason seems to be that suites are larger and more closely represent one's home-away-from-home. Live greenery adds an element of relaxation and home-like decor.

One of the reasons for the slow application of plants in guest rooms has been the difficulty of gaining access to them for routine watering and maintenance. Remember that most commercial plant care services are provided by independent contractors using manual irrigation practices. They have a regular schedule of visits for any given client. It is highly unlikely that most rooms would be vacant during those visits, and it is conceivable that weeks or possibly months could go by before some of the plants could be watered. Most decorative plants can't tolerate that kind of irregular care. Many interiorscapers have minimized the problem by installing self-watering planters. The problems associated with their use have prevented widespread application, however. APM

systems can now be designed into the building as integral facilities management systems, or they can be retrofit into individual suites to serve the same purpose. As an integral system, the control center and water distribution tubing would be installed and laid out much the same as in office or apartment buildings. Special irrigation receptacles mounted on the walls of the rooms provide easy access to irrigation water, no matter where the planters are located.

Inexpensive, small-area systems can also be retrofit to take care of individual rooms or suites. Control centers can be installed under bathroom sinks in the vanity cabinets where they are connected to the water supply. Tubing is distributed under carpeting around the perimeter of rooms.

Resorts

Resort complexes are basically hotels with greatly expanded recreational facilities and other amenities. The hotel portions are generally decorated and planted like any other, and have similar maintenance problems. Many resorts also have out-buildings, such as cabins, cottages, and clubhouses, which could benefit from the extensive use of potted plants. As vacations are often associated with nature, plants become a necessity. Facilities managers and interiorscapers are still faced with the same access problems they encounter with conventional hotel rooms, and for those reasons frequently ignore interior plantscaping in suites and cottages. APM systems can now be designed and installed into guest facilities to provide fully automatic irrigation service, freeing the managers of those access problems.

Resort bars are frequently decorated with both hanging and freestanding greenery, and because of the brighter environment outdoors, require more frequent watering. Small APM systems can easily be installed to care for these automatically.

Clubhouses and Recreation Halls

Clubhouses, found in country clubs, resort hotels, and residential complexes, are generally furnished in much the same way as carpeted areas in lobbies, offices, lounges, and restaurants. They are generally designed and decorated to be casual, comfortable spaces, well suited for sports, social, and community use. Live container plants are frequently used to complement the decor in foyers, game rooms, fitness rooms, hallways, lounges, locker rooms, pro shops, snack counters, solariums, pool areas, and sundecks. These facilities can benefit greatly from the use of automated plant care systems as irrigation is virtually always manual. Because these areas are usually well furnished, APM systems are the main technology of choice. The exceptions are outdoor pool decks and sun decks, which are not as critical. In those cases, either APM systems or drip irrigation can be used.

Restaurants and Lounges

The appeal of live plants in restaurant and lounge settings is long standing. For a great many years restaurateurs have used freestanding and hanging potted planters in the dining rooms of their establishments for ambiance. One is hard put to find eateries without plants—from fast-food chains to five-star establishments. The appeal is the relaxing feeling live foliage lends to an otherwise plain interior setting. Artificial planters have encroached on the territory of live foliage, but many restaurants—particularly upscale ones—recognize the difference and opt for the real thing. Hanging live planters and built-in planter boxes are used in abundance to create the casual atmosphere that management knows draws customers. Because of the extent and location of plant decor of that type, maintenance expenses can be quite high. Until precision irrigation technology was introduced, virtually all of the watering had to be done by hand. That meant a technician had to climb a stool or ladder (in some cases rolling scaffolds are used) to reach the overhead plants with watering cans, tanks, and machines. Freestanding planters have had the option of self-watering containers, which can be used in select applications. APM systems offer a comprehensive, fully automated technique

Figure 13.9: Restaurant interior with live plants.

capable of minimizing manual labor and costs while providing the most consistent care possible. They also eliminate the overflow and spillage of manual irrigation, so annoying to management and customers alike. Plant care contractors service restaurants during off-hours when customers have not yet arrived, and careless maintenance technicians sometimes leave behind unwanted signs of their presence. Proper training of field personnel by competent interiorscape firms keeps that type of annoyance to a minimum.

APM systems are installed in restaurants much the same as they are in office buildings, with the control center mounted in a service area of the building, usually in the kitchen or utility room where there is easy access to water lines. Tubing is routed from there throughout the dining area, being hidden as much as possible. Many restaurants are built with suspended ceilings, which provide a convenient overhead space for tubing lines. Other restaurants have high, vaulted ceilings with planters hanging from joists and beams.

FROM CONTROL CENTER

WATER DISTRIBUTION TUBING LINES HIDDEN WITHIN STRUCTURE

Figure 13.10: A typical APM system layout in a restaurant/lounge.

These are most difficult for the average maintenance technician to service. Ladders are usually required, although manual watering machines with long wands will frequently reach most of them.

Large restaurant chains will be among the major beneficiaries of APM systems. Annual plant maintenance expenditures easily run into the millions of dollars for some of them. Because of the suspended ceiling design in most of these facilities, it is an easy matter to retrofit relatively inexpensive APM systems into the structure to care for hanging planters. Planter boxes in room dividers and freestanding containerized foliage can also be retrofit, but usually with more difficulty. The most cost-efficient installations are designed into the building at the drawing board stage and laid-in during the construction phases. Under any circumstance, restaurant and lounge plant care costs and annoyances can be effectively minimized by incorporating this new technology.

Whenever situations arise that make it impractical to install APM systems throughout, the main system can be supplemented with freestanding, self-watering containers. This way, the facility will have full coverage.

Shopping Malls and Arcades

If there is one segment of interior landscape that should be automatically irrigated it is the shopping mall. Shopping malls have been built in profusion over the past twenty years, and most have been well landscaped with a broad variety of planters. The majority are in situ (built-in) and well integrated into the interior architectural design. They help to break up the stark lines, colors, and finishes of building materials, giving a natural feeling to the interior so that it is comfortable and inviting. Long ago, retailers also learned of the commercial magic live plants can lend to shopping centers of this type. Interiors

with greenery draw people and keep them there longer, meaning they will shop longer as well.

Shopping malls are very expensive to maintain, yet fairly easy to fit with automated plant care systems—so long as it is done during construction. Many malls being constructed today are being fitted with automated irrigation. Inadequate technology is one of the reasons for its having been ignored in the past, but with the advent of more specialized techniques, there is no reason to continue expensive manual irrigation practices. Large trees in planter pits are still being watered primarily with long hoses, sometimes stretching 100 feet from the local hose connection. To water properly and deeply, long periods of time are required. One simple, relatively inexpensive irrigation pipe network installed underground from tree pit to tree pit and controlled by a timer can effectively save hundreds of thousands of dollars over many years of building use. Bubbler, soaker, or subterranean emitters should be used around the roots. They are much more efficient than sprinkler heads and prevent the traffic safety hazards of wet walkways. In this case, a conventional irrigation set-up without spray heads would be fine. Trees generally need lots of water, particularly those that get plenty of sun under skylights. Five-minute irrigation cycles can be programmed, sometimes twice daily. The emitters can be adjusted down if necessary. This is a rare case where APM systems cannot be used to best advantage. The short irrigation cycles are frequently too abbreviated for very large trees growing in a bright environment. The same trees grown in dim light would, however, benefit from the more controlled flow rates of APM systems. Models having larger flow rates and frequent, multiple cycles are available to provide greater capacity.

There are many smaller plants and planters used in malls that can benefit from automated precision systems. The network would be established with one or more control centers in the building, depending on the size and complexity of the mall layout. Overall control could be relegated to the facility's computerized control center, if that is used. Tubing would be laid in under or through concrete slabs to small planter boxes or to locations in the building where potted plants are likely to eventually reside. Irrigation outlets, such as Boca Automation's special irrigation receptacles, can be fitted into the floors, walls, or support columns through which water can be accessed. Planter ledges can be fit with irrigation manifolds to service many potted plants on the shelf. Water supply tubing connects to the manifold and carries the short pulses of irrigation flow.

Offices and stores in the mall can be established as branches of the overall master system. Automated plant care systems can be integrated with the facility's computerized energy-management controller to provide a highly responsive installation.

Shopping arcades frequently use potted plants along the promenade to provide a natural, garden-like atmosphere. Some are on the walkways, while others hang from suspended planters. Both types are difficult to irrigate properly by hand. As these plants are outside, although usually in the shade, they do get more light and so require more water. Hanging planters must be carefully irrigated by hand to make sure enough water has been dispensed, yet not enough to cause an overflow that might lead to slippery pavements. A situation like this one could also be handled with a drip irrigation system if it is designed properly. Freestanding containerized plants along the building wall can frequently be serviced from interior APM systems through appropriate emitters, such as the fountain type. They are mounted on an outside wall next to a plant location. During the abbreviated irrigation cycle, water is squirted the short distance between

Figure 13.11: Fountain-type emitter at shopping arcade.

it and the soil surface (Figure 13.11). The appeal of using this type of emitter over the conventional ones lies in its vandal-proof design.

Retail Outlets

Shops, department stores, and other retail establishments have invested in their share of interiorscaping in recent years. For the same commercial reasons that attract restaurateurs, merchants are using plants to attract customers. In most cases, potted plants are used. Department stores scatter them throughout, on partitions, display cases, and on the floor near them. Room settings in furniture departments, garment fitting rooms, and elegant showrooms are particularly prone to be decorated with various types of greenery.

APM systems are well suited to this type of irrigation, as the furnished interiors of shops demand precise water placement. Control centers can be installed in a rest room or service room where there is convenient access to cold water lines, with tubing overhead or running through partitions to planter locations. Wherever possible, small emitter tubes can be passed under carpeting to isolated container plants. Many stores have suspended ceilings which provide a convenient plenum through which to route tubing. Large department stores require extensive advanced planning. Pre-construction systems design can provide the most cost-efficient installation. Small areas of stores can frequently be retrofit with inexpensive individual systems capable of servicing many plants. If cold water lines are inaccessible, low-pressure APM systems can be used.

Institutional Buildings and Facilities

Banks

These commercial establishments are also being decorated today in a more inviting manner, using live plants to provide color and natural ambiance. Bankers' offices are decorated and plantscaped as any other office might be. Containerized plants sit on desk tops, filing cabinets, wall units, book shelves, room dividers, and work station modules, as well as on the floor. Automated irrigation can be applied in the same way as with corporate offices.

The open service areas one generally finds in banks also use plantings in strategic locations. These environments can be more difficult to automate. In most cases, the key

is to integrate an APM system into the structure. Tubing can be cast into the concrete slab and accessed through service boxes mounted in the floor and hidden by carpeting. Other branches of the tubing can be brought up into room divider, service counter, or partition planter boxes. Other tubes would circle the perimeter of the open area, either along the baseboard or inside the walls, with irrigation receptacles or other connections providing access to the water supply tubing. Tubing can usually be hidden behind decorative moldings and utility channels. If the bank is in a technically advanced building, the APM system can be controlled by the facility's computerized energy-management system.

Hospitals and Medical Offices

Medical buildings of all sorts are being plantscaped in a variety of schemes, all of them aimed at providing a more casual, natural, and relaxing feeling to alleviate patients' anxieties, as well as to enhance the decorative value of the space. Live plants are being used in hospital lobbies, waiting rooms, cafeterias, administrative offices, and solariums, as well as in the waiting rooms of doctors' and dentists' offices.

As with any other building, the inconveniences and costs of plant care services can be minimized by using automated techniques. Large planter areas in hospital lobbies can usually be effectively irrigated with drip systems, or APM systems can be used. The advantage in using the latter is that other branches of the same system can service the furnished areas of the building as well, such as nearby offices. Modern hospitals are being built with sophisticated computer controls for a variety of functions. APM systems can become peripherals to these other systems. In the case of doctors' and dentists' offices, systems can be installed in ways similar to most other office settings, using special irrigation receptacles if the installation can be integrated into partitions.

Residential Buildings and Facilities

Live plants have been widely used in residences as a means of decorating and as a hobby. Now we also know that plants help keep our environment clean. Designers can make our homes healthier by using them in large numbers. The good news is that with modern methods, plant care in the home is easier than ever.

Most houseplants are cared for manually. Except in some upscale homes, plants are usually maintained by the homeowner, who sometimes also uses small, single-plant watering gadgets. Unfortunately, many homeowners lack the knowledge, time, or inclination to care for their plants properly. Plants can be a problem in a second home where people are away for long periods, during vacation time, or for those who travel frequently on business. For some, however, plants are prized specimens. Many become objects of close emotional attachment—"green pets," as some refer to them. For those who can afford it, plant care specialists can be hired. Yet many people don't like the idea of having strangers in their homes while they are away, preferring to impose on friends and neighbors to come in and water the plants instead. The difficulty here is that temporary help generally doesn't know much about plant requirements. APM systems can solve most of the problems associated with the care of house plants by automatically watering plants week after week. Plant care does involve other tasks as well, but the critical, most demanding one— irrigation—is taken care of and in many cases integrated with other tasks. For example, plant nutrients, pesticides, and other chemicals can sometimes be applied systemically, that is, carried in the irrigation water to be absorbed through the root system.

Apartment Buildings

Although one might consider these as residential rather than commercial spaces, most facility maintenance takes place in the common areas of those buildings. Large apartment buildings and condominiums are very commercially-oriented, and are usually handled by property management companies that are as concerned about methods and costs as any commercial building manager. The products and services used are essentially similar.

Large luxury apartments and condos are frequently decorated with lush plantings in the lobby areas. Built-in planter boxes are usually used, supplemented with freestanding containerized plants. Drip systems and APM systems are the prime candidates for automatic plant care in both the planter boxes and freestanding potted plants. Retrofit installations can frequently be made to service all or a part of the lobby area. The project practicality is determined by the construction and layout.

So far as common areas go, container plants are additionally found in hallways, game rooms, fitness rooms, sales and management offices, and on elevator landings. APM systems, if designed into the building prior to construction, can service all of these locations. Outdoors, potted plants can be found around pool areas, sun decks, walkways, snack centers, and tiki bars. In a fully-installed building of this type, the APM system is integrated not only into the common areas, but into the residential part of the structure as well in order to service the apartments. This will be dealt with in more detail in the following discussions.

Apartment Suites

APM systems can be incorporated into individual apartment suites either during construction or later as retrofit installations. High-pressure versions are the systems of choice in most integral installations, yet

209

low-pressure versions are usually used in retrofit situations. Although it is possible to set up a single control center for a string of apartments, the most practical design allows for complete control in each.

An apartment's system is much like those used in hotel suites. The control center would best be mounted in the laundry room (most modern apartments have them), or under bathroom or kitchen sinks. The tubing network is routed from there throughout the partitions to various rooms of the apartment, with access provided by irrigation receptacles mounted in the walls. Emitter tubes are plugged into them and laid under carpeting to planter locations. Control of each apartment system can be provided by a central computer in the management office of the building, allowing for timing or system shut-off if the tenant did not want the service. In this way the building owner can provide a fee-paid amenity to tenants. In other situations, the timer/controller is completely controlled by the apartment owner or tenant.

Apartment suites also have outdoor plant care needs. Plants on balconies or terraces require frequent watering. Many building codes prevent the inclusion of hose bibbs on the balconies of multi-storied buildings to prevent the possibility of water damage by overflow from upper floors. Low-pressure APM systems have self-contained reservoirs that function as the water source.

Figure 13.12: Terrace installation.

AUTOMATED PRECISION MICRO-IRRIGATION IN VARIOUS BUILDING TYPES

Pumps built into the reservoir module provide flow to the tubing network servicing the plants on the balcony. The timer/controller can be mounted outside on a wall (requiring weatherproof equipment), or inside the apartment with wiring extending outside to the pump connections. These systems are ideal for freestanding potted plants as well as for hanging planters. Containerized vegetable gardening can easily be accommodated, as can specialty gardening such as bonsai culture and orchid growing.

Single-Family Houses

Architects and builders are learning to accommodate their clients' use of plants by designing skylights, greenhouse windows, atria, sun rooms, planter shelves, boxes, pits, high-placed windows, and supplementary lighting into new homes and apartments. In many spaces, the design is very much plant-oriented.

As previously discussed, the early fully automatic plant care technology is unsuitable for housing interiors. Exceptions involve the occasional use of sprinkler system branches from outdoor systems to water built-in planter boxes and pits. These would be found in large, expensive homes where the planter is far enough from furnished areas that the owner need not be concerned about accidental water damage. Drip emitters are sometimes used in these planters as well, and they are actually the wiser choice over spray heads. As for the rest of the house, these technologies are seldom suitable. Self-watering planters have been used by some to provide a measure of convenience. But again, it is the more effective APM systems that can provide comprehensive, fully automatic plant watering service in "smart" (technically advanced) homes.

APM systems can be integrated into the structure of the house during the building process, or they can be retrofit in existing homes. They provide service to greenery throughout the entire house, or can be used to irrigate smaller installations that cover only one section. Outdoors, containerized plants can be watered by independent systems installed to cover the patio, pool deck, or entry areas. Other small, dedicated systems can be installed in atria and planter beds.

While some installations require low-pressure versions of the technology, most situations call for high-pressure systems sourced from the home's water supply. It is technically feasible to automatically service every planter in a home, particularly when the system is incorporated in the structure. Integrated high-pressure (Mirage III™) systems are installed with the control center in a laundry room or garage, and the water distribution tubing network is routed from there throughout the house, passing through partitions, floor structures, ceiling and attic spaces, and basements. Irrigation receptacles are mounted on the walls of rooms, generally spaced with one on each wall in appropriate places. Emitter tubes are plugged into them and passed under the carpet edge to wherever freestanding planters might happen to be. There is a great deal of flexibility in that regard, as the emitter tubing can be routed for long distances if necessary. Whenever plants are moved, reinstalling the emitter tubes is a simple matter. Planter shelves and box planters are fitted with special manifolds to distribute water to a number of plants at that location. In high-tech homes containing systems and services that encompass everything from security to energy-management, an APM system can be interfaced with a computerized home control system. Otherwise, the plant care system can be self-controlled.

Retrofit installations can run the gamut from single inexpensive units caring for a couple of plants to more complex devices providing full-house coverage. Obviously, it is more difficult to install tubing networks

Figure 13.13: A home installation with an irrigation receptacle.

in fully constructed, fully furnished homes, making the retrofit installation more costly. Tubing runs in these instances are mostly through attics, basements, and partitions, as well as under carpeting and behind baseboards around the perimeters of rooms. When tiled floors are encountered, special problems are created that require other simple solutions. The most practical retrofit installations involve inexpensive, yet sophisticated carrier-frequency remote control devices, such as the X-10 PowerHouse™⁵ System. These are installed to control small satellite plant care systems scattered wherever necessary throughout the home. Each of these inexpensive low-pressure irrigation units is capable of watering up to about 10 plants as much as about 35 feet away. The complexity of individual unit control is simplified by the carrier-frequency controller. It injects control intelligence into the house's electrical wiring, to be picked up and reacted to by receiving modules plugged into power receptacles wherever they are needed. In this way, plant care units can be placed anywhere inside or outside the home to care for any number of zones and be controlled from a convenient central point. Whenever they can be used in retrofit situations, multi-unit high-pressure systems can be controlled in the same way. A secondary benefit is that a very versatile energy-control system would already be in place, able to control all forms of lighting, appliances, heating/air conditioning, security systems, and the like. The combination makes for a very smart house—at low cost. Other home automation technologies, such as CEBus®,[6] Lon Works™,[7] and SMART HOUSE™,[8] are also gaining a foothold in U.S. housing markets. Boca Automation's APM systems are compatible with all of them.

Many homes have extensive patios around which potted plants can be found in abundance, hanging from trellises, arbors, and covered walkways, or resting on retaining walls, steps, and decks. Many times offshoots of a sprinkler system are insufficient for their maintenance. Drip irrigation could be installed from the lawn irrigation system as an option, but because of their superior control, APM systems could water these plants without overflow.

Marine Applications

Luxury yachts are decorated in the same manner as homes, apartments, or offices, including the latest in high-technology. Live plants are a part of this scheme, and APM systems are a welcome addition to the boater's complement of on-board amenities. Tubing can be threaded through bulkheads and partitions with the same ease as in land-based structures. Irrigation receptacles can be used, as can direct connections. In most cases these systems must be low-pressure versions operating from the yacht's water tanks or from self-contained pump/reservoir modules.

Figure 13.14: Carrier frequency controller, X-10 compatible type. Source: Leviton Manufacturing Co.

FOURTEEN

The Design and Costing of Automated Precision Micro-Irrigation Systems

Previous chapters have discussed automated precision micro-irrigation (APM) systems in general terms. Now comes the practical side, the detail that allows one to translate ideas and concepts into a layout design that can make the project a reality. Each and every project is unique in its requirements, making the design tasks different in each case. Yet all cases share common threads, so in conceptual terms one would be on familiar ground no matter what type of project was under consideration. Integrated systems and retrofit designs each have their own set of problems, just as the challenges of a large office building are much more demanding than those of a small house. In this chapter we will sort through the different criteria in order to gain enough expertise to confidently handle most APM system design projects.

Defining the Design Problem

Before anything else can be done, the design problem must be defined. One must:

1. Know what needs to be accomplished by an installed system.

2. Have a general understanding of the physical attributes of the building under consideration.

3. Be aware of the possible hazards and difficulties.

Later these will be combined with knowledge of the systems themselves to evolve a design plan.

A quick design stage is usually required to get a handle on the nature of the installation and its approximate costs. First, a cursory survey must be made of the building plan. If the building is in place or under construction, a visit to the site is in order to look over the design, structural details, interior finish details, locations of built-in planters and water sources, possible future locations for freestanding planters, etc. Notes should be taken, sketches of the layout made, and at least rough dimensions recorded. If building blueprints are available, the designer should have access to them. The building developer's employees should act as guides, pointing out building features and answering any questions that may be relevant to the design. If the building has not yet been built or is in a remote location that is inaccessible to the designer, this initial study must be made from building plans and other information furnished by the client. The designer should ask for a complete set of plans, at the very least including floor plans of the building sections under scrutiny, elevations of the same, and plumbing and electrical layouts. The client should always be questioned as to what he or she expects from an automated plant care system in the building interior. All this input is necessary to get a clear picture of the nature and objectives of the project, potential installation problems, approximate costs, and what needs to be done to satisfy the client.

A couple of factors have just been mentioned that highlight the need for the designer to have some expertise in building design and construction—at least enough to read blueprints; understand some of the terminology used and the problems associated with building construction; know something about plumbing systems and building codes; and be somewhat familiar with interior design. One does not have to have in-depth knowledge of the areas, but some is definitely necessary.

The Sample Layout

With the information gathered, the designer should plan a quick layout of the system he or she plans to recommend. While the layout merely represents a sketch at this stage, it often comes after many hours of study. The preliminary design should include the following:

- The general type of system required, specifying low-pressure or high-pressure versions.

- Recommended control equipment, including appropriate models of APM systems.

- Specification of system timers and controllers.

- Size of the main water distribution tubing lines.

- Routing of the water distribution tubing network (approximate).

- Type and number of tubing fittings required (approximate).

- Number of irrigation receptacles required (approximate).

- Installation cost calculated from available information (approximate).

- Other relevant details (installation labor, contractor mark-ups, etc.).

A report to the client in the form of an installation proposal can then be generated from the cursory design study.

Many complex projects require so much preliminary study and design work to determine their feasibility that the client must be charged for that service. Other projects are simple to lay out and install, allowing the design process to be accomplished on-site at the time of installation (if done with expertise and care). Most building projects require something between the two extremes. When the installation proposal has been accepted, then a detailed set of working plans must be generated for use by the architect and contractors involved, as well as for the use of the owner and property or facility manager. Discussions of that process follow.

Technical Considerations

There are many technical details that must be dealt with in systems design. Some have to do with engineering data, while others are less complicated.

Technical drawing methods are used to graphically describe the layout of an APM system. Not all installations require a formal design plan, but whenever the system is to be integrated into the structure of a building, such a plan will be required as much as electrical or plumbing design plans are required. This is so the architect and installation contractors know exactly what is contained in the system, where it goes, and how it is to be installed. In a manner of speaking, the automated plant care system might be considered a sort of secondary plumbing system, despite the fact that its purpose, control, and appliances bear no similarity. Most integrated systems will, in fact, be installed by plumbing contractors and a "road map"—the technical working drawing— must be furnished for them to follow. The drawing is called the *interior irrigation system plan* and is drawn with symbols understood by others. Because the expertise involved is similar to that of plumbing, the language of plumbing will be used to graphically describe these special layouts. Figure 14.1 illustrates a few of the important basic plumbing symbols used in APM systems design.

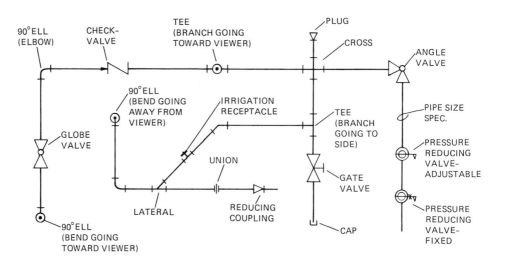

Figure 14.1: The designer borrows symbols used to describe plumbing to make an interior irrigation system plan.

Solenoid Valve and Pump/Reservoir Ratings

One of the keys in specifying a pump or solenoid valve in an APM system is the output rating of the device or, in other words, how much of an irrigation load the pump or valve can carry. Small pump/reservoir modules are flow rated in terms of ounces/10 seconds (ounces of water delivered during a 10-second operating cycle). Ratings for these light-duty pumps will be in the range of 7 to 12 ounces/10 seconds. Larger units for use outdoors are flow rated in the same terms, but output will be much higher, usually about 120 ounces/10 seconds. These ratings are for ground-level service. Flow ratings at 8-foot elevation should also be available from the manufacturer. They represent the lift capabilities of the pump, telling the user whether it is useful for watering hanging planters, potted plants on the floor above, or high-mounted planter shelves. The output port size of a pump tells the user to which tubing size it can be connected and the type of adapter required.

The size of the reservoir is another important consideration, for it determines how long the unit will service the plants without refilling. Reservoirs are supplied in sizes from 2¼ gallons to 32 gallons, although almost any size can be made available for special applications. In the light-duty systems, a 2¼ gallon reservoir, watering 6 or 8 medium-size indoor plants, would hold enough water to last 4 to 6 weeks without refilling. This is highly variable because there are so many factors that determine a plant's moisture requirements. In designing the system, one should attempt to provide it with enough reservoir capacity for at least six weeks of continuous operation. Keep in mind that low-pressure versions of APM systems are automatic only to the extent of their reservoir capacity; then they must be refilled. There are ways of linking two reservoirs in order to multiply capacity. These alternatives can be considered when necessary.

Solenoid valves are commonly flow rated in terms of the *Cv factor* (valve flow coefficient or valve capacity index), which indicates the rate of water flow in gallons per minute under certain standard conditions. They give the designer a general idea as to the flow capacity of the valve. The Cv factor is determined by the inlet and outlet port sizes and the internal architecture of the valve. A more practical flow rating for solenoid valves is the flow rate at various water pressure levels. The flow rate of any solenoid valve varies with

Table 14.1

Relationship Between Solenoid Valve Rating and Flow Rates
(in Gallons per Minute) at Various Water Pressures

Solenoid Valve Cv	20 psi	30 psi	40 psi	50 psi	60 psi	65 psi
0.34	1.6	1.9	2.5	3.0	3.4	3.5
1.4	6	7.5	8.5	9.5	11	11.5
2.8	12	15	17	19	22	23
3.4	15	18	21	23	27	28
3.6	17	20	23	26	28	30
5.5	24	29	34	37	40	43

Sources: Dayton Electric Manufacturing Co., "Solenoid Valves," form 551589 (Chicago, May 1978) and Aqua/Trends.

the water pressure applied to it—the higher the pressure, the greater the flow rate. Flow rates of solenoid valves used in APM systems range from 0.2 gallons per minute to 35 gallons per minute. The size is chosen according to the volume of water required by the particular installation. Most interior systems require relatively low volume. Table 14.1 shows the relationship between Cv factor and flow rates.

In small installations where only a few plants are involved, mini flow rates of only 0.22 gallons per minute can be used. This is common when only one or two guest rooms of a hotel or home need servicing. It is better, however, to choose a higher-rated solenoid valve so that the system coverage can be expanded at a later time if necessary. Temporary reductions can be made at the valve to keep flow rates manageable.

Water Flow Variables

Water flow from the output of a pump or solenoid valve is affected by the tubes or pipes, fittings, and other devices it must pass through on its way to the plants. The direction of flow, as well as friction, also have an effect. Water pressure and flow drop as the water goes along, and the extent of these changes in a system determines the size of the pump or solenoid valve required by the installation. Rather than guessing what is required or trying to determine it by

trial and error, rough calculations are made to zero in on the appropriate equipment. These calculations must be made with a variety of input data, factors that will be discussed in the following sections.

Flow Characteristics of Tubing

The characteristics and diameter of tubing or piping are important to water flow. Materials differ in the way they permit or restrict the flow of water, or any other liquid, for that matter. Due to frictional contact between the two materials, the interior surfaces of a tube or pipe create a drag on the water as it rushes through. The tubing diameter has the same effect. The smaller the tube, the greater the restriction to flow. The distance that the water has to travel through a tube is also brought to bear on the flow characteristics. The greater the distance, the slower the flow rate and the lower the water pressure downstream. This relationship is specified by the industry as the pressure drop per 100 feet of tubing or piping. Table 14.2 shows that for a given flow rate (gpm), as the diameter of the tubing decreases, the pressure losses due to internal friction increase dramatically. For example, many APM system installations require input flow rates of 5 gallons per minute. From the data in Table 14.2 we see that if we use small diameter tubing of the order of 3/8"ID (inside diameter), the pressure drop over 100 feet of tubing is so high that it

Table 14.2

Water Pressure Loss in Plastic Tubing at Various Flow Rates and Tubing Sizes

Water Supply Volume (GPM)	Friction Loss in psi/100 ft of Plastic Tubing (psi)			
	3/8" OD	3/8" ID	1/2" ID	3/4" ID
2.5	200	27	6.4	1.2
5.0	700	100	25	4
10.0	—	360	90	15

Source: Adapted from LCP Chemicals and Plastics, "Friction Characteristics of Water Flow through Rigid Plastic Pipe," monograph (Carlton, Ohio: September 1984)

permits little or no water through. At least 1/2"ID tubing would have to be used for the main water distribution line if the system is to irrigate a large number of plants. Usually the main line is much shorter than 100 feet, so losses of this magnitude are not prohibitive. Branches can be smaller as they carry less water.

Gravity

Another factor that tends to restrict flow is gravity. Whenever risers (vertical tubing lines having uphill water flow) are installed, the weight of the water within the tube creates a drag on its upward motion. Pressure is reduced in the process. This is called *static head*. It takes 0.434psi to push water up a distance of 1 foot. Pushing the water up 20 feet would require 20 x 0.434psi, or 8.68psi for that flow pattern alone. Therefore, in designing these system installations, the number of feet that tubing must rise over the water source has to be taken into consideration. In large buildings, the effects of static head can be particularly significant because of greater vertical distances.

Tubing Fittings

Tubing and pipe fittings, as well as regulators, filters, and backflow preventers, all reduce pressure as the water passes through. The amount of friction loss depends on the design of the device, its material, the sizes of its orifices, as well as on the rate of water flow and the pressure acting on it. That's a complex menu of factors. Suffice it to say that if many of these devices are in the tubing line, the pressure loss can be significant and the system should be adjusted with larger tubes, greater input water pressure, etc. The data in Table 14.3 will provide a guide for accomplishing this.

Fittings are specified in terms of friction loss equivalent to a given length of tube or pipe of the same size. For example, if a certain 1/2" fitting had a friction loss equivalent to 10 feet of 1/2" tubing, it would mean that 10 feet should be added to the total footage of tubing when calculating the tube's friction losses. This is calculated for each fitting in the line. A common practice is to simply add an additional 50% to the length of tubing used in the design to compensate for pressure losses through fittings.[1]

Table 14.3

Allowances for Friction Loss Through Fittings (in Units of Equivalent Length of Similar Size Tubing)*

Tubing Fitting	Friction Loss-Tubing Equivalent		
	3/8" ID	1/2" ID	3/4" ID
90° Ell (elbow)	0.5 ft.	1.0 ft.	1.3 ft.
45° Ell (elbow)	0.3 ft.	0.6 ft.	—
Tee-run (straight through)	0.2 ft.	0.3 ft.	0.4 ft.
Tee-branch (90°)	0.8 ft.	1.5 ft.	2.0 ft.
Globe valve	4.0 ft.	7.5 ft.	10 ft.
Gate valve	0.1 ft.	0.2 ft.	0.3 ft.
Check valve	—	30 ft.	—

Source: Adapted from Frank R. Dagostino, Mechanical and Electrical Systems in Building (Reston, VA: Reston Publishing/Prentice-Hall, Inc., 1982), 43.
*Varies with the type of coupling and other factors.

Emitters

Another type of fitting is the emitter. Its relationship to irrigation flow rates will be discussed separately. Various kinds of emitters are used in APM systems. Each has its own flow characteristics, thus affecting the design in a slightly different way. The flow rates from emitters are important in determining the size of water distribution tubing and of pumps and solenoid valves to be used in the design. The total demand for water in an installation depends on the aggregate amount that is likely to flow from all emitters on the system if they were all in service. Adjustable mini-valve/emitters are the most common variety used in this technology. Figure 14.2 shows the maximum rates of flow from this type of emitter at various pressure levels. These variables are most important, for the systems are designed to operate at different pressures to accommodate different needs.

Another type of emitter that gets some use in APM systems is the Laser Soaker Line™. It differs from the adjustable valve types in that it provides a continuous linear soaking pattern on or in the ground. The laser-drilled emitter holes are spaced at 6"

and 12" intervals. These tubes have different flow rates at various pressure levels (see Figure 14.3). This information will be useful in designing planter box installations and circular emitter patterns in containerized tree planters.

Control Centers

An important design consideration common to all projects is the location (or locations) of the control center. This is where electrical and plumbing connections are made to the APM system's timer/controller—the source and "brain" of the system. The first factor that must be addressed is the control center's proximity to a water source.

In the case of low-pressure versions, the pump/reservoir module acts as the water source, so it can be located almost anywhere that is convenient. But to make a neat, unobtrusive installation, these units should be located in out-of-the-way places not easily seen by the public. The smaller systems can be hidden behind furniture or mounted inside of cabinets, molded architectural furniture, and planter boxes. Larger units can be installed in closets,

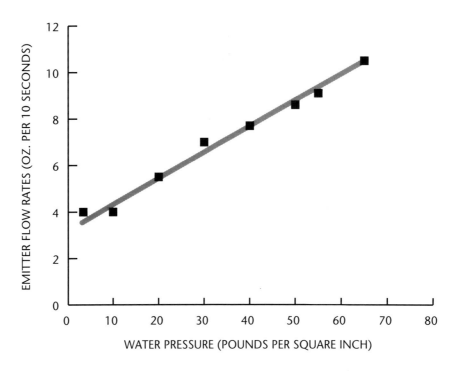

Figure 14.2: The relationship between pressure and flow rates with adjustable mini-valve/emitters. Source: Boca Automation.

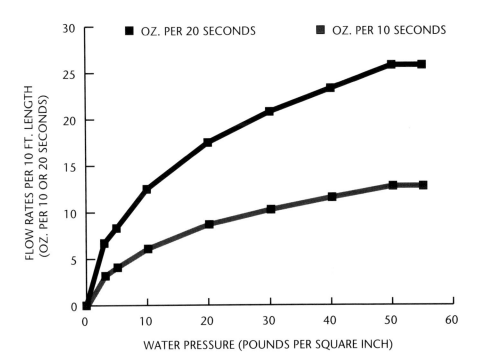

Figure 14.3: Flow rates from Laser Soaker Line™ at various pressure levels. Source: Boca Automation.

utility or service rooms, and garages. Outdoors, they are located in little-used corners of patios, balconies, and pool decks. The control center shouldn't be too far from a faucet so that hauling water to it from time to time will not be a great burden. Hoses or tubes can be connected to faucets to refill reservoirs, so long as the distance is not prohibitive.

High-pressure control centers are located in remote areas of a building with convenient access to a cold water line. The timers and controllers are surface mounted so that plumbing connections can be made externally. The supply line is connected to a nearby cold water pipe. In residential buildings the most practical locations are in laundry rooms, garages, basements, and inside of kitchen and vanity cabinets. In commercial buildings, the control centers should be in a core area location, such as utility or janitors' rooms, mechanical rooms, or rest rooms. Systems meant to service smaller building areas can frequently be centered inside of bathroom vanity cabinets or in office kitchenettes. Outdoor systems can be connected to hose bibbs.

Automation cannot be accomplished without controlled power, so in all cases there must be an electrical connection that provides 24-hour service to the system. Since most available APM system controls are simple plug-in types for ease of installation, power must be made available through a dedicated receptacle. In those versions that are hard-wired into an electrical junction box or time switch, it must be provided at the control center location. Although very little power is required by these systems, some prefer to have the automated irrigation system on an independent power branch with its own circuit breaker. In most cases, however, this is not necessary. Wall outlets can be fitted with mini-breakers if desired. In high-tech homes and commercial buildings with computerized control systems, they would control the switching of power to the electrical box servicing the APM system. Self-powered controllers are available for special applications. They are battery-powered and can be installed in locations not serviced by building electricity.

Water Distribution Networks

The routing of water distribution networks affects flow as well. Each situation is different because of varying building design and construction factors, as well as interior design and plant location. Nevertheless, general rules of thumb do exist that can help the designer to better plan an automated irrigation system.

First, tubing should be routed in such a way that it is hidden from view as much as possible. Completely integrated systems are designed with tubing threaded through the building structure, terminating at irrigation receptacles, emitter tube connections, or in planter boxes. The only tubing seen outside the walls are the small-diameter emitter tube assemblies. If these are hidden under carpeting and behind cabinets, furniture, and planters, they too are unobtrusive. Retrofit installations are a bit more trouble to design. For instance, if wall-to-wall carpeting is not available to hide the tubing, other methods must be sought. Commercial buildings frequently have suspended ceilings, and the spaces above provide a good area through which to route tubing. The building code should always be consulted, however, for many restrict hidden tubing to flame-retardant types exhibiting low, non-toxic smoke generation. The same is true for raised floors in some of the newer office buildings. The basements and attics of houses also provide easy access for tubing installation. When these conveniences are lacking, surface-mounted moldings and channels can be used to hide portions of the tubing run. We will discuss these techniques in greater detail in the chapter on installing APM systems.

Important Flow Controls

There are times when a building's water pressure is too strong for a particular installation, or when flow rates are high for other reasons. Full pressure and/or flow are required only when:

1. Great numbers of plants must be serviced by the system.

2. Very long tubing runs are necessary to reach remote planter location.

3. Vertical rises are extensive.

4. There are combinations of all these factors.

All tend to naturally reduce system water pressure and flow rates. Most installations operate under more moderate conditions, and some sort of flow reduction is necessary. One method is to use flow reducer fittings in the solenoid valve input line. Most of these are simple, inexpensive devices that are pressure-compensating, keeping roughly the same flow rate through a wide range of pressure variations. The other way is to use a water pressure regulator, either variable or fixed. While the variable type is more expensive, it permits

Figure 14.4: Pressure-reduction devices.

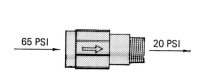

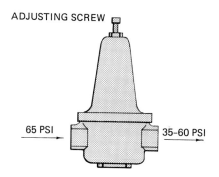

easy adjustment to the levels required by the installation. The fixed types provide only a single, pre-set output pressure level.

Pressure reduction is desirable particularly when there are unsecured (not clamped) tubing connections to barb fittings. High pressure can sometimes blow these junctions apart, causing leaks. High pressure strains all connections, testing the integrity of the system. There are times when only certain branches of a water distribution network require pressure or flow modification, leaving the main part of the network at full operating capacity.

Another important flow control device used in APM system design is the check valve. These are used in main water distribution tubing lines (particularly risers), and, at times, in emitter tubes. The importance of check valve use has already been discussed. They must be used with skill.

The Designing and Costing of a System Installation

While modern, computer-aided design (CAD) methods can significantly reduce the time and effort required to design and cost APM system installations—particularly when dealing with complex configurations—most people still do it the "old-fashioned way," in part because computer software programs are not yet readily available to all practitioners.

The procedure for designing and costing a system installation is as follows:

1. Obtain a set of plans for the building area requiring installation. Floor plans are sometimes adequate but elevations, plumbing, electrical, space and furniture plans are also desirable as they provide insight into available crawl spaces, overhead plenums, basements, furniture locations, power availability, obstructions, etc., and can thus be used to route tubing lines. They also help uncover obstacles to a rapid installation as well as final planter locations. Architectural working drawings are best, but floor plans from sales brochures can often serve the purpose in simpler projects. If plans are not available, make a rough sketch of the area in floor-plan form with detailed dimensions.

2. Check building codes for local requirements.

3. On the floor plan, locate a practical and convenient place for the control center. Draw a small rectangle to represent the control center location, and draw symbolic notes for other control center elements (pressure regulators, filters, backflow preventers, shut-off valves, etc.).

4. Where appropriate, mark the location of irrigation receptacles along the room walls. If receptacles are not to be used, mark anticipated future locations of emitters and potted plants. Some of these are choices based on logic, others on firm knowledge (of fixed planter boxes and pits, for example). It is usually a good idea to coordinate with the interior designer or landscaper working on the job. In early design stages, that may not be possible. It is not necessary to know the exact future location of plants; a close approximation is good enough. Keep in mind that with APM systems plants need not be placed at the receptacles. Flexible emitter tubes will bridge the gap. For instance, containerized decorative plants are generally placed at or near corners of rooms, next to windows, on pieces of furniture, or in front of blank wall space. They are seldom placed in walkway areas, doorways, in dimly lighted locations, or near emergency exits where they might impede traffic.

Most retrofit installations do not use irrigation receptacles. Instead, they use other fittings to connect emitter tubes to the plants. Manifolds are used in cases where a number of plants are grouped together, as in planter boxes or shelves. Mark locations of these manifolds and connecting fittings.

5. Count the number of irrigation receptacles or other planned output fittings and record the figure.

6. Sketch the best routes for tubing lines from the control center to the irrigation receptacles or other anticipated planter locations. Tubing should be routed so that it can be hidden in interior partitions, basements, ceiling joists and beams, suspended ceiling plenums, crawl spaces, cabinets, or plenums below raised floors. The most direct routes should be used. Main tubing lines should be installed overhead or cast into floor slabs wherever possible (new construction and renovation). These are larger in size than branch lines. Lay out branch lines as extensions from the main tubing lines. If overhead, bring them down through partitions, or drops—vertical tubing lines having downhill water flow—to baseboard level, and from there branch out to receptacles or emitter locations, routing tubing through partitions and the like. Try to minimize the number of vertical tubing lines.

In most retrofit installations, tubing is hidden beneath carpeting around the perimeter of rooms, or in cases where there is no carpeting, tubing is installed behind special baseboard moldings.

7. Count the number of vertical tubing lines and record the figure. This will equal the number of main check valves required. There will be a check valve installed at the base of each riser or

drop. Mini check valves may also be installed in emitter tubes to control localized flow.

8. With a rule, measure the length of main tubing lines (trunk lines) on the scaled floor plan. Use the scale of the layout to estimate the length in feet. Record the figure.

9. Calculate the length of risers required. To do this multiply the number of risers in the layout by the estimated riser length (in feet) to equal the total length of vertical tubing. Floor-to-ceiling distances can be estimated at about 8 feet for residential buildings. Commercial buildings generally have about 12 feet between floors.

10. With a rule, measure the length of horizontal branch lines. Using the layout scale, estimate the length in feet. Record the figure.

11. Calculate the total demand of the system as follows: Number of emitters in the system x 0.09gpm avg. demand/emitter = Total demand of system in gallons per minute (gpm).

12. Calculate the flow rate required at the input of the system (pump or solenoid valve output) as follows:

Total demand of system (gpm) x 2.0 loss factor* = Total estimated flow rate required at input. * There are situations where tubing runs are short and only a few fittings and pieces of auxiliary equipment are used in the line. Friction losses are therefore low. The 2.0 loss factor can then be reduced considerably.

13. Choose a solenoid valve controller or pump/reservoir module that can provide the total estimated flow rate. Choose a controller with a built-in solenoid valve having enough flow capacity to provide the required flow

rate (consult Table 14.1) at the building's average water pressure, or at some reduced pressure level if that is appropriate. Valve Cv ratings would be listed in the equipment manufacturer's spec sheet.

14. Choose a pump controller (if low-pressure versions are involved) to meet the power and duty demands of the pump/reservoir module selected in Step 12. That information would be found in the manufacturer's spec sheets.

15. Choose the size of tubing to be used for the main water distribution lines. The inside tubing diameter should be the same as or larger than the inlet/outlet ports of the pump or controller's solenoid valve. Adapter fittings can be used to provide compatibility if necessary.

16. Choose the size of tubing to be used for risers and horizontal branch lines. In most cases 1/2"ID (inside diameter) or 3/8"ID tubing is used for vertical drops or risers, and 3/8"ID or 3/8"OD (outside diameter) tubing for horizontal branch lines. The 3/8"OD tube size is adequate for branches servicing up to about 35 plants.

17. Total the lengths of tubing of each type and size based on the tentative layout (from steps 7, 8, and 9). Record the figures.

18. Count the number of tubing fittings and accessories of each type and size as required by the tentative layout. Record these figures.

19. Calculate material costs as follows: Number of units of each item x unit costs = Estimated material costs. Total all material cost estimates.

20. Estimate labor costs based on installers' rates in the area. An installation quote can be obtained from a contractor if outside services are to be used. One should get several quotes to better compare fees. Factors to be taken into consideration are the extent of installer's training and experience and the estimated number of call-backs for final tubing hook-ups, adjustments, and service. Plumbing installation figures can also be obtained from various publications written about construction cost estimating.

21. Total the estimated material and installation labor costs to arrive at a grand total expense.

22. Add reasonable overhead and profit margins to arrive at the estimated total installation cost.

These figures will enable the designer to reasonably estimate the cost of a proposed installation. They can be refined if required, through further study of the job.

Selection of APM system components can be made easier by using one of the available installation kits. In them all controls, tubing, and fittings have been preselected for compatibility. The down side is that it is impossible for prepackaged kits to predict the exact needs of any given installation, so some components will be in excess while others will be in shortage.

When the project estimates are approved, final working drawings of the interior irrigation system plan should be made on drafting paper or film as an overlay to the architect's floor plan blue prints. They can be reproduced and included with the other project working drawings.

In the sections that follow, we will look at several examples of system design. There are many other applications of APM systems for which we have provided no examples or exercises, but be assured that the principles discussed here are typical of many applications.

Designing for Commercial Buildings

It has been mentioned in previous sections that most commercial buildings are built on partial speculation, and so low-cost installations are required in vacant space to alleviate the financial burden during initial periods of disuse. Skeleton installations of APM systems are designed to meet that need. They involve the "bare bones" of a system and can be installed very economically by pre-fitting building space with the necessities for hook-up and use at a later time. This allows the building owner to advertise the inclusion of high-tech amenities without having first made a large capital investment. The skeleton installation on each floor consists of a control center hooked up to the building's cold water supply, and a main tubing line (usually 3/4" ID copper) installed overhead, down the middle of the vacant tenant areas. Connections about every 20 feet for 1/2" MPT adapters are plugged and left ready for hook-up to branches going to suites as the space is leased. Design work involves the selection and location of control centers and the layout of main tubing runs. Costing is simplified by the fact that few parts are involved.

Figure 14.5: Office building floor plan.

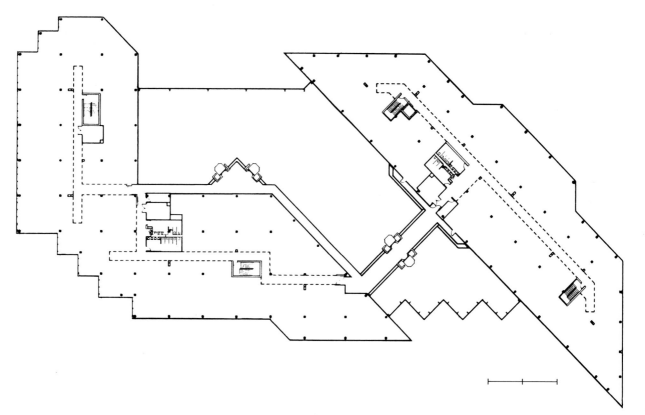

System Design for an Office Building

Figures 14.5 and 14.6 and the discussion that follows take the reader through a step-by-step demonstration design of a skeleton installation. The floor plan is of a modern office building with approximately 33,900 square feet of tenant space on the floor under consideration.

Because of the complex design of the building floor, with major tenant areas split into two sections, or zones, separated by an elevator landing/bridge, it was decided to design two independent high-pressure

irrigation systems, one for each zone. Although the material cost of this approach is slightly higher, the installation is simpler and labor costs are slightly lower as a result. There is also more system flexibility in having independent zones. The floor plan tells us that Zone A is approximately 18,300 square feet, and Zone B approximately 15,600 square feet. A prior inspection of the building disclosed that the overhead space on the floor was fitted with 20" deep steel joists spaced every 4 feet. These are adequate for suspending the 3/4"ID main tubing line over vacant tenant space (building codes permitting). It was also seen

Figure 14.6: Interior irrigation system plan. Boca Automation Model SSI–34 with integral solenoid valve.

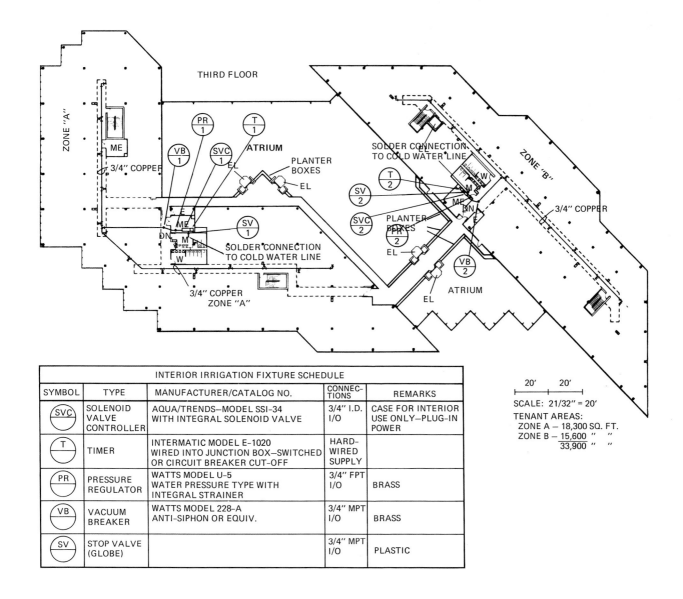

INTERIOR IRRIGATION FIXTURE SCHEDULE				
SYMBOL	TYPE	MANUFACTURER/CATALOG NO.	CONNEC-TIONS	REMARKS
SVC	SOLENOID VALVE CONTROLLER	AQUA/TRENDS–MODEL SSI-34 WITH INTEGRAL SOLENOID VALVE	3/4" I.D. I/O	CASE FOR INTERIOR USE ONLY–PLUG-IN POWER
T	TIMER	INTERMATIC MODEL E-1020 WIRED INTO JUNCTION BOX–SWITCHED OR CIRCUIT BREAKER CUT-OFF	HARD-WIRED SUPPLY	
PR	PRESSURE REGULATOR	WATTS MODEL U-5 WATER PRESSURE TYPE WITH INTEGRAL STRAINER	3/4" FPT I/O	BRASS
VB	VACUUM BREAKER	WATTS MODEL 228-A ANTI-SIPHON OR EQUIV.	3/4" MPT I/O	BRASS
SV	STOP VALVE (GLOBE)		3/4" MPT I/O	PLASTIC

SCALE: 21/32" = 20'
TENANT AREAS:
ZONE A — 18,300 SQ. FT.
ZONE B — 15,600 " "
33,900 " "

that the mechanical room in each zone is next to the rest rooms, convenient sources of water. They were chosen as locations for the control centers. The control equipment could be mounted on a wall, and 3/4"ID input tubing installed up the wall to connect with a cold water line in the overhead space (or other nearby location). Shut-off valves, pressure regulators, and filters are designed into the input lines, and a vacuum breaker into the immediate output line. The 3/4"ID output tubes from the controller also rise into the overhead plenum and connect to a "spine," the 3/4"ID copper trunk line tubing that runs down the center of the tenant space. It should be suspended from the joists or pipe hangers. Every 20 feet a fitting is installed to provide for future connections to office suites. Be sure that access will be available.

The design concept is drawn over the building floor plan (Figure 14.5), either directly or on a tracing paper overlay (Figure 14.6). It then becomes the interior irrigation system plan. Symbols for each of the fittings and accessories are to be included. In this case, they consist mostly of 3/4"ID (sweat) x 3/4"ID (sweat) x 1/2"FPT branch tees, fitted with 1/2"MPT plugs. A fixture schedule (bill of materials) is drawn on, or attached to the interior irrigation system plan. It is a table of the control equipment and fixtures required, but does not include the detail of tubing types and fittings. In this exercise, the interior irrigation fixture schedule (Table 14.4) includes the solenoid valve controller, timer, pressure regulator, and vacuum breaker.

After tubing lines are integrated into the floor plan, a cost estimating worksheet is filled out. It is a detailed schedule of installation labor, materials required, and costs. The design is carefully inspected and each of the fittings, fixtures, and pieces of equipment is recorded on the costing sheet. The worksheet for this example is shown in Table 14.5.

Each zone of the floor plan is costed separately. The cost per unit for each part is obtained from the company database of most recent materials costs, suppliers' current price lists, or an up-to-date quote can be requested from the supplier. The length of each type of tubing is estimated from the floor plan using the scale of the drawing. A rule or architect's scale is laid on the drawing's continuous tubing segments to measure the approximate length. To this is added the estimated length of tubing used in risers and a waste factor of about 5% to get the total amount of tubing (of each type) called for by the installation. Fittings are counted by size and type, and the numbers are recorded. While doing this, a great deal of thought has to go into each connection and the type of fitting needed to make each joint. In the current example, the main tubing lines are rigid copper, and fittings must be soldered in place to join sections and make connections into office suites. Copper ell fittings are used at the end of the main lines. These are 3/4"ID sweat x 1/2"FPT—again, to connect with 1/2" branch tubing at a later time. Plugs are temporarily used in the 1/2"FPT branches of these fittings. Added to the list at this point are hardware and miscellaneous supplies, including tubing clamps and/or pipe hangers, screws, masonry nails, wood support blocks, solder, and flux. Subtotals are calculated for each item on the list and material totals are derived from these. All cost figures should be rounded out to the next higher dollar amount for simplicity. Labor costs for the installation must then be estimated. The basis for these are quotes from installation contractors, past experience, or from data published in recent editions of *Means Mechanical Cost Data Book*.[2] This valuable reference lists installation labor costs by job category. In getting quotes from potential installation contractors, be sure they have all of the facts before making a bid. Labor costs will

TABLE 14.4

Cost Estimates Work Sheet—Office Building 33,900 Square Feet—Skeleton Installation

Materials	Cost/ unit	ZONE A No. Req'd	ZONE A Total cost	ZONE B No. Req'd	ZONE B Total cost
Control Center					
Controller- Model SSI-34AW/3	$300.00	1	$300.00	1	$300.00
Timer- Model E-1020	22.00	1	22.00	1	22.00
Pressure regulator- adjustable, w/strainer	48.00	1	48.00	1	48.00
Backflow preventer- vacuum breaker	15.00	1	15.00	1	15.00
Stop valve- globe type	6.00	1	6.00	1	6.00
Check-valve- adjustable type	6.00	1	6.00	1	6.00
Tee connector- for water line connection	1.00	1	1.00	1	1.00
Tee connector- for anti-water hammer column	1.00	1	1.00	1	1.00
Pipe cap- for anti-water hammer column	1.00	1	1.00	1	1.00
Tubing/Pipe/Hose					
3/4"ID- rigid, type L copper pipe	0.56	290	162.00	240	134.00
Fittings					
Ell connector- 3/4"ID, sweat, brass	0.80	2	2.00	2	2.00
Tee connector-3/4" sweat x 3/4" sweat x 1/2"FPT, brass	1.10	10	11.00	8	9.00
Ell connector- 3/4" sweat x 1/2"FPT, brass	0.85	2	2.00	2	2.00
Plug- 1/2"MPT, brass	0.55	12	7.00	10	6.00
Other (Misc.)	65.00	65.00			

Materials Expense: Zone A		$649.00
Zone B		$618.00
Labor Expense : Installation (incl. labor markup)		$560.00
(1 plumber + helper- 16 man-hrs.@$35 avg./MH incl. O & P @ 45%)		
Other (electric)		$50.00
Grand Total Expense		$1,877.00
Contractor Markup of Materials (Zone A + Zone B @10%)		$127.00
Grand Total Installation Cost		**$2,004.00**
Cost per Square Foot		$0.06

vary from one location of the country to another, and even widely within one area. Quotes will include the subcontractor's profit and overhead on labor. Installation labor costs will be different if a developer has in-house plumbers, as opposed to using an independent contractor. Once labor costs are calculated, they are added to total material costs to obtain grand total expenses. To those must be added a factor for installer's overhead and profits. A 10% subcontractor mark-up on materials is considered a fair figure for estimates. That figure is added to the grand total expense figure to arrive at an estimated grand total cost of installation. In the present example, the total for that floor came to $2,004 or $0.06 per square foot. General contractors will frequently add another 10% to totals.

A recommendation could then be made to the client to extend branches of the system to service the planter boxes flanking elevators in the common area. It might cost

an additional $0.01 per square foot or so for that floor, but the $350 spent during construction would save many thousands of dollars in plant care costs over the life of the building.

System Design for an Office Suite

This example of APM system design will deal with connections from the building's skeleton installation to service a corporate office suite. The irrigation system design work would be done just after the architects and interior designers have completed their layouts, and an office floor plan and finished working drawings are available. In the example at hand (Figure 14.7), the office suite was designed with approximately 5,000 square feet of space.

The interior design calls for the use of about 109 containerized foliage plants, to be

Figure 14.7: A typical 5,000-square-foot office suite floor plan.

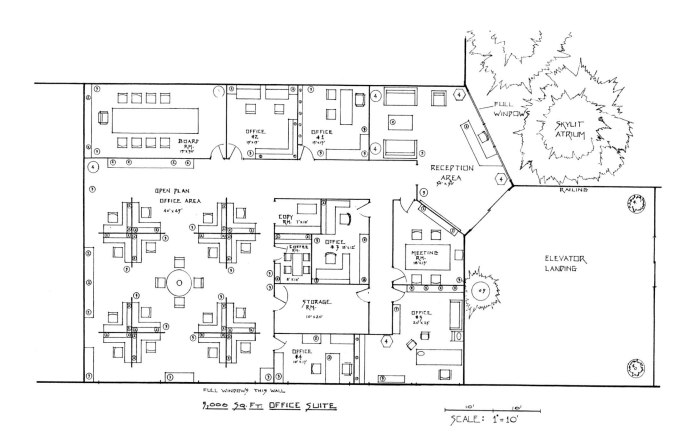

placed on filing cabinets, desks, credenzas, book cases, tables, and freestanding on the floor. The numbered circles and polygons on the floor plan represent tentative locations for the plants. Actually, the plants' final locations have little relevance in designing this installation. Irrigation receptacles must be designed into the walls at logical, yet convenient locations, so plants in the rooms can be serviced easily regardless of where they are eventually placed (or moved to at a later time). The receptacle locations were chosen according to the logic discussed earlier in this chapter. When all were located on the plan, they were counted, and the total was found to be 56. If 109 potted plants are eventually serviced, there would be that many emitters used in this branch of the building's system. Calculating the demand by this branch for irrigation water is done as follows: Number of emitters x 0.09GPM avg. demand/emitter = Total demand; 109 x 0.09 = 9.8GPM Total

demand. Because most of the plants in this particular suite will be small, each using less than 0.09GPM of flow rate, it is not necessary to double the calculated total demand figure with a loss factor. The main irrigation line servicing this floor is 3/4"ID, and the solenoid valve controller used would have an output of at least 40GPM to accommodate all the suites on the system. Only full-pressure output would be considered, although if only one or two suites were on the system during the early leasing stages, pressure levels would be reduced.

Another way of doing this is to design a fixed pressure regulator into each suite's input line so that no matter what the general system pressure is at the time, the suite would be held at a fixed level. This is the preferred method. To be sure flow is well distributed to the suite without too much demand on any one branch input line, it was decided to feed water through

Figure 14.8: Interior irrigation system plan.

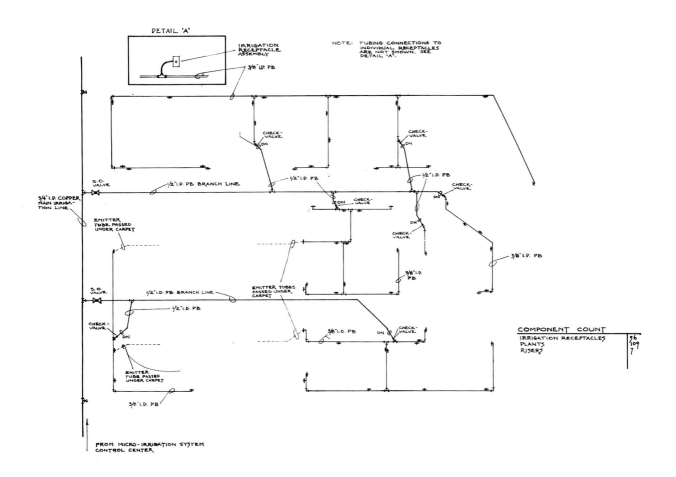

two independent 1/2"ID polybutylene branch lines instead of just one. That means overhead connections to two branch tees in the 3/4"ID main irrigation trunk line. Some building codes do not permit plastic tubing or piping in overhead areas of commercial buildings, so copper or other acceptable tubing material must be used instead. Some will permit fire-rated plastic tubing. (Make sure to always check local codes in the early stages of design work.) The 1/2"ID branch lines are also routed over the office suite, and lateral sub-branches taken from them and dropped down through partitions at six strategic locations. These are marked DN for "down" on the plan. The locations for these drops, or risers, as they are also called, are chosen so that as many receptacles or emitters as possible can be serviced from each. The tubing material can be 1/2" ID polybutylene in this case, without violating most building codes. A check valve must be designed into each vertical line at its base. The smaller lines branching off from the bases of risers are 3/8"ID polybutylene. 3/8"OD PB tubing can sometimes be used as well. They are routed through partitions at baseboard level to irrigation receptacles and other emitter locations. In Figure 14.7 an extra drop was made into the reception area partition as a safety measure, assuring that area of enough water to accommodate a number of larger plants, such as trees.

A common interior design practice is to place more prominent plants in reception areas. The open plan office area must be serviced in a different way. Assuming the floor of the office suite is not raised (as is done in many modern office buildings), one of two design courses can be taken. Each work station island or grouping can be serviced with a low-pressure APM system, with the control center and pump/reservoir module installed in an empty cell of a desk or cabinet. Small-diameter tubing lines

would be routed from there through the work station partitions to planter locations (including those freestanding on the floor). The neatest, most professional installation would be made with irrigation receptacles mounted on the surface of cabinets, desks, and partitions to provide easy, plug-in access to the water lines. The designer can decide to use this more refined method, but must take the extra material and installation cost into consideration.

Emitter tubes from the suite's high-pressure irrigation system can also be used to service the work stations. An emitter tube assembly is simply plugged into a nearby irrigation receptacle and routed under the carpeting to a work station. This works well when the office carpeting is installed with a thick foam underpad. PVC emitter tubing is small in diameter and soft, and will sink easily into the soft underpad, not to be seen from the surface. Other methods of installation make the tubing runs under walkway areas virtually invisible. It is the walkways themselves that are usually the problem. Wherever furniture covers the flooring a slight ridge from below makes little difference, but one across an open floor could be considered unsightly. The same problem exists when trying to retrofit electrical wiring to a work station. It must also be passed under the carpeting and thus creates the same situation. Tubing, being smaller and more flexible than commercial wiring, is less of a problem. Keep in mind that thin-walled PVC tubing of this type tends to flatten down somewhat, taking on an oval configuration. That reduces its propensity to appear as a ridge on the surface. At the same time, water flow is not restricted because so long as the tube is not flattened completely, the interior area remains the same and carries the same amount of water as when its cross-section is round. Obviously, furniture and other heavy objects cannot be placed over the tubing as that would cause flow restriction. More and more residential-type carpets are being used in commercial settings with foam underpads. Aside from the fact that there is more decorative selection among this variety, interior designers find sound absorption qualities are better, they are more comfortable to walk on, and the underpad helps the longevity of the carpeting as it cushions pedestrian pressure and reduces friction on pile fibers. A difficult situation occurs when the office carpet is a commercial type. These are usually thinner and don't use separate foam underpads, but are instead cemented directly to the concrete slab floor with supplementary foam underpads preattached. As a result, it is difficult to pass electrical wiring, tubing, or anything else under these carpets without a ridge showing. Sometimes electrical wiring is passed across the top surface of the carpet and covered with a thin, plastic strip called a cord cover. The same technique can be used with small tubing. Offices having plenums under a raised floor present less difficulty because tubing can be routed under the decking. It can be sheathed in water-tight conduit, if necessary. In any case, the various methods under consideration should be discussed with the client and a final decision made as to how the workstation islands are to be serviced with automated plant care. In this case we will assume that the decision was to plug into irrigation receptacles and pass tubing the short distance under the carpeting to work stations. It is then routed through the work station structure to planter locations. For the best installation, shallow channels can be cut into the concrete floor slab to accommodate this short tubing run.

In costing this project, remember that no control center or main water distribution lines are necessary. Those services are already provided by the building's integral system. A cost estimating worksheet (Table 14.6) was completed when designing the skeleton installation.

Each type and size of tubing is listed and measured for approximate length, as each type and size of fitting is listed and identified on the plan. Accessories and pieces of hardware that are likely to be required are also listed individually. Start with the larger tubing lines first and work down to the smallest, remembering to add some extra to all figures for waste. The amount of actual waste will vary with the skill of the installers, but generally there is a 5% to 10% waste factor on tubing, fittings, and hardware. Waste is not expected when considering electronic equipment, irrigation receptacles, and the like. The total material expense for this design would be about $2,284. There is no such thing as an absolute price when it comes to making cost estimates of any project. The cost of materials and labor varies with so many factors that unless firm quotes have been obtained, and the project is carried out within the period that those quotes are valid, only close estimates can be stated in design and cost studies. This is particularly true of quick, early-stage investigations. Estimated costs can usually be guaranteed, however, within 10% or 15%. Installation labor costs vary widely by geographical location, type of craft, experience levels of the workers, union affiliation, and use of in-house labor as opposed to hiring independent contractors. In the case at hand, installation is predicated on the use of an independent contractor. It is estimated by the contractor that two plumbers and one plumber's helper would be required for 8 hours. Average wage rates were quoted at $36.00 per man-hour. Total labor expense is $864 for the project, making for a grand total expense of $3,148. Another 10% of the material expense is added for subcontractor profit and overhead charges. That brings the total to $3,376. This is what it would cost the building owner in this example to extend an existing APM system into a new tenant suite. On a

233

Table 14.5:

Cost Estimates Work Sheet Office Suite 5,000 Square Feet

Materials	Cost/Unit	No. Req'd	TotalCost
Input Group			
Stop valve- globe type	$6.00	2	$12.00
Pressure regulator- fixed type- @15 psi	10.00	1	10.00
Tubing/Pipe/Hose			
1/2"ID PB	0.35/ft.	280ft.	98.00
3/8"ID PB	0.30/ft.	460ft.	138.00
1/4"OD PVC	0.09/ft.	110ft.	10.00
Fittings			
Tee connector- 1/2"ID I/O/B, barb type, copper	1.30	5	7.00
Check-valve- 1/2"FPT I/O, adjustable, PVC	5.50	7	39.00
Ell connector- 1/2"ID x 3/8"ID barb type,copper	1.10	2	3.00
Tee connector- 3/8"ID I/O/B, barb type, copper	1.60	5	8.00
Ell connector- 3/8"ID I/O, barb type, copper	1.15	12	14.00
Tee connector- 3/8"ID x 3/8"ID x 1/2"ID I/O/B, barb type, copper	1.90	5	10.00
Emitters			
Adjustable, mini-valve emitter, plastic	0.20	130	26.00
Accessories			
Irrigation receptacle (with emitter assembly)- 1/4"OD	32.00	56	1,792.00
Emitter stabilizer- 6" stake	0.14	130	19.00
Crimp rings- for 1/2"ID tubing	0.12	58	7.00
- for 3/8"ID tubing	0.10	180	18.00
Hardware			
Pipe hanger- for 1/2"ID tubing	0.15	20	3.00
Misc.	70.00		
Total Materials Expended			$2,284.00
Total Labor Expense (2 plumbers, 1 helper- 24 man-hrs. @ $36 avg./MH- incl. O & P)			864.00
Grand Total Expense			$3,148.00
Contractor Mark-up of Materials (@ 10%)			228.00
Grand Total Cost of Installation			**$3,376.00**
Cost per Square Foot (@ 5,000 sq. Ft. of office space)			$0.68/sq.ft.

square footage basis, the total represents $0.68 per square foot. The building owner might mark up his cost and charge the installation to the tenant at a higher rate— either a one-time charge or amortized over the period of the lease.

System Design for a Single-Family House

This section will demonstrate the design steps involved in a residential APM system. Assume that a home builder requested the cost of installing a fully integrated version (Boca Automation's Mirage III™ system) into a luxury single-family residence of 3,200 square feet while under construction. The floor plan furnished by the builder (Figure 14.9) shows a three-bedroom, two-and-a-half bath house with family room and den.

Further investigation discloses that above the living room, dining room, and foyer is a high, vaulted ceiling. That fact is relevant here, because it means there is no overhead space through which to route tubing in those areas. The large garage is chosen as the most appropriate location for the control center. Not only is it out of the way, but it is next to the laundry room where there is convenient access to a cold water line. A stop valve is designed into the input water line to shut off the entire branch when necessary, as well as an adjustable, pressure regulator that includes a built-in screen filter (strainer).

Irrigation receptacles are next located at appropriate places along the walls of the rooms. Three are planned for the foyer as potted plants are frequently placed there to provide a casual look to the entrance. All the other rooms are fitted with these special outlets as well, including the kitchen. There, two receptacles are designed into the splashboard above the countertop. Many homeowners like to have plants on kitchen counters and the convenience of having automated plant care there as well as in the other rooms is a welcome amenity. Modern bathrooms are fitted in the same way, particularly those having skylights or windows. That is not the case with our current example, however. The number of irrigation receptacles included in the plan is counted and recorded (28).

Now knowing how many outlets are involved, the total system demand can be calculated. Assuming only one emitter per irrigation outlet on average, there would be a maximum of 28 emitters in operation at any given time. Usually, there would be fewer. The total demand of this system would be as follows: Number of emitters on the system x 0.09GPM avg. demand/emitter = Total demand; 28 x 0.09GPM = 2.5GPM Total demand. From this, the flow rate required at the irrigation system input can be calculated: Total demand (GPM) x 2.0 loss factor = Total flow rate required; 2.5GPM x 2.0 = 5GPM Total flow rate required.

A solenoid valve controller with an output of at least 5GPM must be chosen to control system operation. Referring to Table 14.1, we see that a solenoid valve with a Cv of at least 1.4 is required. The better choice is one having a Cv of 3.4 or 3.6. For this example, we have chosen Boca Automation's Model SSI-34AW/3, as it has enough capacity to service the plan under consideration, as well as other auxiliary branches if required—indoors or out. It has an input/output tubing size of 3/4"ID or 1/2"ID. A short, capped pipe is connected to the controller inlet to act as an anti-water hammer column. It functions like a shock absorber to protect the solenoid valve from sudden changes of pressure. The water pressure regulator can be installed at the controller outlet instead of in the inlet grouping. If more than one irrigation zone is called for, a water distribution manifold would follow the pressure regulator.

Figure 14.9:
Floor plan for
a 3,200-
square-foot
house.

Next we must find the best routing for tubing lines. They must be integrated into the framework of the building so as not to be seen. One of the problems we will encounter is the vaulted ceiling area. Room configurations of this type generally require that tubing and wiring be installed around their perimeter, as space is seldom available overhead. Other problems to be encountered have to do with the many interior and exterior doorways. There are many in houses, and sub-branches running along the baseboard usually do not traverse an open doorway. Nevertheless, there are practical ways of getting around doorways. The line must either be terminated at the door, or routed up and around the door frame to the other side. The former choice is preferable. As most rooms in this house have conventional eight-foot ceilings, there is space above the ceiling joists to route tubing lines. In this example, 1/2"ID polybutylene tubing is routed to the garage ceiling plenum. A vacuum-breaker type of backflow preventer is installed in the line at its highest point. An alternative is to use a

double check valve vacuum breaker at the cold water pipe connection. Its output is branched off in two directions, one toward the building entrance and one toward the back of the house. Once past the vaulted ceiling area, another branch is connected into it to be run through partitions for master suite, living room, and family room service. The other main branch is passed over the den and over the front door frame to service the receptacles on the far side of the foyer. Drops, or risers, down through partitions are made at appropriate places from these 1/2" overhead branches—10 of them in all. At the base of each drop is positioned a check valve and connections to 3/8"ID polybutylene tubing lines that traverse the room perimeters at baseboard level. To these are connected the irrigation receptacle feeder tubes. The interior irriga-tion system plan should be laid out on vellum tracing paper or drafting film if the floor plan furnished by the client is small. The undersized drawing becomes confused with the other elements if the schematic is laid out directly on the floor plan.

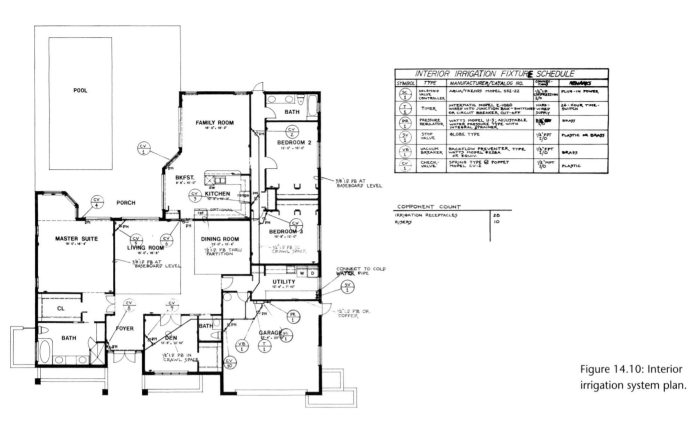

The costing of this installation follows the same procedures we have used in previous examples. Control center elements had previously been chosen while designing the system. They should be listed, along with their latest prices, on the cost estimating worksheet (Table 14.6). The length of tubing runs is measured with a ruler or scale and estimated from the drawing scale. A little extra length is added to compensate for waste. Estimates for 1/2"ID and 3/8"ID tubing are recorded, as are the counts for each fitting size and type, accessories, and hardware. Latest prices for each are extracted from supplier price lists or recent quotes. Labor costs should be obtained from several installation contractors as job quotes. Totals should then be calculated for materials and labor. In this case, grand total expense was estimated at $2,627 or $0.82 per square foot, based on the 3,200 square foot area of the house under air conditioning. Garage area is not counted as it isn't considered part of the living area. Many home builders typically add on another 50% to cover their profit and overhead, making the cost to the homeowner $3,940 for this system. Because capacity is large enough in this case, a suggestion would be made to the homeowner that the APM system be extended outdoors to the pool/patio area. This could be accomplished easily and without much additional cost, and would conveniently service freestanding and hanging, containerized patio plants.

The house used for this example is larger than average but was selected because it contained most of the challenges normally encountered in the design of residential systems. Smaller houses and apartments are typically less difficult to work on from a design standpoint. Note that the high-side expense is largely dependent on the number of irrigation receptacles installed, the local labor rate, and the amount of mark-up the builder adds. There is a trend in the industry for high-tech amenities to be included in homes at builder's cost. This is a marketing strategy currently being pioneered by Lennar, one of the country's largest residential developers.

Table 14.6:

Cost Estimates Work Sheet Single Family Home 3,200 Square Feet

Materials	Cost/Unit	No. Req'd	Total Cost
Control Center			
Solenoid valve controller: Boca Automation Model SSI-34AW/3	$300.00	1	$300.00
Timer: Intermatic Model E-1020 (if home control system is not used)	22.00	1	22.00
Pressure regulator: adjustable, with strainer	48.00	1	48.00
Backflow preventer: vacuum breaker type	15.00	1	15.00
Stop valve: globe type	6.00	1	6.00
Tee connector: for water line connection	1.00	1	1.00
Anti-water hammer column	2.00	1	2.00
Tubing/Pipe/Hose			
1/2"ID PB	0.35/ft.	240 ft.	84.00
3/8"ID PB	0.30/ft.	240 ft.	72.00
Fittings			
Tee connector: 1/2"ID I/O/B, barb type, copper	1.30	8	11.00
Ell connector: 1/2"ID I/O, barb type, copper	1.10	3	4.00
Check-valve: adjustable, 1/2"FPT I/O, PVC	5.50	10	55.00
Tee connector: 3/8"ID I/O/B, barb type, copper	1.60	2	4.00
Ell connector: 3/8"ID I/O, barb type, copper	1.15	18	21.00
Tee connector: 3/8"ID x 3/8"ID x 1/2"ID I/O/B, barb type, copper	1.90	7	14.00
Accessories			
Irrigation receptacle- (with emitter tube assemblies)	32.00	28	896.00
Crimp rings: for 1/2"ID PB tubing	0.12	40	5.00
for 3/8"ID PB tubing	0.10	64	7.00
Hardware			
Pipe hanger: for 1/2"ID PB tubing	0.15	24	4.00
for 3/8"ID PB tubing	0.15	38	6.00
Misc.	70.00		

Total Materials Expense		$1,647.00
Total Labor Expense (1 plumber, 1 helper: 28 man-hrs. @$35 avg./MH— incl. 45% O & P)		980.00
Grand Total Expense		**$2,627.00**
Builder's Overhead and Profit (@ 50% of expense)		1,314.00
Cost to Home Buyer		$3,940.00
Cost per square foot (@ 3,200 sq.ft.)		$1.23

FIFTEEN

Installing Automated Precision Micro-Irrigation Systems

In many respects, installing the elements of automated precision micro-irrigation systems is very similar to installing electric power wiring, plumbing system piping, security system or intercom system wiring, or central vacuum cleaner system ductwork. In each case, the distribution network must be routed through the building in such a way that it is operational, safe, and unobtrusive. Those are the main objectives of APM system installations as well. There are many techniques unique to this concept that were developed over a period of time, mainly through first-hand installation experiences. This chapter contains much of what the reader needs to be knowledgeable, skillful, and versatile in this specialized field.

General Layout Considerations

As we have discussed, there are many impediments to the easy application of this technology in building interiors. The design of the building is a major factor, as are its construction materials. If done with foresight and skill, the designer would have taken all or most of the installation problems into consideration and provided a plan that would make the installer's job much easier. The interior irrigation system plan, fixture schedule, and cost estimating worksheet provide a "road map" for the installation. They show the equipment and parts involved, general layout of the control center, general routing for the water distribution network, types of tubing connections that must be made, installation points for flow control devices, and approximate locations of emitters and decorative plants. The installer, in looking at this material, should be able to get a quick idea of the requirements of the installation. If the installer was involved in the bidding process, the plans and job requirements would already be familiar.

Probably the most difficult part of an installer's work is the routing of tubing throughout the structure. There are many decisions that must be made as the job progresses. This is particularly true of retrofit projects, in which the major problem is hiding tubing lines from view. When rooms are empty, fitted with residential-type carpeting, and there is adequate space beneath for tubing lines, then the installer's job can be relatively easy. Somehow, though, things are never that simple. Problems crop up because of furniture, potted plant locations, partition structures, and the room layout. Many times they cannot be foreseen in the design stages and appropriate action must be taken on the spot.

The integrated versions of APM systems also run into a wide variety of situations that must be dealt with in specific ways. The least difficult to install are skeleton installations in commercial buildings. The floors to which these are applied are vacant and wide open, with few physical impediments to the system. The most difficult situations involve the installation of tubing at inappropriate or inconvenient times, for example, after much of the interior partition drywall has already been installed. Situations like this one are usually accidental, but competent project management should minimize their occurrences.

Control Centers

Control centers are best located in out-of-the-way areas. When working with high-pressure APM systems, that generally means utility rooms of some sort, in the core of commercial buildings, garages, laundry rooms, or basements in residential structures. A dedicated electric receptacle should be mounted nearby. Water source connections are made to the building's cold water supply in a couple of ways. A tee fitting is generally soldered into the copper line and the irrigation supply tubing connected to it, usually with a 1/2"MPT or 3/4"MPT fitting. An appropriate tee compression fitting can also be used. A stop valve (usually globe type) is installed near the connecting point, followed by a strainer or other filter (see Figure 15.1). Sometimes a hose bibb is used to provide both connection and shut off functions. Some adjustable types have built-in screen filters to integrate the two devices. All of these connections can be made with threaded fittings, preferably brass or Schedule 80 PVC. Part of this connection should include an anti-water-hammer air chamber. It is simply a capped bypass tube that absorbs the shock of high-volume water flow that stops abruptly. This device can save wear and stress on fittings and on the solenoid valve itself.

The output side of the solenoid valve is connected to the input side of the water pressure regulator. All Mirage™ system solenoid valve controllers are surface-mounted. The built-in solenoid valve accepts input tubing from water source connections on one side, then sources the water distribution tubing network on its output side. Input tubing can come from inside the wall behind the controller, in which case escutcheons are used to dress up the pass through drywall. When tubing is integrated into a building during construction, it is "roughed in" (only the basic elements, like tubing and fittings, are installed), usually before the electronic control elements are finally installed. At the control center location, tubing stubs are passed through the drywall and loosely capped, ready for inspection and pressure testing of the irrigation tubing network and final connection to the solenoid valve. The temporary caps are later replaced with a bridge of tubing between the input and output stubs, to permit continuous flow through the system during testing. This connection is made temporary by the use of compression fittings. If the irrigation branch shut-off valve is not close to the control center, a globe valve should be installed in the solenoid valve's input line for emergency shut off.

Limited, light-duty systems useful in residences, offices, hotel suites, and restaurants can be sourced from plumbing connections under kitchen or bathroom sinks. Control centers are located in the cabinets, and tubing routed through partitions to irrigation receptacles or other emitter connections. Fixed water pressure regulators can generally be used in these instances to save space and for economy. They should be chosen to provide downstream pressure levels of 15 to 25 psi.

The pressure level depends on the complexity of the installation; the more complex, the higher the pressure, for instance.

Low-pressure versions can be installed in a convenient, hidden place. When large pump/reservoir modules are involved in interior installations, they are located in a closet or utility room of some type. Pump controllers and timers are mounted on the wall near the reservoir. Most controllers are plug-in types, so a timer with a power outlet must be used, or a dedicated outlet remotely controlled. Small low-pressure systems with 2¼ gallon reservoirs can be easily hidden behind or under furniture, behind large planters, and inside of cabinets or desks. With these as well, the small pump controller is fastened to the wall in close proximity to the reservoir. In each case the low-voltage output wire from the controller connects to pump terminals or wire leads. The installer should be careful to observe proper DC polarities (+ power lead gets connected to the + pump terminal, etc.).

If electromechanical time switches are used in the system, they must be mounted next to the controllers. One type commonly used is a simple design which plugs into a power source, with the controller, in turn, plugged into it. Another common type used in APM systems wires into an electrical box with the controller connected to it, either through hard wiring in the same electrical junction box, or by externally plugging into it. Wiring a wall switch to the junction box for power cut off is not recommended unless a key switch is used. Experience has shown that it is too easy to throw the switch accidentally, and the system can languish inoperative for days or weeks before anyone recognizes the problem. Key switches make such mistakes more difficult. Some designers may want to use a separate electrical circuit with its own circuit breaker for the APM system. It is not considered necessary to do so as the power required is seldom greater than 50 watts—and much less in its dormant mode, which is 99% of the time.

Internal fuses protect the control equipment. As a compromise, a designer may want to install a localized fuse or circuit breaker to protect just the irrigation branch of the electrical circuit. If in doubt, it would be a good idea to discuss the situation with local building inspectors or electricians. The main requirement here is that continuous power be made available to the irrigation system control center.

If a centralized power management system is used in the building, it must be able to selectively control the electrical outlets or junction boxes providing power to the irrigation control center. The remote controller must be programmed to apply power to the irrigation control center two or possibly three times per day for at least one minute. It is a good idea to provide a supplementary power lead independent of the computerized control circuit to use when the main supply is dysfunctional.

Water Distribution Networks

The routing and connection of tubing networks for APM systems is a complex subject. There are a variety of materials used in a variety of ways. The commonality is that the tubing must carry water to planter locations, be leak-free, provide local control over water flow, and be sufficiently hidden to make the installation neat and unobtrusive. Each of these requirements will be dealt with in turn, as will the special requirements of various types of installations.

At this stage it should be mentioned that polybutylene tubing is a controversial product in the building trades. Many years ago, when this product was first introduced, the barb fittings available for system connections were made of acetal plastic. Poorly trained and careless plumbers frequently overtightened crimp rings securing the connections, causing stress

Figure 15.1: A typical installation configuration for a high-pressure APM system integrated into a building interior.

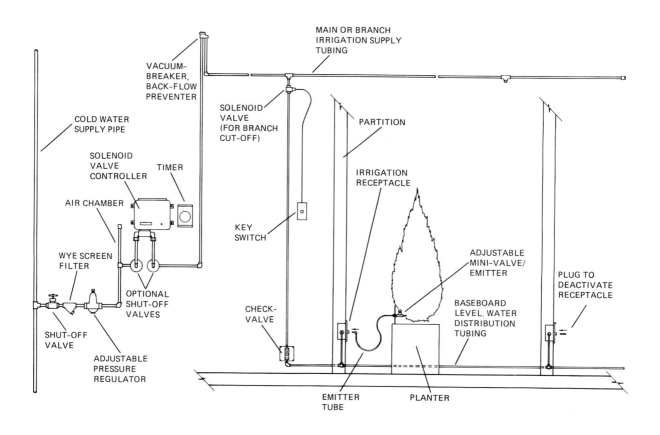

fractures in the acetal fitting. Over a period of time this subtle damage became worse and eventually leaked, causing severe property damage in many cases. As the gravity of the problem became known, Shell Oil Company, Qest (Division of U.S. Brass), and Vanguard—the main industrial developers of the system—took steps to replace the thermoplastic connector fittings with those made of copper and brass. The change solved the problem, and most building codes in the U.S. currently recognize and authorize use of polybutylene plumbing systems in their jurisdictions. However, there are still many lawsuits in U.S. courts which were spawned by early problems. These factors have cast a shadow of uncertainty over all plastic plumbing systems. Nevertheless, the number of successful installations in the U.S. speaks for itself and the industry reports widening use despite the controversy.

Concerning the use of polybutylene in APM systems, remember that water pressure stress on tubing joints in these installations is much less than that found in the main building plumbing. The latter is under constant pressure of up to 75 psi. Most APM systems, on the other hand, operate with pressure levels between 15 and 35 psi, and the tubing networks are pressurized for no longer than about 40 seconds in a 24-hour period. This means that 99% of the day, the water pressure acting on system joints is practically zero. That's a major reduction in system stress, helping to make APM systems one of the safest interior irrigation technologies available.

Routing Tubing Lines for Integral Systems

When APM systems are integrated into the structure of buildings, such as with Boca Automation's Mirage III™ systems, most of the tubing network is installed while the interior partition work is in progress, and while electrical and plumbing wiring and pipes are being "roughed in." The task is easiest in those instances where skeleton installations are made in vacant, commercial floor space, for partitions have not yet been constructed. Competent plumbing contractors should be employed to do this work. Small, secondary installation jobs can be handled by handymen, but keep in mind that the tubing system should be pressure tested and inspected before it is put into use. Local building codes will require this in most instances. The point is that the installer should be knowledgeable about and skillful in the installation of tubing connections. Once partitions are enclosed, leaks are difficult to fix. Of course, the same applies to the primary plumbing system. If the installer is competent in handling that work, chances are good that a little additional training will make him competent in APM system work as well.

Tubing networks in skeleton installations branch out from the solenoid valve controller to overhead trunk lines. It is generally one long trunk line hung from the ceiling. This tubing work is usually made of copper because its stiffness helps in this situation. Where possible, the vertical line (riser) from the controller is installed about 12" higher than the highest tubing line, and fitted at that point with a vacuum breaker and backflow preventer (see Figure 14.1). Some building codes prefer having a double-check valve type of backflow preventer at the water source connection. From there, the trunk line is routed down the middle of the vacant tenant space, fastened to suitable supports or pipe hangers. Every 20 feet a copper tee fitting is soldered into place. A copper ell fitting is soldered to each end of the trunk line, and all threaded outlets are closed off with 1/2"MPT plugs.

Tubing networks routed into rooms and suites sometimes require that their water supply lines be cast into concrete floor slabs and then brought up into partitions. Local building codes differ on these points, but usually the tubing must be sleeved with outer tubing when it is installed in the concrete form. They also require that the tubing be continuous, with no fittings or other joints cast into the concrete. Because of that requirement, tubing runs must sometimes be brought above ground for branch or continuation connections. This can be done most conveniently in a fixed planter box or, if necessary, in a large junction box mounted in a partition. The two ends of tubing lines are simply connected with a fitting bridge between them (see Figure 15.2).

In most instances, water supply tubing for APM systems is introduced into room partitions from overhead connections. When the branch tubes are dropped down into the open partitions, it is important that a spring-loaded check valve be installed in-line, with its one-way flow path pointing toward the baseboard. The check valve must be chosen for a specific location, and its

cracking pressure must be higher than the static pressure in the riser above it. Polybutylene tubing lines (1/2"ID) are normally used in these runs, and the connections to and from the check valve would be made with brass barb fittings, secured with copper crimp rings. The installer will find that slipping barb fittings into polybutylene tubing is made easier if the tubing end is first softened with heat, either from very hot water or a heat gun. The latter method is more effective, so long as the temperature used is not excessive. (This technique can also be used with other plastic tubing.) Building codes generally require that there be convenient access to flow control devices, such as check valves, so they can be removed or repaired easily in case of problems. Access can be provided with these systems by having an access plate mounted in the drywall (gypsum board). An electrical "mud ring" would be attached to the opening in the drywall to provide a mount for a 4" x 4" blank electrical plate, which provides the access when necessary (Figure 15.3). It can simply

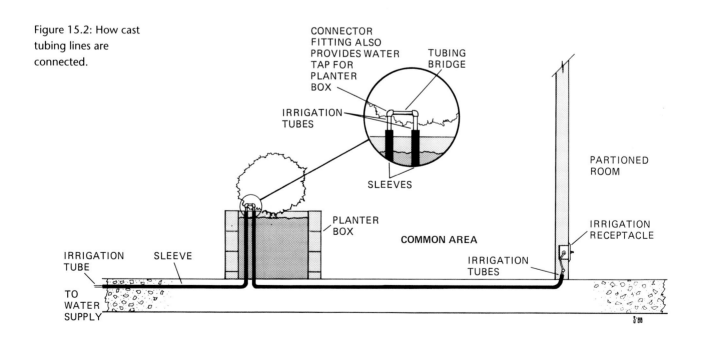

Figure 15.2: How cast tubing lines are connected.

be unscrewed to gain access to the check valve in the partition behind it. Larger access ports are sometimes required. They can be provided by using molded plastic access panels such as those manufactured by Karp Associates (Easi-Access brand).

Just below the check valve, connections are made to branch off further with 3/8"ID tubing which circles the room within the partitions at baseboard level. The input tubing size must be reduced from the 1/2"ID to 3/8"ID. 3/8" ID tee fittings are available with 1/2"ID branches that make the transition easily. These are also barb type fittings, and must be secured with crimp rings. All barb connections of plastic tubing that are to be sealed up within partitions must use authorized crimp rings, and many building codes even require it. The smaller tubing lines that run around the room at baseboard level must be passed through partition studs. Holes are drilled in wooden studs about 4" above the floor. In the case of metal studs, they are generally manufactured with holes already punched into them for electrical and plumbing service lines, and can be used for interior irrigation tubing as well. Protective plastic inserts should be used in those holes supporting irrigation tubes. Whenever properly located service holes are not already available, they must be punched out of the metal stud by stud. This is a routine procedure for plumbing contractors, so the installer will normally know what to do. *It is important when installing APM systems that these lateral branch tubing lines be six to twelve inches below the irrigation receptacles. They need to be placed in such a way that they avoid being punctured by nails and drywall screws.*

During the rough-in stage of installation, the small lateral branches are fitted with irrigation receptacle feeder tubes at appropriate locations. A special tee fitting with a 3/8"OD feeder tube attached comes

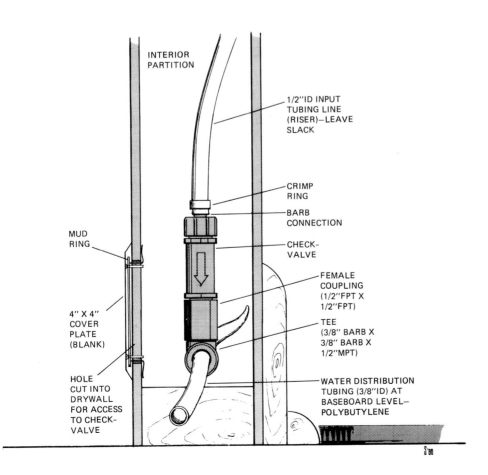

INTERIOR PARTITION

1/2"ID INPUT TUBING LINE (RISER)–LEAVE SLACK

CRIMP RING

BARB CONNECTION

CHECK-VALVE

FEMALE COUPLING (1/2"FPT X 1/2"FPT)

TEE (3/8" BARB X 3/8" BARB X 1/2"MPT)

WATER DISTRIBUTION TUBING (3/8"ID) AT BASEBOARD LEVEL–POLYBUTYLENE

MUD RING

4" X 4" COVER PLATE (BLANK)

HOLE CUT INTO DRYWALL FOR ACCESS TO CHECK-VALVE

Figure 15.3: Check valve connection detail.

with the irrigation receptacle kit. It is a barb type fitting secured by crimp rings that fits into the baseboard tubing line about 9" to the side of where the irrigation receptacle will be installed (see Figure 15.4).

A junction box also comes with the irrigation receptacle installation kit. It should be mounted on a stud at the desired location, with the box located about 12" above the floor. The irrigation receptacle feeder tube should be passed through the side, and then the front of the box. A tag on the tube end should be marked with instructions for the drywall contractor. The note would contain such information as "Attention drywall contractor: Interior irrigation tubing. Cut drywall around box opening."

Routing tubing lines through a house is not very different from routing tubing lines in a commercial structure. The tubing is passed through beams, studs, joists, and partitions in the most practical way possible, making sure that the tubing or pipe is well insulated to prevent freezing in cold-weather locations. (The residential design exercise in Chapter Thirteen gives an idea of the problems likely to be encountered in this type of installation.) If the house has an overhead attic, crawl space, or basement, tubing can then be routed through these accessible yet out-of-sight locations. If desired, any tubing in these plenums can be connected with appropriate compression fittings instead of barb types. Keep in mind that while they are easier to install, compression fittings are more costly.

When routing irrigation lines through basements, attics, or floor joists, it is easy to position an irrigation receptacle feeder line inside a partition in order to service one or more outlets (see Figure 15.6).

Some of the reasons polybutylene tubing is used for irrigation lines is because it is extremely flexible, is easy to cut, and comes in 100-foot coils. This makes it simple to snake the tubing through tight places, and

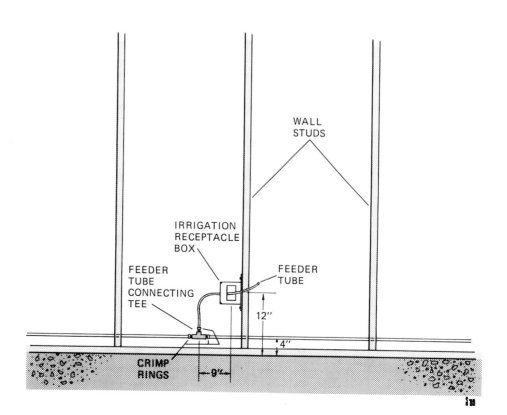

Figure 15.4: Irrigation receptacle installation detail.

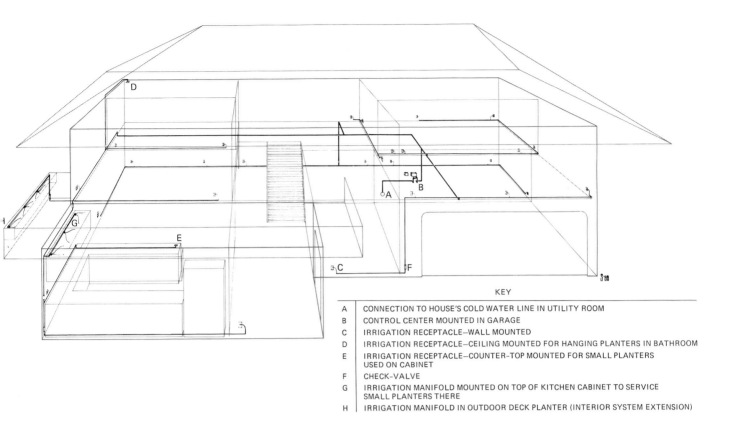

KEY

A	CONNECTION TO HOUSE'S COLD WATER LINE IN UTILITY ROOM
B	CONTROL CENTER MOUNTED IN GARAGE
C	IRRIGATION RECEPTACLE—WALL MOUNTED
D	IRRIGATION RECEPTACLE—CEILING MOUNTED FOR HANGING PLANTERS IN BATHROOM
E	IRRIGATION RECEPTACLE—COUNTER-TOP MOUNTED FOR SMALL PLANTERS USED ON CABINET
F	CHECK-VALVE
G	IRRIGATION MANIFOLD MOUNTED ON TOP OF KITCHEN CABINET TO SERVICE SMALL PLANTERS THERE
H	IRRIGATION MANIFOLD IN OUTDOOR DECK PLANTER (INTERIOR SYSTEM EXTENSION)

Figure 15.5:
Orthographic projection
of a home with a
Mirage III™ system.

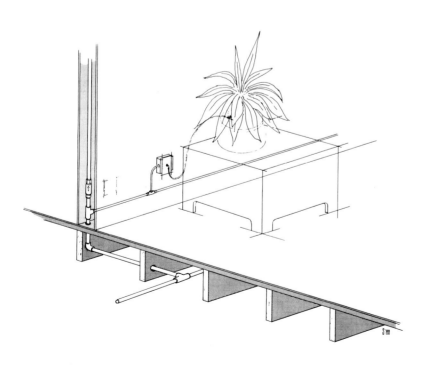

Figure 15.6: Irrigation
receptacle feeder lines
routed from beneath
flooring into a room
partition.

bends can be used wherever possible to replace elbow fittings. The installation will go faster, and the cost of labor and parts is reduced. Where tubing lines are exposed to view, it may be better to use the rigid form of PB tubing for a neater appearance.

Sometimes, as in retrofit installations, it is necessary to route irrigation feeder lines outside the walls. In this case no irrigation receptacles would be used, just connections for emitter tubes or irrigation manifolds. There are a number of ways this type of installation can be handled. For instance, when tubing must be routed to the center of a room in order to service a freestanding planter, a tubing branch is laid in the floor slab form (with sleeving) and terminated in a 4" x 4" junction box (with single-gang mud-ring) that is also set into the form at the desired location. The top of the junction box should be flush with the floor surface (see Figure 15.7). The irrigation tubing extends through the box and is end-capped before the concrete is poured. This tubing would later be connected to an irrigation

receptacle plate screwed to the 4" x 4" box. In the end, an irrigation receptacle is surface mounted on the floor in the middle of the room for future use.

Another way of doing this is to use the type of floor box available for electrical service, which is camouflaged by decorative face plates usually made of brass. The junction box itself is recessed into the concrete floor slab, while its decorative faceplate fits flush with the floor surface. A hole can be drilled into the faceplate to pass an emitter tube connected to the irrigation supply line into the junction box (see Figure 15.8). Other types have screw-in service ports that provide the same pass-through access.

A similar application utilizes a floor channel, which also provides electrical or other service to the center of a room. The system functions in a strip pattern so that access to the service can be gained at more than one spot along its length. This concept can be useful with APM system installations as well. The channel is embedded in the concrete floor slab, with an embedded

Figure 15.7: Isolated irrigation service box with imbedded water service tubing.

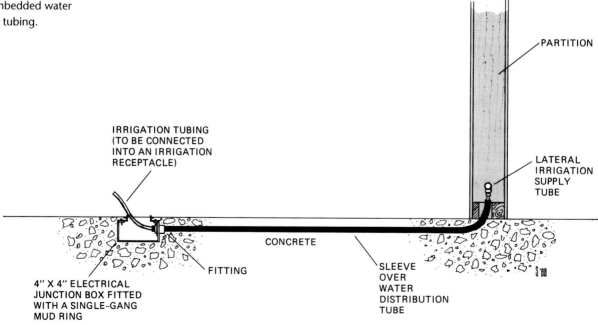

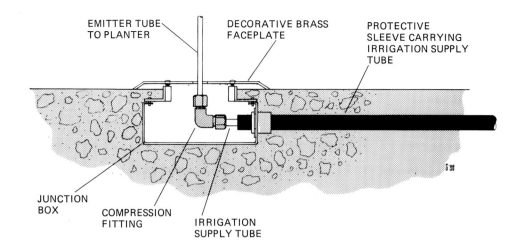

EMITTER TUBE TO PLANTER

DECORATIVE BRASS FACEPLATE

PROTECTIVE SLEEVE CARRYING IRRIGATION SUPPLY TUBE

JUNCTION BOX

COMPRESSION FITTING

IRRIGATION SUPPLY TUBE

Figure 15.8: Floor box being used to access irrigation tubing lines.

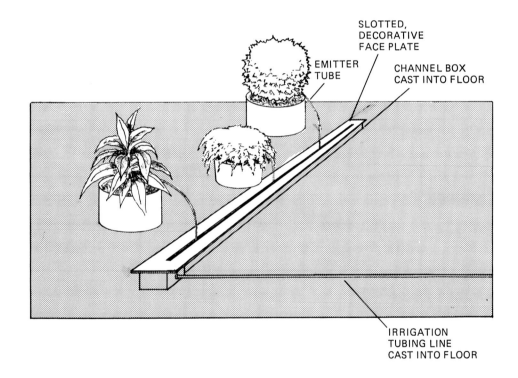

SLOTTED, DECORATIVE FACE PLATE

EMITTER TUBE

CHANNEL BOX CAST INTO FLOOR

IRRIGATION TUBING LINE CAST INTO FLOOR

Figure 15.9: Floor channel installation.

junction box receiving a water distribution tubing line to feed the strip floor fixture. The floor channel has a decorative brass cover plate with slots designed into it. Emitter tubes can be connected to irrigation feeder tubes inside the channel and passed through the cover plate to freestanding planters (Figure 15.9). If vandalism is a concern, emitter tubes of copper, brass, or aluminum can be used.

Tubing is easier to install along the borders of rooms. When working with tile or marble flooring, tubing can first be placed at the bases of partitions, with small branches leading to the surface for later connections. The tubing is subsequently sealed in grout when the flooring is installed (Figure 15.10). Tubing diameters must, of course, be small, as there is not much space in tile seams.

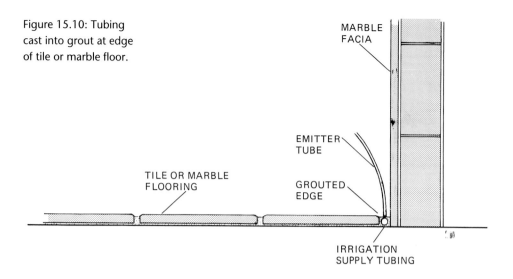

Figure 15.10: Tubing cast into grout at edge of tile or marble floor.

MARBLE FACIA

EMITTER TUBE

TILE OR MARBLE FLOORING

GROUTED EDGE

IRRIGATION SUPPLY TUBING

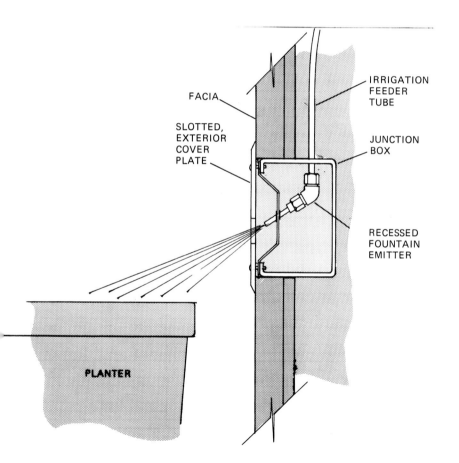

FACIA

SLOTTED, EXTERIOR COVER PLATE

IRRIGATION FEEDER TUBE

JUNCTION BOX

RECESSED FOUNTAIN EMITTER

PLANTER

Figure 15.11: Mounting details of fountain plate emitter.

Vertical wall surfaces—particularly partitions, columns, and area dividers—also require special installation techniques. Irrigation receptacles can be mounted on the surface of drywall partitions, or those faced with tile, marble, wooden paneling, etc. Cut-outs are made in the decorative finish material to accommodate the special receptacle, as is done with electrical outlets. Where abnormal conditions prevail, such as in areas subject to greater than normal vandalism, a different approach may be called for. An owner, fearful that emitter tubing could be destroyed if conventional irrigation receptacles are used to service freestanding planters along building walls (indoors or out), could use other types of integral outlets. One such device is the fountain plate mentioned in Chapter Thirteen. It is sourced from an irrigation feed line as are all other outlets, and uses a 4" x 4" junction box to enclose connections and mount the exterior plate (see Figure 15.11). One fountain plate must be mounted at each planter location. Generally, there is no flow adjustment. During construction, the junction box is positioned in the wall and irrigation tubing routed through its top and out the front, ready for further connections to the emitter assembly.

Routing Tubing in Retrofit Installations

Existing buildings usually make the installation of irrigation equipment more difficult. On rare occasions, though, small APM systems servicing furnished rooms can be a simple affair. The smallest versions are available as kits, with all of the equipment, tubing, and fittings pre-packaged together. Tubing lines in these light-duty kits are not much larger than 3/8"OD, and are usually only about 1/4"OD or 3/16"OD, and their small size helps them hide nicely under carpeting. In a case where only 1 to 15 plants are to be serviced in a relatively small area (possibly one or two rooms), a high-pressure control center would be mounted under a kitchen or bathroom sink. If low-pressure versions are more appropriate, then the pump controller and timer would normally be mounted on a wall behind furniture or planters, or possibly inside furniture or cabinetry, with the pump/reservoir module located nearby. Tubing would be routed from the control center, under the edge of the carpeting, and around the perimeter of the rooms to planter locations. Residential or sometimes commercial carpeting is laid over thick, foam padding with a tack strip holding the edges of the carpet around the walls. There is a gap of approximately 3/4" left between the tack strip and baseboard molding, leaving a convenient channel through which to route the water distribution tubing. It follows the perimeter of the rooms where decorative plants are generally placed (see Figures 15.12, 15.13, and 15.14). Keep in mind that it may be risky to install the tubing before the carpets in renovation projects, as careless edge cutting could damage a tube.

The system illustrated in Figure 15.13 is sourced from the building's water supply. The control center is shown mounted inside of a kitchen (residential) or kitchenette (office or hotel suite) cabinet, with tubing distributed around the room under the edges of the carpet. The number of plants that can be serviced and the layout complexity depend on the tubing size and the duty-rating of the solenoid-valve controller. Tubing fittings in this case should be barb type with crimp rings or compression type. Tubing of 3/8"OD should

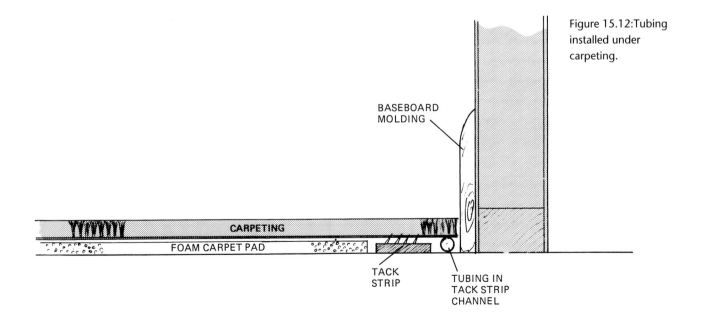

Figure 15.12: Tubing installed under carpeting.

BASEBOARD MOLDING

CARPETING

FOAM CARPET PAD

TACK STRIP

TUBING IN TACK STRIP CHANNEL

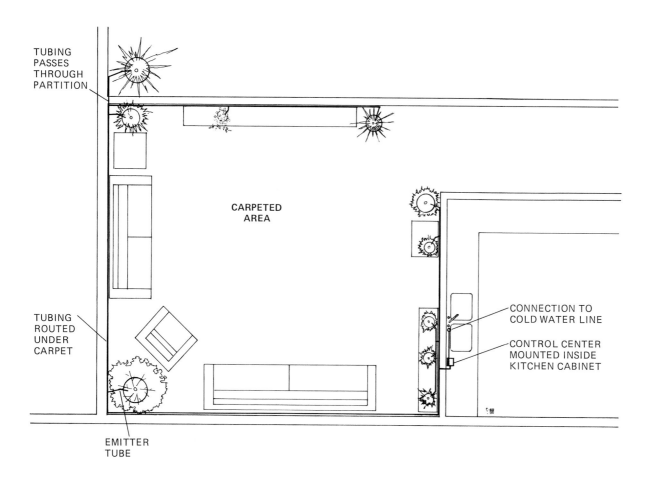

TUBING
PASSES
THROUGH
PARTITION

CARPETED
AREA

TUBING
ROUTED
UNDER
CARPET

CONNECTION TO
COLD WATER LINE

CONTROL CENTER
MOUNTED INSIDE
KITCHEN CABINET

EMITTER
TUBE

Figure 15.13: Typical small, retrofit installation using high-pressure APM system.

be used for the main water distribution lines if possible, so the system can be extended to other locations or to many more plants if desired.

The system illustrated in Figure 15.14 is sourced from a low-pressure pump/reservoir module. The assumption here is that no convenient connection to the building's water supply lines is available. The control center is located in the corner of the room behind a planter, with the pump controller mounted low on the wall to stay out of sight. The small-bore tubing is passed under the carpet edges around the perimeter of the room, and barb-type tee fittings are installed at appropriate points to attach emitter tubes for servicing nearby planters. Because of the low system pressure, it is not necessary to use crimp rings on the fittings. However,

recommended installation practice advises the use of crimp rings or adhesive bonding to secure tubing/fitting joints. Fewer plants are serviced by these small, low-pressure systems than by high-pressure versions. Each kit comes with a duty-rating indicating the number of plants that can be serviced by that particular system.

When tubing must be routed from the perimeter to the center of rooms, it can be passed beneath the carpet in a couple of ways. A slit, 1½" to 2" long, is cut in the carpet backing (between the pile tufts) at the center of the room where the freestanding planter is to be located. A "snake," such as those used to draw electrical wiring through partitions, is passed through the slit and carefully worked under the carpet to the perimeter of the

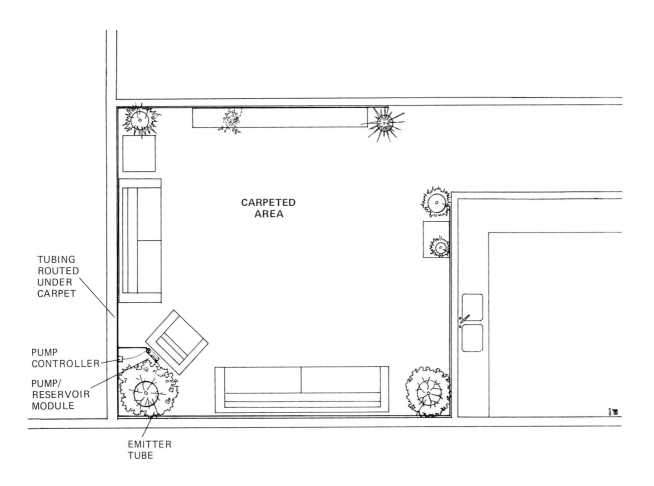

TUBING
ROUTED
UNDER
CARPET

CARPETED
AREA

PUMP
CONTROLLER

PUMP/
RESERVOIR
MODULE

EMITTER
TUBE

room where a water distribution line is located. A 3/16"OD PVC tube is connected to the end of the snake and pulled through the slit, with enough exposed length to route to the planter. The other end is connected into the water distribution line with a barbed tee fitting. The tubing can be run under the carpet and padding, or it can be run between them. The latter is preferable because the tubing is then cushioned by the padding beneath it. Sometimes a slight ridge is distinguishable where the tubing passes beneath the carpet, but it is seldom obvious enough to be objectionable. Anyway, flexible plastic tubing installed under carpeting in this manner will tend to flatten somewhat. This flattening does not interrupt the passage of water, so long as the tube has not

completely collapsed. Elliptically shaped tubing cross sections have the same internal volume as rounded shapes, and therefore allow the same amount of water to pass through them (see Figure 15.15). The best way of installing tubing in this situation is to cut the foam padding along the path of the tubing line, thereby creating a channel for it beneath the carpet (see Figure 15.16). This is normally done before the carpet has been laid.

Figure 15.14: Typical small, low-pressure system installation.

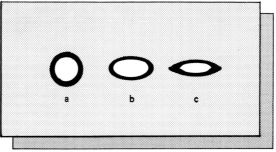

a   b   c

Figure 15.15: Irrigation tubing under carpeting can be flattened to some extent without restricting water flow.

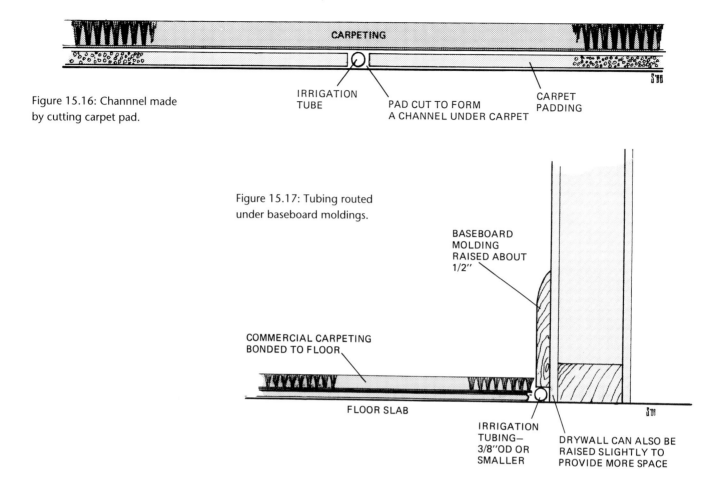

Figure 15.16: Channnel made by cutting carpet pad.

CARPETING

IRRIGATION TUBE

PAD CUT TO FORM A CHANNEL UNDER CARPET

CARPET PADDING

Figure 15.17: Tubing routed under baseboard moldings.

BASEBOARD MOLDING RAISED ABOUT 1/2"

COMMERCIAL CARPETING BONDED TO FLOOR

FLOOR SLAB

IRRIGATION TUBING— 3/8"OD OR SMALLER

DRYWALL CAN ALSO BE RAISED SLIGHTLY TO PROVIDE MORE SPACE

Where most commercial carpet installations are involved, there is no underpadding, or the padding is laminated to the carpet's underside. Commercial carpets are usually cemented to the floor to keep them from slipping or buckling. In these cases, it is more difficult to pass tubing underneath, but it can be done by first cutting a slit (as previously described) and working the carpeting away from the floor with a stiff metal or wooden stick passed through the slit, breaking the adhesive bond along a narrow channel all the way to the wall. Plastic emitter tubing can then be routed through this channel just as an electrical cord would be. Carpet mastics are made to provide only a semi-permanent bond, so this technique is not as difficult as it seems. In these commercial carpet installations there is no tack strip in place to hold the edges, so no channel exists around

the room perimeter. Space can be provided for tubing there, however, by slightly lifting the edges of the carpet and laying small-bore tubing in the resulting space. Another way of creating space is to raise baseboard moldings about 3/4" above bare floor level. This approach creates a channel in the crook between the molding, drywall, carpet edge, and floor (see Figure 15.17). It is adequate to run 3/8"ID tubing (or smaller) around the rooms. This size tubing is large enough to service most room settings, yet small enough to hide easily.

Yet another method uses rubber or vinyl baseboard moldings around the perimeter of the room, hiding small-bore tubing behind the bottom lip of the molding (Figure 15.18).

Tubing runs can be hidden by channel moldings as well (Figure 15.19). They can be used not only at the baseboard, but also

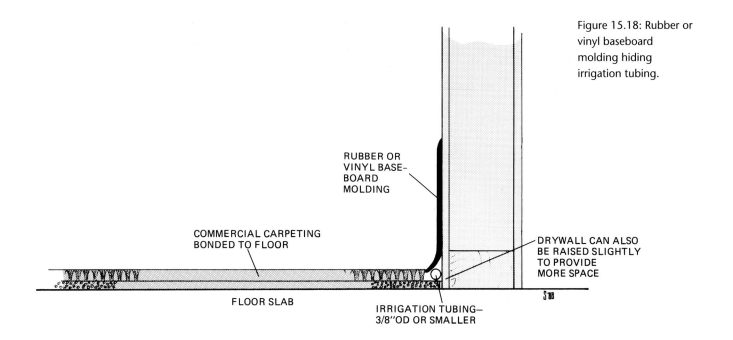

Figure 15.18: Rubber or vinyl baseboard molding hiding irrigation tubing.

RUBBER OR VINYL BASE-BOARD MOLDING

COMMERCIAL CARPETING BONDED TO FLOOR

DRYWALL CAN ALSO BE RAISED SLIGHTLY TO PROVIDE MORE SPACE

FLOOR SLAB

IRRIGATION TUBING— 3/8″OD OR SMALLER

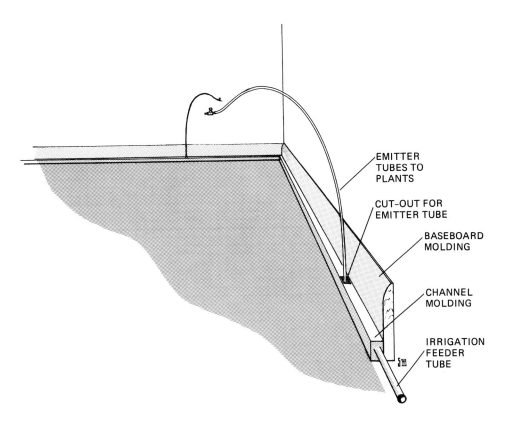

Figure 15.19: Channel molding concealing irrigation tubing around the baseboards of rooms.

EMITTER TUBES TO PLANTS

CUT-OUT FOR EMITTER TUBE

BASEBOARD MOLDING

CHANNEL MOLDING

IRRIGATION FEEDER TUBE

up and across wall and ceiling surfaces. Several types of channel moldings are available for electrical service installations, and they can be used toward the same end in APM systems. Various types of channel moldings are available, with some more decorative than others. Metal types are available, the plastic kind are easiest to install, and some brands even have self-adhesive backing. All can be painted to match the decor, but the self-adhesives are not recommended for many painted surfaces, as loose paint particles clog their surface and cause them to lose their "tack" rapidly. Flat wall paint seems to create the worst problem in this regard, as it is heavily filled with pigment, which tends to migrate to the paint surface before it sloughs off. Self-adhesive strips work best on smooth, metal surfaces finished with lacquer or hard enamel. The surfaces should be clean and dry before attachment is attempted. Other types of channel moldings are attached to surfaces with screws, either directly or through mounting strips, which tend to provide a more secure attachment. They do take longer to install, but the call-backs for repairing separated moldings will be fewer. When using any channel moldings, connections to emitter tubes must be made at appropriate locations near planters, and cut-outs must be made in the molding to allow tubing to pass through.

Figure 15.20: Baseboard molding modified to accomodate irrigation tubing.

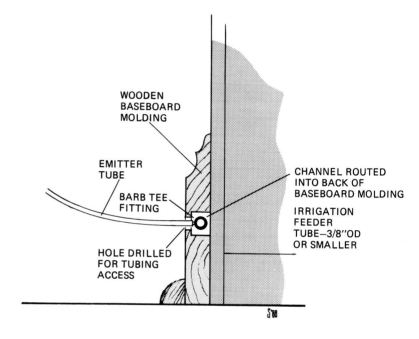

Figure 15.21: Cove molding concealing irrigation tubing.

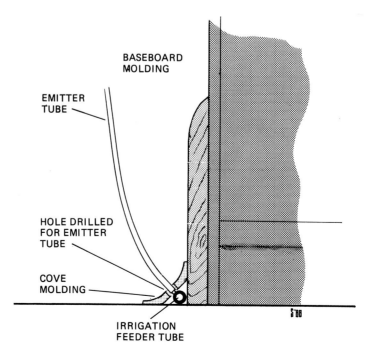

INSTALLING AUTOMATED PRECISION MICRO-IRRIGATION SYSTEMS

Another technique used to hide tubing around baseboards is the modification of existing baseboard moldings. Channels can easily be cut into their back sides with production routing machines or molding cutters (Figure 15.20). Holes drilled into the molding at appropriate locations permit access to the irrigation feeder line for emitter tubes. Carpenters must be cautioned to keep nails away from the tubing area when installing such moldings.

Certain brands of small, common, cove moldings leave a space when mounted that can be used to channel irrigation tubing around baseboards (Figure 15.21). Cut-outs or holes must be cut into these as well for emitter tube passage at appropriate locations.

In situations where no carpeting is used—only tile, marble, terrazzo, or sheet vinyl, among others—the techniques just described can also be used to route irrigation tubing. When large, ceramic tiles are used as flooring, tubing can sometimes be installed into the joints between tiles and covered with grout.

There are other retrofit situations where it will be necessary to cut a channel into a concrete floor slab for passage of irrigation tubing lines. This is commonly done in construction work, and modern tools make the procedure feasible. After the channel is cut, tubing is laid in and cemented over. If done in conjunction with other building renovations, a good deal of disruption can be avoided.

Tubing/Fitting Connections

In all APM system installations, providing secure tubing connections is a paramount concern. Because of the wide variety of fittings used in the various situations encountered, each requires a different technique.

Barb-type fittings are most commonly used in APM systems. They simply slip into tubes and hoses. Low-pressure systems don't usually require any additional joint security; the natural friction between parts provides a good enough fit. However, more cautious installation practice dictates that tubes and fittings in low-pressure systems be secured either with an appropriate adhesive, tubing clamps, or with crimp rings. The adhesive types that experience has shown to work best are natural latex or neoprene-based, with volatile solvent thinners, such as solvent-type contact cements (Weldwood, Pliobond contact cement, or another equivalent).

Crimp rings provide the most secure connections with barb fittings. They are slipped over the tubing end prior to its receiving the fitting, and then crimped down over the tubing with a special tool. The crimp should be evenly made around the joint, otherwise localized tubing distortion could occur, the result of which could be a leak. Copper crimp rings are typically used for polybutylene tubing. After installation, they should be gauged to assure a proper crimp configuration. Steel, single-, and double-eared crimp rings can be used safely with polyethylene and PVC tubing.

Compression fittings are probably the easiest of all types to use. The tubing is simply slipped into the socket provided, and a nut tightened down until the joint is secure. A gripping collar within the fitting socket crimps down on the tube when the nut is tightened. Plastic compression fittings require not much more than hand-tightening, but an extra 1/4 turn or so with a wrench makes the joint even more secure. Even though they are easy to use, quality compression fittings carry surprisingly high pressure ratings. Most carry the approval seals of the important organizations in the field—IAPMO (International Association of Plumbing and Mechanical Officials), UPC (Uniform Plumbing Code), NSF (National

Sanitation Foundation), and CSA (Canadian Standards Association). Properly installed, they are as safe as any tubing connection. When compression fittings are used with softer, plastic tubing, particularly PE and vinyl, a brass insert should be used in the tube end to prevent its collapse when the fitting is tightened down with a wrench.

Threaded fittings require an adapter of some sort to connect the device to tubing. For example, most pressure regulators are designed with threaded connections at inlet and outlet. Tubing obviously has no threads, so a threaded adapter must be attached to the pressure regulating valve. These fittings are also simple to install, using a wrench for tightening. A few wraps of Teflon tape or a paste thread sealer like silicone should be used when connecting threaded fittings.

Control Center Equipment

The installation of tubing lines is a relatively small part of the job, particularly in integrated systems. After most of the finish work has been completed on the building, the controller and timer are mounted and connected into the rest of the system, at which time irrigation receptacles and manifolds are connected. Boca Automation's controllers are surface mounted on a partition wall at a particular location. Tubing lines have been terminated there, ready to receive the control equipment. Water distribution connections to the solenoid valve are either barb-type/crimp ring or compression fittings. Depending on the model, electrical connections are made either by hard wiring into a junction box installed behind the controller, or by simply plugging into the timer receptacle (or remote controlled receptacle). The timer itself is installed in a similar way; some models require hard-

wiring into a junction box, while others plug into a power receptacle. The most professional installations are made with hard-wired equipment. The easiest installations are made with plug-in equipment.

Before turning on the water supply, check the operation of the control center. Timers have a manual operating mode—usually a switch—that permits the timer to be bypassed and overridden. (Consult the timer instructions.) By means of this switch, apply power to the controller. A red indicator on it will light up. Listen for the click of the solenoid valve as it opens and closes. Then time the interval between opening and closing. It should roughly coincide with the irrigation cycle rating of the device, normally 10 or 15 seconds in duration. After manually turning off the timer's power switch (the controller's red indicator light will go off), wait about 15 seconds and try it again. Run this test at least three times to be sure the equipment comes close to specifications. The operating duration should be within +/– 2 seconds of published specs. With power off, throw the irrigation cycle switch on the controller to the longer cycle position (generally 20 or 30 seconds). Perform the same tests as with the shorter cycle to again check for proper operation. The operating duration in this case should be within +/– 3 seconds of the published specs. While performing these tests, the shorting plug must be removed from the remote control jack on the controller. Next, check its operation. Apply power to the controller and let it complete its irrigation cycle. After the click is heard, denoting closing of the solenoid valve, insert the plug in the remote control jack. The click of the solenoid valve should be heard as it opens again. It will remain open for as long as the plug is in the jack. *Do not leave it plugged in for more than 2 minutes.* If a remote control cord has been purchased (this is optional equipment), test it by plugging it into the remote control jack at the appropriate time. When first plugged in, nothing will happen. Press the switch on the end of the remote cord. It should open the solenoid valve and keep it open for as long as the switch is pressed.

At this point, the timer must be programmed to operate the system at the desired times. Most interior installations of APM systems will require operation twice a day. Occasionally a third cycle is added, and in very large installations with big trees, four or five short operations per day may be needed. If an electromechanical timer is being used, changeable tabs or pins on the clock wheel are positioned to switch power on or off at the times indicated. If a central, microprocessor-controlled timer is used, it must be programmed to switch the power on at the appropriate times *for at least one minute*. This gives the controller a long enough power window to generate a complete irrigation cycle.

The times of day during which the system is operational are important only for reasons of convenience. In natural environments, rain may water the plants at any time, day or night, so they are adapted to variation. The irrigation cycles should be spaced as far apart as possible to permit water from the last cycle to diffuse fully into the soil. If two daily cycles are used, space them 12 hours apart. If three daily cycles are used, space them 8 hours apart, etc. The precision of these schedules is not critical, but should be close for most efficient operation. It is a good idea to have at least one daily cycle while someone is there to check on the consistency of operation and occasionally make sure that all emitters are flowing as they should. As a suggestion, cycles are practical at 9 o'clock in the morning and 9 o'clock at night. In residences, someone is usually there in the evenings at that time, yet it is not late enough to disturb sleep cycles. In offices, someone is usually there at 9 A.M. The

installer's judgment should be used, or better yet, the irrigation schedule should be discussed with the building occupant and interiorscaper, if one is involved.

In large buildings, there would normally be an independent APM system installed on each floor. They should not all be activated at once. Even though flow rates through each would not be large, in aggregate they would strain the building's water supply. The best irrigation schedule would have the systems operate sequentially at night, when the load on a building's water system is least heavy. A practical schedule might include one cycle between 6 and 9 P.M, and another between 6 and 9 A.M. These schedules may be best for the interiorscapers as well, for many try to make their rounds during off-hours. It would give them a chance to observe system operation and make adjustments as necessary.

The installation of low-pressure APM systems follows essentially the same pattern as that described for high-pressure versions. Controller connections are different, of course. After the pump controller has been mounted on a partition wall, the low-voltage power cord is connected to the pump terminals. In small, light-duty models, these are on the pump itself, or in larger systems, there are power leads (wires) from the pump/reservoir module. As these are usually DC pumps, polarity must be carefully observed when making connections.

Irrigation Receptacles

Irrigation receptacles are installed at locations provided for them by making a simple connection to the receptacle feeder tube, which should have been positioned through the front of the receptacle junction box during rough in. The tubing connection is either a barb/crimp ring or

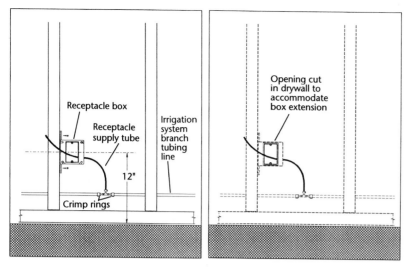

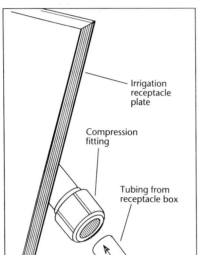

Figure 15.21: Connecting irrigation receptacles.

Receptacle box

Receptacle supply tube

Irrigation system branch tubing line

12"

Crimp rings

Opening cut in drywall to accommodate box extension

Irrigation receptacle plate

Compression fitting

Tubing from receptacle box

compression fitting, depending on the model. At this point it is likely that the building inspector will want to run a pressure test on the system, with all receptacles connected. The receptacle assembly comes fitted with deactivating plugs. Leave them in place during the pressure test. Once those procedures are out of the way, the irrigation receptacle assembly is attached to the junction box with screws through its decorative plate.

Irrigation Manifolds

By now, irrigation feeder tubes should have been routed to the areas where manifolds are needed. They would normally be passed through holes in the adjoining partition. Recommended installation procedure calls for mounting an escutcheon over the tube where it exits the wall. This makes a tidier passage (Figure 15.22).

Connections are made to the manifold with a barb fitting secured by a crimp ring,

Figure 15.22: Typical irrigation manifold installation.

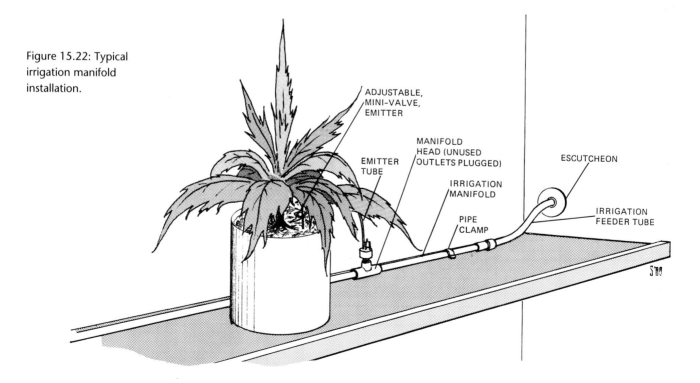

ADJUSTABLE, MINI-VALVE, EMITTER

MANIFOLD HEAD (UNUSED OUTLETS PLUGGED)

EMITTER TUBE

IRRIGATION MANIFOLD

ESCUTCHEON

IRRIGATION FEEDER TUBE

PIPE CLAMP

or with a compression fitting. The manifold would have been fastened to the base or wall of whatever it services during the rough-in stages. A check valve is frequently installed at the manifold inlet to control flow more precisely. Emitter tubes are connected to manifold outlets wherever needed. Other outlets are plugged. Adjustable mini-valve/emitters are connected to the ends of emitter tubes and the adjustment screws opened a bit to permit flow.

Emitter Tubes

Emitter tubes can now be plugged into irrigation receptacles and other fittings to make them ready for duty. The emitter tube assembly that comes with the unit is simply plugged into the receptacle *after the deactivating plug is removed*. Pushing in on the receptacle's release ring will permit removal of the plug. The tube is routed to the locations of freestanding, containerized plants in the room. Each emitter tube should service the plant(s) closest to it. Emitter tubes can be placed under the edge of carpeting and brought to the surface in the vicinity of planters, even 20 or 30 feet from the receptacle. Generally up to eight plants can be watered from a single receptacle emitter tube. They can be branched off into two or more sub-branches using 1/4" tees, each with its own adjustable, mini-valve emitter. Whenever a tube must be raised to heights greater than about 1½ feet, it should be fitted with a mini check valve, with the one-way flow direction pointing upwards. This keeps water in the tube after system shut-off, and prevents undue air purge time during the next watering cycle. This is not a hard-and-fast rule, and applies mainly to low-pressure systems, or to high-pressure systems where the flow rate has been greatly reduced.

It may be necessary to bring emitter tubes close to the ceiling in order to water hanging planters or planters on high shelves. Although clear emitter tubes which don't show up very easily against their background can be used, it may be preferable to hide them inside partitions. Small holes are first cut in the partition at the top and base, and the tube "fished" through the wall from one to the other, much the same as when electrical wiring is installed. Connections are made on top and bottom with supply and emitter fittings. Holes in the wall around the tubes can be patched with Spackle or crack filler for a neater installation.

The emitters themselves are installed by simply plugging them into the end of the tube after it has been cut to a convenient length, while still leaving a little slack in the tube. It can be difficult to install fittings in some flexible tubes, such as PE and PB, because of their inherent stiffness. The process can be facilitated by first softening the tube end with heat. The emitter is held in place with an emitter stabilizer, which is no more than a notched stake that is pushed into the planter soil. The notch holds the emitter and tube to the stake.

Systems in Planter Boxes

Planter box installations of APM systems are different than those for freestanding planters. In many ways they are less difficult, for the aesthetic and safety requirements are not as stringent. Irrigation supply tubing is routed to the built-in planter box through partitions or flooring, depending on the situation. When the APM system is designed into the building, the most efficient way of routing supply tubing is to cast a line into the concrete floor slab between a remote irrigation supply branch and the planter box (Figure 15.23). The supply branch is connected to an irrigation manifold, premounted in the planter. Emitter tubes connect to the manifold and

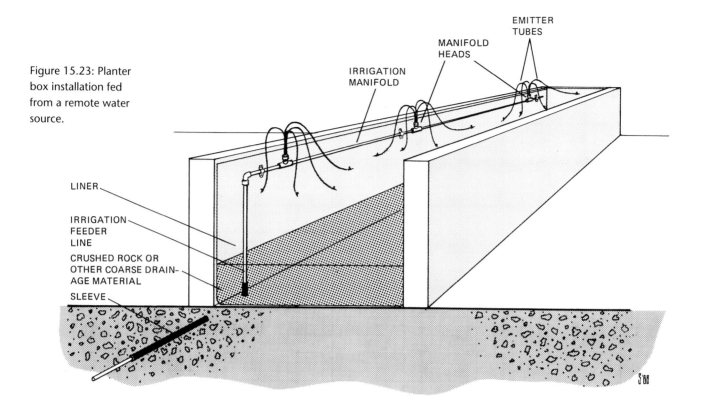

Figure 15.23: Planter box installation fed from a remote water source.

LINER

IRRIGATION FEEDER LINE

CRUSHED ROCK OR OTHER COARSE DRAINAGE MATERIAL

SLEEVE

IRRIGATION MANIFOLD

MANIFOLD HEADS

EMITTER TUBES

service the plants closest to them. Bubbler heads can be used in place of emitter tubes to distribute water. Mini-spray heads can also be used on the manifold when the plant types in question are well suited to this type of watering.

When electrical and water service have been designed into a built-in planter box, a different type of installation is required. Proper design practice provides hose bibbs and electrical outlets in each planter box or pit. The hose bibb is usually specified there to allow the plant maintenance technician to connect a hose for manual watering of a tree or smaller plants in the local area. The electrical outlet is usually used for accent or holiday lights. Hose bibbs and electrical outlets can also be used to operate a small, independent APM system, installed for that planter alone. The type of solenoid valve controller used can be a light-to-medium-duty unit, but it must have an all-weather case to protect it from the damp or wet conditions it would encounter. It should be

mounted on the wall of the planter near the hose bibb and electrical junction box. The timer—also an all-weather type—is mounted next to it. The input side of the solenoid valve is connected to the hose bibb (with a small backflow preventer) and the power cord plugged into the timer's outlet (Figure 15.24). The output side of the solenoid valve is routed to the water distribution network, which can be as simple as a loop of laser soaker tubing ringing the roots at the base of a tree, or as complex as a multi-branched irrigation manifold distributing water throughout a large planter box. If light-duty use is expected, it would be wise to use a fixed pressure reducer to modify the flow rate.

Outdoor Systems

The following discussion refers not only to installations of outdoor APM systems, but also to indoor atrium-type settings. Features and requirements are similar for both.

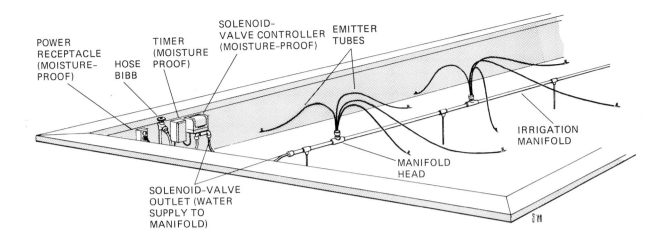

POWER RECEPTACLE (MOISTURE-PROOF)

HOSE BIBB

TIMER (MOISTURE PROOF)

SOLENOID-VALVE CONTROLLER (MOISTURE-PROOF)

EMITTER TUBES

IRRIGATION MANIFOLD

MANIFOLD HEAD

SOLENOID-VALVE OUTLET (WATER SUPPLY TO MANIFOLD)

Outdoors, APM systems provide the same service as sprinkler or drip systems, but in a more precise manner so that planter overwatering and overflow do not become a problem. They are very suitable for potted plants around patios, pool decks, terraces, apartment balconies, storefronts, and shopping promenades where not only foliage plants are grown, but flowers, bonsai, and containerized vegetable gardens as well. Both high-pressure and low-pressure systems can be used outdoors. Regardless of the choice, all must have all-weather control center equipment to withstand the elements. It's also a good idea to install control centers in sheltered locations.

Low-pressure system use is common for outdoor installations. Part of the reason has to do with the fact that many building codes prohibit the use of hose bibbs, or any other type of water service, on high-rise apartment balconies. The low-pressure system provides its own water source (pump/reservoir module) and so long as electrical service is readily available, an installation can be made. The pump/reservoir module is generally large, and should be located in an out-of-the-way place (a sheltered location is preferable), yet it must be near an electrical power source or located where a power line can reach it. The pump controller and timer are

mounted on an exterior wall next to the module, and the low-voltage power cord plugged into the pump leads (with polarity intact) (see Figure 15.25). The controller power cord is plugged into the timer's power outlet, and the timer's power cord is plugged into the closest power receptacle having continuous or controlled service. The pump output tubing is connected to water distribution tubing lines, which are usually a network of 1/2", Schedule 40, PVC sprinkler system pipes. They can be fitted with manifold outlets, emitter tubes, bubbler heads, or spray heads to accommodate installation needs.

Figure 15.24: APM system installed in a planter with self-contained services.

Figure 15.25: Low-pressure control center connections in an outdoor installation.

High-pressure systems are installed in a similar way, except that the water source is generally a hose bibb connection. They are most commonly used around residential and commercial patios and pool decks, store fronts, shopping promenades, and interior atria. To avoid incapacitating the hose bibb, irrigation system connections should be made to a wye fitting, with shut-off valves in each leg. The leg connected to the APM system should have its valve open at all times. The other is for utility purposes and is always closed when not in use. It is important to remember that the hose bibb valve must be kept open at all times. It's a good idea to remove the valve handle to prevent accidental shut-off.

Atria are generally well-lit from skylights and oversized windows, so their moisture requirements are high, albeit somewhat lower than outdoors. Keep in mind that atria can become extremely hot when the sun is

overhead, and so a shade screen of some sort is sometimes used in order to modify lighting conditions. Also, air does not circulate as much in atria as outdoors, and moisture can build up to a dangerous point. Mildew and fungus problems are common in these settings. Supplementary fans are frequently required. One advantage of APM systems is that watering rates are more controlled than with other technologies, and proper moisture can be maintained at the root ball without overdosing.

Output tubing from the solenoid valve is connected to the water distribution network, which again is usually PVC sprinkler pipe. This can be routed into patio areas, planter boxes, overhead canopies, pool decks, building overhangs, along walkways, and around vegetable gardens. In cold-weather areas of the country, provisions should always be made for drainage prior to frost to protect tubing and fittings. The system

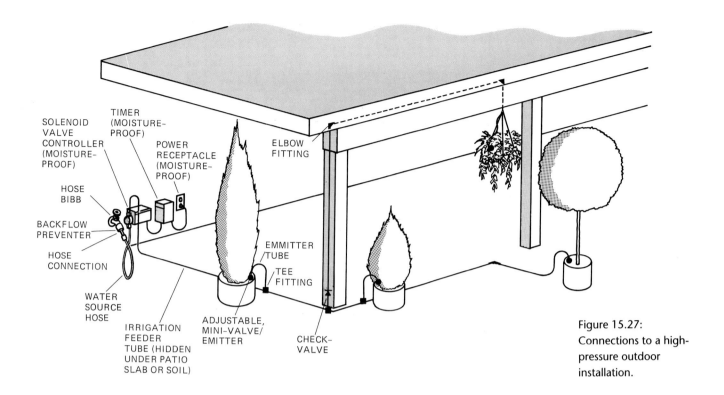

SOLENOID
VALVE
CONTROLLER
(MOISTURE-
PROOF)

TIMER
(MOISTURE-
PROOF)

POWER
RECEPTACLE
(MOISTURE-
PROOF)

ELBOW
FITTING

HOSE
BIBB

BACKFLOW
PREVENTER

HOSE
CONNECTION

WATER
SOURCE
HOSE

IRRIGATION
FEEDER
TUBE (HIDDEN
UNDER PATIO
SLAB OR SOIL)

EMMITTER
TUBE

TEE
FITTING

ADJUSTABLE,
MINI-VALVE/
EMITTER

CHECK-
VALVE

Figure 15.27:
Connections to a high-
pressure outdoor
installation.

should be purged of water by blowing out or draining tubing lines, and the hose bibb is then closed down.

Interfacing With Other Technologies

It has been mentioned in other chapters that there are many ways of activating APM systems. The simplest, of course, is the electromechanical time switch. The most complex are multi-purpose, computer-based control systems, made for large building management. The ones most useful in the application of APM systems are fairly simple as modern, technical devices go. One of the most versatile of the middle-ground devices for residential use is the carrier-frequency, energy control system. X-10 (U.S.A.), Incorporated, the main supplier of this technology, calls it the X-10 Powerhouse[1] System. Its main functions have to do with the computerized automatic, or manual

remote switching of lights, appliances, security devices, heating/cooling equipment, home entertainment systems, etc. The controllers are capable of operating as self-timed, automatic switches, or as manually triggered remote switches (Figure 15.28). Manual activation can be done by using button control panels and radio-controllers from somewhere in the same building, or from thousands of miles away by telephone.

In all cases, the control signals are superimposed onto the building's electric power wiring and eventually picked up by small receiving modules plugged or wired into power outlets in other parts of the building (Figure 15.29). Into these modules are plugged the device (or devices) to be controlled. The receiving modules have programmable device codes that correspond to similar codes on the remote controller. When properly coded signals reach the receiver through the power wiring, they cause power to be applied to the devices plugged in.

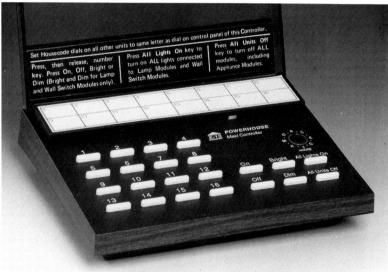

Figure 15.28: X-10 controllers.

The X-10 controllers are capable of orchestrating up to eight power control programs, each switching devices at different times of day for different periods of "on" time. The activation/deactivation cycle can be repeated twice daily with the inexpensive models, and more than twice daily with other equipment. Small satellite systems can be scattered around a house or office, each plugged into a receiving module. Most (or all) would have the same power application program, and would therefore be coded into the same control channel. Another control channel can be used for supplementary plant lighting, in the form of artificial lights that would come on for several hours during the day or night to supplement natural daylight. And yet another control channel can be programmed to operate outdoor APM systems at other times of the day.

Installing these carrier-frequency remote control systems is an easy matter. In the simplest of cases, all elements of the system are plugged into wall outlets at convenient locations. The timer/controller is placed in a practical space as well, like a living room, bedroom, or office. The receiving modules are plugged or wired into junction boxes or outlets wherever a satellite APM system can be placed, but always near the potted plants being serviced. Almost any number of these satellite systems can be used in the building at any location, so long as they are on the same electrical wiring network. The combination of technologies makes a highly versatile system, capable of automatically controlling not only the APM systems installed in the building, but all lights, appliances, and other electrical devices as well (Figure 15.30).

Another version of this technology is sold by Leviton Manufacturing. It has a more versatile timer/controller with a greater number of features. It wires into an electrical junction box, rather than plugging in as with the X-10 U.S.A. controllers. This feature makes for a more professional-looking installation.

Still other remote, energy-control technologies are coming into use. Protocols are now available for CEBus®, LonWorks™, and Smart House™ technologies.[2] All are based on a computerized timer/controller installed in the home or office, which automatically switches lighting, appliances, heating/cooling equipment, and the like. They are simplified implementations of the complex building management systems commonly used in "smart" buildings. The peripheral devices are either hard-wired to the controller, or receive control intelligence through carrier-frequency signals. The idea is to bring some of this usefulness to private homes and light commercial applications.

Adaptations of these themes are being introduced in other concepts. One technology just becoming recognized uses local video cable companies to transmit control and video signals to their customers. A customer subscribing to the service would have special receivers installed that pick the control signal out of the overall reception and distribute it throughout the building for various control chores. The timing and program manipulation in this case are handled at the cable company. A similar concept is being introduced by some

telephone companies. Timing and programming are done at the phone center, with control signals transmitted through the phone lines. Receiving modules are installed to turn this into a useful system at the remote location.

With all of these energy-management concepts, the APM system beomes a peripheral to the main control system, along with the lights, appliances, video and other devices. Installation techniques will depend on the nature of the control technology involved.

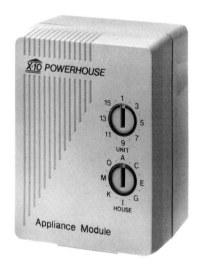

Figure 15.29: X-10 receiving modules.

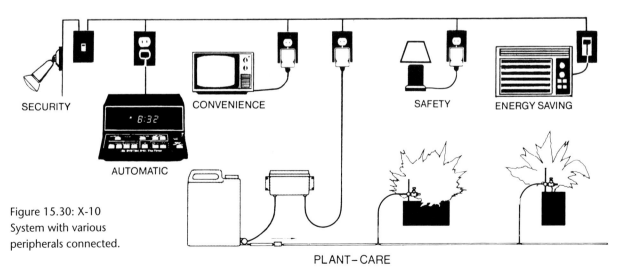

Figure 15.30: X-10 System with various peripherals connected.

SIXTEEN

Starting and Operating a New Installation

Once the mechanical work of installing an automated precision micro-irrigation system has been completed, established procedures must be followed to ensure that everything functions correctly. This is also the time when initial adjustments should be made to the system so that it will henceforward require minimal attention. After that, routine operating and maintenance procedures are instituted. Some of this is done by the installer, some by the installer and plant maintenance technician together, and some by the plant maintenance technician working as the sole custodian of the plants and their electromechanical/hydraulic life-support system. While most procedures are simple, they often become complicated by the idiosyncrasies of the project. Techniques have been developed to cope with most situations, and these will be discussed in detail in the following pages.

Start-Up Procedures

The installer is responsible for starting up the APM system after the mechanical part of the job is finished. Outlined below are the steps that should be followed:

1. Check all connections to exposed tubing to be sure they are complete and secure.

2. Once plants are in place, insert the emitter stabilizer stake with emitter into the potting soil of each. Adjust the height of the emitter 2" to 3" above the surface of the soil. The emitter outlet should be above the root mass near the plant's stem.

3. Open the adjustable mini-valve/emitters about halfway to permit some flow.

4. Be sure an overflow saucer is beneath each freestanding planter.

5. With small, light-duty systems, check to see if the mini check valve is operating properly. This is done by removing it from the pump outlet and blowing into its inlet side, feeling for air coming from the outlet side. If it seems operable, refit it into the tubing line. If not, replace it.

6. Check to be sure that all power connections have been made and electrical service is available to the system.

7. Check the timer's irrigation cycle program settings to be sure it is on the proper schedule. If a computer-based, energy-management controller is used to supply power for the automatic irrigation system, it should be checked by requesting a screen read-out of the programmed schedule.

8. Check the controller's irrigation cycle setting. It should be switched to the shortest cycle (normally 10 or 15 seconds).

9. If the water distribution tubing network is multi-zoned, shut off all zones except the one to be tested and adjusted. Home, office suite, and restaurant installations typically use shut-off valves to deactivate a zone. This is sometimes a manually operated, globe-type valve in overhead irrigation feed lines, and sometimes a key-switch-operated solenoid valve in a tubing riser. The globe valve should be opened only slightly at first.

10. In large installations, two people should work together in adjusting emitters. It is recommended that the actual adjustment be done by the interiorscape technician assigned to the routine maintenance task. One person should be stationed at the control center, and the other at the planters. There should be some means of communication between them. If too far apart to be heard normally, a walkie-talkie system can be used.

11. Turn the unit on via the timer's manual power switch. The system will begin timing for the programmed duration of operation. Water will flow during this 10- or 15-second period. The controller's red indicator will be lit, showing that power is being applied. At this point the stop valve can be opened fully.

12. Insert the shorting plug into the controller's remote-control jack. This causes the solenoid valve or pump to operate and water to flow again. Water will flow for as long as the plug remains in the jack, which should be no more than about one minute at a time. Repeat the process until all tubing lines

Figure 16.1: Flow
patterns of various
emitter adjustments.

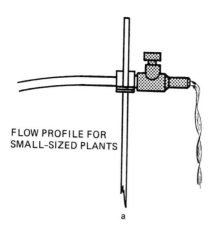

FLOW PROFILE FOR
SMALL-SIZED PLANTS

a

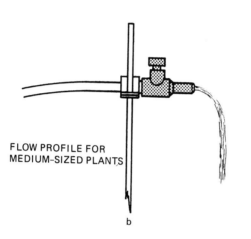

FLOW PROFILE FOR
MEDIUM-SIZED PLANTS

b

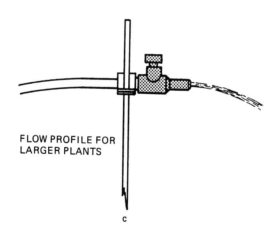

FLOW PROFILE FOR
LARGER PLANTS

c

are filled with water. Some planters could overflow during this operation if they are serviced by tubing near the source. Keep a close watch on them and close down their emitters temporarily, if necessary. If water refuses to flow from an emitter, it is usually because all the air has not yet been purged from its feed tube. Check to see that the emitter adjustment is open enough to allow air to escape.

13. After the tubing network has been filled, reinsert the shorting plug for one minute. During that time, emitters can be adjusted one by one. The amount of flow permitted by each will be determined by the type of plant it services, its size, location, as well as other factors. These judgments should be made by a person knowledgeable in *interior* plant-care matters. Approximate settings can be made without taking measurements by simply judging visually. As a rule of thumb, small plants in 5" to 8" containers should have the following flow pattern illustrated in Figure 16.1a. Remember, minimum flow with these adjustable emitters is a mere two drops during a 10-second irrigation cycle. That would be suitable for small, dry-loving plants.

Medium-sized plants in 10" to 14" containers should have a flow pattern similar to that shown in Figure 16.1b. Larger plants in 17" to 30" containers should have a flow pattern similar to that shown in Figure 16.1c.

It is recommended that a remote-control cord or electronic remote-control device be used while adjusting emitters. If a remote-control cord of sufficient length is used, it can be extended to the planter locations. Irrigation will continue for as long as the switch button is held down, and with this accessory, flow can be closely controlled to prevent excesses. The electronic remote-control switch also permits precise on/off operation of the controller from planter locations, but does it by more sophisticated switching means. As long as the control button is held down, signals will be received by the controller to keep the flow of water going. Keep in mind that while individual plant emitters are being adjusted, the other plants are receiving flow as well. When making initial adjustments to large numbers of plants, it is not uncommon to have some overflow from bottom drain holes. The soil gets saturated and can absorb no more, so it gives up the excess. Plastic plant saucers should be placed under all containers to catch any possible overflow. Flow should be permitted just long enough to make the adjustment at each plant. If only a short period of time is required to adjust the system, as would be the case with a simple installation, plant soil may not be moist enough. The plants should be hand watered to bring soil moisture up to recommended levels. Remember that the function of the system is to consistently maintain an optimum level of soil moisture, not to wet out dry planters.

Do not be overly concerned about how precisely or evenly adjustments are made from plant to plant. The technology is very forgiving, and approximations usually suffice— particularly for the initial adjustments. Fine-tuning comes later, after a week or more of operation.

14. After all plants in a zone have been adjusted individually, check their flow again and readjust where necessary. This is the way the system is balanced.

15. Adjust each zone in sequence, shutting down all zones on which no work is being done. After all have been initially adjusted, recheck them. The installer will find that in adjusting an extensive system servicing many plants, flow to the first plants drops off as the succeeding emitters are opened; some water is being taken from the first plants to service the last. Once the system has been roughly balanced, additional adjustments make little difference.

16. Inspect emitter tubes that rise over 1½ feet. If they have been fitted with mini check valves, be sure that backflow has been eliminated. If water level in the tube declines after the system shuts down, the check valve is leaking and should be replaced. Sometimes a second mini check valve used in series (one behind the other) with the first will suffice.

17. If low-pressure systems are being used, dissolve the recommended soluble fertilizer in the reservoir. A weak solution should be prepared. If the fertilizer is colored, solutions should be pale.

18. Before leaving the project, a meeting should be held with the interiorscaper and the building/facility management or homeowner to instruct them on the proper use of the system. It should be made clear that from that point on, the responsibility for operation becomes theirs, and that the installer does not become involved with plant care (unless of course, the installer is also an interiorscaper). A quantity of spare parts should be left at the site, particularly emitter tubes, adjustable mini-valve/emitters, emitter stabilizers, as well as ell and tee fittings for emitter tubes.

Operating Procedures

After the mechanical installation has been completed and the APM system has been checked and coarsely adjusted, the interior plant maintenance expert (in-house or under contract) begins overseeing its operation. The following guidelines and procedures should be observed:

1. A newly installed system should be monitored weekly for about one month to six weeks, and emitter adjustments made in response to the maintenance person's inspection. Because of the small quantities of water used daily, it may take a week or two for the soil moisture to reach equilibrium.

2. Use a good moisture meter. It reads relative levels of moisture around the root ball, penetrating where fingers and gauge sticks can't. In many cases, the soil surface may be dry to the touch, yet the root ball is properly damp. The meter will be able to discover such situations.

3. If a plant appears dry after adjustments have been made to the slightly opened emitter, the soil should be manually watered to bring moisture to the desired level.

4. If all plants seem to be drying out despite emitters feeding their maximum amounts, then the system should be reprogrammed to water more frequently. Perhaps a schedule with three waterings daily would be more suitable than twice daily, for example. This is accomplished by rescheduling the timer or electronic power controller. Also, for a given irrigation schedule, watering rates can be doubled by means of the irrigation cycle switch on the pump and solenoid valve controllers. Most light- and medium-duty interior controllers can be switched between 10 seconds and 20 seconds. Medium- and heavy-duty interior controllers can be switched between 15 seconds and 30 seconds. Controllers made for outdoor use are normally switched between 20 seconds and 40 seconds. High-pressure systems have additional adjustments that can be used, if necessary. For instance, water pressure can be increased (if originally reduced with a regulator), or flow rates can be increased (if restricted by a flow-control washer).

   These coarse adjustments become an important part of seasonal irrigation control. As the hotter months approach, soil moisture levels will decline. Summer months require greater water application because of increased soil surface drying and higher plant transpiration rates. Heating systems in winter months also tend to be drying. Appropriate adjustments should be made when necessary.

5. The system can be calibrated by determining exact flow rates. This is done after the maintenance technician is satisfied that emitter settings are acceptable. The amount of water dispensed to a plant over a given period (a day or week, for example, or even a single watering cycle) is measured by simply catching it in a cup or other small container as it leaves the emitter (Figure 16.2).

   A measuring cup or laboratory graduate is used to determine the number of ounces accumulated. Calculations are made to extrapolate the values to a chosen time period. For example, this could be ounces per 10 seconds, ounces per day or week, gallons per hour, per day or week, etc. For most purposes a single irrigation cycle is tested, in which case ounces per 10 seconds would be the unit of measurement. This must be done at each plant and can become quite tedious if many plants are involved, but it is the most accurate way to determine water application rates. The readings will be found useful for keeping the system uniform over long periods. However, plant needs will increase with growth, and flow readjustments must be made accordingly. New measurements can then be made to recalibrate the system. This type of adjustment is infrequent.

6. Plants in professionally maintained interiorscapes are turned to the light regularly. Care should be taken that system tubing is not disturbed when this is done. If necessary, the maintenance technician should remove the emitter assembly by pulling up the stake before turning the container, replacing it afterward. This prevents tubing lines from becoming twisted, tangled, and crimped.

7. The control timing should be checked periodically to be sure everything is in order. Accidental or deliberate changes can go unnoticed until plant health declines. By then it could be too late.

8. As a general rule, plant leaves should be closely inspected for a number of reasons. One has to do with the fact that leaf tips start to turn yellow, then dry out and turn brown when soil moisture levels are improper. Unfortunately, it happens when there is too much water, as well as when there is not enough. If these signs appear, soil moisture must be carefully checked.

9. During routine inspections, check that the adjustable mini-valve/emitters are above soil level and not covered by mulch.

10. When control centers are installed within built-in planters, be sure mulch does not come near the electronic

equipment. It can be damaged by damp mulch (or other materials) around it, and the condition could also pose a fire hazard. A type of retaining wall or moisture-proof enclosure can be installed in this case. It could even be as simple as a piece of stiff plastic sheet secured to the wall and bent around the controls. A moisture-proof pump or solenoid valve controller case (as well as timer case) should be used under such circumstances.

Figure 16.2: Flow measurement techniques.

11. Mulch should be used to prevent excessive evaporation from the soil surface.

12. A supply of emitters, emitter stabilizers (stakes and clamps), and tubing should be kept near the installation for occasional repair and replacements.

13. Fertilizer and other plant-care chemicals can be applied with the irrigation water. Water-soluble fertilizers, systemic pesticides, and fungicides may be used in dilute solutions when the system is one of the low-pressure types. The chemical solution would be stored in the reservoir. If there is any appearance of sludge or jelly-like accumulations in the reservoir, it may be caused by the mixture of incompatible chemicals. Stop the practice, and clean out the

system. These accumulations can cause tubing and fittings to clog.

14. A similar condition frequently occurs when algae builds up in reservoirs and tubing lines, particularly those near windows and other light sources. Clear tubes should be replaced with opaque types where that problem exists.

15. Fertilizer injectors are not recommended for use in high-pressure systems. The chemicals can deteriorate metal fittings and control parts.

16. Periodic inspection and cleaning of input filters and screens is important, and should not be overlooked in the routine maintenance schedule.

17. In cold-weather climates, the outdoor systems should be purged of water before the coming of frost, and the electronic equipment should be shut down for the duration of the cold season.

18. Periodically inspect emitter tubing for crimps or other constrictions. Furniture legs are sometimes accidentally moved on top of tubing.

If an installation is prepared with care, and someone with the proper training and sensitivity looks after the interiorscape, it will provide trouble-free performance for many years.

Automated building management systems such as these will become commonplace in the years to come, bringing our sheltered environments into the twenty-first century. Clearly, designers will be an important part of this transition from passive buildings to "smart" structures that anticipate our needs and desires. Ultimately it is they who will provide us with the comprehensive, multi-functional homes and businesses that will possess beauty worth admiration and unparalleled functional practicality.

Appendixes

Interiorscaping Plants and Their Preferred Conditions

Mini-encyclopedia of houseplants

COMMON NAME	BOTANICAL NAME	SOIL MIX					LIGHT				WATER				TEMPER-ATURE			HUMIDITY			PROPAGATION
		All purpose	High humus	Gritty lean	Loose medium	High acid	Sunny	Semi-sunny	Semi-shady	Shady	Keep wet at all times	Keep evenly moist	Approach dryness between waterings	Let dry out between waterings	Cool	Average house	Warm	Very moist	Moist	Average house	
Acalypha	Acalypha	•					•	•				•				•				•	Cuttings in fall
Achimenes	Achimenes		•					•	•			•				•				•	Rhizome division, seed, stem cuttings
Acorus	Acorus	•							•	•	•				•			•			Division in spring or fall
African hemp	Sparmannia africana	•						•				•				•				•	Cuttings
African violet	Saintpaulia		•					•	•			•				•			•		Seed, leaf cuttings, division
Agapanthus	Agapanthus	•					•	•	•			•			•	•				•	Division in early spring
Allamanda	Allamanda	•						•				•				•			•		Cuttings of half-ripened stems in spring
Amaryllis	Hippeastrum		•				•	•				•				•				•	Remove offsets at potting time; sow spring seed
Anemone	Anemone	•					•	•				•			•				•		Seed or offsets
Anigozanthus	Anigozanthus	•					•					•			•					•	Seed or root division
Anthurium	Anthurium				•				•			•					•	•			Cuttings or offsets
Apostle plant	Neomarica gracillis	•					•	•				•				•			•		Division of rhizomes

COMMON NAME	BOTANICAL NAME	SOIL MIX					LIGHT				WATER				TEMPERATURE			HUMIDITY			PROPAGATION
		All purpose	High humus	Gritty lean	Loose medium	High acid	Sunny	Semi-sunny	Semi-shady	Shady	Keep wet at all times	Keep evenly moist	Approach dryness between waterings	Let dry out between waterings	Cool	Average house	Warm	Very moist	Moist	Average house	
Aralia	*Dizygotheca elegantissima*, also see: *Polyscias* and *Fatsia*		•					•	•			•				•			•		Cuttings
Ardisia	*Ardisia*	•						•	•			•			•				•		Seed or cuttings
Asparagus fern	*Asparagus*	•						•	•	•		•				•				•	Seed or clump division
Aspidistra	*Aspidistra*	•						•	•	•		•			•					•	Division of roots in late winter or spring
Aucuba	*Aucuba japonicia*	•						•	•			•			•					•	Seed or cuttings
Azalea	*Azalea*	•			•	•	•					•			•			•			Stem cuttings
Baby's tears	*Helxine*		•					•	•			•				•		•			Division of clumps or cuttings
Bamboo	*Bambusa*		•				•	•				•				•				•	Division of large clumps
Bat-wing tree	*Erythrina indica*	•						•	•			•				•				•	Seed
Begonia	*Begonia rex; Begonia semperflorens;* Rhizomatous species; Fibrous-rooted, cane species; Tuberous-rooted species; and Fibrous-rooted species		•					•	•	•		•				•			•	•	Cuttings or seed
Bird-of-Paradise	*Strelitzia*	•						•	•			•					•			•	Division of rhizomes, remove suckers in spring
Bougainvillea	*Bougainvillea*	•					•					•				•			•		Seed in spring or cuttings of half-ripe wood
Bromeliad:	*Aechmea*				•		•	•						•		•				•	Remove offsets
Pineapple	*Ananas*		•				•	•						•		•		•			Root top of fruit
	Billbergia				•		•	•				•				•				•	Detach suckers
Earth stars	*Cryptanthus*		•					•	•					•		•				•	Remove offsets
	Neoregelia				•			•	•					•		•				•	Detach suckers
Living vase or Flaming-sword	*Vriesia*		•					•	•			•				•			•		Remove suckers or plantlets
Brassaia (Schefflera)	*Brassaia*	•					•	•	•	•		•				•				•	Cuttings of half-ripened stems
Cactus:	*Aporocactus; Astrophytum; Cephalocereus; Chamaecereus; Cleistocactus Echinocactus; Echinocereus; Echinopsis; Gymnocalycium; Lobivia; Mammillaria; Notocactus;*			•			•	•						•	•	•				•	Offsets or cuttings

COMMON NAME	BOTANICAL NAME	SOIL MIX					LIGHT				WATER				TEMPERATURE			HUMIDITY			PROPAGATION
		All purpose	High humus	Gritty lean	Loose medium	High acid	Sunny	Semi-sunny	Semi-shady	Shady	Keep wet at all times	Keep evenly moist	Approach dryness between waterings	Let dry out between waterings	Cool	Average house	Warm	Very moist	Moist	Average house	
	Opuntia; Pereskia; Rebutia;																				
	Ephiphyllum; Hylocereus; Selenicereus;	●						●	●			●				●			●		Cuttings in spring or summer
	Schlumbergera; and *Zygocactus*	●						●	●			●				●			●		Cuttings
Caladium	Caladium	●						●	●			●					●		●		Divide tubers or clumps in spring
Calceolaria	Calceolaria	●							●	●		●			●				●		Seed in April or August
Calla-lily	*Zantedeschia*	●			●						●					●			●		Seed or offsets
Camellia	*Camellia japonica*		●			●	●	●				●			●			●			Cuttings of current season's new wood
Chinese evergreen	*Aglaonema*	●						●	●	●		●				●				●	Root stems
Chlorophytum (spider)	*Chlorophytum*	●						●	●	●		●				●				●	Remove aerial plantlets or division
Chrysanthemum	*Chrysanthemum*	●					●	●				●			●					●	Cuttings
Cineraria	*Senecio cruentus*	●					●	●				●			●				●		Seed in summer
Citrus	*Citrus*	●					●	●				●				●				●	Cuttings of half-ripened wood in spring
Clematis	*Clematis*		●				●					●				●				●	Seed, layering, division, cuttings, or grafting
Clerodendrum	*Clerodendrum*		●				●	●				●				●				●	Cuttings of half-ripened wood or remove suckers
Clivia	*Clivia*	●						●	●			●			●	●				●	Division
Cobra plant	*Darlingtonia californica*		●		●			●	●	●							●		●			Seed or shoots in summer
Coccoloba (Seagrape)	Coccoloba	●						●	●			●				●				●	Seed, layering, wood cuttings
Coffee	*Coffea*	●						●	●	●		●			●	●			●		Seed or wood cuttings
Coleus	*Coleus blumei*	●					●	●				●				●				●	Seed or stem cuttings
Columnea	*Columnea*		●				●	●				●				●		●			Tip cuttings or seed
Creeping Charlie	*Pilea nummularifolia* (also see: *Plectranthus*)		●					●	●			●				●				●	Cuttings

		SOIL MIX					LIGHT				WATER				TEMPER-ATURE			HUMIDITY			
COMMON NAME	BOTANICAL NAME	All purpose	High humus	Gritty lean	Loose medium	High acid	Sunny	Semi-sunny	Semi-shady	Shady	Keep wet at all times	Keep evenly moist	Approach dryness between waterings	Let dry out between waterings	Cool	Average house	Warm	Very moist	Moist	Average house	PROPAGATION
Creeping fig	*Ficus pimula* or *Fradicans*	•						•	•	•		•				•			•		Cuttings
Crossandra	Crossandra		•					•				•				•			•		Seed or tip cuttings
Croton	Codiaeum		•			•	•					•				•			•		Cuttings
Cup-and-saucer vine	Cobaea scandens	•					•	•				•				•				•	Seed
Cyclamen	Cyclamen		•					•	•			•			•			•			Seed
Cyperus	Cyperus	•						•	•	•	•				•				•		Division
Cycas fern or palm	Cycas	•						•				•				•				•	Seed or dormant suckers
Dieffenbachia (Dumb cane)	Dieffenbachia	•						•	•	•			•			•				•	Stem cuttings or layering
Dipladenia	Dipladenia splendens	•					•	•				•				•		•			Stem cuttings or seed
Dracaena	Dracaena	•						•	•	•		•				•				•	Stem cuttings, layering, root division
	Pleomele	•						•	•	•		•				•				•	Stem cuttings, layering, root division
Easter lily	Lilium longiflorum	•						•						•	•					•	Plant bulbs
Euonymus	Euonymus	•						•	•			•			•				•		Cuttings of half-ripened wood in fall or winter
Elaeagnus	Elaeagnus	•						•	•			•			•	•			•		Cuttings in spring
Fatshedera	Fatshedera lizel	•			•			•	•			•			•	•			•		Cuttings
Fatsia	Fatsia japonica		•					•				•			•	•			•		Cuttings of branches
Ferns: Bird's-nest	Asplenium		•					•	•			•			•				•		Remove offsets or root plantlets
Boston or sword	Nephrolepis		•					•	•			•				•				•	Division of clumps
Bear's-paw	Polypodium		•					•	•			•				•				•	Division of clumps
Holly	Cyrtomium		•					•	•			•			•				•		Rhizome division
Maidenhair	Adiantum		•		•				•	•	•					•		•			Division of clumps
Miniature	Polystichum		•						•			•				•				•	Division
Rabbit's-foot	Davallia		•						•			•			•				•		Rhizome division
Staghorn	Platycerium				•			•	•			•				•			•		Remove offsets
Table or brake	Pteris		•						•			•			•				•		Division
Ficus or fig	Ficus	•						•	•	•		•					•			•	Air layering
Fittonia	Fittonia	•						•	•			•			•				•		Tip cuttings
Flame violet	Episcia		•					•	•			•					•		•		Root stolens

279

COMMON NAME	BOTANICAL NAME	SOIL MIX					LIGHT				WATER				TEMPER-ATURE			HUMIDITY			PROPAGATION
		All purpose	High humus	Gritty lean	Loose medium	High acid	Sunny	Semi-sunny	Semi-shady	Shady	Keep wet at all times	Keep evenly moist	Approach dryness between waterings	Let dry out between waterings	Cool	Average house	Warm	Very moist	Moist	Average house	
Flowering maple	Abutilon	●						●				●				●				●	Stem cuttings
Flowering tobacco	Nicotiana	●						●	●		●					●				●	Seed
Fragrant gladiolus	Acidanthera	●						●				●				●				●	New corms in spring
Freesia	Freesia	●						●				●			●				●		Seed or offsets
Fuchsia	Fuchsia	●						●	●			●			●				●		Cuttings in spring
Gardenia	Gardenia	●				●	●	●				●				●			●		Cuttings of half-ripened wood
Gerbera	Gerbera	●					●	●				●				●				●	
Geranium	Pelargonium	●					●	●					●		●	●			●	●	Cuttings
Ginger:	Amomum	●						●	●			●				●			●	●	Clump division
Spiral	Costus		●					●	●			●				●			●		Clump division in spring
	Curcuma		●					●	●			●				●	●	●			Division of tubers in spring
Ginger lilies	Hedychium	●						●			●	●				●			●		Division of tubers at rest time
Peacock plant	Kaempferia		●					●	●			●				●	●	●			Seed or clump division
Commercial ginger root	Zingiber		●					●	●			●				●	●	●			Division of clumps in spring
Gloriosa	Gloriosa rothschildiana		●				●	●				●				●			●		Seed or tuber division
Gloxinia	Sinningia	●						●				●				●			●		Seed, leaf or stem cuttings, tuber division
Gynura	Gynura	●					●					●				●				●	Cuttings
Haemanthus	Haemanthus	●					●	●				●				●			●		Remove offsets when repotting
Hawaiian ti	Cordyline terminalis	●						●	●	●		●				●				●	Stem cutting, layering, root division
Hibiscus	Hibiscus	●					●					●				●			●		Stem cuttings
Homalomena	Homalomena	●						●	●			●				●			●		Stem cuttings
Hydrangea	Hydrangea	●			●	●	●				●	●			●					●	Stem cuttings
Hypoestes	Hypoestes		●				●	●				●				●			●		Seed or cuttings
Impatiens	Impatiens	●					●	●	●				●			●		●			Cuttings
Iresine	Iresine	●					●						●		●	●				●	Cuttings
Ivy, English	Hedera helix	●					●	●	●	●		●	●		●				●	●	Cuttings
Ixia	Ixia	●					●					●	●		●				●		Bulb offsets

COMMON NAME	BOTANICAL NAME	SOIL MIX					LIGHT				WATER				TEMPER- ATURE			HUMIDITY			PROPAGATION
		All purpose	High humus	Gritty lean	Loose medium	High acid	Sunny	Semi-sunny	Semi-shady	Shady	Keep wet at all times	Keep evenly moist	Approach dryness between waterings	Let dry out between waterings	Cool	Average house	Warm	Very moist	Moist	Average house	
Ixora	Ixora	•					•	•				•				•				•	Strong cuttings
Jatropha	Jatropha	•					•	•				•				•			•	•	Seed or cuttings
Jerusaleum cherry	Solanum	•					•	•				•					•			•	Seed
Jessamine, night-blooming	Cestrum nocturnum		•				•	•				•					•			•	Cuttings
Joseph's coat	Alternanthera	•					•	•				•				•				•	Cuttings
King's crown	Jacobina carnea	•						•				•				•			•		Cuttings
Leopard plant	Ligularia tussilaginea	•						•	•			•					•			•	Dividing plants with more than one crown
Liriope or lily turf	Ophiopogon	•						•	•			•					•		•		Division
Lipstick vine	Aeschynanthus		•		•			•	•			•				•		•			Stem or tip cuttings
Miniature rose	Rosa	•					•	•				•				•			•		Seed or cuttings
Montbretia	Crocosmia	•					•					•				•				•	Seed or offsets
Myrtle	Myrtus communis	•					•	•						•	•					•	Cuttings of ripened wood
Nandina	Nandina	•						•	•			•				•				•	Stem cuttings
Norfolk island pine	Araucaria excelsa	•						•	•			•			•	•			•		Seed or root tops of old plants
Oleander	Nerium oleander	•					•	•				•				•				•	Cuttings of firm tip growth in spring or summer
Orchid:	Brassavola				•		•	•						•		•		•			Division in late winter
	Cattleya				•		•	•						•		•		•			Division in late winter
Swan	Cycnoches	•			•			•	•			•				•		•			Division in spring or summer
	Epidendrum				•			•	•				•			•		•			Air layering or division in spring
Tiger	Odontoglossum				•				•				•		•			•			Division in spring or summer
Butterfly	Oncidium				•			•	•			•				•		•			Division in spring
Lady slipper	Paphiopedilum				•				•			•				•		•			Division in spring
Dogwood or moth	Phalaenopsis				•			•	•			•				•		•			Division in spring
Oxalis	Oxalis	•					•	•				•				•			•		Offsets or division
Palms: Bamboo	Chamaedorea	•							•	•		•				•				•	Seed or remove suckers
Butterfly	Chrysalidocarpus	•						•	•			•				•				•	Seed or clump division in spring

COMMON NAME	BOTANICAL NAME	SOIL MIX					LIGHT				WATER				TEMPER-ATURE			HUMIDITY			PROPAGATION
		All purpose	High humus	Gritty lean	Loose medium	High acid	Sunny	Semi-sunny	Semi-shady	Shady	Keep wet at all times	Keep evenly moist	Approach dryness between waterings	Let dry out between waterings	Cool	Average house	Warm	Very moist	Moist	Average house	
Date	*Phoenix*	●						●	●			●				●				●	Seed or remove suckers
Fan	*Chamaerops*	●						●	●		●	●			●					●	Seed or suckers
	Licuala	●						●	●			●				●			●		Seed or suckers
	Livistona	●						●	●			●				●			●		Seed or suckers
	Rhapis	●						●	●			●			●					●	Seed or suckers
Fishtail	*Caryota*	●						●	●			●				●			●		Seed in March
Pandanus	*Pandanus*		●				●	●				●				●		●			Remove suckers
Passion flower	*Passiflora*		●				●	●				●				●			●		Seed or cuttings
Pellionia	*Pellionia*	●							●	●		●				●			●		Cuttings
Peperomia	*Peperomia*	●						●	●	●			●			●				●	Stem or leaf cuttings
Philodendron	*Philodendron*	●						●	●	●		●				●			●	●	Stem cuttings or offsets
Pilea (Artillery, Aluminum, Moon Valley)	*Pilea*		●					●	●			●				●			●	●	Cuttings
Pittosporum	*Pittosporum*	●						●	●			●			●				●		Cuttings of half-ripened wood
Plectranthus (Swedish ivy)	*Plectranthus*	●						●	●	●		●				●				●	Seed or stem cuttings
Podocarpus	*Podocarpus*	●							●			●			●				●		Seed or ripened wood cuttings
Polyscias	*Polyscias*	●					●	●	●	●		●			●	●		●			Cuttings
Prayer plant	*Maranta*		●						●			●				●			●		Division
Pregnant onion	*Ornithogalum caudatum*	●						●					●			●				●	Remove offsets
Primrose	*Primula*		●					●	●			●			●				●		Seed
Privet	*Ligustrum*	●					●	●				●				●				●	Stem cuttings
Pyracantha	*Pyracantha*	●					●					●			●					●	Soft wood cuttings in early summer
Radar plant	*Desmondium gyrans*	●					●					●				●				●	Seed in February
Ranunculus	*Ranunculus*	●					●					●			●				●		Seed in March; roots in autumn
Redwood burl	*Sequoia sempervirens*						●	●	●	●		●				●				●	Plantlets can be rooted
Resurrection plant	*Selaginella lepidophylla*						●	●	●	●		●				●				●	Purchase in dried form

		SOIL MIX					LIGHT				WATER				TEMPERATURE			HUMIDITY			
COMMON NAME	BOTANICAL NAME	All purpose	High humus	Gritty lean	Loose medium	High acid	Sunny	Semi-sunny	Semi-shady	Shady	Keep wet at all times	Keep evenly moist	Approach dryness between waterings	Let dry out between waterings	Cool	Average house	Warm	Very moist	Moist	Average house	PROPAGATION
Rhododendron	Rhododendron	●				●	●	●				●			●				●		Stem cuttings
Rhoeo (Moses-in-the-Cradle)	Rhoeo	●					●	●	●			●				●				●	Remove offset or transplant seedlings from parent
Rosary vine	Ceropegia woodi	●					●	●	●					●		●				●	Cuttings or plant bulblets along stems
Sansevieria	Sansevieria	●					●	●	●	●			●			●				●	Division of rootstock or leaf cuttings
Saxifraga	Saxifraga	●					●	●			●	●			●				●		Remove young plants
Scindapsus	Scindapsus aureus	●						●	●	●		●					●			●	Cuttings
Selaginella	Selaginella		●					●	●		●					●		●			Cuttings
Sensitive plant	Mimosa pudica	●					●	●	●		●	●				●			●		Seed or transplants
Shoo-fly plant	Nicandra physalodes	●					●	●				●				●				●	Seed
Shower plant	Cassia	●					●	●				●				●				●	Seed
Shrimp plant	Beloperone guttata	●					●	●						●		●			●		Cuttings
Spathiphyllum	Spathiphyllum		●				●	●				●				●			●		Division of rootstock
Stephanotis	Stephanotis floribunda		●				●	●				●				●			●		Cuttings of half-mature stems in spring
Succulents: Century plant	Agave	●					●							●		●				●	Remove offsets
	Aloe	●					●	●					●			●				●	Seed or offsets
Ice plant	Aptenia	●					●						●			●				●	Stem cuttings
Pony-tail	Beaucarnea	●					●	●					●			●				●	Remove offset
	Bowiea	●						●	●			●			●					●	Remove offsets
Propeller, rattlesnake, scarlet paintbrush, etc.	Crassula	●					●	●					●	●		●				●	Seed or cuttings
	Eschiveria	●					●	●						●		●				●	Offsets or stem cuttings
Poinsettia, Crown-of-thorns, etc.	Euphorbia	●					●	●						●		●				●	Cuttings
Tiger jaws	Faucaria			●			●							●		●				●	Seed or cuttings
Baby toes	Fenestraria			●			●							●		●				●	Seed or cuttings
Ox-tongue	Gasteria	●						●	●				●			●				●	Seed or offsets

COMMON NAME	BOTANICAL NAME	SOIL MIX					LIGHT				WATER				TEMPERATURE			HUMIDITY			PROPAGATION
		All purpose	High humus	Gritty lean	Loose medium	High acid	Sunny	Semi-sunny	Semi-shady	Shady	Keep wet at all times	Keep evenly moist	Approach dryness between waterings	Let dry out between waterings	Cool	Average house	Warm	Very moist	Moist	Average house	
Zebra or wart	*Haworthia*	•					•	•						•		•				•	Seed or offsets
	Kalanchoe	•					•	•						•	•	•				•	Potting plantlets, seed, or tip cuttings
Living stones, stone face	*Lithops*			•			•							•		•				•	Seed in spring
	Pachyveria	•					•	•						•		•				•	Offsets or stem cuttings
Devil's backbone	*Pedilanthus*	•					•	•					•			•				•	Cuttings in spring
Mistletoe cactus	*Rhipsalis*	•			•			•	•			•					•	•			Cuttings
	Scilla	•						•	•			•				•			•		Offsets in autumn
Donkey's tail, coral beads, etc.	*Sedum*	•					•	•						•	•	•				•	Seed, cuttings, or division
Starfish flower	*Stapelia*		•				•	•				•				•				•	Division or cuttings in late spring or summer
String-of-pearls	*Senecio rowleyanus*	•					•	•					•			•				•	
Sweet-olive	*Osmanthus fragrans*	•					•	•				•			•				•		Cuttings of half-ripened wood in summer
Tibouchina	*Tibouchina*	•						•	•			•			•				•		Cuttings
Tolmeia (Piggy-back)	*Tolmeia*		•				•	•			•	•				•			•		Pin baby plants into damp soil
Tulbaghia	*Tulbaghia*	•					•	•				•				•				•	Offsets in spring or fall
Voodoo plant	*Hydrosme rivieri*	•					•	•				•				•				•	Remove offsets from tuber
Walking iris	*Neomarica northiana*	•					•	•				•			•				•		From small plants formed by flowers
Wandering Jew	*Gibasis*	•					•	•	•			•			•				•		Cuttings anytime
	Setcreasea	•					•	•	•				•		•					•	Cuttings anytime
	Tradescantia	•					•	•	•				•		•					•	Cuttings anytime
	Zebrina	•					•	•	•			•				•			•		Cuttings anytime
Yesterday, Today, and Tomorrow	*Brunfelsia calycina*	•					•					•				•			•		Cuttings
Zebra plant	*Aphelandra*	•					•					•				•			•		Tip cuttings in spring

Source: "House Plants: Indoors/Outdoors"; Ortho Books, Ortho Div. of Chevron Chemical Co.; San Francisco, 1974.

Tubing and Pipe Fitting Nomenclature

TEE FITTINGS

UNION TEES (SAME SIZE ALL AROUND)	COMPRESSION TYPE	BARB TYPE	SLIP — SLIP OR PIPE THREAD (FPT) / SOLVENT-WELD TYPE	FEMALE PIPE THREAD / THREADED TYPE (PIPE FITTING)
MALE BRANCH TEES (MALE THREAD ON BRANCH)	MALE PIPE THREAD (MPT) / COMPRESSION TYPE	MALE PIPE THREAD / BARB TYPE		MALE PIPE THREAD (MPT) / THREADED TYPE / FEMALE PIPE THREAD (FPT)
REDUCING TEES (BRANCH IS SMALLER THAN RUN)	SMALLER COMPRESSION / COMPRESSION TYPE	SMALLER BARB / BARB TYPE	SMALLER SLIP / SLIP — SLIP / SOLVENT-WELD TYPE	SMALLER THREAD (FPT) / SLIP — SLIP / COMBINATION TYPE (SOLVENT-WELD/THREAD)
FEMALE BRANCH TEES	FEMALE PIPE THREAD OR SLIP SOCKET ON BRANCH, MOST COMMON IN PVC PIPE FITTINGS.			

ELBOW FITTINGS (ALSO CALLED "ELLS")

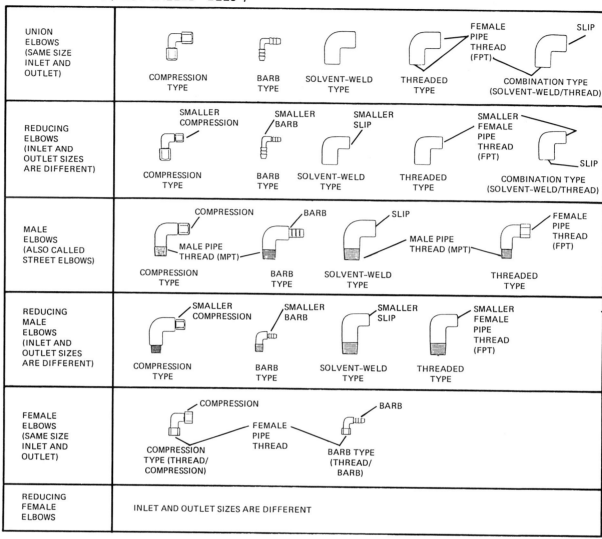

UNION ELBOWS (SAME SIZE INLET AND OUTLET)	COMPRESSION TYPE — BARB TYPE — SOLVENT-WELD TYPE — THREADED TYPE — COMBINATION TYPE (SOLVENT-WELD/THREAD) with FEMALE PIPE THREAD (FPT) and SLIP
REDUCING ELBOWS (INLET AND OUTLET SIZES ARE DIFFERENT)	COMPRESSION TYPE (SMALLER COMPRESSION) — BARB TYPE (SMALLER BARB) — SOLVENT-WELD TYPE (SMALLER SLIP) — THREADED TYPE (SMALLER FEMALE PIPE THREAD FPT) — COMBINATION TYPE (SOLVENT-WELD/THREAD) with SLIP
MALE ELBOWS (ALSO CALLED STREET ELBOWS)	COMPRESSION TYPE (COMPRESSION / MALE PIPE THREAD MPT) — BARB TYPE (BARB) — SOLVENT-WELD TYPE (SLIP / MALE PIPE THREAD MPT) — THREADED TYPE (FEMALE PIPE THREAD FPT)
REDUCING MALE ELBOWS (INLET AND OUTLET SIZES ARE DIFFERENT)	COMPRESSION TYPE (SMALLER COMPRESSION) — BARB TYPE (SMALLER BARB) — SOLVENT-WELD TYPE (SMALLER SLIP) — THREADED TYPE (SMALLER FEMALE PIPE THREAD FPT)
FEMALE ELBOWS (SAME SIZE INLET AND OUTLET)	COMPRESSION TYPE (THREAD/COMPRESSION) with COMPRESSION and FEMALE PIPE THREAD — BARB TYPE (THREAD/BARB) with BARB
REDUCING FEMALE ELBOWS	INLET AND OUTLET SIZES ARE DIFFERENT

STRAIGHT FITTINGS

MALE CONNECTORS, ADAPTERS OR COUPLINGS (SAME SIZE INLET AND OUTLET)	COMPRESSION — MALE PIPE THREAD (MPT) — COMPRESSION TYPE	BARB — BARB TYPE	SLIP — MALE PIPE THREAD (MPT) — SOLVENT-WELD TYPE	FEMALE PIPE THREAD (FPT) — THREADED TYPE
REDUCING MALE CONNECTORS	INLET AND OUTLET SIZES ARE DIFFERENT			
FEMALE CONNECTORS, ADAPTERS OR COUPLINGS (SAME SIZE INLET AND OUTLET	COMPRESSION — FEMALE PIPE THREAD (FPT) — COMPRESSION TYPE	BARB — BARB TYPE	SLIP — FEMALE PIPE THREAD (FPT) — SOLVENT-WELD TYPE	FEMALE PIPE THREAD (FPT) — THREADED TYPE
REDUCING FEMALE CONNECTORS	INLET AND OUTLET SIZES ARE DIFFERENT			
SLIP COUPLINGS (SAME SIZE INLET AND OUTLET)	SLIP — SLIP — SOLVENT-WELD TYPE			
REDUCER SLIP COUPLINGS	INLET AND OUTLET SIZES ARE DIFFERENT			
BUSHINGS (SIMILAR TO REDUCING ADAPTERS BUT MORE COMPACT)	SMALLER FEMALE PIPE THREAD (FPT) — MALE PIPE THREAD (MPT) — THREADED TYPE (PIPE FITTING)	SMALLER SLIP — SLIP — SOLVENT-WELD TYPE	SMALLER FEMALE PIPE THREAD (FPT) — SLIP — COMBINATION TYPE	
NIPPLES (OR MALE UNIONS)	MALE PIPE THREAD (MPT)			
PLUGS AND CAPS	NO OUTLET — MALE PIPE THREAD (MPT) — THREADED PLUG (PIPE FITTING)	NO OUTLET — SLIP — SOLVENT-WELD TYPE PLUG	NO OUTLET — BARB — BARB TYPE PLUS (TUBING FITTING)	NO OUTLET — FEMALE PIPE THREAD (FPT) — THREADED CAP / NO OUTLET — SLIP — SOLVENT-WELD CAP

287

HOSE ADAPTERS

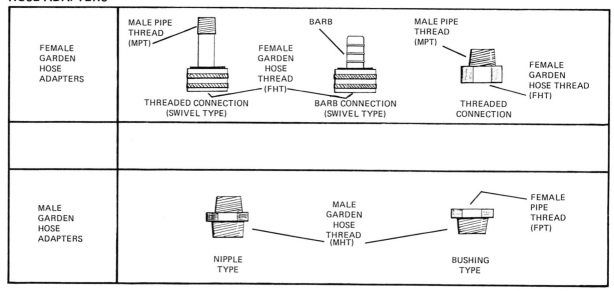

| FEMALE GARDEN HOSE ADAPTERS | MALE PIPE THREAD (MPT) · THREADED CONNECTION (SWIVEL TYPE) · FEMALE GARDEN HOSE THREAD (FHT) · BARB · BARB CONNECTION (SWIVEL TYPE) · MALE PIPE THREAD (MPT) · THREADED CONNECTION · FEMALE GARDEN HOSE THREAD (FHT) |
| MALE GARDEN HOSE ADAPTERS | NIPPLE TYPE · MALE GARDEN HOSE THREAD (MHT) · BUSHING TYPE · FEMALE PIPE THREAD (FPT) |

APPENDIX C

Sources and Suppliers

The following lists are by no means complete, but they represent some of the more important sources of interiorscaping equipment and services.

Manual Watering Machines— Manufacturers

Aquamatic Systems, Inc.
Division of American Granby
1111 Vine Street
Liverpool, NY 13088
Telephone: (800) 726-9889

Cascade Designs, Inc.
(The Watering Machine Brand)
157 Clifford Street
Providence, RI 02903

Automatic Sprinkler Systems— Manufacturers

Champion Brass Manufacturing Co., Inc.
1460 North Naud Street
Los Angeles, CA 90012
Telephone: (213) 221-2108

K-Rain Manufacturing Corp.
1640 Australian Avenue
Riviera Beach, FL 33404
Telephone: (407) 844-1002
Fax: (407) 842-9493

L. R. Nelson Corp.
1 Sprinkler Lane
Peoria, IL 61615
Telephone: (309) 692-2200
Fax: (309) 692-5847

Rain Bird Sprinklers, Inc., Turf Division
145 North Grand Avenue
Glendora, CA 91740
Telephone: (818) 963-9311

Rain Master Irrigation Systems
1825-103 Surveyor Avenue
Simi Valley, CA 93063
Telephone: (805) 527-4498
Fax: (805) 527-2813

Richdel, Inc.
1851 South Roop Street
Carson City, NV 89701

Roberts Irrigation Products, Inc.
700 Rancheros Drive
San Marcos, CA 92069
Telephone: (619) 744-4511
Fax: (619) 744-0914

Ross Sprinkler Co.
2543 Strozier Avenue
South El Monte, CA 91733

Buckner Sprinklers, Inc.
4381 North Brawley Avenue
Fresno, CA 93722
Telephone: (209) 275-0500
Fax: (800) 997-0500

Safe-T-Lawn, Inc.
5350 N.W. 165th Street
Hialeah, FL 33014

The Toro Company—Irrigation Division
5825 Jasmine Street
Riverside, CA 92504
Telephone: (909) 688-9221

Telsco Weather-matic
3301 West Kingsley Road
Garland, TX 75041
Telephone: (214) 278-6131
Fax: (214) 278-5710

**Drip/Trickle Irrigation Systems—
Manufacturers**

Agrifim Irrigation, Inc.
336 W. Bedford #107
Fresno, CA 93711
Telephone: (209) 431-2003
Fax: (209) 435-2922

Chapin Watermatics, Inc.
740 Water Street
Watertown, NY 13601
Telephone: (315) 782-1170
Fax: (315) 782-1490

Garden America Corporation
(Drip Mist Brand Watering Systems)
Post Office Box A
Carson City, NV 89702

Global Irrigation Corp.
8405 Artesia Boulevard
Buena Park, CA 90621

Indigo Technologies, Inc.
(Agro-Drip Brand)
2405-650 West Georgia Street
Vancouver, British Columbia
V6B 4N8 Canada

Natafim Irrigation, Inc.
104 South Central Avenue
Valley Stream, NY 11580

Pepco Extruded Products, Inc.
Nibco Irrigation Products
4870 West Jacquelyn Avenue
Fresno, CA 93722
Telephone: (209) 275-3555
Fax: (209) 275-5021

Rain Bird Sprinklers, Inc.—Turf Division
145 North Grand Avenue
Glendora, CA 91741
Telephone: (818) 963-9311

Reed Irrigation Systems
Post Office Box X
El Cajon, CA 92022

Roberts Irrigation Products, Inc.
700 Rancheros Drive
San Marcos, CA 92069
Telephone: (619) 744-4511
Fax: (619) 744-0914

Toro Company—Irrigation Division
5825 Jasmine Street
Riverside, CA 92504
Telephone: (909) 688-9221

Wade Manufacturing Company
Nibco Irrigation Products
2851 East Florence Avenue
Fresno, CA 93721
Telephone: (209) 485-7170
Fax: (209) 485-7623

**Subirrigation Systems—
Manufacturers**

Hydrachem Corp.
(Hydropore Brand Pipe)
17400 Dallas Parkway—Suite 105
Dallas, TX 75252

Pepco Extruded Products, Inc.
Nibco Irrigation Products
4870 West Jacquelyn Avenue
Fresno, CA 93722
Telephone: (209) 275-3555
Fax: (209) 275-5021

Rain Bird Sprinklers, Inc.—Turf Division
145 North Grand Avenue
Glendora, CA 91740
Telephone: (818) 963-9311

Reed Irrigation Systems
(Bi-Wall Brand Pipe)
Post Office Box X
El Cajon, CA 92022

Subsurface Industries
(Leaky Pipe Brand)
Post Office Box 18069
Fort Worth, TX 76118

Subterrain Irrigation Co.
1534 East Edinger
Santa Ana, CA 92705

TPR Products
(MPS Capillary Irrigation/Mona Brand)
Post Office Box 710
Deerfield, IL 60015
Telephone: (708) 634-4125
Fax: (708) 634-4126

Self-Watering Planters

Akvamatik
2312 Central Avenue
Middletown, OH 45042

Chatelain Industrie
Post Office Box 532
Chester, NY 10918

International Concepts, Inc.
(Grossfillex Brand)
11200 Westheimer—#320
Houston, TX 77042

Hydro-Planter Designs, Inc.
(Genie Brand)
5510 Ambler Drive—#7
Mississauga, Ontario
Canada L4W 2V1

Dr. Jardinier Self-Watering Planter Systems,
   Inc.
(Dr. Jardinier Brand)
Fresno, CA

TPR Products
(Mona System Brand)
Post Office Box 710
Deerfield, IL 60015
Telephone: (708) 634-4125
Fax: (708) 634-4126

Planter Technology
(Natural Spring Brand)
999 Independence Avenue
Mountain View, CA 94043
Telephone: (415) 962-8982
Fax: (415) 962-8875

Plant Minder, Inc.
(Plant Minder Brand)
22582 Shannon Circle
Lake Forest, CA 92630

Riviera Systems, U.S.A.
(Riviera Brand)
2800 NW 5th Avenue
Miami, FL 33127

City Gardens, Inc.
(Water Disc Brand)
455 Watertown Street
Newton, MA 02160
Telephone: (800) 696-8130

Plasticom, Inc.
(Watermatic Brand)
Post Office Box 368
Southbridge, MA 01550

Automated Precision Micro-Irrigation Systems—Manufacturers

Boca Automation, Inc.
(Mirage, EnvironMate, Aqua/Trends brands)
P.O. Box 810444
Boca Raton, FL 33481
Telephone: (407) 272-9838
Fax: (407) 272-2539

Consulting, Design and Engineering Services—automated interior plant care systems

Boca Automation, Inc.
Post Office Box 810444
Boca Raton, FL 33481
Telephone: (407) 272-9838
Fax: (407) 272-2539

Moisture Meters—Manufacturers

AMI Marketing Services
(Instamatic Brand)
Post Office Box 148
Ronkonkoma, NY 11779

Green Thumb Products
(Green Thumb Brand)
Apopka, FL 32703

Endnotes

Introduction

1 A.C. Hill, "Vegetation: A Sink For Atmospheric Pollutants," *Journal of the Air Pollution Control Association*21(6) (Pittsburgh, 1971): 341; Environmental Health Sciences Center, *The Role of Plants in Environmental Purification* (Corvallis, OR: Oregon State University, 1972); J.H. Bennett and A.C. Hill, "Absorption of Gaseous Air Pollutants by a Standardized Plant Canopy," *Journal of the Air Pollution Control Association.* 23(3) (1973): 203; A.M. Townsend, "Sorption of Ozone by Nine Shade Tree Species," *Journal of the American Horticultural Science* 99(3) (1974): 206; J.H. Bennett and A.C. Hill, "Interactions of Air Pollutants with Canopies of Vegetation," in *Responses of Plants to Air Pollution* by Mudd & Koslowski (New York: Academic Press, 1975), 273; T. Yoneyama, T. Totsuka, A. Hashimoto and J. Yazaki, "Absorption of Atmospheric NO_2 by Plants and Soils III," *Soil Science and Plant Nutrition* 25(3) (1979):337; W. Knabe, "Capacity and Efficiency of Vegetation in Reducing Airborne Pollution in Urban and Industrial Areas," Symposium on the Effects of Airborne Pollution on Vegetation, United Nations Economic Commission for Europe (Warsaw, Poland: August 1979); U. Luttge and K. Fischer, "Light-Dependent Net CO-Evolution by C3 and C4 Plants," *Planta* 149 (1980): 59; G.P. Hanson and L. Thorne, "Vegetation to Reduce Air Pollution," *Lasca Leaves* 20 (1972): 60–65; E. Robinson and R.C. Robbins, "Sources, Abundance and Fate of Gaseous Atmospheric Pollutants Supplement," SRI Project PR-6755 (Menlo Park, CA: Stanford Research Institute, 1969); A.R. Meetham, "Natural Removal of Pollution from the Atmosphere," *Quarterly Journal of the Royal Meteorological Society* 76 (1950): 359–371.

2 John Naisbitt, Megatrends (New York: Warner Books, 1982).

3 Paul N. Klaus, Decreasing Stress Through the Introduction of Microenvironments (Sunnyvale, CA: NASA, August 1987).

4 S. Kaplan and R. Kaplan, *Humanscape: Environments for People* (North Scituate, MA: Duxbury Press, 1978), 193.

5 J.A. Wise and E. Rosenberg, *The Effects of Interior Treatments on Performance Stress in Three Types of Mental Tasks* CIFR Technical Report No. 002-02-1988 (Grand Rapids, MI: Grand Valley State University, 1988).

6 Bruce Allsopp, *Towards a Humane Architecture* (London: Frederick Muller, Ltd., 1974).

7 Lang, Burnette, Moleski and Vachon, *Designing for Human Behavior* (Stroudsburg, PA: Dowden, Hutchinson and Ross, 1974).

8 Byron Mikellides, *Architecture for People* (New York: Holt, Rinehart and Winston, 1980).

9 Walter B. Kleeman, Jr., *The Challenge of Interior Design* (Boston: CBI Publishing Company, 1981).

10 Habitability Technology Section, *Habitability Data Handbook—Volume 2, MSC-03909* (Houston: NASA Spacecraft Design Division, July 31, 1971).

11 Roger S. Ulrich and Russ Parsons, "Influences of Passive Experiences with Plants on Individual Well-being and Health," Texas A&M University College of Architecture, paper presented at the National Symposium on the Role of Horticulture in Human Well-being and Social Development (Washington, DC: April 19, 1990): 16.

12 Mary Gilliatt, *The Complete Book of Home Design* (Boston: Little, Brown and Co., 1984), 94.

13 Michael Wright, editor, *The Complete Indoor Gardener* (New York: Random House, 1979), 16.

14 Judy Graf Klein, *The Office Book* (New York: Facts On File, Inc., 1982), 120.

15 Norma Skurka, *The New York Times Book of Interior Design and Decoration,* (New York: Quadrangle/ The New York Times Book Company, 1976), 92.

16 Michael Brill, *The Impact of Office Environment on Productivity and Quality of Working Life* (Buffalo: Buffalo Organization for Technological and Social Innovation, 1982).

17 Judy Graf Klein, *The Office Book* (New York: Facts On File, Inc., 1982), 36, 40, 120.

18 Stephen Scrivens, *Interior Planting in Large Buildings* (New York: Halsted Press/John Wiley & Sons, 1980), 1.

19 Jack W. Stuster, *Space Station Habitability Recommendations Based on a Systematic Comparative Analysis of Analogous Conditions* (Houston: NASA, 1986), 84.

20 *Statistical Abstract of the United States* (1986).

Chapter 1

1 B.C. Wolverton, "Space Biotechnology in Housing," presented at the National Association of Home Builders Convention, Dallas (January 19, 1986): 2; I.I. Gitelson, *Biotechnological Life-Support Systems: Their Role in Moulding Ecological Morality and Ethics* (Krasnoyarsk: Institute of BioPhysics, USSR Academy of Sciences, 1991).

2 Irving Skeist, *Plastics in Building* (New York: Reinhold Publishing,1966), 1.

3 While the provenance of this quotation is a controversial subject, it is generally attributed to Chief Seattle (speech, 1854).

4 Devra L. Davis, Gregg E. Dinse and David G. Hoel, "Decreasing Cardiovascular Disease and Increasing Cancer Among Whites in the United States From 1973 Through 1987," *Journal of the American Medical Association* (February 9, 1994): 431.

5 United States Environmental Protection Agency, Office of Air and Radiation, *Report to Congress on Indoor Air Quality* II, EPA/400/1-89/001C (Washington, DC: Environmental Protection Agency, August 1989), 4–27.

6 Fenton Communications, "We're losing the War on Cancer, Experts Say: Seek Reform of National Cancer Institute to Stress Environment and Prevention," (press release, Washington, DC: February 4, 1992).

7 The North Atlantic Treaty Organization's Committee on the Challenges of Modern Society Pilot Study on Indoor Air Quality, *The Implications of Indoor Air Quality for Modern Society* (report from meeting held at Erice, Italy, February 13 through 17, 1989), 21.

8 United States Environmental Protection Agency, Office of Air and Radiation (see chap. 1, n. 6), 5–15.

9 Lance A. Wallace, *The Total Exposure Assessment Methodology (T.E.A.M.) Study* I, EPA/600/6-87/002a (Washington, DC: Environmental Protection Agency, Office of Acid Deposition, Environmental Monitoring and Quality Assurance, June 1987).

10 John Naisbitt, *Megatrends* (New York: Warner Books, 1982), 39.

11 Stuart D. Snyder, *Building Interiors, Plants and Automation* (Englewood Cliffs, NJ: Prentice-Hall, 1990), 30.

12 Keppy Arnoldsen, "Interiorscape Irrigation: Water Within," *Landscape Design Magazine* (March 1994): 27; Robert Hyland, "Modern Technology Solves Personnel Problems: Interior Landscape Irrigation," *Western Landscaping News* (February 1983): 28.

Chapter 2

1 Larry Tye, "The Menace Within: Indoor Pollution, A Crisis in the Making, Perils That Need Not Be," *The Courier-Journal Magazine* (September 15, 1985): 4.

2 L. Mølhave and J. Moller, *The Atmospheric Environment in Modern Danish Dwellings: Measurements in 39 Flats* (Copenhagen: Danish Building Research Institute, 1979).

3 B.C. Wolverton, (see chap. 1, n. 1): 2.

4 United States Environmental Protection Agency, *Report to Congress on Indoor Air Quality: Executive Summary and Recommendations* I (Washington, DC: Office of Air and Radiation, Office of Research and Development, August 1989), p.1.

5 John C. Topping, Jr. and Adrien Waller Helm, *Clean Air Handbook* (Rockville, MD: Government Institutes, Inc., 1990), 147.

6 Senate of the United States, "Indoor Air Quality Act of 1991: Senate Bill S.455," (February 21, 1991): 1.

7 John F. Brundage, M.D. et al (Walter Reed Army Institute of Research), "Building-Associated Risk of Febrile Acute Respiratory Diseases in Army Trainees," *Journal of the American Medical Association* (April 8, 1988): 2108.

8 Fenton Communications, (see chap. 1, n. 7).

9 Jonathan M. Samet and John D. Spengler, *Indoor Air Pollution: A Health Perspective* (Baltimore: The Johns Hopkins University Press, 1991), 389.

10 Kenneth Lelen, "Firms Paying More Attention to Indoor Air Quality Issues," *The Philadelphia Inquirer* (August 8, 1994): D1.

Chapter 3

1 Lance A. Wallace, (see chap. 1, n. 10), 7; United States Environmental Protection Agency, (see chap. 2, n. 4), 1.

2 The North Atlantic Treaty Organization's Committee on the Challenges of Modern Society, (see chap. 1, n. 8).

3 United States Environmental Protection Agency and the United States Consumer Product Safety Commission, *The Inside Story: A Guide To Indoor Air Quality* (Washington, DC: September 1988); Lance A. Wallace, *The Sick Building Syndrome: A Review* No. 88-110.6 (Washington, DC: United States Environmental Protection Agency, 1988).

4 Paavo Airola, *How To Get Well* (Sherwood, OR: Health Plus Publishers, 1993), 227.

5 Harriet A. Burge, et al, "Evaluation of Indoor Plantings as Allergen Exposure Sources," *Journal of Allergy & Clinical Immunology* 70:2 (1982): 101.

6 Sol Miller, *Position Paper: The Possibility of Biological Contamination by Plants* (Fairfield, CA: Safety Systems and Services, 1988).

7 *Formaldehydes and Other Aldehydes* (Washington, DC: National Research Council/National Academy Press, 1981).

8 C.W. Bayer and M.S. Black, *Indoor Air Quality Evaluations of Three Office Buildings* (Atlanta: Georgia Institute of Technology, 1988).

9 R. Zweidinger, et al, *Direct Measurement of Volatile Organic Compounds in Breathing Zone Air, Drinking Water, Breath, Blood and Urine* NTIS No.PB82-186 545 (Washington, DC: United States Environmental Protection Agency, 1982).

10 L. L. Sheldon, et al, *Indoor Air Quality in Public Buildings* I and II (Washington, DC: United States Environmental Protection Agency, September 1988).

11 Benjamin A. Goldman, *The Truth About Where You Live: An Atlas for Action on Toxins and Mortality* (New York: Times Books/Random House, 1991), 21.

12 L. Mølhave, et al (Institute of Environmental and Occupational Medicine, University of Aarhus, Aarhus, Denmark), *Human Reactions to Low Concentrations of Volatile Organic Compounds* (Aarhus: Environ Internat, 1986), 167.

13 United States Environmental Protection Agency, *Report to Congress on Indoor Air Quality: Assessment and Control of Indoor Air Pollution* II (Washington, DC: United States Environmental Protection Agency, Office of Air and Radiation, Indoor Air Division, August 1989), 3–9, 4–27, 4–29.

14 NASA, *The Proceedings of the Skylab Life Sciences Symposium* (Johnson Space Center: NASA, August 27–29, 1974).

15 Benjamin Goldman, (see chap. 3, n. 11), 16.

16 *Energy Answers '87* (Stockholm: Swedish Council for Building Research, 1988).

17 Ellen J. Greenfield, *House Dangerous: Indoor Pollution in Your Home and Office and What You Can Do About It* (New York: Vintage Books/Random House, 1987), 105.

Chapter 4

1 The Burton Goldberg Group, *Alternative Medicine: The Definitive Guide* (Puyallup, WA: Future Medicine Publishing, 1993), 313.

2 Dan Katchongva, *A Message for All People* (New York: Akwasasne Notes, 1973), i–ii.

3 Carl Sagan, *Cosmos* (New York: Random House, 1980), 32, 338.

4 David M. Moore, *Green Planet: The Story of Plant Life on Earth* (London: Cambridge University Press/Equinox Books, 1982).

5 David M. Moore, (see chap. 4, n. 4); G. Ray Noggle and George J. Fritz, *Introductory Plant Physiology* (Englewood Cliffs, NJ: Prentice Hall, 1983), 85, 160, 163, 165.

6 Park S. Nobel, *Plant Cell Physiology* (San Francisco: W. H. Freeman & Co., 1970) 165.

7 "The Miracle of Trees," *Life Magazine* (May 1990): 67.

8 I.I. Gitelson, I.A. Terskov, B.G. Kovrov, G.M. Lisovsky, Y.N. Okladnikov, F.Y. Sid'ko, et al, *Long-term Experiments on Man's Stay in Biological Life-Support Systems* 9:8 (London: Institute of Biophysics, USSR Academy of Sciences, Advanced Space Research, 1989), 65; I.I. Gitelson, G.M. Lisovsky, B.G. Kovrov, Y.N. Okladnikov, M.S. Rerberg, F.A. Sid'ko, Terskv, *Problems of Space Biology: Experimental Ecological Systems Including Man* 28 (Moscow: Institute of Biophysics, USSR Academy of Sciences/Navka Press, 1975); L.V Kirensky, I.A. Terskov, I.I. Gitelson, G.M. Lisovsky, B.G. Kovrov, Y.N. Okladnikov, *Experimental Biological Life Support System II: Gas Exchange Between Man and Micro-Algae Culture in a 30-Day Experiment* VI (Inst. of Biophysics, USSR Academy of Sciences, Life Sciences and Space Research, 1968), 37; L.V. Kirensky, I.A. Terskov, I.I. Gitelson, G.M.

Lisovsky, B.G. Kovrov, Y.N. Okladnikov, *Theoretical and Experimental Decisions in the Creation of an Artificial Ecosystem for Human Life-Support in Space* IX (Institute of Biophysics, USSR Academy of Sciences, Life Sciences and Space Research, 1971), 76; L.V. Kirensky, I.A. Terskov, I.I. Gitelson, G.M. Lisovsky, B.G. Kovrov, Y.N. Okladnikov, *Biological Life-Support Systems Including Lower and Higher Plants* (Institute of Biophysics, USSR Academy of Sciences, 20th International Astronautic Congress, 1972); A. Terskov, I.I.Gitelson, G.M. Lisovsky, B.G. Kovrov, Y.N. Okladnikov et al, *The Experiment on Introducing Vegetable Plants in a Closed Gas-Exchange Biological Life-Support System* 3 (Institute of Biophysics, USSR Academy of Sciences, Space Biology & Airspace Medicine, 1974), 33; I.I. Gitelson, I.A. Terskov, G.M. Lisovsky, B.G. Kovrov, Y.N. Okladnikov, F.Y. Sid'ko, et al, *Life Support Systems with Autonomous Control Employing Plant Photosynthesis* 3 (Institute of Biophysics, USSR Academy of Sciences/Acta Astronautica, 1976), 9; G.M. Lisovsky, *Closed System: Man-Higher Plants* (Novosibirsk: Institute of Biophysics, USSR Academy of Sciences/Navka Press, 1976); I.A. Terskov, G.M. Lisovsky, S.A. Ushakova, et al, *The Possibility to Use Higher Plants in Life-Support Systems on the Moon* 3 (Institute of Biophysics, USSR Academy of Sciences, Space Biology & Airspace Medicine, 1978), 63; B.G. Kovrov, I.A. Terskov, I.I. Gitelson, G.M. Lisovsky, et al, *Artificial Closed Ecosystem "Man-Plants" with a Full Regeneration of Atmosphere, Water and Ration Vegetable Part* (Institute of Biophysics, USSR Academy of Sciences, 32nd International Astronautics Congress, 1981); G.M. Lisovsky, I.A. Terskov, I.I. Gitelson, et al, *Experimental Estimation of the Functional Possibilities of Higher Plants as Medium Regenerators in Life Support Systems* (Institute of Biophysics, USSR Academy of Sciences, 32nd International Astronautic Congress, 1981); I.I. Gitelson, I.A. Terskov, B.G. Kovrov, G.M.Lisovsky, et al, *Closed Ecosystems as the Means for the Outer Space Exploration by Men: Experimental Results, Perspectives* (Institute of Biophysics, USSR Academy of Sciences, 32nd International Astronautic Congress, 1981).

9 W.W. Heck, R.B. Philbeck and J.A. Dunning, *A Continuous Stirred Tank Reactor (CSTR) System for Exposing Plants to Gaseous or Vapor Contaminants* Series No. ARS-S-181 (Raleigh, NC: Agricultural Research Service/North Carolina State University, 1978); F.W. Went, *The Experimental Control of Plant Growth* (1957); M. Treshow, *Environment and Plant Response* (1970); Boyd Stram, *Physiological Effects of Simulated Environments on Green Plants* (Ann Arbor, MI: Ann Arbor Science Series, 1981), chapter 5.

10 Lance A. Wallace, "Emission Rates of Volatile Organic Compounds," *Building Materials and Surface Coatings* (Proceedings of the 1987 EPA/APCA Symposium on Measurement of Toxic and Related Air Pollutants/Air Pollution Control Association, 1987): 115.

11 B.C. Wolverton, Rebecca C. McDonald and E. A. Watkins, Jr. (NASA, Environmental Research Laboratory), *Foliage Plants for Removing Indoor Air Pollutants from Energy-Efficient Homes* 38:2 (New York: Economic Botany/New York Botanical Garden, 1984), 227; B.C. Wolverton, Rebecca C. McDonald and Hayne H. Mesick (NASA, Environmental Research Laboratory), "Foliage Plants for Indoor Removal of the Primary Combustion Gases Carbon Monoxide and Nitrogen Dioxide," *Journal of the Mississippi Academy of Sciences* XXX (1985): 5; B.C. Wolverton, *Houseplants, Indoor Air Pollutants and Allergic Reactions* (Missouri: NASA, National Space Technology Laboratories, December 1986).

12 Barbara T. Walton and T. A. Anderson, "Microbial Degradation of Trichloroethylene in the Rhizosphere: Potential Application to Biological Remediation of Waste Sites," *Applied and Environmental Microbiology* 56:4 (1990): 1012.

13 B.C. Wolverton, Anne Johnson, Keith Bounds (NASA Environmental Research Laboratory), *Interior Landscape Plants for Indoor Air Pollution Abatement* (Stennis Space Center, MS: NASA and Associated Landscape Contractors of America, September 15, 1989), 12.

14 J.K. Nelson, S. O. Montgomery and P. H. Pritchard, "Trichloroethylene Metabolism by Microorganisms that Degrade Aromatic Compounds," *Applied and Environmental Microbiology* 54:2 (1988): 604; Melissa L. Rochkind, J.W. Blackburn and G.S. Sayler, *Microbial Decomposition of Chlorinated Aromatic Compounds, EPA Contract #68-03-3074* EPA/600/2-86/090 (Washington, DC: United States Environmental Protection Agency, 1986); Michael Gabb and M. Chinery, *The World of Plants* (New York: Foundations of Science Library/Greystone Press, 1966); Alan R. Harker and Y. Kim, "Trichloroethylene Degradation by Two Independent Aromatic Degrading Pathways in Alcaligenes Eutrophus JMP 134," *Applied and Environmental Microbiology* 56:4 (Stillwater, OK: Oklahoma State University, 1990): 1179-1181; C. Deane Little, A.V. Palumbo, S.E. Herbes, M.E. Lidstrom, R.L. Tyndall and P.J. Gilmer, "Trichloroethylene Biodegradation by a Methane-Oxidizing Bacterium," *Applied and Environmental Microbiology* 54:4 (Oak Ridge National Laboratory/Florida State University, 1988): 951–956; Michael J.K. Nelson, S.O. Montgomery, W.R. Mahaffey and P.H. Pritchard, "Biodegradation of Trichloroethylene and Involvement of an Aromatic Biodegradative Pathway," *Applied and Environmental Microbiology* 53:5 (Gulf Breeze, FL: TechnologyApplications, Inc./Environmental Protection Agency, 1987): 949–954; Melissa Rochkind, J.W. Blackburn and G. Saylor, *Microbial Decomposition of Chlorinated Aromatic Compounds, EPA Contract #68-03-3074* EPA/600/2-86/090 (Washington, DC: United States Environmental Protection Agency, February 1986).

15 B.C. Wolverton, R.C. McDonald and W.R. Duffer, "Microoganisms and Higher Plants for Wastewater Treatment," *Journal of Environmental Quality* 12:2 (1983): 236.

16 "Wastewater Treatment the Natural Way," *Spin-off 1988* (Washington, DC: NASA Technology Utilization Division, 1988): 92; John Todd, "Report from Ocean Arks: The Solar Aquatics Story," *Annals of Earth, 1989* II:2: 16; Harriet A. Burge, W.R. Solomon and M.L. Muilenberg (University of Michigan Dept. of Internal Medicine under grant from the National Institute of Allergy and Infectious Diseases), "Evaluation of Indoor Plantings as Allergen Exposure Sources," *Journal of Allergy and Clinical Immunology* 70:2 (August 1982): 101.

17 Sol Miller, *Position Paper: Plant-Borne Microorganisms and Human Health* (Fairfield, CA: Society of American Florists/Safety Systems and Services, Inc., October 10, 1988).

18 *Mirage III System: Integral Interior Irrigation* (Boca Raton, FL: Aqua/Trends).

19 John R. Porter, Philadelphia College of Pharmacy & Science, Dept. of Biological Sciences, Philadelphia, PA, letter to the author, November 5, 1991; Frank B. Salisbury, Utah State University, Deptartment of Plants, Soils, Micrometeorology, Logan, UT, letter to the author, December 18, 1991.

20 Harriet Burge and Thomas Platts-Mills, *Indoor Air Assessment: Indoor Biological Pollutants* (Washington, DC: United States Environmental Protection Agency, Office of Health & Environmental Assessment, December 1990).

21 R.C. McDonald, "Vascular Plants for Decontaminating Radioactive Water and Soils," *NASA Technical Memorandum TM-X-72740* (National Space Technology Laboratories, MS: 1981).

22 John R. Porter, *Studies of Plants Under Stress: Toluene Removal from Contaminated Air and Field Chlorophyll Analysis* (Stennis Space Center, MS: NASA/American Society for Engineering Education and Southern University, September 1991), 109.

23 George H. Manaker, *Interior Plantscapes* (Englewood Cliffs, NJ: Prentice Hall, 1987), 36.

24 E.F. Jansen and A.C. Olson, "Metabolism of Carbon-14-Labeled Benzene and Toluene in Avocado Fruit," *Plant Physiology* 44: 786.

25 B.C. Wolverton and John D. Wolverton, *Plant/Microbial Ecology: Nature's Solution to Sick-Building Syndrome* (Picayune, MS: Wolverton Environmental Services, September 1994), 4.

26 B.C. Wolverton and John Wolverton, *Removal of Formaldehyde From Sealed Experimental Chambers by Azalea, Poinsettia and Dieffenbachia* (Picayune, MS: Wolverton Environmental Services, January 1991).

27 John Wolverton and B.C. Wolverton, "Improving Indoor Air Quality Using Orchids and Bromeliads," *Interiorscape* (January/February 1992): 6.

28 B.C. Wolverton and John D. Wolverton, *Bioregenerative Life-Support Systems for Energy-Efficient Buildings* (Huntsville, AL: Proceedings of International Conference on Life Support and Biospherics, February 18, 1992).

29 B.C. Wolverton and John D. Wolverton, "Plants and Soil Microorganisms: Removal of Formaldehyde, Xylene and Ammonia from the Indoor Environment," *Journal of the Mississippi Academy of Sciences* 38:2 (August/September 1993):1.

30 M. Giese, U. Bauer-Doranth, C. Langbertels and H. Sandermann, Jr., "Detoxification of Formaldehyde by the Spider Plant (Chlorophytum Gomosum L.) and Soybean (Glycine Max L.) Cell Suspension Cultures," *GSR-Forsschungszentrum f,r Umvelt und Gesundheit GMBH* (Oberschleissheim, Germany: Institute f,r Biochemische Plantenpathologie, January 7, 1994).

31 I.I. Gitelson, *Biotechnological Life-Support Systems: Their Role in Moulding Ecological Morality and Ethics* (Krasnoyarsk: Institute of Biophysics, USSR Academy of Sciences, 1991).

32 Margo T. Oge, EPA Director of the Office of Radiation and Indoor Air, letter to the author, June 4, 1993.

33 Letter from the author to Robert Axelrad, EPA Director of the Office of Air and Radiation, Indoor Air Division, March 31, 1992.

34 *Energy Answers '87* (Stockholm: Swedish Council for Building Research, 1988).

Chapter 5

1 United States Environmental Protection Agency, (see chap. 3, n. 15).

2 United States Environmental Protection Agency, (see chap. 5, n. 1), 61.

3 Kim Leclair and David Rousseau, *Environmental by Design: Interiors* I (Point Roberts, WA: Hartley & Marks, 1992).

4 *New York Times* March 23, 1989.

5 United States Environmental Protection Agency, (see chap. 3, n. 15), 1–3.

6 Lance Wallace, (see chap. 1, n. 10).

7 G.R. Amols, K.B. Howard, A.K. Nichols and T.D. Guerra, *Residential and Commercial Buildings Data Book* PNL-6454/UC-98 (Richland, WA: Pacific Northwest Laboratory, 1988).

8 A. Persily, "Ventilation Rates in Office Buildings," paper presented at the ASHRAE Conference on IAQ, The Human Equation: Health and Comfort, San Diego, CA, 1989.

9 G.P. Hanson and L. Thorne, *Vegetation to Reduce Air Pollution* 20 (Lasca Leaves, 1972).

10 D.I. Cook and D.F. Van Haverbeke, "Trees and Shrubs for Noise Abatement," *United States Forest Service Research Bulletin* 276 (1971).

11 Roger S. Ulrich and Russ Parsons, "Influences of Passive Experiences with Plants on Individual Well-Being and Health," Texas A & M University Symposium on Role of Horticulture in Human Well-Being, Washington, DC, April 19, 1990.

12 B.C. Wolverton and R.C. McDonald, "Vascular Plants for Decontaminating Radioactive Water and Soils," *NASA Technical Memorandum TM-X-72740* (National Space Technology Laboratories, MS: 1987).

Chapter 6

1 "Flowers and Foliage Plants: Production and Sales," USDA Crop Reporting Board, Sp. Cr. 6–1; "Floriculture Crops: Annual Summaries," USDA National Agriculture Statistics Service, Sp. Cr. 6–1; "Foliage, Floriculture and Cut Greens," Florida Agriculture Statistics Service, Sp. Cr. 6–1, May 1995.

2 "1991 Contractor 25," *Interiorscape Magazine* (November/December 1991): 31.

3 "1982 Survey of the Landscape Business," *Western Landscaping News Magazine* (November 1982).

4 Robert Hyland, "Modern Technology Solves Personnel Problems: Interior Landscape Irrigation," *Western Landscaping News Magazine* (February 1983): 28

5 Gregory M. Pierceall, *Interiorscapes—Planning, Graphics, and Design* (Englewood Cliffs, NJ: Prentice Hall, 1987).

6 Mirage™ brand automated precision micro-irrigation systems are a trademark of Boca Automation, Inc.

Chapter 7

1 T. A. Prince and T. L. Prince, "How Many Are Saying It With Flowers?" *Interiorscape Magazine* (September/October 1985): 46.

2 George H. Manaker, (see chap. 4, n. 44), 36.

3 Richard L. Gaines, *Interior Plantscaping: Building Design for Interior Plants* (New York: Architectural Record Books/McGraw-Hill, 1977).

4 Foliage for Clean Air Council, *Plant Tips for Commercial and Residential Environments* (Fall Church, VA: 1991); B.C. Wolverton and John D. Wolverton, "Plant and Soil Microorganisms: Removal of Formaldehyde, Xylene and Ammonia from the Indoor Environment," *Journal of the Mississippi Academy of Sciences* 38:2 (1993):14; B.C. Wolverton and John D. Wolverton, *Bioregenerative Life-Support Systems for Energy-Efficient Buildings* (Huntsville: International Conference on Life Support and Biospherics, February 18, 1992), 121; B.C. Wolverton, Rebecca C. McDonald and E.A. Watkins Jr. (NASA Environmental Research Laboratory), "Foliage Plants for Removing Indoor Air Pollutants from Energy-Efficient Homes," *Economic Botany* 38:2 (Bronx, NY: 1984): 227; B.C. Wolverton, Rebecca C.

McDonald and Hayne Mesick (NASA Environmental Research Laboratory), "Foliage Plants for Indoor Removal of the Primary Combustion Gases Carbon Monoxide and Nitrogen Dioxide," *Journal of the Mississippi Academy of Sciences* XXX (1985): 5; B.C. Wolverton (NASA Environmental Research Laboratory), *Houseplants, Indoor Pollutants and Allergic Reactions* (NASA National Space Technology Laboratories, MS: December 1986); B.C. Wolverton, Ann Johnson and Keith Bounds (NASA Environmental Research Laboratory), *Interior Landscape Plants for Indoor Air Pollution Abatement* (Stennis Space Center, MS: NASA/Associated Landscape Contractors of America, September 15, 1989), 12; John Wolverton and B.C. Wolverton, "Improving Indoor Air Quality Using Orchids and Bromeliads," *Interiorscape Magazine* (January/February 1992): 6; NASA research data sheets.

Chapter 8

1 *Houseplants—Indoors/Outdoors* (San Francisco: Ortho Books [Chevron Chemical Co.], 1974).

2 *All About Fertilizers, Soils and Water* (San Francisco: Ortho Books [Chevron Chemical Co.], 1979).

3 *Mini-Encyclopedia of Houseplants* (San Francisco: Ortho Books [Chevron Chemical Co.], 1979).

4 George H. Manaker, (see chap. 4, n. 44), 233–238.

5 Richard L. Gaines, (see chap. 7, n. 3), 80–106.

6 Mirage™ is a trademark of Boca Automation, Inc.

7 Richard L. Gaines, (see chap. 7, n. 3), 37; George H. Manaker, (see chap. 4, n. 44); Nelson Hammer, *Interior Landscape Design* (New York: McGraw-Hill, 1992), 143–149.

8 George H. Manaker, (see chap. 4, n. 44), 46–64.

9 Ibid., 80.

10 (See chap. 8, n. 2), 13.

Chapter 9

1 Robert Hyland, (see chap. 6, n. 4), 28.

2 *Aqua-Mate Catalog* (Providence: Aquamatic Systems, Inc., 1985).

3 JoAnn Johnston, "Specimen Containers and Specimen Weights," *Interiorscape Magazine* (May/June 1986): 14.

4 Robert Hyland, (see chap. 6, n. 4), 28.

5 George H. Manaker, (see chap. 4, n. 44), 119.

Chapter 10

1 Mirage™ is a trademark of Boca Automation, Inc.

2 Jack Kramer, *Drip System Watering* (New York: W.W. Norton & Co., 1980), 16, 17.

3 *Irrigation Products Catalog* (Riverside, CA: The Toro Company—Irrigation Division, 1987); *Turf Irrigation Equipment Catalog* (Glendora, CA: Rainbird, Inc.—Turf Division, 1987).

4 Jack Kramer, (see chap. 10, n. 2), 36; *Basic Drip Irrigation Design for Landscaping* (Riverside, CA: The Toro Company—Irrigation Division, 1985), 1.

5 Judy Smith, "The Friendly Skies Add Greenery at LAX: Drip System to Reduce Maintenance Costs in Airport Interiorscape," *Interiorscape Magazine* (July/August 1983): 48.

6 U.S. Patent #4,834,265.

7 Aqua/Trends™ and EnvironMate™ are trademarks of Boca Automation, Inc.

Chapter 11

1 Michael Wright, *The Complete Indoor Gardener* (New York: Random House, 1979), 220.

2 Maggie Oster, *The Green Pages* (New York: Ballantine Books, 1977), 216.

3 *Sunset House Plants: How to Choose, Grow, Display* (Menlo Park, CA: Lane Publishing, 1983), 19.

4 Joan Lee Faust, *New York Times Book of Houseplants* (New York: Quadrangle/The New York Times Book Co., 1973), 12.

5 Richard L. Gaines, (see chap. 7, n. 3), 10.

6 Ibid.

7 George H. Manaker, (see chap. 4, n. 44), 179.

8 Ibid.

9 "101 Ways to Love, Grow and Care for House Plants," *Woman's Day Magazine* (March 1981): 80.

Chapter 12

1 Robert M. Hettema, *Mechanical and Electrical Building Construction* (Englewood Cliffs, NJ: Prentice-Hall, 1984), 74.

2 Registered Trademark of Pepco Extruded Products, Inc.

Chapter 13

1 Mirage III™ Systems is a trademark of Boca Automation, Inc.

2 Stephan Scrivens, *Interior Planting in Large Buildings* (New York: Halsted Press/John Wiley and Son, 1980), 79.

3 Ibid, 47.

4 Ann Nydele, "Future Trends in Hotel Design," *Buildings Magazine* (March 1988): 60.

5 X-10 Powerhouse™ is a trademark of X-10 U.S.A., Inc.

6 CEBus® is a registered service mark of the Electronic Industries Association (EIA).

7 Lon Works™ is a trademark of Echelon Corporation.

8 SMART HOUSE™ is a trademark of the Smart House Limited Partnership.

Chapter 14

1 Frank R. D'agostino, *Mechanical and Electrical Systems in Building Construction* (Reston, VA: Reston Publishing/Prentice-Hall, 1982).

2 *Annual of the R.S. Means Company* (Kingston, MA).

Chapter 15

1 X-10 PowerHouse™ is a trademark of X-10 U.S.A., Inc.

2 CEBus™ is a registered service mark of Electronic Industries Association (EIA); LonWorks™ is a trademark of Echelon Corporation; Smart House™ is a trademark of Smart House Limited Partnership.

References

1981. 101 Ways to Love, Grow and Care for House Plants. *Woman's Day Magazine*. 80.

1982. 1982 Survey of the Landscape Business. *Western Landscaping News Magazine*.

1983. *Sunset House Plants: How to Choose, Grow, Display*. 19.

1989. *New York Times*.

1990. The Miracle of Trees. *Life Magazine*. 67.

1991. 1991 Contractor 25. *Interiorscape Magazine*. 31.

Airola, Paavo, 1993. How To Get Well. *227.*

Allsopp, Bruce, 1974. Towards a Humane Architecture.

Amols, G.R., Howard, K.B., Nichols, A.K., Guerra, T.D. 1988. Residential and Commercial Buildings Data Book.

Arnoldsen, Keppy, 1994. Interiorscape Irrigation: Water Within. Landscape Design Magazine. *27.*

Axelrad, Robert, 1992. EPA Director of the Office of Air and Radiation, Indoor Air Division, letter to the author.

Bayer, C.W. and Black, M.S., 1988. Indoor Air Quality Evaluations of Three Office Buildings.

Bennett, J.H. and Hill, A.C. 1973. Absorption of Gaseous Air Pollutants by a Standardized Plant Canopy. Journal of the Air Pollution Control Association.

Bennett, J.H. and Hill, A.C. 1975. Interactions of Air Pollutants with Canopies of Vegetation. Responses of Plants to Air Pollution. *273.*

Brill, Michael, 1982. The Impact of Office Environment on Productivity and Quality of Working Life.

Brundage, M.D., John F. et al (Walter Reed Army Institute of Research), 1988. Building-Associated Risk of Febrile Acute Respiratory Diseases in Army Trainees. Journal of the American Medical Association. *2108.*

Buildings Data Book. PNL-6454/UC-98.

Burge, Harriet A. et al, 1982. Evaluation of Indoor Plantings as Allergen Exposure Sources. *Journal of Allergy & Clinical Immunology.* 70:2-101.

Burge, Harriet A., Solomon, W.R., and Muilenberg, M.L. 1982. Evaluation of Indoor Plantings as Allergen Exposure Sources. *Journal of Allergy and Clinical Immunology.*

Burge, Harriet and Platts-Mills, Thomas, 1990. *Indoor Air Assessment: Indoor Biological Pollutants.*

Cook, D.I. and Van Haverbeke, D.F. 1971. Trees and Shrubs for Noise Abatement. *United States Forest Service Research Bulletin.* 276.

D'agostino, Frank R. 1982. *Mechanical and Electrical Systems in Building Construction.*

Davis, Devra L., Dinse, Gregg E. and Hoel, David G. Decreasing Cardiovascular Disease and Increasing Cancer Among Whites in the United States from 1973 through 1987. *Journal of the American Medical Association.* 431.

Environmental Health Sciences Center, 1972. *The Role of Plants in Environmental Purification.*

Faust, Joan Lee, 1973. *New York Times Book of Houseplants.* 12.

Fenton Communications, 1992. We're Losing the War on Cancer, Experts Say: Seek Reform of National Cancer Institute to Stress Environment and Prevention. Press release, Washington, DC.

Foliage for Clean Air Council, 1991. *Plant Tips for Commercial and Residential Environments.*

Gabb, Michael and Chinery, M. 1966. *The World of Plants.*

Gaines, Richard L. 1977. *Interior Plantscaping: Building Design for Interior Plants.*

Giese, M., Bauer-Doranth, U., Langbertels, C., Sandermann, Jr., H. 1994. Detoxification of Formaldehyde by the Spider Plant (Chlorophytum Gomosum L.) and Soybean (Glycine Max L.) Cell Suspension Cultures. *GSR-Forsschungszentrum f,r Umvelt und Gesundheit GMBH.*

Gilliatt, Mary, 1984. *The Complete Book of Home Design.* 94.

Gitelson, I.I. 1991. *Biotechnological Life-Support Systems: Their Role in Moulding Ecological Morality and Ethics.*

Gitelson, I.I., Terskov, I.A., Kovrov, B.G., Lisovsky, G.M., Okladnikov, Y.N., Sid'ko, F.Y. et al, 1989. *Long-term Experiments on Man's Stay in Biological Life-Support Systems.* 9:8.

Gitelson, I.I., Lisovsky, G.M., Kovrov, B.G., Okladnikov, Y.N., Rerberg, M.S., Sid'ko, F.A., Terskov, I.A., 1975. *Problems of Space Biology: Experimental Ecological Systems Including Man.* 28.

Gitelson, I.I., Terskov, I.A., Kovrov, B.G., Lisovsky, G.M. et al. 1981. *Closed Ecosystems as the Means for the Outer Space Exploration by Men: Experimental Results, Perspectives.*

Gitelson, I.I., Terskov, I.A., Lisovsky, G.M., Kovrov, B.G., Okladnikov, Y.N., Sid'ko, F.Y. et al. 1976. *Life Support Systems with Autonomous Control Employing Plant Photosynthesis.* 9.

Goldman, Benjamin A., 1991. *The Truth About Where You Live: An Atlas for Action on Toxins and Mortality.* 21.

Graf Klein, Judy, 1982. *The Office Book.* 120.

Greenfield, Ellen J. 1987. *House Dangerous: Indoor Pollution in Your Home and Office and What You Can Do About It.* 105.

Habitability Technology Section, 1971. *Habitability Data Handbook—Volume 2, MSC-03909.*

Hanson, G.P. and Thorne, L. 1972. *Vegetation to Reduce Air Pollution.*

Harker, Alan R. and Kim, Y. Trichloroethylene Degradation by Two Independent Aromatic Degrading Pathways in Alcaligenes Eutrophus JMP 134. *Applied and Environmental Microbiology.*

Heck, W.W., Philbeck, R.B., Dunning, J.A. 1978. *A Continuous Stirred Tank Reactor (CSTR) System for Exposing Plants to Gaseous or Vapor Contaminants.* Series No. ARS-S-181

Hettema, Robert M. 1984. *Mechanical and Electrical*

Building Construction. 74.

Hill, A.C. 1971. Vegetation: A Sink For Atmospheric Pollutants. *Journal of the Air Pollution Control Association.*

Hyland, Robert, 1983. Modern Technology Solves Personnel Problems: Interior Landscape Irrigation. *Western Landscaping News.* 28.

Jansen, E.F. and Olson, A.C. Metabolism of Carbon-14-Labeled Benzene and Toluene in Avocado Fruit. *Plant Physiology.* 44: 786.

Johnston, JoAnne, 1986. Specimen Containers and Specimen Weights. *Interiorscape Magazine.* 14.

Kaplan, S. and Kaplan, R. 1978. *Humanscape: Environments for People.* 193.

Katchongva, Dan, 1973. *A Message for All People.* i-ii.

Kirensky, L.V., Terskov, I.A., Gitelson, I.I., Lisovsky, G.M., Kovrov, B.G., Okladnikov, Y.N. 1968. *Experimental Biological Life Support System II: Gas Exchange Between Man and Micro-Algae Culture in a 30-Day Experiment.*

Kirensky, L.V., Terskov, I.A., Gitelson, I.I., Lisovsky, G.M., Kovrov, B.G., Okladnikov, Y.N., 1971. *Theoretical and Experimental Decisions in the Creation of an Artificial Ecosystem for Human Life-Support in Space.* 76.

Kirensky, L.V., Terskov, I.A., Gitelson, I.I., Lisovsky, G.M., Kovrov, B.G., Okladnikov, Y.N., 1972. *Biological Life-Support Systems Including Lower and Higher Plants.*

Klaus, Paul N. 1987. *Decreasing Stress Through the Introduction of Microenvironments.*

Kleeman, Jr., Walter B. 1981. *The Challenge of Interior Design.*

Knabe, W. 1979. Capacity and Efficiency of Vegetation in Reducing Airborne Pollution in Urban and Industrial Areas. Symposium on the Effects of Airborne Pollution on Vegetation, United Nations Economic Commission for Europe.

Kovrov, B.G., Terskov, I.A., Gitelson, I.I., Lisovsky, G.M. et al. 1981. *Artificial Closed Ecosystem "Man-Plants" with a Full Regeneration of Atmosphere, Water and Ration Vegetable Part.*

Kramer, Jack, 1980. *Drip System Watering.* 16, 17.

Lang, Burnette, Moleski and Vachon, 1974. *Designing for Human Behavior.*

Leclair, Kim and Rousseau, David, 1992. *Environmental by Design: Interiors.*

Lelen, Kenneth, 1994. Firms Paying More Attention to Indoor Air Quality Issues. *The Philadelphia Inquirer.* D1.

Lisovsky, G.M. 1976. *Closed System: Man-Higher Plants.*

Lisovsky, G.M., Terskov, I.A., Gitelson, I.I., et al. 1981. *Experimental Estimation of the Functional Possibilities of Higher Plants as Medium Regenerators in Life Support Systems.*

Little, C. Deane, Palumbo, A.V., Herbes, S.E., Lidstrom, M.E., Tyndall, R.L., and Gilmer, P.J. 1988. Trichloroethylene Biodegradation by a Methane-Oxidizing Bacterium. *Applied and Environmental Microbiology.*

Luttge, U. and Fischer, K. 1980. Light-Dependent Net CO-Evolution by C3 and C4 Plants. *Planta.* 149:59.

Manaker, George H. 1987. *Interior Plantscapes.* 36.

McDonald, R.C. 1981. Vascular Plants for Decontaminating Radioactive Water and Soils. *NASA Technical Memorandum TM-X-72740.*

Meetham, A.R. 1950. Natural Removal of Pollution from the Atmosphere. *Quarterly Journal of the Royal Meteorological Society.*

Mikellides, Byron, 1980. *Architecture for People.*

Miller, Sol, 1988. *Position Paper: Plant-Borne Microorganisms and Human Health.*

Miller, Sol, 1988. *Position Paper: The Possibility of Biological Contamination by Plants.*

M⁻lhave, L. and Moller, J. 1979. *The Atmospheric Environment in Modern Danish Dwellings: Measurements in 39 Flats.*

M⁻lhave, L. et al (Institute of Environmental and Occupational Medicine, University of Aarhus, Aarhus, Denmark). *Human Reactions to Low Concentrations of Volatile Organic Compounds.* 167.

Moore, David M. 1982. *Green Planet: The Story of Plant Life on Earth.*

Naisbitt, John, 1982. *Megatrends.*

NASA, 1974. *The Proceedings of the Skylab Life Sciences Symposium.*

NASA, 1988. Wastewater Treatment the Natural Way. *Spin-off 1988.* 92.

National Research Council, 1981. *Formaldehydes and Other Aldehydes.*

Nelson, J.K., Montgomery, S.O., Pritchard, P.H. 1988. Trichloroethylene Metabolism by Microorganisms that Degrade Aromatic Compounds. *Applied and Environmental Microbiology.*

Nelson, Michael J.K., Montgomery, S.O., Mahaffey, W.R., Pritchard, P.H. 1987. Biodegradation of Trichloroethylene and Involvement of an Aromatic Biodegradative Pathway. *Applied and Environmental Microbiology.*

Nobel, Park S. 1970. *Plant Cell Physiology.* 165.

Noggle, G. Ray and Fritz, George J. 1983. *Introductory Plant Physiology.* 85, 160, 163, 165.

North Atlantic Treaty Organization's Committee on the Challenges of Modern Society Pilot Study on Indoor Air Quality, 1989. *The Implications of Indoor Air Quality for Modern Society.* Report from meeting held at Erice, Italy. 21.

Nydele, Ann, 1988. Future Trends in Hotel Design. *Buildings Magazine.* 60.

Oge, Margo T. 1993. EPA Director of the Office of Radiation and Indoor Air, letter to the author.

Ortho Books, 1974. *Houseplants—Indoors/Outdoors.*

Ortho Books, 1979. *All About Fertilizers, Soils and Water.*

Ortho Books, 1979. *Mini-Encyclopedia of Houseplants.*

Oster, Maggie, 1977. *The Green Pages.* 216.

Persily, A. 1989. Ventilation Rates in Office Buildings. Paper presented at the ASHRAE Conference on IAQ, The Human Equation: Health and Comfort.

Pierceall, Gregory M. 1987. *Interiorscapes—Planning, Graphics, and Design.*

Porter, John R. 1991. *Studies of Plants Under Stress: Toluene Removal from Contaminated Air and Field Chlorophyll Analysis.* 109.

Porter, John R. 1991. Philadelphia College of Pharmacy & Science, Dept. of Biological

Sciences, Philadelphia, PA, letter to the author.

Prince, T.A. and Prince, T.L. 1985. How Many Are Saying It With Flowers? *Interiorscape Magazine.* 46.

Robinson, E. and Robbins, R.C. 1969. Sources, Abundance and Fate of Gaseous Atmospheric Pollutants Supplement. SRI Project PR-6755.

Rochkind, Melissa L., Blackburn, J.W., and Sayler, G.S. 1986. *Microbial Decomposition of Chlorinated Aromatic Compounds, EPA Contract #68-03-3074.* EPA/600/2-86/090.

Sagan, Carl, 1980. *Cosmos.* 32, 338.

Salisbury, Frank B. 1991. Utah State University, Department of Plants, Soils, Micrometeorology, Logan, UT, letter to the author.

Samet, Jonathan M. and Spengler, John D. 1991. *Indoor Air Pollution: A Health Perspective.* 389.

Scrivens, Stephan, 1980. *Interior Planting in Large Buildings.* 1, 79.

Senate of the United States, 1991. Indoor Air Quality Act of 1991: Senate Bill S.455. 1.

Sheldon, L.L. et al, 1988. *Indoor Air Quality in Public Buildings.*

Skeist, Irving, 1966. *Plastics in Building.* 1.

Skurka, Norma, 1976. *The New York Times Book of Interior Design and Decoration.* 92.

Smith, Judy, 1983. The Friendly Skies Add Greenery at LAX: Drip System to Reduce Maintenance Costs in Airport Interiorscape. *Interiorscape Magazine.* 48.

Snyder, Stuart D. 1990. *Building Interiors, Plants and Automation.* 30.

Stram, Boyd, 1981. *Physiological Effects of Simulated Environments on Green Plants.*

Stuster, Jack W. 1986. *Space Station Habitability Recommendations Based on a Systematic Comparative Analysis of Analogous Conditions.* 84.

Swedish Council for Building Research, 1988. *Energy Answers '87.*

Terskov, A., Gitelson, I.I., Lisovsky, G.M., Kovrov, B.G., Okladnikov, Y.N. et al. 1974. *The Experiment on Introducing Vegetable Plants in a Closed Gas-Exchange Biological Life-Support System.* 33.

Terskov, I.A., Lisovsky, G.M., Ushakova, S.A. et al. 1978. *The Possibility to Use Higher Plants in Life-Support Systems on the Moon.* 63.

The Burton Goldberg Group, 1993. *Alternative Medicine: The Definitive Guide.* 313.

Todd, John, 1989. Report from Ocean Arks: The Solar Aquatics Story. *Annals of Earth, 1989.* II:2: 16.

Topping, Jr., John C. and Waller Helm, Adrien, 1990. *Clean Air Handbook.* 147.

Townsend, A.M. 1974. Sorption of Ozone by Nine Shade Tree Species. *Journal of the American Horticultural Science.*

Treshow, M. 1970. *Environment and Plant Response.*

Tye, Larry, 1985. The Menace Within: Indoor Pollution, A Crisis in the Making, Perils That Need Not Be. *The Courier-Journal Magazine.* 4.

Ulrich, Roger S. and Parsons, Russ, 1990. Influences of Passive Experiences with Plants on Individual Well-being and Health. Texas A&M University College of Architecture, paper presented at the National Symposium on the Role of Horticulture in Human Well-being and Social Development. 16.

United States Environmental Protection Agency and the United States Consumer Product Safety Commission, 1988. *The Inside Story: A Guide To Indoor Air Quality.*

United States Environmental Protection Agency, Office of Air and Radiation, 1989. *Report to Congress on Indoor Air Quality.* II, EPA/400/1-89/001C: 4-27.

Wallace, Lance A. 1987. *The Total Exposure Assessment Methodology (T.E.A.M.) Study.*

Wallace, Lance A. 1987. Emission Rates of Volatile Organic Compounds. *Building Materials and Surface Coatings.* 115.

Wallace, Lance A. 1988. *The Sick Building Syndrome: A Review.* No. 88-110.6.

Walton, Barbara T. and Anderson, T.A. 1990. Microbial Degradation of Trichloroethylene in the Rhizosphere: Potential Application to Biological Remediation of Waste Sites. *Applied and Environmental Microbiology.*

Went, F.W. 1957. *The Experimental Control of Plant Growth.*

Wise, J.A. and Rosenberg, E. 1988. *The Effects of Interior Treatments on Performance Stress in Three Types of Mental Tasks.* CIFR Technical Report No. 002-02-1988.

Wolverton, B.C. 1986. *Houseplants, Indoor Air Pollutants and Allergic Reactions.*

Wolverton, B.C. 1986. Space Biotechnology in Housing. Presented at the National Association of Home Builders Convention, Dallas. 2.

Wolverton, B.C. and McDonald, R.C. 1987. Vascular Plants for Decontaminating Radioactive Water and Soils. *NASA Technical Memorandum TM-X-72740.*

Wolverton, B.C. and Wolverton, John D. 1992. *Bioregenerative Life-Support Systems for Energy-Efficient Buildings.* 121.

Wolverton, B.C. and Wolverton, John D. Plant and Soil Microorganisms: Removal of Formaldehyde, Xylene and Ammonia from the Indoor Environment. *Journal of the Mississippi Academy of Sciences.* 38:2-14.

Wolverton, B.C. and Wolverton, John, 1991. *Removal of Formaldehyde from Sealed Experimental Chambers by Azalea, Poinsettia and Dieffenbachia.*

Wolverton, B.C. Wolverton, John D. 1994. *Plant/Microbial Ecology: Nature's Solution to Sick-Building Syndrome.* 4.

Wolverton, B.C., Johnson, Ann, and Bounds, Keith, 1989. *Interior Landscape Plants for Indoor Air Pollution Abatement.* 12.

Wolverton, B.C., McDonald, R.C., and Duffer, W.R. 1983. Microorganisms and Higher Plants for Wastewater Treatment. *Journal of Environmental Quality.*

Wolverton, B.C., McDonald, R.C., and Mesick, Hayne, 1985. Foliage Plants for Indoor Removal of the Primary Combustion Gases Carbon Monoxide and Nitrogen Dioxide. *Journal of the Mississippi Academy of Sciences.* 5.

Wolverton, B.C., McDonald, R.C., and Watkins Jr.,

E.A. 1984. Foliage Plants for Removing Indoor Air Pollutants from Energy-Efficient Homes. *Economic Botany.*

Wolverton, B.C., McDonald, Rebecca C., Mesick, Hayne H. 1985. Foliage Plants for Indoor Removal of the Primary Combustion Gases Carbon Monoxide and Nitrogen Dioxide. *Journal of the Mississippi Academy of Sciences.* 5.

Wolverton, John and Wolverton, B.C. 1992. Improving Indoor Air Quality Using Orchids and Bromeliads. *Interiorscape.* 6.

Wright, Michael (editor), 1979. *The Complete Indoor Gardener.* 16, 220.

Yoneyama, T., Totsuka, T, Hashimoto, A. and Yazaki, J. 1979. Absorption of Atmospheric NO2 by Plants and Soils III. *Soil Science and Plant Nutrition.*

Zweidinger, R. et al, 1982. *Direct Measurement of Volatile Organic Compounds in Breathing Zone Air, Drinking Water, Breath, Blood and Urine.* NTIS No.PB82-186 545.

Index